D1713065

Mediaeval Institutions
SELECTED ESSAYS

Mediaeval Institutions

SELECTED ESSAYS

By CARL STEPHENSON

Edited by BRYCE D. LYON

Cornell Paperbacks

Cornell University Press

ITHACA, NEW YORK

Contents

CONTENTS

Introduction

WHAT does the document say? In Carl Stephenson's long career as a scholar and teacher probably no other question was more frequently addressed to himself or to his students. With this direct approach to the sources Carl Stephenson has launched all his historical investigations. It is the dominant theme running through the articles brought together in this volume—one which the editor hopes will serve to give suitable recognition to Carl Stephenson upon his retirement from teaching as well as to make readily available some of his most important contributions on various historical subjects. The conclusions reached in these articles have, to be sure, found popular expression in such books as his *Mediaeval History* and *Mediaeval Feudalism,* but the necessarily brief treatment there given to them is no substitute for fuller exposition. It has been thought unnecessary in this volume to republish the articles by Carl Stephenson on urban origins and institutions because they have found eloquent expression in *Borough and Town.*

Carl Stephenson's methodological approach and his concern with mediaeval institutions reflect in part the influence of the masters under whom he studied. As a graduate student at Harvard University he chose to work with Charles Gross, who introduced him to English municipal history and proposed as a thesis subject "The Military Obligations of the English Boroughs." But his work under Gross was cut short by the sudden death of that fine scholar. He then came to work under Charles Homer Haskins, who suggested a preliminary study of towns on the Continent. The institutions of England, France, Germany, and the Low Countries could never be understood in isolation; they should rather be considered institutions of western Europe. This advice Carl Stephenson has continued to follow, as will be seen from data presented below.

Another early influence, less direct but equally decisive, came from John Horace Round. That scholar's brilliant criticism of Domesday Book and fine essay on the introduction of knight service into England captivated Carl Stephenson. Never were the two to meet except through correspondence, but the decisive influence of Round is apparent in the earliest of Carl Stephenson's work. Like Round, he came to regard the principal canon of historical scholarship as the necessity of going straight to the relevant sources and through them to the core of the problem itself. Once the problem had been apprehended, the next step was to present it as simply and clearly as possible. No greater tribute to Round has been expressed than that of Carl Stephenson: "I came to appreciate as fundamental to our knowledge of the Norman records the searching criticism of Round, whose essays, for the sheer power of straight thinking there exhibited, have been to me a constant joy and incentive." If Carl Stephenson has differed from Round in broadening the scope of his investigations on early mediaeval institutions, he confesses to having followed Maitland, "whose marvelous sense of historical values, combined with an uncanny faculty of vivid expression, has given us our truest picture of early English institutions."

For a number of years Carl Stephenson remained primarily interested in the problem of municipal taxation. His first article, "The Aids of the English Boroughs," was followed by two others: "Les 'aides' des villes françaises" and "La taille dans les villes d'Allemagne." Then, in 1924, he gained the opportunity of a year's study with Henri Pirenne at Ghent. Thus Haskins' earlier advice was confirmed. To comprehend the origin of the town and its institutions, as well as mediaeval taxation, one must view them as parts of the social and economic revolution that transformed western Europe in the eleventh and twelfth centuries. Particularistic and nationalistic theorizing did not suffice to explain the town, feudalism, taxation, and the status of the peasant; neither did patriotic romanticism and juristic reasoning. Under Pirenne, Carl Stephenson did substantial research on the growth of taxation on the Continent, took note of the numerous suggestive leads continually let fall by the genial Belgian, and finally came to see that the mercantile-settlement theory of Pirenne and Rietschel on the origin of the town could be applied to the English borough. This was done in *Borough and Town*. There, in particular, he appealed to British scholars for a better appreciation of topographical study as essential to the understanding of urban development—such study as had already been inspired by the work of Pirenne and Rietschel.

This is not the place for detailed comment on the essays printed below, but certain of their contributions should be noted. The advantages of the comparative approach are seen in the articles on taxation. Carl Stephenson has pointed out that the *taille* of French-speaking regions was the same as the *Bede* of German-speaking regions. The right to it was not a remnant snatched up from the shattered remains of Carolingian authority, nor did it spring from centralization of princely authority; it was a local development of taxation in the post-Carolingian period of political chaos when every lord took what he could from his dependents. The Normans had introduced the *taille* into England, where it was also known as tallage. Restricted to seignorial organization it was not different from the continental *taille,* but as applied to boroughs it corresponded to the extraordinary aids that came to be levied by various princes in the twelfth century. This royal tallage was secured from the boroughs by individual negotiation with each, a practice that was common throughout western Europe. From this practice it was a logical step for the princes to summon representatives of the towns to meet with the clergy and feudal aristocracy in a parliament, diet, or meeting of estates. There the representatives generally bargained to secure wanted privileges. The story of taxation here told has little place for juristic theory on the right of princes to so-called feudal imposts, but sensibly portrays the ordinary tax, whatever it was called, as developing informally through trial and error. When the economic revolution had made the bourgeoisie the obvious class to tap for money, individual negotiation was constantly increased until finally it came to be superseded by negotiation in assemblies. The summoning of these assemblies was dictated by numerous motives, but the presence of the third estate is satisfactorily accounted for only by the prince's need of money.

In his articles on Domesday Book Carl Stephenson has followed the paths blazed by Maitland and Round, but this has never deterred him from challenging their conclusions when he believed them unwarranted by the evidence. He thus took issue with Round who, though hedging, had finally agreed with Maitland that Domesday Book testified to freedom of commendation. Carl Stephenson again based his argument on the insufficiency of legal evidence as against the practical evidence of economic dictation. Perhaps the ordinary inhabitant of Anglo-Saxon England could legally alienate his land, but his economic status would render this action almost unthinkable. In reality, commendation was a bond between lord and economic dependent that was not easily broken and, when so understood, depicts the seignorial organization of Anglo-Saxon England not unlike that which the Normans had known and practiced after 1066. Such a seignorial pattern was not, as Carl Stephenson was to argue a few years later, peculiar to Anglo-Saxon England. Examining the continental historical narratives, charters, and *leges barbarorum* of the early mediaeval period, he could find merely the picture of a fundamentally aristocratic society resting, as in England, upon the simple peasant who had no freedom of commendation. His conclusion, though not revolutionary, was so closely knit with the evidence and so far removed from Germanist argument that it gave a solid blow to the beloved *Markgenossenschaft* of Möser, Maurer, and Below, as well as to the idyllic township of Kemble, Freeman, and Green. Rather than beginning with a vague sort of democratic freedom which he somehow lost and finally won back, the common man started in the early

Middle Ages with no actual freedom and was only to achieve it in the later Middle Ages.

On the origin of feudalism Carl Stephenson has lent his support to the explanation that traces vassalage to the Germanic *comitatus* of Tacitus and then links it to fief-holding, which dates back to Charles Martel, who granted land in return for the service of heavy-armed cavalry. When in the course of the eighth century vassalage and fief-holding were united, real feudalism had arrived. Carl Stephenson thus corroborates the early suggestions of Montesquieu and the later arguments of Heinrich Brunner and Ferdinand Lot. While agreeing with George Burton Adams that no real feudalism existed in England prior to 1066, Carl Stephenson takes issue with him on the basis for this conclusion. Adams believed that his failure to find the *patrocinium* in Anglo-Saxon England was proof of the lack of feudalism. Carl Stephenson contends that, whether or not such an arrangement existed in Anglo-Saxon England, no true feudalism was to be found there because knight service and fief-holding came only with the Norman Conquest. In this connection he has put forward the suggestion that one explanation for lack of knight service in pre-Norman England may have been the absence of the *destrier*, the large war charger which enabled heavy-armed men to fight on horseback; for until 1066 the Anglo-Saxon thegn possessed only a much smaller horse incapable of such a task. Carl Stephenson then goes on to ask whether on the Continent the introduction of the *destrier* had a bearing upon the development of knight service in the eighth century. This question yet awaits the attention of a specialist.

Of even greater value than Carl Stephenson's opinions on the origin of feudalism is his concept of its significance. In sharp contrast to the prevalent view that feudalism was a destructive political force responsible for the break-up of the Carolingian Empire, he insists that feudalism was a constructive and useful political system. The Carolingian Empire was doomed to fall, not because of feudalism, but because it was too large to be supported by an agrarian economy. Actually feudalism was the only system that could provide for essential political and military needs during the tenth and eleventh centuries. Proof of its constructive political force is that in Flanders, Normandy, Anjou, the Ile de France, and England it was employed by local rulers to forge strong centralized states that survived. Feudalism worked well if limited to an area not too large for the conditions imposed by a manorial economy and small enough to be controlled by a feudal lord.

It will now be left to the articles that follow to impart more clearly what Carl Stephenson envisions as the task of the historian and the proper approach to it. Here arid speculation is absent; here documentary evidence, interpreted by common sense, abounds. Here is no grand view of history portrayed on a large canvas; here is history that shows realistically how the typical feudal lord, bourgeois, or simple peasant carried on his daily life and ordered his affairs. Is not this, after all, the kind of history we want from a mediaevalist?

BRYCE D. LYON

Harvard University
April, 1954

xii

Acknowledgments

THE editor wishes to thank the following publishers for granting permission to reprint the articles that appear in this volume: The editors of *Le Moyen Age*. "Les 'aides' des villes françaises aux XIIᵉ et XIIIᵉ siècles," Second Series, XXIV (1922), 274–328.
The editors of *La Revue Belge de Philologie et d'Histoire*. "The Origin and Nature of the *Taille*," V (1926), 801–70.
Houghton Mifflin Company. "Taxation and Representation in the Middle Ages." *Anniversary Essays in Mediaeval History*, by Students of Charles Homer Haskins (Boston and New York, 1929), pp. 291–312.
Columbia University Press. "The Beginnings of Representative Government in England." *The Constitution Reconsidered* (New York, 1938), pp. 25–36.
Longmans, Green and Company. "The *Firma Noctis* and the Customs of the Hundred," and "Commendation and Related Problems in Domesday." *The English Historical Review*, XXXIX (1924), 161–74; LIX (1944), 289–310.
The Mediaeval Academy of America. "Notes on the Composition and Interpretation of Domesday Book." *Speculum*, XXII (1947), 1–15.
The Macmillan Company. "The Origin and Significance of

Feudalism," "Feudalism and Its Antecedents in England," and "The Problem of the Common Man in Early Medieval Europe." *The American Historical Review,* XLVI (1941), 788–812; XLVIII (1943), 245–65; LI (1946), 419–38.

The editor is also deeply grateful for the financial support of Cornell University, which made this volume possible. Professor Paul W. Gates, chairman of the History Department, has greatly helped in launching the project and has given generously of his time. The staff of the Cornell University Press has contributed friendly and expert assistance. Professor Carl Stephenson has kindly lent his aid in preparing the manuscript for publication. As his footnotes to particular essays show, the purpose has been to present reprints, rather than works brought up to date by thorough revision.

Without such hearty co-operation, the editor repeats, this book could not have appeared.

The Aids of the French Towns in the Twelfth and Thirteenth Centuries *

THE parliamentary system, which in the political evolution of western Europe constitutes the intermediate stage between the feudalism of the twelfth century and the absolutism of the sixteenth, was principally characterized by the advance of the so-called Third Estate; and that directly resulted from the newly developed wealth of the bourgeoisie. These facts are evident, but how such changes originated remains obscure. When, in the fourteenth century, the kings of France took subsidies voted by regular assemblies, by virtue of what right did the representatives of the *bonnes villes* appear alongside the members of the clergy and nobility? To believe certain authors, feudal law was the basis of the whole system. The bourgeoisie, like the two superior orders, had come to be bound to the monarchy by essentially feudal ties; it was therefore necessary that representa-

* Published as "Les 'aides' des villes françaises aux XIIe et XIIIe siècles," *Le Moyen Age,* Second Series, XXIV (1922), 274–328; French translation by Maurice Prou. The original manuscript was long since thrown away. The Cornell University Press now wants a version in English; so a retranslation has been made by the author, who has thus been enabled to revise a good many paragraphs. Such revision has necessarily been influenced by knowledge acquired in years after 1922; but the substance of the article, with its central thesis, remains unaltered.

tives of the towns should be summoned for consent to all extraordinary measures, whether financial or otherwise. But if, according to the ruling opinion, only communes enjoyed the rank of vassal, why was it that other *bonnes villes* were also represented? Or if, as has been stated, emancipation was itself a feudal procedure, resulting from a contract between a *seigneur* and his *roturiers,* why were so many of the latter left out of the estates? What principles other than feudal could the men of that age supply? To answer these questions, we must examine the scanty evidence provided by documents of the twelfth and thirteenth centuries.

Thus necessarily coming to consider the origin of the mediaeval town, we are at once confronted by a number of contradictory opinions. Yet it will suffice, as an introduction to the present study, to note certain points on which there is general agreement. The elementary advance of the town was that it became free of seignorial control, securing emancipation from various rights held over the population by a lord or various lords. Furthermore, the means of assuring this first step was the conclusion of an agreement that provided, not merely an improvement for the local residents, but also one for the lords concerned. Up to a certain point, accordingly, the bourgeois and the peasant marched along the same road; in this first stage of the journey they both sought to free themselves from their most oppressive obligations, such as the arbitrary *taille* (a sort of manorial tax) and unlimited *ost et chevauchée* (a sort of manorial military service).[1] These two obligations are well known; but, for the sake of a clear understanding, it is well to remember some of their characteristics. In the first place, neither was by strict definition feudal; since the lord did not require them from his vassals. No more were they purely manorial, for they were often exacted from men outside the demesne proper— as by the king when he demanded them from the tenants of many

[1] H. Sée, *Les classes rurales et le régime domanial en France au moyen âge* (Paris, 1901), pp. 245 ff., 263, 267 ff.; A. Luchaire, *Les communes françaises,* ed. L. Halphen (Paris, 1911), pp. 53, 133, and *Manuel des institutions françaises* (Paris, 1892), pp. 319 ff., 373, 383; H. Pirenne, in *La Revue Historique,* LVII, 59 ff.

ecclesiastics.[2] Whether or not the *taille,* as has been asserted,[3] was originally servile, it was generally regarded as a detestable mark of inferior status. Its arbitrary character, as well as that of *ost et chevauchée,* was generally ended by enfranchisement.[4] In this connection two matters deserve emphasis. First, to any special expense faced by a nobleman during the agrarian age his peasants had to contribute, usually through a *taille.* Secondly, until a charter or other settlement had ended the primitive *taille,* there was no reason for an extraordinary *taille.* If custom permitted, the needy lord could exact an aid from his vassals or, in default of precedent, he could ask for a voluntary subsidy. In either case the payment could be called a feudal aid; whether the money was got from the men of the vassals was no concern to the lord. With or without such a feudal aid, he could address himself to his own peasants. If they were *taillables à merci,* he merely took what he pleased; if they had been enfranchised, their charters might have reserved special *tailles* and the reserved cases might correspond with those when vassals were required to contribute. Peasants could thus be expected to pay a *taille* or aid when their lord was taken prisoner or again when he had to help in ransoming his own lord. In neither case can it be correctly said that the peasants gave him a feudal aid.[5] But explicit res-

[2] Sée, 318 ff., 374; Luchaire, *Histoire des institutions monarchiques de la France sous les premiers Capétiens* (Paris, 1891), II, 113, 138 ff.; F. Senn, *L'institution des avoueries ecclésiastiques en France* (Paris, 1903), pp. 132 ff., and *L'institution des vidamies en France* (Paris, 1907), pp. 137 ff.

[3] Sée, pp. 175 ff., 308 ff., 323 ff.

[4] *Ibid.,* pp. 311, 357 ff., 367 ff.; Luchaire, *Manuel,* pp. 309, 348. For specific examples see below.

[5] The origin and nature of the aids called feudal remain uncertain. The classic sketches, such as that in A. Vuitry, *Études sur le régime financier de la France* (Paris, 1878), pp. 384 ff., are based on customals of the thirteenth and fourteenth centuries, which reflect legalistic doctrines hardly formulated in the age of municipal origins. The feudal aid is generally defined as an extraordinary subsidy taken on certain occasions by a lord from all persons, noble or non-noble, under his authority—Vuitry, as above; Luchaire, *Manuel,* pp. 206–07. It is to be regretted that, in this regard, Luchaire did not maintain the distinction he had earlier made (*Institutions monarchiques,* I, 126 ff.) and insist on the term *aide seigneuriale;* cf. *Manuel,* p. 331, n. 1. To call the feudal aid money paid by a peasant is perhaps a matter of slight importance, but the confusion of the aid given by a vassal with the sums levied by him on his tenants to make up that aid renders impossible an

ervation of extraordinary *tailles* was by no means common in the twelfth century; quite generally the usage was left to be decided by custom, by persuasion, or by force. These questions concern also the towns. For further evidence we must examine the pertinent charters, and in that connection it will be convenient to begin with the royal towns of the twelfth century.

Here we have to note a remarkable fact: restriction of the *taille* is absent from many charters granted by Louis VI, Louis VII, and Philip Augustus to powerful communes, while it appears in most charters to less important towns.[6] Thus the clearest and fullest exemption is found in the famous grant of Louis VI to Lorris:[7]

Nullus, nec nos nec alius, hominibus de Lorriaco talliam nec ablationem nec rogam faciat.

This article, together with another restricting *ost et chevauchée* to one day, was regularly inserted in the numerous *filiales* of the charter to Lorris.[8] Likewise the charters to Bourges

---

understanding of seignorial taxation. The discussion of this question by even so lucid a writer as M. Sée (*Les classes rurales*, p. 485) leaves much to be desired. The evidence generally cited for the collection of aids or extraordinary *tailles* from peasants does not antedate the thirteenth century. Besides, except for the dubious levy of 1147, there is no proof that any French king before Louis IX obtained a feudal aid (Luchaire, *Manuel*, pp. 578–79). But see the letters patent issued in 1222 by William, bishop of Paris, to record an agreement with Philip Augustus (A. Teulet, *Layettes du Trésor des Chartes*, I, 554): "Habet siquidem dominus rex et successores sui in burgo Sancti Germani, in cultura episcopi, et in clauso Brunelli exercitum et equitacionem, vel taillam propter hoc factam, et guetum sicut in communi ville Parisiensis; et habet super homines illius burgi et culture episcopi et clausi Brunelli taillam quotiens filios suos faciet milites novos, et quando filias suas maritabit, et etiam si redimeretur de captione proprii corporis sui facta in guerra; et eodem modo habebunt successores sui super homines predictos. Propter alias autem causas non possunt a domino rege vel successoribus suis tailliari dictorum locorum homines sine assensu episcopi."

[6] Luchaire, *Louis VI le Gros* (Paris, 1890), pp. clxxix ff., and *Institutions monarchiques*, II, 177 ff.; M. Prou, "Les coutumes de Lorris," *La Nouvelle Revue Historique de Droit Français et Etranger*, VIII, 167. For other examples of charters containing a restriction of *taille* and of military service see Luchaire, *Etude sur les actes de Louis VII* (Paris, 1885), nos. 299, 318; H. F. Delaborde, *Recueil des actes de Philippe-Auguste* (Paris, 1916), nos. 5, 16, 21, 84, 194, etc.

[7] *Ibid.*, no. 202; Prou, p. 448. In a translation cited by M. Prou *oblatio* is rendered by *tousse* (i.e. *tolte*) and *roga* by *demande*.

[8] Given by Louis VI to Moulinet and La-Chapelle-la-Reine; by Louis VII and Philip Augustus to seventy other small towns (*ibid.*, pp. 301 ff.).

4

THE AIDS OF THE FRENCH TOWNS

and Dun-le-Roi, two towns that never attained the rank of commune, contain the following provision: [9]

Ab omni tolta et tallia et botagio et culcitrarum exactione omnino quieti et liberi erunt.

These bourgeois, therefore, were definitely freed of all arbitrary impositions, including *gîte;* and the following article guarantees that they should not be called for military service outside the country of Berry.

Among the communal charters that of Laon, in 1128, is especially famous as having provided the model for a series of charters to rural communes created by the French kings in the twelfth century. It contains a provision which, however common in grants to small towns, is rare in those to communes: the *taille* is limited to a poll tax of four *deniers* on four occasions, not specified.[10] In the other communes of the Laonnais the payment of *taille* remained an individual obligation, rather than a communal charge. But Montdidier, to which the liberties of Laon were extended in 1195, received complete exemption.[11] Com-

[9] Delaborde, no. 40; confirmation by Philip Augustus of the charters granted to Bourges and Dun-le-Roi by Louis VII. Of these charters only the latter is extant (Luchaire, *Actes de Louis VII*, p. 692).

[10] Delaborde, no. 279: "Consuetudinarias autem tallias ita reparavimus ut unusquisque hominum ipsas tallias debentium singulis terminis quibus tallias debet quatuor denarios solvat." The first of the rural communes to be established after the model of Laon was the group of Bruyères-sous-Laon, originally set up by Louis VI in 1129 and confirmed by Philip Augustus in 1186 (*ibid.,* no. 197). From this charter it appears that the *taille* was due three times a year: "Consuetudinarie autem tallie ita temperate sunt ut . . . tria placita per annum solvent et per singula placita quatuor denarios bone monete." Cf. another document of 1129 (Luchaire, *Louis VI*, p. 337), which refers to "placitis sive talliis." All this is a.bit confusing but seems to indicate a close connection between the holding of the seignorial court, generally three times a year, and the levy of *taille*. Hence *placitum* was sometimes used to mean or imply the *taille*. Cf. the charter of Meaux (below, n. 14) and Luchaire, *Manuel*, p. 343. On the other rural communes of the Laonnais see Luchaire, *Les communes françaises*, pp. 79 ff.; Delaborde, no. 110; *Ordonnances des rois de France*, XI, 276, 279; and below, n. 43. The eight villages of the Cerny group, according to their charter of 1184, were to pay fifteen *livres* as *droit de commune* and all but two a double *cens* in addition. A precedent for this arrangement, also applied to Crépy-en-Laonnais (Delaborde, no. 129), had been established by Louis VII who in 1134 freed Alluets-le-Roi of all *taille, tolte, ost et chevauchée, corvées,* and other exactions in return for double rents (*Ordonnances*, VII, 275).

[11] *Ibid.,* XII, 288: "Nullus hominum hujus pacis talliam persolvat."

5

parable are the customs of Soissons, which also enjoyed wide influence. The original charter from Louis VI begins with the following article: [12]

Infra firmitates civitatis Suissionensis alter alteri recte secundum suam opinionem auxiliabitur, et nullatenus pacietur quod aliquis alicui eorum aliquid auferat vel ei talliatam faciat, vel quidlibet de rebus ejus capiat, excepto hoc quod homines civitatis episcopo per tres menses de pane et de carne et de piscibus creditionem facient.

The same clause, or nearly that, appears in most of the affiliated charters that M. Bourgin has so excellently described. But a variant in the charter of Compiègne adds the information that the association for mutual resistance to the levy of *taille* was sworn as part of the communal oath.[13] If any doubt remains as to the meaning of this custom derived from Soissons, comparison with the privilege granted to Mantes about the same time should be decisive: [14]

Ut omnes qui in eadem permanebunt communitate ab omni talliata, injusta captione, creditione et ab omni irrationabili exactione, cujuscumque sint homines, liberi et immunes jure perpetuo permaneant.

In both towns, for the benefit of all inhabitants, we find the abolition of the same exactions: the *taille,* arbitrary seizure of goods, and compulsory credit. From the charter of Mantes were derived those of Bruyère in 1170, of Chevrières and Chaumont in 1182, of Pontoise and Poissy in 1188, and of Les Andelys in 1204.[15]

[12] Delaborde, no. 35; G. Bourgin, *La commune de Soissons* (Paris, 1908), p. 424. The same expressions are found in the charter of Vailly (Delaborde, no. 159).

[13] *Ibid.,* no. 169: "Juraverunt videlicet quod infra firmitates . . ." etc. Cf. the charters of Senlis, Sens, La-Neuville-Roi, and Crépy-en-Valois. M. Bourgin does not discuss the question of *taille* at Soissons and interprets the quoted article (p. 117) as "interdisant aux membres de la commune de se tailler mutuellement." But the essential purpose of the passage in question was clearly to prohibit exactions by all lords, with an exception made for the bishop. At the last moment I find I have been anticipated in this conclusion by N. P. Ottokar, *Essays on the History of French Towns in the Middle Ages* (published in Russian; Perm, 1919). I owe this reference to the kindness of my colleague Professor Rostovtseff.

[14] Confirmation of 1151, *Ordonnances,* XI, 197. See Luchaire, *Les communes françaises,* p. 137.

[15] *Ordonnances,* VI, 619; Delaborde, nos. 51, 59, 233, 234; L. V. Delisle, in *Mémoires de la Société des Antiquaires de Normandie,* XVI, xv, n. 1.

From the evidence provided by these five groups of royal charters, including most if not all that mention the *taille*,[16] certain definite conclusions may be drawn. First, the arbitrary *taille* was ended in these towns, being either wholly abolished or commuted into a fixed contribution; and in no instance did the king reserve extraordinary *tailles* or aids on particular occasions.[17] Secondly, similar exemption must have been granted in many cases when express mention of the fact is not made by the charters; for it is improbable that mere villages like those in the Lorris group obtained privileges not enjoyed by powerful communes to the north.[18] Precisely what had been the original condition of the bourgeois in the latter remains uncertain. We do not know to whom they had owed *taille* or how it had been assessed; but that it had somehow come to be ended is certain. This is a subject that may be elucidated by a comparative study of the more important seignorial towns.

In the great fiefs, as in the royal domain, grants of franchises were somewhat haphazard. The oldest charters tended to have

[16] Other examples: Dizy (*Ordonnances*, IV, 341) and Vézelay (Delisle, *Catalogue des actes de Philippe-Auguste*, no. 750); also Chateauneuf-de-Tours, to which Louis VII promised that neither he nor his successors would take any money from them by force—A. Giry, *Les établissements de Rouen* (Paris, 1883–85), I, 190, n. 1.

[17] It would seem that, in this respect, there was absolutely no distinction between the communes and other privileged towns. So far as military service was concerned, the question has already been discussed by L. L. Borrelli de Serres, *Recherches sur divers services publics* (Paris, 1895), I, 507; and in consequence certain remarks by Luchaire in *Les communes françaises* have been modified by M. Halphen. But proof to justify the generally accepted opinion that communes like vassals were obliged to pay feudal aids is equally hard to find. The mistake may perhaps be attributed to a remark by L. G. Bréquigny (*Ordonnances*, XI, lvi), that the communes regularly had to pay aids on three or four occasions. The only reference he gave is to the charter of Doullens, which enjoyed the liberties of Abbeville—a town later made famous by the studies of Thierry. See Luchaire, *Les communes françaises*, p. 100, and *Manuel*, p. 413; E. Glasson, *Histoire du droit et des institutions de la France* (Paris, 1887–96), V, 105; Giry, *Rouen*, I, 440; J. Flammermont, *Histoire des institutions municipales de Senlis* (Paris, 1881), p. 100; L. H. Labande, *Histoire de Beauvais* (Paris, 1892), p. 241. Speaking of the communes, Giry and Réville, in E. Lavisse et A. Rambaud, *Histoire générale*, II, 445, make the following generalization: "Toutes, sans exception, au même titre que des feudataires, étaient tenues de fournir des subsides, les *aides féodales*, dans les *quatres cas déterminés*." For further discussion of this subject see below.

[18] Thus the fact that certain communal charters, like those of Noyon and Beauvais, do not mention the *taille* has no especial significance. See Labande, *Beauvais*, pp. 90–91.

7

superior influence, and chance quite frequently decided whether a particular liberty was or was not expressly mentioned. Absence of such documentary evidence by no means proves that the bourgeois concerned did not enjoy the liberty. In Flanders, for example, the men of the greater towns seem to have been so firmly possessed of elementary rights that, by the twelfth century, there was little need of recording them in formal charters. Thus the *keures* issued by Philip of Alsace are essentially restricted to details of law, civil or criminal, and hardly refer to communal obligations.[19] Nevertheless, it happened that in 1127 Saint-Omer received from William Clito a very different kind of charter. It gives us valuable information, not only about the liberties of the town, but also about the prevailing custom of the county:[20]

Et sicut meliores et liberiores burgenses Flandriae ab omni consuetudine liberos deinceps esse volo; nullum scoth, nullam talliam, nullam pecuniae suae petitionem ab eis requiro.

Held at an earlier time by the count of Flanders, the two fiefs of Vermandois and the Amiénois were brought into the royal domain by Philip Augustus. Thus extending his direct authority over the towns of Saint-Quentin, Amiens, and Péronne, he established or confirmed communes in all three; and their charters fail to mention *taille*. The customs of Amiens had slight influence; but those of Péronne were spread to at least a half-dozen towns of Picardy, and those of Saint-Quentin to Ham, Chauny, Roye, and Eu.[21] Although we do not know just what

---

[19] For example to Nieuport, Arras, Audenarde, Ghent, Bruges, and Ypres— C. Giraud, *Essai sur l'histoire du droit français* (Paris, 1846), I, 38; Delaborde, no. 473; L. A. Warnkönig, *Histoire de la Flandre*, ed. A.-E. Gheldolf (Brussels, 1835–64), II, 421, IV, 463, V, 426.

[20] *Ibid.*, II, 412; Giry, *Histoire de la ville de Saint-Omer* (Paris, 1877), p. 370. It is possible that charters then granted to other Flemish communes have been lost (*ibid.*, p. 56).

[21] Charters to Amiens, Péronne, and Saint-Quentin; *Ordonnances*, XI, 264, V, 159, XI, 270. See Giry, *Etude sur les origines de la commune de Saint-Quentin* (Saint-Quentin, 1887), pp. 16 ff.; also Luchaire, *Les communes françaises*, p. 137. The first article in the charter of Saint-Quentin somewhat reminds us of the Soissons custom: "Quod homines communiae omnibus rebus suis quieti et liberi permaneant; neque nos neque alius super aliquem de communia quicquam, nisi judicio scabinorum clamare possit." Like Hesdin, Cappy, Athies, and Aire, Bray-sur-Somme acquired the liberties of Péronne; but for the decision of dubious matters it asked for advice from Saint-Quentin and Arras. Although Giry thought this

fiscal privilege was enjoyed in the towns of this first group, we have exceptionally precise information about such privilege in the second group. The men of Eu, in 1151, wrote to those of Saint-Quentin, asking for an authentic statement of their liberties. A translation of the response has been preserved and it contains the following provisions: [22]

Les bourgeois de Saint-Quaintin de doivent nulle ayde en nulle maniere à leur seigneur, ne ne se assemblent pour faire li taille, mais se aucun li veut donner de son grè, conme requis du seigneur, selonc son plaisir il li donra.

This liberty of voluntarily granting all aid is, it is true, not specified in the charter obtained by Eu in 1155, which merely accords the customs of Saint-Quentin. Yet such liberty was actually maintained by the bourgeois, as is proved by letters patent dating from the next century.[23]

The archives of Saint-Quentin also contain a statement of 1158 concerning the liberties of Ham. In it we read the following articles: [24]

Concessum est quoque ut nullus dominus hujus castri aliquando faciet ullam captionem neque ablationem neque violentiam cuiquam de communia . . . Si dominus captus fuerit, vel filium suum militem fecerit, vel filiam suam maritaverit, burgenses debent ei xx libras.

It should be noted that we encounter here, in connection with municipal finance, the famous three aids of northern French custom. Whether or not they were listed among the original customs of Saint-Quentin we do not know; but they reappear in the charter of a neighboring town.

Abbeville, in 1184, received from Count John of Ponthieu the liberties of Amiens, Corbie, and Saint-Quentin.[25]

article implied no borrowing of customs, it is noteworthy that the charter of Bray included a guarantee very much like that to be reported for Saint-Quentin (*Ordonnances*, XI, 295).

22 Giry, *Saint-Quentin*, p. 77.

23 A. Legris, *Le livre rouge d'Eu* (*Société de l'histoire de Normandie*, 1911), pp. 1, 91.

24 Giry, *Saint-Quentin*, p. 79.

25 *Ordonnances*, IV, 53; Teulet, *Layettes*, I, 141.

Praeterea statutum est quod nec ego Johannes comes Pontivi, nec heredes mei, nec alii domini terrarum que infra Abbatis Villam siti sunt, aliquam exactionem a burgensibus exigere poterunt, nec credent michi nec alicui dominorum sine vadimonio nisi ex propria voluntate, nisi tale fuit tenementum cujus possessor certam summam domino suo ex debito credere teneatur . . . Nec silentio pretereundum est quod tantum tria auxilia idem burgenses michi tenentur ex debito solvere; centum videlicet libras Pontivensis monete ad filium meum militem faciendum, centum libras filie mee conjugande, centum libras ad redemptionem meam de captione.

This charter, in turn, became the model for other towns within the county.[26]

We meet with a different form of exemption in the charters issued by the counts of Beaumont-sur-Oise, of which the prototype seems to be that granted to Chambly in 1173. The bourgeois were held for unrestricted *ost et chevauchée,* but a fixed payment of five *sous* per house was substituted *pro talliis, corveis, et demandis.*[27] The same provision reappears in the charters of Méru and Beaumont. Bonvilliers was freed in another fashion, while Chauny had already obtained exemption by receiving the liberties of Saint-Quentin.[28]

It is well known that in Normandy municipal autonomy was not so complete as in Flanders and Picardy. Nevertheless, the charter of Duke Henry (later Henry II of England) to Rouen in 1150, eventually confirmed by John and Philip Augustus, wholly abolished the arbitrary *taille*: [29]

26 F. C. Louandre, *Histoire d'Abbeville et du comté de Ponthieu* (Abbeville, 1883), pp. 156 ff. Some of these charters were confirmed by Philip Augustus in 1222 (*Ordonnances,* XII, 297).

27 L. C. Douët d'Arcq, *Recherches historiques et critiques sur les anciens comtes de Beaumont-sur-Oise* (Amiens, 1855), p. 165.

28 *Ibid.,* pp. 158, 160, 170. These charters were confirmed, some by Philip Augustus, the rest by Louis VIII. That of Bonvilliers is especially noteworthy because it clearly excluded all customary *taille* without specific reserve: "Pro his vero redditibus et consuetudinibus qui in hac karta enumerantur, do eis omnem libertatem et sint quieti et liberi de omnis arveriis, et de omnibus corveis, et de omnibus interrogationibus, et de omnibus taliis; ita quod nichil ab eis exigere potero nisi quod michi retineo et quod karta dicit."

29 Giry, *Rouen,* II, 58. The charter of Philip Augustus in 1207 seems to establish the same franchise in different terms: "Nec eos cogemus ad reddendum nobis talliam per consuetudinem nisi sponte sua nobis dare voluerint."

Quod nec tailliam faciam super eos nec res eorum capiam nisi sua bona voluntate prestare voluerint michi.

Extended to many Norman towns by the dukes, the *établisse-ments de Rouen* were confirmed by Philip Augustus for Falaise, Pont Audemer, Alençon, and Verneuil; though, as has been seen, Les Andelys received a different charter modeled on that of Mantes. In Poitou these same privileges of Rouen were accorded to La Rochelle, Saintes, Oléron, Saint-Jean d'Angély, Cognac, Angoulême, and Poitiers, most of which kept them under the French kings.[30] In the region to the east municipal development was slower; most towns did not obtain charters until the thirteenth century. The oldest commune of Champagne was Meaux, which in 1179 received a charter influenced by that of Soissons. After stipulating the payment of a yearly *droit de commune,* the count renounces the *taille* in the following terms: [31]

Sub prenotatis itaque constitutionibus omnes homines meos, quicumque in prescripta communia fuerint, quietos et immunes a tallia et a placito quod dicitur generale imperpetuum esse concedo, salvo quidem jure meo per omnia.

It is probable that the final clause vaguely refers to certain customary payments claimed by the count; for the charter subsequently refers to *collectae* or *misae* established by the commune "pro auxilio meo vel expeditione vel quacumque de causa." Similar grants were made to Provins in 1190, to Fismes in 1227, and to Ecueil in 1229.[32] The smaller towns of Champagne ordinarily received the liberties of Lorris.[33]

Tonnerre was freed of its customary *taille* in 1174 by Count Guy of Nevers who, however, reserved *ost et chevauchée,* a tithe of all crops, and a *cens* of six *deniers* per house.[34] His successor

---

[30] *Ibid.,* I, 47 ff.

[31] Teulet, *Layettes,* I, 124; R. Bourgeois, *Du mouvement communal dans le comté de Champagne aux XIIᵉ et XIIIᵉ siècles* (Paris, 1904), p. 115. Bourgin, *Soissons,* p. 296.

[32] Teulet, *Layettes,* I, 164, II, 115, 160; Bourgeois, p. 122; Bourgin, pp. 302 ff.

[33] Prou, *Lorris,* pp. 303 ff.; H. d'Arbois de Jubainville, *Histoire des ducs et des comtes de Champagne* (Paris, 1859–66), IV, 711; Bourgeois, *Du mouvement communal,* p. 157.

[34] *Ordonnances,* XI, 217.

Pierre likewise took care of future revenue when, in 1190, he conceded to Auxerre that "pro tallia et corvatis et aliis exactionibus quitandis" the richer bourgeois should annually pay him twenty *sous* and the others less in proportion to their means.[35] Dijon, the foremost commune of Burgundy, received the liberties of Soissons in 1187.[36] As at Meaux, permanent relief from *taille* was given in return for a yearly *droit de commune;* the language of the two charters is, indeed, identical. Blois obtained complete exemption in 1196 from Louis, count of Blois, by a charter including this provision: [37]

Omnes homines Blesis et infra banlivam Blesis manentes talliam michi debentes et eorum heredes a tallia, ablatione, imprumtato, et roga coacta de cetero penitus quitto et immunes esse concedo.

In the Midi enfranchisement from the *taille* or *quête,* as it was often called, was a virtually universal characteristic of town charters; and when the privilege first appears, it seems to have been already old. Thus Bernard-Aton V, viscount of Nîmes, wrote to the bourgeois of that town in 1145: [38]

Et insuper laudo et concedo et dono per me et omnes successores meos eis omnibus . . . illam indulgenciam quam pater meus et mater et fratres mei fecerunt eis, videlicet, toltas et quistas coactas.

Indeed, all the great communes of eastern Languedoc—Beaucaire, Alais, Mende, Calvison, and others—seem to have enjoyed similar immunity at least from the beginning of the thirteenth century.[39] A town to the west, Saint-Antonin-en-Rouergue, obtained from its viscount about 1144 a charter containing this provision: [40]

Donamus et absolvimus in perpetuum illam malam consuetudinem quae vocatur questa; praeter hoc quod nobis dare voluerint sua

[35] E. Baluze, *Miscellanea* (Lucca, 1761–64), III, 85.

[36] J. Garnier, *Chartes de communes et d'affranchissements en Bourgogne* (Dijon, 1867), I, 4; Bourgin, *Soissons,* p. 362.

[37] J. Soyer et G. Trouillard, *Cartulaire de la ville de Blois,* p. 50. A similar grant was made to Clermont-en-Beauvaisis in 1197 (Teulet, *Layettes,* I, 192).

[38] L. Ménard, *Histoire . . . de la ville de Nismes* (Paris, 1750), *Preuves,* no. 19.

[39] R. Michel, *L'administration royale dans la sénéchaussée de Beaucaire au temps de Saint Louis* (Paris, 1910), pp. 211, 215, 217, 225, 241, 373; Anon., *Recherches historiques sur la ville d'Alais* (Alais, 1860), p. 453.

[40] Teulet, *Layettes,* I, 55.

propria voluntate . . . ita quod numquam queramus eis suam pec-
cuniam vel aliquid de suo extra suam voluntatem.

The privileges of Toulouse date at least from 1147, when Count
Alphonse gave to the city a charter recognizing its freedom from
questa et tolta, forced credit, and military service except that
required to repel invasion.[41] Essentially the same custom prevailed at Montpellier, Carcassonne, Albi, and Agen; as well as in
many other towns whose charters, to avoid monotonous repetition, need not be cited.[42]

With regard to the seignorial towns we thus have to conclude
that their enfranchisement everywhere included abolition of the
arbitrary *taille.* Although, as has been seen, such abolition was
not specified in many royal charters to communes, we may surely
agree that it was somehow granted also to them. For many this
meant only the confirmation of a *fait accompli*—the established
independence from ecclesiastical rule, which naturally implied
the abrogation of such manorial customs as the *taille.* This
argument is supported by the fact that episcopal and monastic
towns which never attained the autonomy of communes were
regularly freed of *taille* in return for a promise of extraordinary
subsidies on special occasions.[43] And it should here be noted

[41] C. Devic et J. Vaissete, *Histoire générale de Languedoc,* V, column 1096.

[42] Teulet, *Layettes,* I, 261: "Consuetudines villae Montispessulani. . . . Toltam
vel quistam vel mutuum coactum vel aliquam exactionem coactam non habet nec
unquam habuit dominus Montispessulani in habitoribus Montispessulani presentibus vel futuris." See A. Germain, *Histoire de la commune de Montpellier*
(Montpellier, 1851), I, 112. Carcassonne claimed the same privilege (Teulet, *Layettes,* I, 272). Cf. the charter of 1220 for Albi (Giraud, *Histoire du droit français,*
I, 84). In 1248 Raymond VII of Toulouse confirmed as an old franchise "quod in
civibus Agenni supradictis universaliter vel singulariter quistam, talliam, vel
mutuum non habebimus nisi ipsi talliam nobis vellent dare vel mutuum facere de
eorum spontanea voluntate" (*Archives municipales d'Agen, Chartes, 1189-1328,*
p. 67). See the charters of other towns in Devic et Vaissete, VIII, columns 873,
1081, 1248, 1725.

[43] Certain examples will at least serve to show the diversity of custom in this
respect. Langres was freed in 1168 of all *taille* and *tolte* by a charter of the
bishop (E. Petit, *Histoire des ducs de Bourgogne,* III, 81). In 1194 the bishop of
Mende ended a dispute with his bourgeois by renouncing all unjust exactions and
bad customs that he and his predecessors had established, promising that he would
not levy "alberguos, toltos, talhadas nisi quas evidens necessitas vel utilitas ecclesie
vel civitatis proposcerit et sanior pars populi approbaverit"—C. Porée, *Le con-
sulat de Mende* (Paris, 1901), pp. 49 ff. One of the commonest obligations of an

that the so-called *aides aux quatre cas* do not appear in the
municipal charters of the twelfth century. When lay lords made
reservations, it was rather for the familiar three aids of feudal
custom in Normandy; but examples of even such usage are
rare in the north and entirely absent in the south.[44] It was

ecclesiastical town was a *taille* paid for a campaign of the king when he had no
direct right to *ost et chevauchée* from the bourgeois; thus the "tallia pro exercitu
regis," demanded from Saint-Riquier in 1126 (*Ordonnances,* XI, 184). According
to a charter of 1185 (Delaborde, no. 156), the men of Ferrières were freed by their
abbot "ab omni demanda, exactione, et tallia"; but the king kept his right to *ost et
chevauchée,* and the bourgeois paid doubled rents on the election of a new abbot.
In the same year Philip Augustus confirmed an agreement between the bishop of
Laon and his men of Anizy (*ibid.,* no. 145), by virtue of which a yearly payment was substituted for the old *tailles en trois cas*: "pro exercitus nostri servitio,
pro domino papa, pro guerra Laudunensis ecclesie manifesta." A much more complicated settlement between the abbot of Tournus and his bourgeois was made in
1170 through the intervention of Louis VII (*Ordonnances,* XI, 205): "Talliam
quam singulis annis exigebant temperavimus hoc modo. Abbas super burgenses
nullam deinceps faciet talliam nisi pro auxilio aut procuratione nostra aut procuratione domini pape aut alicujus cardinalium." But the abbot could still take a
reasonable aid for any other important emergency facing his church. In 1181 the
abbot of Saint-Benoît-sur-Loire granted to men in certain villages (Delaborde,
no. 23) that they owed "nomine tallie" merely definite sums, but that the latter
should be doubled in case of a trip by the abbot to the papal court. At Molesme
the bourgeois customarily paid *ruis* (see below, notes 60, 63) on four occasions:
when the abbot went to Rome, when buildings other than the church and the
cloister were burned, when the abbot needed money for paying his debts, or
when he bought lands worth two hundred *livres* (Garnier, *Chartes de communes,*
II, 308). See also the case of Neuilly cited by Sée (*Les classes rurales,* p. 594), when
the abbot of Saint-Maur proved that four *tailles* had been reserved to him: for a
visit to the pope in France, the burning of the abbey, the king's coronation, or a
subsidy taken by him from churches within his domain.

[44] This statement is based only on the foregoing discussion, which is not presumed to be exhaustive. It is quite possible that someone may be able to cite a
charter of the twelfth century that specifies the *aides aux quatre cas,* but there
cannot be many such. Nor is the number three at all sacred; a charter of Raoul
de Coucy for Vervins in 1163 requires a subsidy only for his ransom or for that
of his son—N. LeLong, *Histoire ecclésiastique et civile du diocèse de Laon* (Cha-
lons, 1783), p. 607. Aumale, which had enjoyed the rank of commune since 1166,
was recognized in 1258 as owing *taille* to the count only in two cases: for his ransom and *l'ost du roi*—E. Semichon, *Histoire de la ville d'Aumale* (Paris, 1862),
I, 52. Even in the thirteenth century the documents evince no uniform practice in
this connection. Examples from one region will suffice. The Burgundian charters
published by Garnier prove that La-Roche-Pot, Chagny, and three other little
towns paid the so-called *aides aux quatre cas* (II, 94, 133, 153, 186, 189). Ampilly-
le-Sec paid two, for knighthood or crusade (II, 338); Noyers three, for marriage,
ransom, or crusade (II, 131); Seurre three, for marriage, crusade, or acquisition of

generally left for custom to determine the fiscal relations between the towns and their lords; the charters merely provided that special contributions should be voluntary.

Logically, then, we are confronted by the problem of how great lords actually obtained needed money from their towns. It is clear that they, according to strict interpretation of the charters, could expect little; for at least in the larger towns they reserved no *taille* or reserved it only on occasions that would rarely arise. Special provision was made neither for a crusade nor for any other war. Besides, the almost universal restriction of *ost et chevauchée* to a single day or to a limited neighborhood tended to interdict the raising of local troops for a major campaign or the substitution of an equivalent tax. In this connection the policy of the king is of prime importance; yet it should be remembered that he hardly ranked among the greatest French lords until the thirteenth century, when he could merely follow examples already set by his vassals. So, before turning to records of the royal government, we may try to learn something about methods adopted in the great fiefs to get money from the towns.

The slight evidence we have from the twelfth century comes from Normandy, and it is so fragmentary as to exclude very satisfactory explanation. From the exchequer rolls of 1180 and 1184 only remnants are extant. They show that a *taille* had been assessed on both urban and rural communities of the duchy; but the nature of the levy has to be conjectured through comparison with the rolls of subsequent years.[45] In 1195 the great aid for the ransom of King Richard was levied in both England and Normandy. According to established practice in the former, various classes of men throughout the duchy were required to contribute in various ways. We thus find accounts of an aid, of a *taille,* and of loans taken from lay nobles, ecclesiastics, and communities. It is possible that certain towns acquitted themselves by paying lump sums. At least at Caen, however, a tax was

---

land worth 500 *livres* (II, 207); Sagy four, on these three occasions plus knighthood (II, 328). Pontailler merely contributed a double *cens* when the lord was knighted (II, 299).

45 T. Stapleton, *Magni Rotuli Scaccarii Normanniae sub regibus Angliae* (London, 1840–44), I, 66, 74, 76, 117.

assessed by the viscount on the bourgeois individually.[46] Loans were exacted from Rouen, Pont-Audemer, Argentan, and Bernay.[47]

Better evidence concerning taxation of the Norman towns is provided by the roll of 1198, when *auxilia exercitus* or *tallagia servientium* were levied in the duchy. All the towns, however privileged, seem to have contributed in much the same way—by paying round sums instead of sending troops to the frontier.[48] If it is remembered that very similar taxes were developed in England under Henry II,[49] it will seem quite probable that those of Normandy originated at about the same time and in the same way. Whatever may be thought of this suggestion, it is certain that the *établissements de Rouen* did not prevent the dukes from getting money from the towns when it was needed. That famous set of liberties, indeed, merely required the lord to ask his bourgeois for the voluntary grant of a wanted subsidy. To what extent this article of the Rouen charter was observed by the successors of the Angevins in Normandy and Poitou will be seen below.

A group of customs with equal influence in regions to the east was that of Soissons. As already remarked, the charter of Soissons became the model for the most important towns of Champagne, headed by Meaux, and of Burgundy, headed by Dijon. Under this system the bourgeois were freed of all *taille* and various other obligations through annual payment of a lump sum as *droit de commune*. At Tonnerre, on the other hand, a different plan was put into effect: the *taille* was replaced by a fixed *cens,* taken from the bourgeois individually. At Auxerre, and a little later at Nevers, the *cens* was graduated in such fashion that each of the richer paid a yearly sum not to exceed a particular amount, while the poorer were assessed by a commission

46 *Ibid.,* I, 112, 221, 270.   47 *Ibid.,* I, 156, 209, 213, 247.

48 *Ibid.,* II, *passim.* In some cases a forced loan was exacted to supplement the *taille,* as at Caen (p. 346). It seems that the men of Pont-Sainte-Marie resisted the payment of this loan; for they were acquitted after an inquest had proved them entirely free of all *tailles* and military service (p. 382).

49 See "The Aids of the English Boroughs," in *The English Historical Review,* XXXIV, 457 ff.

of four citizens.[50] Precisely the same system was adopted in 1213 by Eudes III, duke of Burgundy, for Chaumont and his portion of Châtillon-sur-Seine.[51]

Meanwhile Thibaut IV of Champagne had introduced an amended scheme of municipal taxation. For his wars, apparently, the regular income from his towns, though supplemented by special grants,[52] had proved inadequate. So in 1230 Troyes, receiving its first charter, was thereby freed "de totes toltes et de totes tailles," on condition that each citizen annually pay six *deniers* per *livre* of chattels and two *deniers* per *livre* of real estate.[53] Every man must assess himself under oath unless he preferred to buy exemption through payments of twenty *livres* a year. This new system, characterized by the name of *jurée*, was rapidly extended to many other towns—for example to Provins, which had earlier acquired the liberties of Meaux.[54] That the count thus gained considerable profit is evident, but pretexts for increased demands were always available. Before the end of the century it became customary for the count, whenever he needed extra money, to request the grant of additional *jurées* by the towns.[55]

At about the same time a similar game was being played in

[50] Teulet, *Layettes*, II, 1, 211.   [51] Garnier, *Chartes de commune*, I, 329.

[52] Chablis, which belonged to Saint-Martin de Tours under the protection of the count, obtained the following letters in 1190 (M. Quantin, *Cartulaire général de l'Yonne*, II, 417): "Ego Henricus Trecensis comes palatinus notum facio presentibus et futuris quod, cum Jerosolimam proficisci decrevissem, ab hominibus de Chableya trecentas libras cepi. Non aliquo tamen jure aut consuetudine quam in ipsos haberem, sed ob Christi negocium et auxilium vie et peregrinacionis nostre, memorata pecunia de assensu et permissione Turonensis capituli ibidem mihi est collata." Similar letters were issued by Thibaut IV on the occasion of his crusade. It is quite probable that the counts requested aids from all their towns at the same time, though no existing document provides evidence for such a general levy. Blanche of Navarre seems likewise to have taken an aid from her towns in 1209, when her son was placed under the wardship of Philip Augustus, as well as when he was relieved of it in 1214. See the letters for Lagny in N. Brussel, *Nouvel examen de l'usage général des fiefs en France* (Paris, 1750), I, 415; also d'Arbois de Jubainville, *Comtes de Champagne*, IV, 838.

[53] Bourgeois, *Du mouvement communal*, p. 135.

[54] *Ibid.*, pp. 141, 147, 154; d'Arbois de Jubainville, IV, 724, 732; Teulet, *Layettes*, II, 185, 205, 218, 228.

[55] D'Arbois de Jubainville, IV, 837; and *catalogue*, nos. 401 *bis*, 3495, 3649.

Burgundy. In 1220 Dijon, with entire success, opposed the arbitrary levy of a tax for the crusade by invoking guarantees in its charter of 1187.[56] In 1231 the city received from Hugh IV an amended charter, said to provide an easing of previous burdens. The annual responsibility for 500 *livres* was so changed that each of the richer bourgeois should pay one mark per year. Any surplus was to go to the duke; any deficit was to be made up by additional assessments.[57] This so-called *liberté des marcs*—eventually extended to Montbard, Beaune, and many other communities—had a disastrous effect on municipal finance. At Dijon, for example, the accumulation of arrears, enhanced by periodical doubling or tripling for special subsidy, produced a debt of 13,999 *livres* in the course of twenty years.[58]

In Flanders, where the autonomy of the towns was much more complete than in the fiefs to the east, we find no trace of any such direct tax as was established by the counts of Champagne and the dukes of Burgundy. Yet it would be a mistake to suppose that the Flemish towns were not financially exploited by the central government. Until the archives of the great northern communes have been thoroughly studied, our knowledge of such exploitation must depend on slight evidence; but it is eloquent. Approximately when Louis IX launched his second crusade, the magistrates of Douai found it advisable to draw up a list of the sums that on various occasions had been paid to Countess Margaret.[59] Here is the summary of their report.

First of all, the town of Douai gave 3700 *livres* to Margaret on her accession in 1244. Three years later the crossbowmen sent to Ruppelmonde cost 300 *livres*. Then, in 1248, a *bonté* of 1500 *livres* was provided for the overseas expedition of her son William and, on his return, presents raised the amount by 100 *livres*. The war occasioned by her succession was an expensive affair: 2500 *livres* in 1252 for persuasion of Louis IX, 1500 *livres* in 1253 for release from military service in Holland, 2200 *livres*

---

[56] Garnier, *Chartes de commune*, I, 32; Petit, *Ducs de Bourgogne*, IV, 6; Bourgin, *Soissons*, pp. 373 ff.

[57] Garnier, I, 39.

[58] *Ibid.*, I, 40, n. 1, 53, n. 1, and II, 96, 364; Petit, IV, 59.

[59] G. Espinas, *Les finances de la commune de Douai des origines au XVe siècle* (Paris, 1902), pp. 418–20.

given to the countess in 1254 during the siege of Mons and Athies by the count of Anjou, and 500 *livres* lent during the same year "par la prière me Dame." Besides, the town had furnished troops to the army seven times during the twenty years of Margaret's previous government. In the single year 1256 Douai paid 1050 *livres* for dispensation from military service, 150 *livres* to arm galleys at Gravelines, and 4000 *livres*, plus remission of 500 *livres* from a loan of 1254, for the ransom of her son Guy taken prisoner in Holland. Two years later the town paid an additional 4000 *livres*, 1200 *livres* more in 1262, and 1000 *livres* for dispensation from the Namur campaign in 1263. In the next year Margaret got 1500 *livres* "dou ruef qu'elle rouvra quant les autres villes li donnèrent," and in 1266 another *ruef* of 500 *livres*.[60] For "l'arriest des Englais" the countess asked for a loan from her towns, and Douai furnished 400 *livres* sterling. Finally, for the crusade of 1268, the town contributed 6000 *livres*.[61]

In the face of such evidence it is idle to theorize about *aides aux quatre cas*.[62] Whenever the rulers of Flanders needed money from the towns, it was obtained—by politely asking for it and then exerting pressure to make the grant as large as possible. The letters of acquittal for Douai in 1270 [63] seem to prove, not

[60] *Ruef* or *Bede* is ordinarily translated in Latin as *petitio*. Cf. the *demanda, questa, rogatio, interrogatio*, etc., of French charters.

[61] The document does not say that these levies were taken from all the Flemish towns; but it is probable that, like those following, the two were not restricted to Douai. Ghent received letters of no prejudice for sending troops to Zeeland in 1248 (Warnkönig, III, 277). See also the letters of acquittal for 2000 *livres* paid to ransom Guy in 1258 (II, 458), and for a *donum* of 2000 *livres* in 1260 (III, 292). Besides, there should be other evidence in unpublished records. The role of the French towns in the Angevin expedition will be considered below.

[62] Warnkönig, II, 255, attributes to the count the right of exacting from his towns the aids for the marriage of a daughter, the knighting of a son, and ransom; while, he says, other subsidies had to be gracious. M. Espinas, p. 297, expresses the opinion that Margaret was entitled to the *aides aux quatre cas* and to sums paid in substitution for military service; on other occasions the communes could refuse aid. He has to admit, however, that the precise nature of many contributions is hard to determine.

[63] The *échevins* and the community of Douai declare that they have been reimbursed for all they have given the countess, acquitting her and her heirs "de tous douns, de tous rues, et de toutes prises; et de toutes les choses qu'il ont eut de nous et de nostre vile de Douwai" (*ibid.*, p. 442).

so much the zeal of the bourgeois, as the end of a controversy to which the foregoing list of exactions may have given rise.

Fortunately, in studying the fiscal policy of other French states with regard to the bourgeoisie, we do not have to depend so largely on conjecture. Details lacking elsewhere are abundantly supplied by the *Correspondance administrative d'Alphonse de Poitiers*.[64] Alphonse was the brother of the sainted Louis IX and from him received great fiefs in the Midi: Poitou, Saintonge, and Auvergne. Eventually, through marriage to the daughter of Raymond VII, he inherited the county of Toulouse. Having taken the cross along with the king, he shared captivity in Egypt. Later he revived the project of a crusade, but did not live to carry it out. Alphonse of Poitiers must always be ranked among the foremost statesmen of thirteenth-century France.

Of the first subsides taken by Alphonse we know little—only what is mentioned by way of precedent for his later ones. Clearly, however, he had asked the towns of Auvergne for various aids before he became count of Toulouse: for his knighting (1241), for his war in Poitou (1242), for his crusade (1249), and for his ransom (1250).[65] At least on the first and third of these occasions the towns of Poitou contributed *dona*.[66] But it is only about 1261,

---

[64] A. Molinier, in *Documents inédits* (Paris, 1894). The book of E. Boutaric, *Saint Louis et Alphonse de Poitiers* (Paris, 1870) contains many documents, often inexactly transcribed, with abundant commentary that usually is lacking in clarity. Other fragments of this correspondence have been published in Devic et Vaissete, VII—a volume that also contains excellent notes by Molinier, particularly nos. 46 and 59, pp. 132 ff., 462 ff. See furthermore Sée, *Les classes rurales*, p. 591.

[65] This information comes from memoranda sent to the count in the course of his final disputes with Riom and Montferrand (Molinier, *Correspondance administrative*, nos. 747, 1191; Boutaric, pp. 279–80. For his first crusade, said his agent in 1268, Alphonse had received from the towns of Auvergne the sum of 7500 *livres;* of which Riom had given 4000, Palluet 60, Châtel-Guyon 70, Montboissier 60, Nonette 60 or 80. He could not remember the amounts given by other towns.

[66] Boutaric, as above. In 1241 La Rochelle, Saint-Jean-d'Angély, Niort, and Poitiers paid *dona:* the first of these 1000 *livres,* the others 500 each. In 1249 Alphonse wrote to the same towns that he was prepared to forward letters of no prejudice whenever they had given him the *fouage* promised for the expulsion of the Jews (Teulet, *Layettes,* III, 72). It is probable that the subsidy was originally granted for the crusade and that the towns, as often happened later, assured themselves of a desired concession before agreeing to payment. The *dona* of La Rochelle and Poitiers in 1251 (Devic et Vaissete, VIII, column 1281) seem to have been aids for the ransom of their lord. It should be remembered that Alphonse had confirmed the *établissements* of Rouen for all these towns (Giry, as above).

when Alphonse took the cross for the second time, that detailed information about his fiscal activity begins. His seneschals were then instructed to the following effect. All men of his lands— including ecclesiastics, barons, and knights for their men—have promised a *fouage* for the crusade. But he has learned that his towns will pay more *ex dono*. Therefore his commissioners should inquire as to what each town will offer, whether it is his own or that of a vassal. The seneschals are to find out how much each of these towns promised to Raymond for his crusade and are authorized to accept any offer through which Alphonse is not due to lose.[67]

Particular instructions were added for commissioners in each district.[68] First, said Alphonse, they should go to one of his own towns, especially to one they think best disposed to meet his desire. There they should get into touch with a dozen or so of the town's representatives and remind them that since his accession he has given them his protection and always treated them justly; that he has exacted from them "ne questes ne dons ne bontez," but only the dues that were owed him. And the commissioners should add that the king of France, since his return from the Holy Land, has had "aides granz en deniers de ses villes de leur volonté et de grace, et l'a faite lever par ii fois ou par iii par homes jurez de chaucune ville, si comme de Paris et de ses autres villes"; also that the king of Navarre (the count of Champagne), the count of Anjou, the countess of Flanders, the duke of Burgundy, and the count of Nevers have likewise received good aids in money. Therefore, since it is the opinion of the count and of other well-informed persons that the men of his lands ought willingly to pay what they have promised, the commissioners should ask them courteously to do so. Next a dozen men of the town, because they know the fortune of each bourgeois, should be chosen and sworn fairly to assess every citizen. The commissioners should write down what each bourgeois possesses together with the total assessment for the town. A copy of this statement is to be kept by the seneschal and

[67] Molinier, nos. 1962, 1965, 1974, 1975; Devic et Vaissete, columns 1488–92; Boutaric, p. 280.

[68] Molinier, no. 1968, which seems to be the *cedula* referred to by no. 1965; Devic et Vaissete, VIII, column 1493; Boutaric, p. 297.

another transmitted to the count. "Et en ceste maniere le fait
fere li rois de France en ses villes, quant elles li font aides." Then
the commissioners are to visit the other towns of the count, as
well as those of his vassals, in each case notifying the immediate
lord. And if they find that Raymond adopted another plan which
the men of the count regard as better, they shall follow his
example. Moreover, if the *bonnes villes* of the count wish to
give, instead of *fouage,* a sum not inferior to what *fouage* would
produce, and if the towns of his vassals likewise prefer that procedure, such sums may be accepted from the communities offering them. Within towns refusing to make the substitution the
fouage shall be levied as it was originally granted.[69]

Only a small number of towns in the Agenais had already
made acceptable offers [70] when the expedition was abandoned,
and with it the proposed subsidy. Later the project was revived
and the commissioners resumed their task—to enter into fresh
negotiations and eventually obtain a series of grants from the
count's various lands. Generally throughout the Midi, except in
territories that had paid a subsidy five years earlier, a *fouage*
was levied.[71] In Poitou and Saintonge, however, the aid took

[69] The exact nature of the promise referred to in the preamble of the instructions—how the grant was made and whether local lords could lawfully bind all
their men to it—does not appear. Alphonse dodged the question by asking gratuitous sums from each community. Since rather confused statements have been made
about this tax, it might be well to emphasize certain points clearly shown by the
pertinent documents. First, the vassals of Alphonse gave him an aid for his crusade; but, instead of collecting the money from their tenants, they allowed him to
levy the imposition himself. Secondly, the aid thus granted was a *fouage*—a form
of *taille* assessed on each home with a fireplace. Therefore, if previous observations are correct, nobles paid a feudal aid though no *fouage* was levied on them
personally; non-nobles did not pay a feudal aid, being liable as always for contributions—however called—to make up those of their superiors. The novelty in
this affair, if there was one, consisted in the extension of the count's direct authority. Judging from later practice, we may suspect that the local lords got a
percentage of the return. See above, n. 5.

[70] Thus we have commissions to various persons, instructing them to talk with
the representatives of Agen and Millau about the *fouage* (Molinier, nos. 1840,
1976, 1977); also letters in which Alphonse says he is disposed to accept 1500 *livres*
from Agen, and the same amount from Pont-Sainte-Marie (no. 1978).

[71] The preliminary instructions of 1267 (nos. 238, 323) were followed by letters
telling what ought to be done in case of opposition. The seneschal should post-

the form of a double *cens* assessed on all non-nobles.[72] Whatever the normal tax, the towns were permitted, on the same conditions as in 1261, to substitute the payment of lump sums.[73] Discussion of the matter with Toulouse, begun in 1266, continued for two years before a definite agreement was reached.[74] The bourgeois asked and finally obtained confirmation of many franchises; in the end the count was assured a grant of 6000 *livres*. It is also interesting that in this connection Alphonse held ready letters of no prejudice for Toulouse and any other town that wanted them; but in return he demanded written receipts according to another form kept in reserve.[75] Such letters seem to

pone assessment of *fouage* on the men of ——, while waiting to find out whether they, or another for them, had promised a *fouage;* whether they had ever paid a *fouage* to the late Count Raymond; "seu eidem aliquam aliam gratiam vel subvencionem in denariis vel taliis seu alio modo fecerunt, et utrum teneantur de jure vel consuetudine, usagio, vel alia justa causa, nihilominus tractantes cum predictis hominibus si quid nobis dare voluerint pro focagio seu nomine focagii seu eciam nomine alterius gracie, ex gratia et spontanea voluntate" (nos. 152, 158, 162, 164, 168, 170, 255, 257, 267, 268, etc.). Alphonse was interested in appealing to precedent, but his main object was to get the money. Thus we find him in 1268 ordering the seneschal of Rouergue to inquire whether certain men have ever paid to his predecessors "focagium vel subventio seu auxilium, quocumque nomine censeantur"; and particularly whether the counts of Toulouse have levied money from their men for a crusade, the knighting of a son, or the marriage of a daughter; also whether, on such occasions, the immediate lord got anything (no. 546). The doubt of Alphonse here expressed led Molinier to the opinion that the *aides aux quatre cas* had been unknown in the Midi (Devic et Vaissete, VII, 165; *Correspondance administrative*, p. xxvi). Yet, whatever the occasions, it is certain that the earlier counts of Toulouse had received extraordinary subsidies from their towns. Bollène admitted such grants (*ibid.*, no. 1732; cf. nos. 1812, 1826); and see the complaint of Murles to Louis IX, saying that earlier it had paid *fouage* exceptionally and then "propria voluntate, non ex debito" (Devic et Vaissete, VII, column 155).

[72] Alphonse tried to obtain a grant from the nobles; yet, in spite of alleged precedent, he encountered stubborn opposition, and there is no proof that they ever paid. From *roturiers*—presumably those of his own domain—he required a double *cens,* described as a *gracia liberalis* by the custom of the country (Molinier, nos. 622, 623, 707). It is hard to agree with the opinion of Boutaric based on these letters (pp. 281–83). On the double *cens* see above, notes 10, 43, 44.

[73] *Villes neuves* or *bastides* were generally exempted, but they could be urgently requested to make a gratuitous offering (Molinier, nos. 244, 265, 1895).

[74] *Ibid.*, nos. 325, 338, 341, 363, 620, 2058; Devic et Vaissete, VIII, columns 1560–65, 1619, 1650.

[75] *Ibid.*, no. 2060: "Alfonsus universis etc. Cum dilecti et fideles nostri con-

have been exchanged only with the most powerful communes. Yet, to avoid all possible controversy, the aids taken from the humblest villages, whether those of the count or of his vassals, were regularly described as graciously accorded.[76] Meanwhile negotiations had likewise been undertaken with the towns of Poitou, Saintonge, and Auvergne. Before the end of 1267 La Rochelle had granted 2000 *livres* and Saintes 1000, both towns under guarantee of no prejudice for the future.[77] Other communities—particularly Niort, Poitiers, Saint-Jean-d'Angély, Riom, and Montferrand—had either declined to act or had offered sums declared inadequate. Consequently letters were sent to the various agents of the count, urging them to bring pressure upon the recalcitrant bourgeois. Thus, in 1268, the seneschal of Saintonge was told that he should impart to the men of Saint-Jean-d'Angély the astonishment of the count at their paltry offering; since during the last sixteen years or more they had given him "ne aide, ne secours, ne taille," as should be done by loyal subjects bound to love and serve their lord—especially on the occasion of a crusade to the Holy Land. He would remind them that the king of France, the king of Sicily (his brother Charles of Anjou), the king of Navarre, the count of Brittany, and the countess of Flanders have had "maint don en deniers, mainte taille, et maintes aides de leurs villes plusieurs foiz";

---

sules et communitas urbis et suburbii Tholose ex mera liberalitate et dono gratuito subventionem gratiosam nobis fecerint usque ad summam sex milium librarum turonensium, de quibus tenemus nos plenarie pro pagatis, nos subventionem hujusmodi profitemur ab eisdem gratis et liberaliter nobis factam, nec volumus seu intendimus nomine focagii vel promissionis ab eis nobis facte super eodem vel cujuscunque alterius servitutis, nunc vel in posterum, occasione dicte subventionis, spontane ab eis facte, ipsis prejudicium generari." Similar assurances were sent to other communes. In return sealed letters to the count were required, stating with rich phraseology that the bourgeois of their free will had given the count a certain "subventio peccunaria et donum"; and that they had acquitted him and his heirs of all expense and damage thereby incurred (nos. 2060, 2961; Devic et Vaissete, VIII, column 1561; Boutaric, p. 309).

[76] See the negotiations with Millau, Amelan, and Basiège (Molinier, nos. 350, 517, 545; Devic et Vaissete, VIII, columns 1625, 1668; Boutaric, pp. 300 ff. Numerous other details in this connection will be found in Molinier, nos. 1732, 1734, 1785, 1797, 1799, 1813.

[77] *Ibid.*, nos. 24, 96, 98, 100, 110–13. The letters given by the communes use almost the same form as that cited above, n. 71.

also that he enjoys many rights which he could enforce against the town if he chose to do so.[78]

A month later similar arguments were marshaled for the benefit of Riom, which Alphonse said had promised him 4000 *livres* for his first contemplated expedition.[79] The bourgeois denied this allegation, making to their lord, as the record states, only "ineptas responsiones." At last the threat of a poll tax on the richer citizens, the testimony of one appointed to collect the aid of 1249, and the promise of a new charter resulted in a *don gratuit* of 4000 *livres;* but the count still had trouble in collecting the money.[80]

Another great commune of Auvergne, Montferrand, was also led to offer resistance; though the methods previously used, together with the threat to hasten the collection of an unpaid fine, induced the bourgeois to satisfy the count before the end of 1269.[81] Also by this time the towns of Poitou had made submission after some local disorders, and the financial operations of the great count came to an end.[82] Alphonse of Poitiers was assuredly no less mercenary than his contemporaries, among them the sainted Louis IX. As Alphonse said, he asked nothing more than other princes had often obtained. We cannot doubt that, in default of regular taxes, he based his demands for money on such precedents as he had. But in that connection we must remark that bourgeois pride, especially in the Midi, forbade the payment of an aid by a respectable commune without protracted bargaining.

The documents thus discussed at considerable length teach us

[78] Molinier, no. 689; Boutaric, p. 286. Alphonse wrote to the seneschals of Poitou and Saintonge that they should insistently demand aids from the towns that had as yet offered none, "maxime cum ad hoc de generali et notoria consuetudine Francie teneri dicuntur." Besides they should determine the names of three or four hundred upper-class bourgeois at Poitiers, of two or three hundred at Niort, and of proportionate numbers in other towns to find out what each would individually give (no. 654).

[79] *Ibid.*, no. 725; Boutaric, p. 289.

[80] Molinier, nos. 224, 739, 743, 746–49, 756. Alphonse was still trying to collect his 4000 *livres* in 1270 (no. 1197) and it was finally left for the *parlement* under Philip III to enforce collection of sums due from certain bourgeois—A. A. Beugnot, *Les Olim* (Paris, 1839–42), I, 406.

[81] Molinier, nos. 1163, 1191; Boutaric, pp. 191–93.

[82] Molinier, nos. 973, 978, 1043, 1044; Boutaric, pp. 287 ff.

at least one important truth: although a primary motive of the bourgeois in trying to get a charter was their desire to escape arbitrary *taille,* they eventually saved little more than their dignity; for such privilege as they obtained was of no avail against the demands of a powerful lord. His charters may have pretended to abolish his title to despotic exactions, but he remained in position to ask irresistibly for so-called voluntary contributions. By the thirteenth century municipal charters often came to specify compulsory aids in certain cases; perhaps earlier they had been unusual and truly gratuitous. Yet even after they had been legalized by general consent, the great lords by no means limited their requisitions to so narrow a field. Appeals to precedent, to the worthiness of a cause, or to a moral obligation were supplemented by assurances of no prejudice for the future. Despite all polite verbiage, however, the true basis of such taxation was the power of the lord, checked only by the ability of the town to resist. And in that respect the communes of the south were unquestionably stronger than those of the north.

It remains to consider the king's taxation of his *bonnes villes.* The first evidence we have in this connection has to do rather with military service than with payments of money. It is the well-known *prisia servientium* of Philip Augustus which, as has been shown by M. Audouin, was drawn up in 1194 and somewhat amended during the next ten years.[83] In view of the research to which this document has been subjected,[84] detailed criticism will hardly be necessary; but it might be well to emphasize a few of its features that directly relate to the subject under discussion. Being a record of *service roturier* in general, it includes contributions of men and carts taken from *prévôtés* and abbeys, as well as from towns of every rank. Most of these communities are set down as owing contingents in round numbers, multiples of ten with one cart for every fifty serjeants; but there are exceptions. Nine towns or groups of towns are recorded as possibly giving sums of money. Arras and Beauvais are said to furnish either men or money; Etampes 1000 *livres* or more if the king

[83] E. Audouin, *Essai sur l'armée royale au temps de Philippe-Auguste* (Paris, 1913), p. 17.
[84] In addition to Audouin; Borrelli de Serres, *Recherches,* I, 467 ff.

26

wishes; Lorris 500 or 1000 *livres* if the king wishes; Melun and Corbeil "in voluntate regis." It is therefore clear that this levy of foot soldiers, presumably for the war against Richard of England, was replaced at least in some towns by payment of money. But in 1202, as we learn from the first extant account of the royal government, a cash subsidy was taken from all towns of the king's domain at the rate of three *livres* per man and fourteen *livres*, ten *sous*, per cart.[85] Thus the practice of taxing the royal towns as a substitute for military service seems to have been inaugurated by Philip Augustus,[86] and it becomes necessary to seek a legal basis for such exaction.

It is perfectly clear that, whatever the status of men within the royal *châtellenies* who were required to contribute, the *bonnes villes* could not have been thus charged under the name of *taille*. Nor, by strict interpretation of their charters, were they bound for more than very limited military service. To escape this difficulty, Borrelli de Serres was led to invent a distinction between feudal service and royal service, and to understand the charters as restricting only the former.[87] Applied to the age of Philip Augustus, such a theory seems rather farfetched, and there is a simpler explanation. Although the king was not formally entitled to definite contingents of troops from his towns,[88] he could still negotiate for grants of them from each community. We may guess that, to avoid any embarrassment

---

[85] *Ibid.*, I, 12 ff.; also discussed in detail by Audouin, pp. 19 ff.

[86] See the remarks of Luchaire in Lavisse, *Histoire de France*, III², 239.

[87] *Recherches*, I, 508. His thesis inevitably encounters many difficulties. For example, he affirms (p. 507) that all towns received their liberties *en fief* and so were held for the customary feudal service. But will this apply to every village that obtained restriction of *taille* or *ost et chevauchée*? See above, notes 6, 13. His thesis also involves the assertion (p. 514) that the *tallia servientium* was owed merely to the king; not, like the feudal aids, to every lord. Yet the first known tax of this kind was that of a Norman duke. Aside from the trials reported in the *Olim*, which belong to a much later and vastly different age, Borrelli de Serres presents almost no evidence to support his thesis. It is true that the charters of some towns—as Bray-sur-Somme (*Ordonnances*, XI, 295)—reserve contributions *nomine belli;* but this does not prove that equivalent reservations were understood in all cases.

[88] Except for Tournay which, according to the charter of Philip Augustus, owed the king 300 foot soldiers for each campaign (Delaborde, no. 224; Borrelli de Serres, I, 486).

of law or custom, his commissioners merely requested men or money by way of special aid. The comments included in the *prisée* of 1194, cited above, would appear to indicate that the document was a report drawn up by royal agents after conversation with the townsmen but before decision had been made as to precisely what service would be required in every case. A gap in the records prevents our knowing about the later policy of Philip Augustus. But the fortunate preservation of a fragment from an account of 1226 proves that Louis VIII asked a subsidy from his towns for the Albigensian crusade. It is there stated that Douai, Hesdin, Abbeville, Bruyères-sous-Laon, Etampes, Bourges, and Saint-Omer paid round sums *pro servientibus.*[89] For the levies of Louis IX the sources, though incomplete, are more decisive. We have a complete roll of accounts for 1248, portions of others, and various excerpts made by Brussel from documents now lost. But beside such direct evidence of contributions then exacted from the royal towns, we have the testimony of the king's brother Alphonse,[90] the accounts drawn up by various communes in 1260, and the record of certain legal proceedings occasioned by the king's financial operations.

Until departing for the famous crusade of 1248, Louis IX undertook no military expeditions more serious than *chevauchées* against Henry III of England and his allies in Brittany and Champagne. Yet each of these campaigns seems to have cost the towns something; for we find scanty reports of aids paid in 1231, 1234, and 1238–39.[91] The complete account

[89] C. Petit-Dutaillis, *Etude sur la vie et le règne de Louis VIII* (Paris, 1894), p. 522; Borrelli de Serres, I, 176 ff. In most cases the sums are recorded as levied *de burgensibus*, without indication of their purpose. We thus find the receipt: "De taliis Alencone, Britolii, et aliarum villarum, ıxxx libre cxıı solidi." Cf. "Pro tallia Parisius ᴍᵛᶜ libras," cited from a roll of 1217 by Brussel, *Usage des fiefs*, I, 529. Whether these payments may justly be called *dons obligatoires* depends on the character of the military service they replaced, and in some cases it was not obligatory.

[90] See above, n. 68.

[91] Thus in 1231 and 1234 "De burgensibus Sancti Audomari de dono xvᶜ libras"; "De burgensibus Sancti Audomari pro ultima medietate doni sui vᶜ libras" (Brussel, I, 417). The author compares these payments to the *dons gratuits* of the clergy and provincial estates in his own day. A fragment from another roll of 1234 adds payments made by Bourges, Dun-le-Roi, Aubigny, and Saint-Pierre-le-Moutier

roll of 1248 more fully reveals the royal procedure in such connections.[92] All sorts of towns, from the greatest communes down to mere villages, were called upon to contribute *pro auxilio viae transmarinae*. It is this levy that serves to introduce the municipal accounts of 1260, and the most eloquent of them is that of Noyon.[93]

Here is how, the bourgeois declare, they had come to be burdened with so heavy a debt. When the king went overseas, they gave him 1500 *livres*. But while he was there, the queen informed them he needed a larger sum; so they sent him 500 *livres* more. Then, on his return, he borrowed from them 600 *livres*, five-sixths of which were eventually turned into a gift. When the count of Anjou undertook his expedition into Hainaut, the men of Noyon were first told that he needed wine; they gave him ten tuns, costing 100 *livres*. Later, on hearing that he must have "mestier de sergents" to safeguard his honor, they provided him with 500 men at similar cost. Next the count came to Saint-Quentin and there summoned the commune of Noyon "pour son cors garder"—service that entailed the ex-

(*Recueil des historiens de la France*, XXII, 575), which the editor took to be sums *auxilii nomine* for the Breton war. In 1260 Roye is mentioned as having paid 600 *livres*, "donum pro exercitu Britannie" (Teulet, *Layettes*, III, 531, 569). Then, in what remains from an account of 1238 (*Historiens*, XXI, 251), we find enrollments of contributions, presumably *aides de l'ost*, made by Saint-Quentin and Rouen; and Brussel (as above) cites another from Arras. This levy should be the same as that reported by the count of Roye as being after the king's return from Brittany (Teulet, as above). See also the inquest of 1247 (*Historiens*, XXIV, 111 G, 309 F). There the bourgeois of Tours complain that the royal bailiff, by order of the king, has put upon them a *taille* that violates their liberties; and the citizens of Roullens assert that Louis VIII has demanded from them 140 *livres* as *fouage*, although they have never been his men. To affirm with Borrelli de Serres and A. Callery, *Histoire du pouvoir royal d'imposer* (Brussels, 1879), pp. 48, 50, 76, that all these *dona* were made in place of obligatory service in the army would seem, for reasons stated above, somewhat hazardous.

[92] *Historiens*, XXI, 260 ff. Among the numerous articles concerning the towns there is not one that refers to the way in which the money was obtained: e.g., "De Hamo per gratiam." Reims also contributed, and letters of no prejudice were sent both to the church and to the town (P. Varin, in *Documents inédits*, I², nos. 216, 218, 220).

[93] Teulet, *Layettes*, III, 515; A. Lefranc, *Histoire de la ville de Noyon* (Paris, 1883), p. 223; Luchaire, *Les communes françaises*, p. 198; Langlois, in Lavisse, *Histoire de France*, III², 79. On the general character of these accounts see Borrelli de Serres, *Recherches*, I, 95 ff.

penditure of 600 *livres.* "Et tout che fist li vile de Noion au conte pour honneur dou roi." Then, after the dismissal of the army, they heard that the count still needed money and would suffer "vilenie" if they failed to aid him; so they lent him 1200 *livres* and gave him acquittal of 300 to receive letters acknowledging the remainder of the debt. Finally there was the gift of 1200 *livres* to the king for his peace with England.

From Montdidier comes the following account which, though briefer, is likewise explicit: [94]

Hec est causa tanti debiti. Primo pro dono regi quando ivit ultra mare M libre. Item, eidem quamdiu fuit in dicta terra duobus vicibus M libre. Item, eidem in redditu suo II^c libre. Item, pro mutuo facto comiti Andegavensi pro exercitu Hanonie IIII^c libre. Item, pro expensis factis a dicta communia in dicto exercitu IIII^c libre. Item, pro dono facto domino regi pro pace Anglie VIII^c libre. Summa XXXVIII^c libre.

Cerny-en-Laonnais, La-Neuville-Roi, and Roye provide a statement of their expenditures in similar form.[95] Crandelain and Chauny report theirs in the same way, but without so many details.[96] Many other towns, like Amiens, merely send the totals of what had been paid to the king during the period.[97]

The evidence, though incomplete, clearly shows that Louis IX authorized no less than six levies from his towns in the course of a dozen years: aid for the crusade in 1248, aid for his

[94] Teulet, *Layettes,* III, 568.

[95] *Ibid.,* III, 568–69. As already seen, the account includes various older payments going back to 1234. Since then, in another report (*ibid.,* III, 531), the bourgeois say they have provided the king with 4200 *livres.* And they still owe him 400 *livres;* "kar chil qui doivent la taille sunt si povre et au desouz qu'il ne porroient paier à une fois, et chest poverté leur est venue par les deniers que li rois a eu de la ville."

[96] *Ibid.,* III, 524, 564. Crandelain pleads such poverty as is shameful to confess and asks for relief. The men of Chauny say that the king has had from them 1500 *livres* since he took the cross, while the count of Anjou has cost them at least 500 *livres.*

[97] *Ibid.,* III, 515, 532, 536, 541, etc. The sums due to the king are ordinarily payments on the *don,* or *ruef,* for the peace with England. Rouen states that the count of Anjou yet owes the town 3000 *livres,* with this interesting memorandum: "Item, Ludovicus bone memorie, genitor vester, debebat ville Rothomagi, tempore quo viam universi carnis fuit ingressus, V^c libras turonensium, de quo villa Rothomagi habet suas litteras patentes (*ibid.,* III, 544).

ransom in 1250, troops etc. for the Hainaut campaign in 1253, aid for the marriage of his daughter in 1255, and aid for the peace with England in 1259. For the first of these levies, as already noted, the original account roll still exists. For the second there are merely the statements of the communes already cited. With regard to the expedition undertaken by the count of Anjou, we have a copy of a summons dispatched to eighteen northern towns; [98] while others probably contributed sums of money, for Paris paid a *donum* of 4000 *livres* in the same year.[99] It is worth remarking that, whatever had been the case in 1194, an appeal for general war in defense of France could hardly have been made in 1253.[100] The identification of the aid vaguely reported as paid to the king when he returned with one taken for the marriage of his daughter comes from an entry in the *Olim*.[101] Finally, in 1259, contributions were exacted for the unpopular treaty with Henry III of England.[102] Under the name of *dona,* these aids were apparently forced upon a definitely recalcitrant bourgeoisie; for the king was induced to order an inquest so that the alleged causes of delinquency might be determined. As has been seen, the towns quite frankly blamed their royal lord. He had, in truth, squandered enormous sums for a disastrous crusade, for an unprofitable adventure of his brother Charles, and for a peace with the English that to contemporaries seemed ruinous. Yet the benign Joinville was able to dictate this tribute: [103]

Li roys ne requist ne ne prist onques aide des siens barons, n'à ses chevaliers, n'à ses hommes, n'à ses bones villes, dont on se plainsist.

98 *Historiens,* XXIII, 730; Borrelli de Serres, *Recherches,* I, 428.

99 Brussel, *Usage des fiefs,* I, 530.

100 See the remarks of Borrelli de Serres, I, 95 ff.

101 Beugnot, *Les Olim,* I, 848–49: "Auxilium pro milicia domini Philippi, primogeniti sui, . . . et pro maritagio regine Navarrie, filie sue primogenite."

102 Outside the accounts of 1260, these *dona* are referred to in the *Olim,* I, 458, 464, 467. Callery, *Histoire du pouvoir royal d'imposer,* p. 52, makes the levy of 1259 wholly feudal by calling it an aid "en accroissement de fief." For Borrelli de Serres (as above) it was an abuse of power because, like the service of 1253, it was not owed.

103 *Histoire de Saint Louis,* ed. de Wailly (Paris, 1869), p. 39. On the interpretation of this remark by Joinville see Boutaric, p. 306; Luchaire, *Manuel,* p. 579; Borrelli de Serres, as above; Langlois, in Lavisse, *Histoire de France,* III², 78.

The bitter discontent revealed in the municipal accounts of 1260 did not remain in the stage of polite remonstrance. When the king, with the double excuse of knighting his son and preparing for a second crusade, asked for another aid in 1267, several towns refused and serious disturbances broke out in many localities. The result, as we learn from the *Olim,* was a series of trials before the *parlement.* The most interesting of these cases was that concerning Bourges.[104]

Solicited by the king for the aids of 1255 and 1267 "tanquam jus suum et de jure communi sibi debitum," the bourgeois claimed exemption. They had never paid such aids, which violated the custom of their country, and they especially invoked their royal charter as freeing them "ab tolta, tallia, botagio, et culcitrarum exactione." To this the king's counsel replied that their charter availed them nothing; what they had been asked for was none of the exactions mentioned there, but another subsidy to which the king was entitled by the general custom of the kingdom. Their allegation that no such aid was lawful in their country was likewise worthless; for men who had been subject to the royal will before their emancipation could justly claim no exemptions beyond those which the king had chosen to give them when he emancipated them. In consequence judgment was rendered against the town, and it was arbitrarily taxed at 2000 *livres.* Dun-le-Roi, which had a charter like that of Bourges, suffered the same fate. Issoudun, appealing to a charter obtained from its lord before incorporation in the royal domain, was also forced to pay. Certain other trials affecting smaller towns provide no further information of any importance.[105]

This whole affair is marked by noteworthy features, and it is unfortunate that lack of evidence prevents a more exact appraisal of its significance. As has been seen,[106] it is unlikely that

[104] Beugnot, *Les Olim,* pp. 848–49; Callery, pp. 53–54; Flammermont, *De concessu legis et auxilii tertio decimo saeculo* (Paris, 1881), p. 48; Prou, *Lorris,* p. 170.

[105] Thus four little towns, who appealed to the custom of their country in refusing an aid for the knighting of the king's son, were likewise required to pay (Beugnot, I, 832). The aid is mentioned in many other articles of this report, sometimes vaguely and sometimes specifically; thus "facta tallia Parisius pro dono facto domino regi a civibus Parisiensibus pro milicia domini Philippi primogeniti sui et pro via transmarina" (*ibid.,* I, 810).

[106] See above, n. 5; Vuitry, *Etudes,* p. 396; Luchaire, *Manuel,* p. 579.

the *aides aux quatre cas* had been customary in the royal domain since the reign of Louis VI. No royal charter reserved them to the crown, and the levy of 1146 was regarded as an unjustified innovation. Therefore, so far as we may judge, the case for Bourges was well founded. Also noteworthy is the fact that the claim of the bourgeois never to have paid such aids as demanded from them was hardly contested. Bourges had indeed contributed to the aid of 1248, and that of 1267 was officially attributed in part to the crusade. Yet the main question was not so much whether the town should contribute special aids as whether it had the right of granting them freely—and that right the court refused to admit.[107] It is quite possible that since the reign of Philip Augustus compulsory *aides aux quatre cas* had come to be established; though, in the opinion of M. Prou, no exception had been foreseen by the charter of Louis VI. However that may be, while the towns of the south were being treated with great courtesy by the king and his brother,[108] those of the north had begun to feel the encroaching absolutism of the monarchy. But before making further conclusions with regard to the royal policy, we must examine the acts of Philip III.

That this king did more than follow precedents established by his sainted father is improbable; yet the first protests of the towns against the imposition of military service date from his reign. As noted above, such exactions had been frequent since the time of Philip Augustus and, according to the available evidence, all the royal towns had on various occasions, and without invoking privileges in their charters, furnished troops or equivalent aids. Nevertheless, when Philip III summoned his towns for the campaign of Foix in 1272, a good many of them

---

[107] Another pertinent bit of information is the decision rendered with regard to a bourgeois of Etampes. Having left the town after the king had asked for an aid, but before the town had granted it, he was later assessed for his share. The judgment refused his claim to exemption (Beugnot, I, 804).

[108] Devic et Vaissete, VII, columns 165, 518. See the letters given to Narbonne (VIII, column 1671) and those drawn up by Albi (VIII, column 1669): the bourgeois have agreed to give the king "in adjutorium passagii sui" 100 marks sterling; but on condition that he send them letters of no prejudice before the money is paid. At Cahors there was a riot that did not end until Louis VIII had died; then Philip III collected a *don* as well as a fine—E. Dufour, *La commune de Cahors* (Cahors, 1846), p. 10; Langlois, *Le règne de Philippe III* (Paris, 1887), p. 249.

seem to have refused to send either troops or the *financiones* that had been officially substituted.[109]

In the ensuing trials the bourgeois won considerable success. Thus Lorris and a number of other towns that enjoyed the same liberties—especially the restriction of *ost et chevauchée* to a single day—were adjudged not liable for the demanded service.[110] Still other towns, such as Bourges and Dun-le-Roi, were likewise freed by virtue of royal charters that limited their military service to the province of Berry.[111] Issoudun, however, had to pay a *tallia pro exercitu;* presumably because its charter, like that of Pomponne, was seignorial rather than royal.[112] There was a sequel in 1275–76, when wars with Navarre and Castille provided occasion for another series of imposts, from which only a few exemptions are recorded.[113] At least some of the towns whose charters restricted military service are known to have paid *dona*—apparently contributions that were alleged to be voluntary.[114] Although the king gained a decision in the *parlement*

[109] Langlois, pp. 249, 348 ff.; Callery, p. 77; Vuitry, I, pp. 400 ff. See the summonses for the army of Foix: *Historiens*, XXIII, 234; Giry, *Documents sur les relations de la royauté avec les villes de France de 1180 à 1314* (Paris, 1885), p. 107.

[110] Beugnot, I, pp. 887, 889, 901. After examination of the charters in question, "pronunciatum fuit quod homines dictarum villarum non tenentur ad exercitum domino regi pro quo, cum submoniti non venissent, emenda petebatur ab eis." See Prou, *Lorris*, p. 168.

[111] Beugnot, I, 902–03. The case of Waquemoulin (p. 889) seems to be quite comparable.

[112] *Ibid.*, I, 882, 887: "Major et communia Pomponii proponebant quod domino regi ad exercitum minime tenebantur, eo quod a comite Sancti Pauli tunc domino suo eis fuit concessum quod non tenebantur ire in exercitum seu in expedicionem. E contra dicebatur pro domino rege quod, non obstante concessione hujusmodi, tenebantur solvere emendam sibi impositam pro eo quod submoniti in exercitum non venerunt, cum eos liberasse de exercitu domino regi debito nequiverit dictus comes." The men of Villeneuve-en-Hez were condemned to pay a similar fine, because their charter freed them from *taille* but not from "emenda pro defectu exercitus" (p. 886).

[113] Langlois, pp. 349–50; Callery, pp. 78–80. There is scattered evidence with regard to the levy of 1276—Borrelli de Serres, *Recherches*, I, 132; Delisle, *Mémoire sur les opérations financières des Templiers* (Paris, 1889), p. 109; E. Lemaire, *Archives de la ville de Saint-Quentin* (Saint Quentin, 1887), I, 99. The towns of Auvergne had their claim to exemption refused for reasons not stated (Beugnot, II, 84), though Brioude somehow came to receive it (II, 121).

[114] See the grant of 1000 *livres* by Narbonne on condition of no prejudice (Devic et Vaissete, X, column 36); also other cases reported by Langlois, p. 350.

against certain communities that had refused an aid for the knighting of his son in 1284, the cause of royal absolutism had not been greatly advanced.[115] Having inherited such precedents, Philip IV does not appear, at least in respect to royal policy toward the towns, as a great innovator. It is rather the mounting of his levies that characterizes a new age—one in which taxation was chronic rather than occasional. Throughout the maze of his fiscal experiments, one constant practice seems to have been that of letting the towns compound for every obligation—and he did not invent the procedure. We thus find them paying *dona* instead of the *denier par livre* in 1292,[116] of the forced loan in 1294,[117] of the fiftieth and hundredth in 1295,[118] of the fiftieth and *fouage* in 1297,[119] of the fiftieth in 1300,[120] of the *ban et arrière-ban* in 1302,[121] etc. Philip was also ready, whenever necessary, to issue letters of no prejudice in the north as well as in the south, where

115 Lorris and eleven other towns enjoying the same privileges were condemned to pay the *auxilium milicie* of 1285; but Cépoy and Chessy were declared exempt "quia rex fuit ibi associatus per quosdam religiosos qui talem redibenciam supra dictos homines non habebant" (Beugnot, II, 249). Opinions differ as to the meaning of these judgments. Callery and Borrelli de Serres cannot, of course, agree. M. Prou believes that the decisions of the *parlement* tended to quash the grants made in early charters, but his view is not shared by Glasson, *Droit français*, VI, 58. In any case the towns continued to protest the levy of similar aids under Philip IV and Philip V; see the inquest of 1314 in Prou, *Lorris, pièces justificatives*, no. 22. The bourgeois seem, indeed, to have adopted a policy of resisting all imposts in the hope of forcing some concessions from a government that tended to become more and more despotic.

116 M. Jusselin, *L'impôt royal sous Philippe-le-Bel*, in *Positions de thèses de l'Ecole des Chartes* (1906), pp. 115 ff.; Vuitry, *Etudes sur le régime financier de la France*, New Series (Paris, 1883), I, 143; Boutaric, *La France sous Philippe-le-Bel* (Paris, 1861), p. 254; Callery, *Histoire de l'origine, des pouvoirs, et des attributions des Etats Généraux* (Brussels, 1881), p. 39; also in *Notices et extraits des manuscrits*, Académie des Inscriptions et Belles-Lettres, XX, 103 ff.; Beugnot, *Les Olim*, II, 411–12, 425.

117 Jusselin, p. 116; Vuitry, I, 146; Boutaric, p. 259; *Notices et extraits*, XX, 123.

118 Jusselin, pp. 118–19; Vuitry, I, 146–47; Boutaric, pp. 259 ff. See the letters addressed to Douai, Lille, Bruges, Ypres, and Messines (Espinas, *Douai*, p. 39, n.; *Ordonnances*, I, 380; Warnkönig, IV, 118 and V, 110, 226).

119 Jusselin, p. 121; Boutaric, pp. 264–65. See the letters addressed to Albi; Devic et Vaissete, X, column 345.

120 Jusselin, p. 123; Boutaric, p. 265. See the letters addressed to Montpellier; Devic et Vaissete, X, column 368.

121 Jusselin, pp. 124–27; Vuitry, I, 150 ff.; Boutaric, pp. 266 ff.

Alphonse of Poitiers had set a good example. Herein is one proof of the power now exerted by the towns. Another can be seen in the fact that they resisted aids for the marriage of the king's daughter in 1307 and for the knighting of his son in 1313—at both times winning concessions.[122] But with the opening years of the fourteenth century we enter the age of estates and, after a few concluding remarks, must end our study.

Although much has been written about the origin of royal taxation in France, the problem has remained obscure principally because of difficulty in explaining how the so-called Third Estate became subjected to it. The obligations of the two superior orders have always been clear. Since the clergy paid *dons gratuits* down to the eve of the Revolution, and the lay nobility made good its claim to exemption from ordinary imposts, they were legally recognized as having the right of free consent. Such a right for the *bonnes villes,* though hardly recognized under the absolute monarchy of Louis XIV, had not only been asserted but to some extent obtained in the mediaeval period. Was their claim as legitimate as that of the superior orders? At least since the memorable happenings of 1789 historians have considered this question more or less impartially and, for the most part, answered in the affirmative.

Thierry confidently asserted the right of the Third Estate to vote taxes; on the ground that the *bonnes villes,* through receipt of privileges, had become "partie intégrante de la hiérarchie féodale." [123] The opinion of Boutaric seems to have inclined in the same direction, although his remarks on municipal liberty are hard to reconcile with his theory of taxation under Philip IV.[124] It was left for Vuitry more fully to justify the thesis of Thierry. In a series of essays containing much excellent analysis he clearly expressed the idea that the royal impost was merely "l'aide féodale transformée, généralisée quant aux personnes, étendue quant aux territoires et quant aux cas où elle serait

[122] Vuitry, I, 157; Boutaric, pp. 272–74. See the letters addressed to Carcassonne (Devic et Vaissete, X, column 473).

[123] *Documents inédits,* I, xxxv–xxxvi.

[124] *Les premiers Etats Généraux* (1860), p. 5; *La France sous Philippe-le-Bel* (1861), pp. 253 ff.; *Les institutions militaires de la France* (1863), p. 23; *Saint Louis et Alphonse de Poitiers* (1870), p. 306.

levée." [125] But to call a town a member of the feudal hierarchy and to describe any municipal contribution as being potentially a feudal aid is, after all, a superficial explanation. Besides, whatever plausibility this argument had was rejected by the later one, that only communes enjoyed the rank of vassal, paid feudal aids, and had the right to make voluntary grants.[126] In the meantime criticism from another quarter had forced the reopening of the whole question. According to Callery,[127] the only subsidies taken by the French kings were those to which they were regularly entitled on certain occasions or which were paid in place of owed military service. Since consent was required neither for the customary aids nor for the levy of troops, the sole reason for the calling of estates was the feudal contract; applied to *roturiers* as well as to nobles, it did not permit the lord at discretion to substitute money for men. Although Callery made a number of unjustifiable assertions, his central argument has never been refuted.[128] If all the royal taxes of the

[125] *Etudes* (1870), p. 532; New Series (1883), I, 144, 150 ff., and II, 3–4.

[126] The theory according to which the commune was a *seigneurie* constituted a *seigneurie collective* was popularized by *Les communes françaises* of Luchaire (1890); but its origin goes back to Giry, being clearly expressed in *Les établissements de Rouen* (1883), I, 440. Flammermont sought to apply it in explaining the origin of the estates—*Histoire des institutions municipales de Senlis* (1881), pp. 97 ff.; *De concessu legis et auxilii* (1883), pp. 115 ff. Speaking of "cette idée erronée qu'au moyen âge nul ne payait l'impôt sans son consentement et que le peuple votait lui-même la taille," he remarks that this was true only of the communes (*Senlis*, p. 100). Strangely enough, he adds, such privilege was recognized even after the suppression of a commune; but in a more general manner, as in the case of the *bonnes villes* who owed their lords suit to court and therefore sent deputies to the estates (p. 97).

[127] *Histoire du pouvoir royal d'imposer* (1879) and *Histoire . . . des Etats Généraux* (1881).

[128] Thus Luchaire, in his *Manuel des institutions françaises* (1892), followed Callery in a subtle distinction between *aides féodales* and *aides de l'ost*—while taking into account the criticism of Langlois, *Philippe III* (1887), p. 349. Callery's theory with regard to the origin of the estates did not have great success. See L. Cadier, *Les Etats de Béarn* (1888), pp. 2 ff.; A. Coville, *Les Etats de Normandie* (1894), pp. 3 ff. The authors of these excellent monographs have clearly shown the close connection between taxation and the system of estates. Yet, because they restricted their attention to the fourteenth century, they did not see fit to challenge Callery on the subject of municipal obligations for extraordinary aids. See the remarks of Molinier concerning the origin of estates in Languedoc; Devic et Vaissete, VII, 510.

thirteenth century, aside from the regular feudal aids, were exactions in place of military service, and if they bore upon all *fidèles* of the king, the old theory about the origin of the estates was no longer tenable. The new one presented by Callery, however, was not found acceptable and served only to complicate the problem under discussion. Nor did a solution proposed by Borrelli de Serres bring entire conviction.[129] Going beyond Callery, he attributed to the king an unlimited right to collect not only feudal aids but also *aides de l'ost,* whence were derived the various forms of his well-known impost. Therefore the only reason for the representation of the *bonnes villes* in the estates was the administrative necessity of fixing through negotiation the amount of the sum to be demanded from each community.

In consequence, no definitive explanation of our problem has yet been made, and none can be made without more thorough research than has been attempted. It nevertheless seems that, by the preceding study, however superficial, the problem has been to some extent simplified. In the first place, we may ignore the troublesome distinction between communes and other towns for the simple reason that all had the same obligations, both financial and military, to their royal lord. In the second place, we have to admit that such obligations were those, not of vassals, but of bourgeois—men who, in this respect, differed from free peasants largely because of organization in tight communities where they could act together. Therefore, if the representation

[129] *Recherches sur divers services publics,* I, 515 ff. It is not surprising that more recent books have been somewhat confused as to the origin of the royal *impôt.* M. Sée, despite an illuminating commentary on the government of the king as a *grand seigneur,* derives his power to tax from "espèces de l'aide féodale," from the "aide gracieuse," and from the "aide militaire" (*Les classes rurales,* pp. 591, 593, 596). M. Brissaud says that the king, as "suzerain universel," asked feudal aids from his vassals, whether lords or communes, and especially for the crusade. Then, for wars or other causes, when the aid was not obligatory for his vassals, it was gratuitous and constituted a *don gratuit.* Hence the necessity for consent, either individually or collectively in meetings of estates. "En somme, l'impôt public est sorti de l'aide féodale; il a été aussi, dans une certaine mesure, le rachat de service militaire. . . . En admettant que l'impôt soit le rachat de l'ost en certain cas, il ne l'est pas toujours; c'est aussi une aide"—*Manuel d'histoire du droit français* (1903), pp. 922–24. See also A. Esmein, *Cours élémentaire d'histoire du droit français* (1905), pp. 545 ff.

of the *bonnes villes* depended on the nature of their contributions, the reason for it must be sought outside feudalism proper. It was emancipation, rather than communal charters, that destroyed the power of arbitrary taxation earlier enjoyed by lords over their bourgeois. The precise character of the burdens that remained upon the populace is today uncertain, and was probably so in the twelfth century—differing with local custom, the provisions of charters, and the requirements of feudal states. The first effort to establish a general law with regard to municipal obligations appears in the reign of Louis IX. The *parlement* then held that, according to the custom of the kingdom, all royal towns were obliged to pay certain aids. But this judgment was continually attacked, and not without success. Even if we accord the king of thirteenth-century France the right of arbitrarily taking the *aides aux quatre cas,* we do not have to make him into a sovereign who could levy any tax he wanted at any time. Yet the king's right of exacting military service, or a payment of money in its place, was incontestable so far as many *roturiers* were concerned, in and out of towns. Should the same right have been valid throughout the kingdom, there would have been no legal check upon royal taxation whenever the excuse of a campaign could be provided. It was not so. Many *roturiers,* ordinarily but not exclusively bourgeois, had been wholly or partially exempted.

The only method, it is submitted, by which a king of France could lawfully get a general tax at any time was to negotiate for a freely granted subsidy—a ready procedure successfully used by all the great lords of western Europe. To such request would be added the precious letters of no prejudice—"un instrument," says M. Langlois, "très efficace au service des puissants pour périmer tous les privilèges de leurs sujets." [130] So it was that the king, following the example of his vassals, exploited the bourgeoisie without regard to charters or previous custom, and in time it became more and more evident that he would eventually come to tax at pleasure the entire country. The reaction was proportionately violent. From Louis IX to Philip

[130] *Philippe III,* p. 258.

IV the record is one of remonstrance, then resistance, and finally revolt. The power of the bourgeoisie, based on local organization, was time and again set against the royal will.

Thus was placed upon the king the practical, if not legal, necessity of giving his towns a privilege like that enjoyed by the clergy and nobility—though he could easily ignore the equally valid rights of peasants who were free but individually isolated. If Philip IV had been able to enforce his asserted title to the *ban et arrière-ban,* and then to exact money in place of the required service, a despotic tax throughout the kingdom would have been created at one stroke. But public opinion was too strong for him. It was rather his request of a subsidy from the *bonnes villes* in 1314 that established the precedent for the following century.[131]

The connection of this usage with that preceding is apparent. As the aids demanded by a king like Louis IX surpassed the needs foreseen under the earlier feudalism, the method of solicitation adopted by him and his contemporaries was new and not feudal. So the system of estates, which developed from separate negotiations for particular grants, does not evince the logical application of twelfth-century principles, but a practical application of those demanded by an age becoming modern. For the principle then coming to be recognized was that underlying modern taxation—the supreme need of the state. Accordingly the governmental system which then arose was, as we say, constitutional because it regarded, not merely what was owed by vassals, but what subjects were disposed to pay. It was a matter of politics rather than of law.

[131] See the sketch of Philip IV's financial measures presented by M. Langlois in Lavisse, *Histoire de France,* III², 250 ff.—a model of clarity which the author presents only "sous reserve." Yet how are we to determine the "cas de nécessité," that came to demand a subsidy from the Third Estate?

The Origin and Nature
of the *Taille**

IN 1186 Hugh, abbot of Saint-Denis, issued a charter with a
remarkable preamble; which explains why the bourgeois of Saint-
Denis had repeatedly come before him to beg relief from *taille*.
"For that custom," he says, "seemed to the said bourgeois in-
ordinately bad and hateful, in that it kept them in constant fear;
and so, not daring to display their goods, they made little gain.
Wherefore, not only were outsiders afraid to settle in the town,
but even the natives were impelled to move elsewhere." The
abbot accordingly abolishes forever all *tailles* and forced exactions, on condition that the bourgeois pay an annual *cens* of 123
livres parisis, to be assessed by ten men of good repute, jointly
selected by him and the bourgeois. And this privilege is to be
shared by all immigrants to the town.[1] The *taille* is thus shown

* Reprinted from *La Revue Belge de Philologie et d'Histoire,* V (1926), 801–70.
Correction of misprints and other minor changes by the author.

[1] *Gallia Christiana* (Paris, 1716), VII, Instrumenta, p. 75: "notum fieri volumus
quod burgenses villae nostrae, ubi sanctissimum corpus gloriosissimi martyris
Dionysii requiescit, praesentiam nostram saepius adeuntes, devota nos supplicatione
rogarunt quatinus ob amorem Dei et praefati martyris reverentiam eos a consuetudinibus talliae et toltae, necnon et omnis rapinae liberos faceremus. Erat enim
memorata consuetudo praefatis burgensibus molesta nimis et odiosa, eo quod
semper in timore positi res suas exponere non audentes, minus lucri intenderent;
eatenus ut non solum forenses ad hanc villam confugere formidarent, verum etiam

to have been an arbitrary tax taken by the lord from all inhabitants of the town: a tax, moreover, which on account of its capricious nature proved incompatible with mercantile pursuits and prevented the growth and prosperity of the community. For his own advantage, as well as for that of his bourgeois, the abbot commutes the old exaction into an annual fixed rent and leaves the raising of the money to the citizens themselves.

By this time, however, it was not only men of bourgeois status who were able to force the modification of the old *taille*. Groups of peasants had begun to assert new claims and eventually they secured liberties analogous to those of the towns. Thus when, about the middle of the thirteenth century, the chapter of Notre-Dame de Paris demanded the customary *taille à plaisir* from the men of Rozoy, the latter declined payment, alleging that they were not liable for it, and on being summoned to court to answer for their conduct, refused to appear. Instead, they offered eighteen *livres* a year as *cens*—and the church saw fit to agree to a settlement on this basis.[2] At Rozoy the *taille* was obviously like that enjoyed by the abbey of Saint-Denis—an impost

---

indigenae ad alias transfugere cogerentur. Nos igitur eorum preces honestas, et tam nobis quam ipsis utiles judicantes, eos imperpetuum a tallia et tolta, necnon et omni rapina, liberos facimus, ea tamen conditione, quod ejusdem villae burgenses et haeredes eorum, nobis et successoribus nostris imperpetuum sex viginti et tres libras Parisiensis monetae constitutis temporibus annuatim persolvant . . . Hujus etiam libertatis participes esse concessimus omnes qui, aliunde venientes, in terris nostris et in terris eorumdem burgensium ejusdem villae habitatores exstiterint . . . Praetaxatus autem census hoc modo colligetur. Abbas qui pro tempore fuerit, consilio praefatorum burgensium, decem viros eliget boni testimonii, qui praestito jurejurando praedicti census assisiam fideliter facient."

2 B. Guérard, *Cartulaire de l'église de Notre-Dame de Paris* (Paris, 1850), I, 389: "Ideo ego Clemens, Dei gratia Parisiensis ecclesie decanus, cum universis ejusdem ecclesie fratribus, omnibus tam presentibus quam posteris notum fieri volumus, qualis fuerit diffinitio querele quam Parisiensis ecclesia in homines de Roseio cognoscitur habuisse. Exigebat siquidem ecclesia nostra ab eis, jure consuetudinis, talliam secundum voluntatem capituli nostri; illi vero se talliam debere pernegaverunt; unde ad justitiam capituli, ordinario jure, submoniti venire recusaverunt. Tandem vero nostre miserationi supplicantes, ut se suosque posteros qui in territorio Roseii permanerent a taliis, interrogationibus, reiis, et quibusdam corveiis, quas mense augusti illi debebant qui terre culturam absque adjumento animalium exercent, penitus redderemus absolutos, decem et octo libras Pruviniensium apud Roseium in festo Sancti Remigii singulis annis, census nomine, se suamque posteritatem Parisiensi ecclesie in perpetuum reddituros, sub juramento constituerunt."

resting on all inhabitants of the village, arbitrary, and apparently annual. In both cases its place was taken by a fixed rent; and although we may imagine that the churches lost no money by the transaction, their tenants undoubtedly breathed more easily under an arrangement that gave them a new feeling of dignity and security.

The abolition of the *taille,* therefore, was one phase of the great social revolution that was already well under way in France by the opening of the thirteenth century. Its progress and results as affecting the fiscal responsibilities of the people come to be well illustrated by an increasing wealth of sources, some investigation of which has already been made.[3] In the other direction, however, all is dark; and even the most laborious research effects the collection of only a few scraps of evidence which, though clear enough in themselves, leave a great deal to be desired. Nevertheless, the student of mediaeval institutions must feel amply rewarded if, by putting together his stray fragments of information, he is able to show in a slightly clearer light the way men thought and lived—organized their state and society—in a world so different from our own as the eleventh century. This, I think, the study of the *taille* will do, for it is there that we find the nearest approach to regular taxation known to the men of that age. Moreover, further interest is given the question by the fact that, unlike the other familiar obligations of the peasant, the *taille* suddenly appears in the eleventh century with scarcely an indication of what its previous history may have been; and that down to the present the most irreconcilable opinions have continued to be held as to its original nature.

Now any valid solution of this problem must, I believe, be based mainly on eleventh- and twelfth-century charters, for the sources of the later period inevitably reflect the centralizing innovations of the kings and their princely rivals. In the following pages, accordingly, a representative selection of such docu-

---

[3] For literature on this subject, see "Les 'aides' des villes françaises au xiie et xiiie siècles," *Le Moyen Age,* XXIV, 274 ff.; and "La taille dans les villes d'Allemagne," *ibid.,* XXVI, 1 ff. The latter in particular should be considered as supplemented and corrected by the present study.

ments will be presented from a fairly comprehensive region—northern France and the Low Countries—one which has the added advantages of extending on both sides of the mediaeval linguistic and political frontiers, and of embracing those provinces where the economic forces that revolutionized northwestern Europe first manifested themselves. But even with this restricted scope, the present study cannot lay claim to completeness: it is the result of wide but not exhaustive reading of cartularies, and pretends only to examine enough evidence to warrant a few preliminary conclusions.[4]

Such documents of the eleventh and twelfth centuries as mention the *taille*—and they are comparatively rare—can be roughly classified in two main groups: charters defining the rights of churches, and charters of liberties to towns or other communities. But since the latter do not begin till after the year 1100, all our materials for the previous century must be included in the former group; and if we turn our attention to these ecclesiastical charters, the great majority will be found to deal with the privileges of such persons as may be called *avoués*—either because they are so described in the documents, or because their relation to certain church properties was much the same as that of the others. Consequently, although much has already been written on the *avoué*, it will be necessary to review the subject of his peculiar powers.

Whatever his rank, and whatever the origin of his functions, the *avoué* of the eleventh century was very generally recognized as being entitled, first, to share the profits of justice on the lands that he protected; secondly, to make various levies for military purposes; and lastly, to collect certain special rents in money or food. These payments seem always to have been well defined; over and over again the charters minutely specify what the *avoué* may take and when and from whom he may take it. This is part

---

[4] Although reference will be made below to several of his works, no amount of citation can properly acknowledge the debt that I owe to M. Henri Pirenne, under whose personal guidance the present bit of research has been undertaken and carried out. Moreover, it is recognizing only an obvious fact when I state that many of the fundamental ideas of this article, as well as of those cited above, are the same as have been most recently expressed by that genial scholar in his *Mediaeval Cities* (Princeton, 1925).

of his just due (*servitium debitum*), his right (*jus advocati*); and the *salvamentum* or *tensamentum* of the French sources was exactly the same sort of thing.[5] Sharply distinguished from such rents are the *tailles* or *Beden* when they first appear in the charters: instead of being fixed, they were vague; instead of being the acknowledged perquisites of the *avoué*, they were the cause of endless recrimination and controversy. Indeed, no uniform custom in this respect was ever established. In a great many cases the levying of *tailles* was strictly forbidden the *avoué;* in many others it became part of his regular income; not infrequently the proceeds were shared between the church and its official protector.

Thus in 1015 Balderic, bishop of Liége, declared that he had absolved Lambert, count of Louvain, and restored him as *avoué*, since he had given back the lands of the church "absolutum et liberum ab omni extranea potestate, ab omni placito, exactione, precaria, et pernoctatione, et omnibus violentis hospitiis." In return he was to have a third of the profits of justice, certain definite *corvées*, together with two *deniers*, one fowl, and four *setiers* of oats from each house.[6] Nineteen years later Bishop Reginald, on founding a new abbey, provided that the *avoué* should have no right of exaction over its territory: "nullum ibi obsonium, nullam precaturam habebit, nihil omnino praeter quod abbas sua manu ei dederit usurpabit." [7] And in 1067, when the same church gave a certain allod to Notre-Dame de Huy, the bishop established that the *prévôt* could name as *avoué* someone to hold office during good be-

---

5 For examples of the *tensamentum* see below. References to the literature on the *avoué* will be found in *Le Moyen Age*, XXVI, 34. In the second part of A. Waas, *Vogtei und Bede in der deutschen Kaiserzeit (Arbeiten zur deutschen Rechts- und Verfassungsgeschichte*, V, Berlin, 1923), the author develops the thesis that all mediaeval *tailles* were *Vogteisteuern*. In view of the evidence cited below, I am unable to accept this conclusion.

6 C. Duvivier, *Recherches sur le Hainaut ancien* (Brussels, 1865), p. 372. Cf. the charter in L. Halphen, *Le comté d'Anjou au XIe siècle* (Paris, 1906), p. 346, by which Fulk Nerra announces the rights of the *avoué* for Saint-Florent de Saumur: "nullus ibi advocatus aliquam exactionem inferre praesumeret nec sibi quaestum aliquem adquirere."

7 J. F. Foppens, *Auberti Miraei . . . opera diplomatica et historica*, 2d ed. (Brussels, 1723-48), III, 301.

havior, "ceterum nec licitum sit precariam facere nec quemquam exactione gravare." [8] To the same effect was Henry III's well-known privilege for the abbey of Saint Maximin at Trier in 1054, and the foundation charter of Laach, issued by Henry, count palatine of the Rhine, in 1093.[9] Meanwhile, in 1079, an agreement between the abbot of Saint-Remi de Sens and Dreux, *avoué* of Sièges, had specified that the latter utterly abandoned "captionem illam quam taliam vocant," [10] and in 1094 the archbishop of Reims removed his excommunication from Hugh, count of Rethel, who had renounced "exactiones quas talias vulgo vocant, quas in villa S. Remigii exercebat." [11] Other examples from the following century could be cited by the score.[12]

[8] *Bulletin de la Commission Royale d'Histoire,* Fourth Series, I, 96. Compare the similar provisions in charters of 1091 and 1106 (pp. 100, 103): "id tantummodo ibi exigeret quod in presentia domini episcopi tota congregatio ei determinaret"; "interdictum est ei ne quid ab aliquo rustico ibi violenter exigeret." Cf. also S. Bormans and E. Schoolmeesters, *Cartulaire de l'église de Saint-Lambert de Liége* (Brussels, 1893), I, 52, 71; C. Duvivier, *Actes et documents anciens intéressant la Belgique* (Brussels, 1898–1903), I, 272: "abjuravit itaque taliis et gistiis, toltis et precibus, et omni exactione praeter rectam advocationem quam juste debet habere."

[9] H. Beyer, *Urkundenbuch zur Geschichte der . . . mittelrheinischen Territorien* (Coblenz, 1860 ff.), I, 401–3: "nullus eorum per inscisiones aut petitiones homines gravare . . . presumat." *Ibid.,* I, 444: "neque violentas exactiones quas precarias vocant aliquando exigat."

[10] M. Quantin, *Cartulaire général de l'Yonne* (Auxerre, 1854–59), II, 13.

[11] *Gall. Christ.,* X, *Instr.,* 31.

[12] For instance, the charter of the bishop of Utrecht (1105), recognizing the count of Zutphen as sole *avoué* of Saint-Walburgis, and cursing all who there oc· casion "vel rapinam, vel exactionem, vel peticionem aliquam"—L. Sloet, *Oorkondenboek der Graafschappen Gelre en Zutfen* (The Hague, 1872–76), I, 206. Of the bishop of Metz to Longueville (1121): "Nullus etiam advocatus ecclesiae vestrae exactiones vel violentas hospitalitates et precationes facere praesumat"—Dom Calmet, *Histoire de Lorraine* (Nancy, 1745–67), V, Preuves, cxli. Of the archbishop of Cologne (1121) to Steinfeld, recognizing the sole *avouerie* of the count of Ahr and prohibiting all *exactio* and *precaria*—T. J. Lacomblet, *Urkundenbuch für die Geschichte des Niederrheins* (Düsseldorf, 1840–58), I, 191. Of the bishop of Laon (1129): "Cum in Triniaco villa S. Theoderici praedicti comitis vicecomes Levoldus novas exactiones agere vellet, sub occasione vicecomitatus sui, annua scilicet placita, et tallias de nummis, de frumento, et vino, contradicente abbate Guillelmo, et rusticis ejusdem villae, sicut rem novam et inauditam"—J. Mabillon, *Annales ordinis S. Benedicti* (Paris, 1703–39), VI, 654. Of Lothair III to Stavelot (1131–39): "non precarias vel inscisuras facere"—J. Halkin and C. G. Roland, *Recueil des chartes de l'abbaye de Stavelot-Malmédy* (Brussels, 1909), I, 314, 329, 365.

In these charters a variety of authorities, both lay and ecclesiastical, are seen co-operating to check what they denounce as iniquitous oppressions. But it by no means follows that all *tailles* were thought unjust; what was wrong for one *avoué* might be right for another, or for the prince who frequently acted as protector or *avoué-en-chef* of many churches. The truth of this statement will be at once apparent from an examination of a series of acts issued by the counts of Flanders. The oldest of these is the regulation of the *avouerie* of Marchiennes by Baldwin IV in 1038.[13] The *avoué* is to have the usual third of the profits of justice, certain amounts of food and drink, special payments in case of war, and eight palfreys for service in the king's army.[14]

Praeter haec, nihil debet habere advocatus in ecclesia, nec ista accipere nisi per manus ministrorum abbatiae . . . Non bannum faciet, nec precarias, nec latronum accipiet, nec corveias, nec palefridos; nec ministri ejus aliquid accipient . . . Nec licet ei nec alicui terrenae potestati in aliqua villa S. Rectrudis contra voluntatem abbatis vel monachorum manere, vel convivia praeparare, nec placita tenere, nec denariorum vel pecuniae collectionem ab incolis exigere, nec ullam violentiam inferre.

Here, then, the count as superior over the local *avoués* prohibits to all lay authorities the taking of *Beden* from the tenants of the abbey. Acting in somewhat the same way, Baldwin V in 1055 confirms an agreement between the abbot of Corbie and a certain *avoué,* by which the latter is to make no *rogatio*

Of Conrad III to Saint-Remi de Maestricht: "exactiones, tallias, quas quidem precarias vel petitiones nominant, vel accubitus vastatorios, regia censura contradicit penitus advocato"—Miraeus-Foppens, I, 105. Of the counts of Limburg: S. P. Ernst, *Histoire du Limbourg* (Liége, 1837–48), VI, 136; C. Piot, *Cartulaire de Saint-Trond* (Brussels, 1870), pp. 92, 128; Lacomblet, II, 41.

13 L. A. Warnkönig, *Flandrische Staats- und Rechtsgeschichte* (Tübingen, 1835–37), III, Urkunde CLV. On the power of the count of Flanders as *avoué,* see H. Pirenne, *Histoire de Belgique,* 3d ed. (Brussels, 1909), I, 114, 124.

14 Cf. the charter of Count Thierry in 1137, A. Van Lokeren, *Chartes et documents de Saint-Pierre au Mont Blandin à Gand* (Ghent, 1868), I, 134: "Volo igitur ut universa terra quam S. Watenensis ecclesia sub tuitione meae advocationis iam possidet ab omni importuna rogatione et vexatione, talliis et exactionibus tam castellanorum quam ceterorum virorum ab hodierno die usque in sempiternum immunis sit et libera, salvo dumtaxat redditu meo, quem mihi haereditario iure annuatim persolvere debet."

on any of the abbey's lands,[15] and in the next year he intervenes to settle a dispute between the abbey of Saint-Bertin and certain men who are pretending to be its defenders. The annual *Bede* which they have been claiming as their due is abolished, and the *gîte* and other services allowed them are strictly limited.[16] The same count also issues a similar prohibition for Douchy, a village of Saint-Pierre at Ghent, but various lords are later found in possession of regular *tailles* on other lands of the abbey.[17] In fact, about the year 1070, Count Robert already recognizes an *avoué* of Saint-Bavon as being entitled to one *Bede* every year; which, nevertheless, shall be so levied that no one shall be forced to pay more than he reasonably can.[18]

In these cases we have to do with abbeys of ancient establishment, and no explicit evidence is forthcoming as to the origin, either of the *avoueries* in question, or of the count's regulative authority. We have, however, two foundation charters of the same Robert which give us decidedly interesting information on these very points. The first of them, dated 1093, attests the endowment of a new abbey at Ham by his vassal Enguerrand, *châtelain* of Lille, who had for this purpose placed certain manors in the count's possession.[19]

Et ego predictas possessiones et omne dominium, libertatem, et omnem prorsus justiciam, et quidquid etiam juris habebam vel

[15] Duvivier, *Actes*, I, 132.

[16] B. Guérard, *Cartulaire de l'abbaye de Saint-Bertin* (Paris, 1841), p. 184: "Insuper vero volebant petitionem annuatim, quasi ex debito, facere."

[17] Van Lokeren, *Chartes de Saint-Pierre*, I, 81: "ut nullus judex, nullus advocatus, licentiam habeat, ibi placitum tenere, vel cuicquam per vim tollere, vel hospitare, vel precarios facere; sed omnia in jure et potestate abbatis constituit." In 1070 the abbot paid 40 *livres* to Eustace, count of Saint-Pol, to secure his abandonment of all injustices at Harnes (*ibid.*, I, 100): "precaria ibidem nulla habeat; statutiones que plebeia lingua kerve vocantur super quoslibet S. Petro attinentes non agat." But see the settlement of 1163–77 with William, seigneur d'Avelghem, wherein the latter renounces all *iniurias* at Avelghem, "excepta tantummodo tallia, quam tamen cum omni discretione et mensura facere debebit" (*ibid.*, I, 165). Cf. I, 232.

[18] Warnkönig, III, Urk. cxxxxii; C. P. Serrure, *Cartulaire de Saint-Bavon à Gand* (Ghent, 1836–40), p. 21. This was the settlement of an old quarrel ("intolerabile retroactis diebus litigium"): "ipse vero advocatus unam tantum per annum petitionem in abbatia faceret, ita duntaxat ut qui posset daret, illi vero qui non posset nullam vim aut preceptum inferret." This *Bede* was taken in pigs.

[19] Miraeus-Foppens, II, 1142.

habere poteram in praedictis quoquomodo, abbati et monachis dicti loci ad opus dicti monasterii dedi, tradidi, et deliberavi perpetuo possidenda . . . Insuper volo et statuo ut nullus successorum meorum, Flandrensium videlicet comitum, seu aliorum quorumcumque, exactionem, tailliam, expeditionem, equitationem, aut servitium exercitus, seu manuperationem super homines ecclesiae de cetero habeat; sed tantummodo abbati et ecclesiae Hamensi in omnibus, et non aliis subjecti erunt. Homines etiam extranei undecumque advenerint, si alicujus advocationis exstiterint, quamdiu in terra ecclesiae commorati fuerint, praeter censum capitalem in omnibus abbati et monachis subjacebunt.

By the second charter Robert makes known that certain noblemen of his county, some of whom are mentioned by name, have built a church at Beuvrières near Béthune, and that they, in his presence and with his assent, have established various customs for the benefit of the monks who shall reside there. Together with the lands and possessions granted, they surrender all rights of justice and lordship; and they specifically provide that none of them, whatever his rank, shall have over the new church or its properties any right of exaction, *taille, corvée,* or *ost*. They offer the sole *avouerie* of the church to the count, who accepts and promises not to alienate it.[20]

Now, although these two charters are differently framed, their effect was certainly the same. In each case lands belonging to individuals were unconditionally bestowed upon a church through the mediation of the count, and the *avouerie,* which was often reserved by donors, was granted him alone. In each case, also, the count gave not only what he had received for that purpose from his vassals, but added franchises that only

20 *Ibid.,* IV, 187: "Ego Robertus, Dei gratia Flandrensium Comes, tam futuris quam praesentibus notum facio, quod quidam nobiles viri de comitatu nostro . . . construxerunt quamdam ecclesiam apud Beuvrariam . . . Praefati autem nobiles viri in praesentia nostra venerunt, et devotiones suas nostro assensu confirmaverunt, et constituerunt ut terras et possessiones et quaecumque beneficia eis contulerunt libere et quiete et cum omni justitia et cum omni prorsus dominio teneant et possideant . . . Constituerunt etiam praefati nobiles ut nullus . . . dominorum vel militum quamlibet exactionem vel talliam vel manoperacionem vel expeditionem super ecclesiam S. Christinae, vel super omnia quae monachorum sunt, habeat; vel quidcumque hujusmodi vel super omnem terram, vel super omnes homines, hospites, monachos Beuvrariae possit exigere vel reclamare; sed in omnibus omnino rebus monachis subjecti erunt."

he could grant—for instance, complete immunity for the abbey's men throughout his dominions or for all settlers on the abbey's lands. The count might, of course, act on his own initiative and concede whatever was his own to give; as, when Baldwin V endowed Saint-Winnoc-lez-Bergues in 1067, he promised that men living on the estates of the monastery, whether old or reclaimed from the adjoining waste, should be subject only to the justice of the abbot, should serve in no army except on his summons, and should be exempt "a taliis ac exactionibus et edicto et servitio comitis." [21] And on other ecclesiastical properties, where the rights had not been abandoned, the counts continued to levy *taille* and military service for many years to come.[22] However, it is interesting to note that neither the one nor the other was a monopoly of the count at the close of the eleventh century, since what lesser lords might relinquish they might also keep.[23]

With these Flemish charters may be compared a host of others, for in every region of feudal Europe the princes and their vassals were founding and endowing churches after the same fashion. Thus when Enguerrand, count of Ponthieu, gives a village to Saint-Riquier in 1052, he forbids "ne aliquis amplius in illa villa neque per vim, neque per deprecaturam, neque per advocaturam de omissis consuetudinibus amplius aliquid expeteret." [24] The foundation charter of Tréport issued by Robert, count of Eu, seven years later contains the pledge that the count and his heirs will take from the donated lands "nulla servitia, nulla auxilia, nullas tallias sive collectas; nullas omnino exactiones exigant." [25] In 1077 the count of Aquitaine promises, with considerable prolixity, that none of his family, relatives, officials, or servants shall exact *gîte* or *taille* from the monks of Moustier-Neuf at Poitiers or from their men, wherever

[21] *Ibid.*, I, 511.

[22] See in particular L. Devillers, *Chartes de Sainte-Waudru de Mons* (Brussels, 1899), I, 30, 56, 58, 66, 95. Cf. H. F. Delaborde, *Recueil des actes de Philippe-Auguste* (Paris, 1916), I, 292, and Duvivier, *Actes*, II, 322–23.

[23] For further discussion of the count's power to grant *tailles* over *hôtes*, and the possession of such rights by the feudal baronage, see below.

[24] Hariulf, *Chronique de l'abbaye de Saint-Riquier*, ed. F. Lot (Paris, 1894), p. 230.

[25] *Gall. Christ.*, XI, Instr., 15.

located.[26] And in the same way Manasses, count of Guisnes, renounces for himself and his successors the laying of any "coactivam petitionem seu incisuram" upon the men of the abbey of Andres.[27] On the other hand, if we may believe the charters, the dukes of Lorraine were guilty, not only of retaining, but also of inventing *tailles* on monastic lands under their protection; [28] and the count of Champagne, while recognizing the immunity of some ecclesiastical properties, maintains his right to *tailles* on others.[29]

Now it must be noticed that throughout all the wrangling over *tailles*, which fill so many records of the eleventh, twelfth, and thirteenth centuries, the aim of the church was always clear and steadfast: to free its lands and its men of all lay control. Since our sources deal almost exclusively with privileges issued to churches or settlements of disputes to their advantage, the evidence against secular *tailles* on ecclesiastical lands seems

26 *Ibid.*, II, Instr., 351.

27 A. Duchesne, *Histoire généalogique des maisons de Guisnes, d'Ardres, de Gand et de Coucy* (Paris, 1631), p. 37.

28 About 1150 the monks of Saint-Michel complained to the pope of the usurpations of the duke (*Gall. Christ.*, XIII, Instr., 571): "nostri quoque temporis comes Raynaldus, qui quinto illis gradu successit, quod majores sui numquam fecerant, pecuniarum rapinas, quas vulgus talliatas vocant, per terram nostram primus agere coepit." And in 1152 Duke Matthew renounced, in favor of the abbess of Remiremont (*ibid.*, XIII, Instr., 507), "tallias autem quas ipse dux et advocati sui injuste super homines ecclesiae facere consueverant." Somewhat earlier the duke of Lorraine had abandoned as a "prava exactio" all *taille* on the lands of the monks of Saint-Dié, except a special aid when he was summoned to the imperial army—G. Waitz, *Urkunden zur deutschen Verfassungsgeschichte*, 2d ed. (Berlin, 1886), p. 8.

29 H. d'Arbois de Jubainville, *Histoire des ducs et des comtes de Champagne* (Paris, 1859–66), III, 442: "Ego Henricus, Trecensium comes palatinus, presentibus et futuris notum fieri volo, inter me et abbatem S. Medardi Suessionensis ecclesie Ingrannum nomine discordiam habuisse propter talliam quam in villis subscriptis feceram, videlicet . . . Sed servientes mei, qui consuetudines meas recipere consueverunt, de prescriptis villis nullam talliam me habere recognoverunt. Quapropter talliam in villis prenominatis relinquo, atque in perpetuum dimitto . . . In aliis vero villis, si quas in potestate mea habuerint, nec talliam nec consuetudinem dimitto." Cf. C. Lalore, *Collection des principaux cartulaires du diocèse de Troyes* (Paris, 1875–83), V, 36. For other examples from various regions see d'Achery, *Spicilegium* (Paris, 1723), III, 459; J. Tardif, *Monuments historiques* (Paris, 1866), p. 238; Delaborde, *Actes de Philippe-Auguste*, I, 24; *Gall. Christ.*, XI, Instr., 90; Miraeus-Foppens, II, 1195; B. Guérard, *Cartulaire de l'abbaye de Saint-Père de Chartres* (Paris, 1840), II, 669; J. Flach, *Les origines de l'ancienne France* (Paris, 1886 ff.), I, 393, n. 1, 417, n. 2.

greatly to outweigh that in its favor. We should remember, however, that when a lord possessed the indisputable right to such *tailles,* no record of it would need to be made, and it would continue as a customary burden on the land until a more generous heir saw fit to abolish or restrict it. Many nobles unquestionably enjoyed perquisites of this sort as part of their ancient property and, to judge from their actions, the unanimous opinion of *avoués* was that *tailles* should normally accompany such other rights as justice and *ost.* Whether there may not have been good cause for this notion will be seen later; but with or without it, *tailles* were frequently established by force.

In this connection an interesting story is told by Roger Guenchi, *avoué* of Romigny; for his charter of 1117 to the church of Compiègne not only recites what concessions he has made, but frankly tells why he has made them and why he has not granted more. "I therefore," he says, "by the same right that others have to customs within their *avoueries,* have annually collected one measure of oats and three *deniers* from each householder there; which income, since I have held it by virtue of the original establishment under my ancestors, and have continued to enjoy it without contradiction, I have determined to retain for myself and my successors. Likewise I have yearly three other *deniers* from each of the aforesaid householders, imposed by my predecessors for *gîte,* which also I have not agreed to give up. The *taille,* however, which my predecessors, though by usurpation and lawlessness, annually levied from the harvested crops, and which I myself, falling into their evil ways and similarly undergoing excommunication, have also had, I have seen fit to moderate." In this magnanimous spirit, accordingly, Roger promises henceforth to take as *taille* only five measures of grain from all tenants belonging to the *avouerie* of Romigny— and it was this settlement that, *faute de mieux,* became the established custom of the locality.[30]

30 E. Morel, *Cartulaire de l'abbaye de Saint-Corneille de Compiègne* (Compiègne, 1904), no. 39; also published in F. Senn, *L'institution des avoueries ecclésiastiques en France* (Paris, 1903), p. 226: "Ego igitur, jure quo ceteri suas in suis advocationibus habent consuetudines, de singulis mansionariis singulas avene minas tresque denarios per singulos annos ibi colligebam. Quod, quoniam a prima institucione a patribus meis habui et absque ulla contradictione possedi, michi

What could be more explicit than this naïve account? The primitive arrangement had given Roger's ancestors the usual *tensamentum*, but they in the course of the eleventh century had supplemented this income by exacting also *gîte* and *taille*, which, in spite of the bitterest opposition, was levied year after year. Finally, to avoid the pains of hell, Roger agreed to limit the amount of the exaction, and it thus became a fixed charge on the land. Altogether, this is a remarkable example of a process that was everywhere taking place, but which in most cases left but little trace in the records.[31] Failing for some reason or another to secure the complete relinquishment of *tailles* on its property, a church would try to protect its tenants by determining the maximum that they could be forced to pay; for toward them the *avoué* would naturally have none of the scruple that selfish interest would prescribe in dealing with his own men.[32] Often, too, the levy of *tailles* was restricted to specified occasions or to such times as might be agreed on between the two parties, when quite commonly both were to share the proceeds.

So in 1067 the canons of Notre-Dame de Paris came to an agreement with the *avoué* of Viry by which he should have *salvamentum* only from occupied houses and not more than three *gîtes* a year; that pleas should be held jointly by a minister of each party, and that no *deprecatio* should be made except by

meisque successoribus censui retinendum. Habeo quoque de singulis predictis mansionariis tres alios quotannis, denarios, predecessoribus meis pro pastu a rusticis institutos, quos etiam dimittere non consensi. Talliam vero, quam pro libitu suo antecessores mei, usurpative tamen et contra vetitum, collectis annuatim fecerant segetibus, egoque, per vias eorum incedens et simile subjacens excommunicatione, tenueram, pro consilio temperavi." It was this charter of Roger Guenchi that, after further troubles with his successors, was made the basis of a new settlement in 1144 (*ibid.*, pp. 231–32).

31 Most of the evidence regarding the limitation of *tailles* comes from the later twelfth or the thirteenth century. For example, A. Luchaire, *Etude sur les actes de Louis VII* (Paris, 1885), p. 424 (1164–65); Senn, *Avoueries*, p. 234 (1170); Guérard, *Cartulaire de N.-D. de Paris*, I, 233 (1193); G. Kurth, *Chartes de l'abbaye de Saint-Hubert en Ardenne* (Brussels, 1903), I, 225 (1216); Miraeus-Foppens, IV, 539 (1226), II, 853 (1230). But Flach (*Origines de l'ancienne France*, I, 392, n. 1) cites an interesting example from the early twelfth century. And see below. In thirteenth-century extents the *taille* usually appears as fixed; see Pirenne, *Le livre de l'abbé Guillaume de Ryckel* (Brussels, 1896), p. 50.

32 Pirenne, *Histoire de Belgique*, I, 143. But see below, n. 38.

their common consent.[33] The same provision was made in 1080 by Richard Mansell in a grant to the abbey of Conches: neither one should take an aid from the men of the land called Baliol without the knowledge of the other, and whatever was taken should be equally divided.[34] Typical of quite a number of *partages* entered into by the abbey of Saint-Père de Chartres was that sponsored before 1111 with Peter, mayor of Sainte-Croix, and his uncle. Certain lands belonging to the latter, but now deserted, are henceforth to be held in common and all income from them is to be shared.[35]

Statutum est etiam ab utraque parte concessum quod nec ipsi nec successores eorum ab habitatoribus terre illius aliqua gravamina exigant, nisi forte eos vel aliquem eorum ab hostibus capi contigerit; tunc enim facient exactionem illam que vulgo tallia vocatur convenienter, secundum laudem nostram et nostrum consilium; et cum facta fuerit, nos medietatem ejus habebimus. Et nos similiter, pro nostra necessitate, eodem modo eandem exactionem poterimus facere; et cum facta fuerit, ipsi medietatem accipient.

The *tailles* foreseen in this charter were obviously in the nature of more or less infrequent imposts, and the one specified

[33] Guérard, *Cartulaire de N.-D. de Paris*, I, 308.

[34] *Gall. Christ.*, XI, Instr., 130: "adjutorium seu forifacturam de aliquo homine ipsius terrae nullus capiet alio ignorante, capta quoque per medium dividetur." This grant is quoted in a confirmation by Henry I of England. Cf. the agreement made in 1120 between the chapter of Angoulême and certain brothers over rights in L'Isle-d'Espagne (*Bulletin et mémoires de la Société archéologique et historique de la Charente*, 6e Série, IX, 128): "Concessum est enim a fratribus illis . . . quod propriam terram S. Petri, quae est in predicta Insula et in circumadjacente riperia, et homines in ea manentes, libere et quiete possideant canonici, ut nemo alius ibi aliquam consuetudinem habeat, neque per vim, neque per quesitionem, neque aliquo alio modo. Communis vero terra canonicorum et predictorum fratrum, ubi est habitatio hominum, communiter habeantur, ita ut redditus equaliter inter canonicos et predictos fratres dividantur, tallede vel quesitiones communi consilio fiant et simili modo equaliter dividantur. De quesitione vero avenae, quae civada dicitur, retinuit Guilelmus et frater ejus ut in singulis rusticis, communis terrae unusquisque eminam querat, quod est sextarius, et canonici similiter querant sextarium." Similar settlements may be found in d'Arbois de Jubainville, *Comtes de Champagne*, III, 456 (c. 1168); *Mémoires de la Société de l'histoire de Paris*, XXIX, 218 (1171); Lacomblet, I, 336 (1180); *Gall. Christ.*, VIII, Instr., 524 (1202).

[35] Guérard, *Cartulaire de Saint-Père*, II, 432. With this compare two other agreements of the same period: *ibid.*, II, 340, 530.

occasion, ransom from captivity, was of course one on which aids were customarily demanded of noble tenants also. Alongside it appear in other documents, though somewhat irregularly, the other familiar occasions. Thus in a charter of the early twelfth century William "Goetus" grants to Saint-Père for colonization ("ad hospitandum") a certain portion of his fief. He is to receive "pro defensione et protectione" various payments in food and money from every *hôte* there settling; and furthermore, if he marries his daughter (by his wife!), buys a castle, or is taken prisoner, "talliam in hospitibus terre illius facere ei licebit, per manum tamen prioris S. Romani." [36] With this may be compared a grant of about the same period to the bishop of Angers. By it Robert Ivon cedes a ruined church and a cemetery on the following conditions: [37]

Hoc etiam dictum fuit, quod episcopus solveret dimidium servitii debiti ipsis dominis a quibus habeo terram illam: videlicet, ad custodiendum castrum Segreii dum homines loci illius essent in exercitu, et ad redimendos dominos terrae illius si caperentur, et ad faciendos milites primogenitos filios dominorum, et ad maritandas primogenitas filias eorum, quod servitium fiet secundum mensuram terrae illius. Nec quaereretur ab hominibus terrae illius vel hoc vel aliud, nisi per voluntatem et manum episcopi. Si autem contigeret ipsum episcopum aliqua cause quaerere ab hominibus terrae illius, de hoc quod ipse caperet dimidium sibi retineret et dimidium michi aut successoribus meis redderet. Similiter, si contigeret me aut meos haeredes aliquid velle quaerere rationabiliter ab hominibus in cimiterio illo habitantibus, per manum episcopi quaereretur, et de hoc quod quaereretur dimidium sibi retineret et dimidium mihi redderet.

It should be noticed that, according to the preceding charter, the bishop might lay a *taille* on the lands in question for no less than three purposes: first, for his own benefit; secondly, for the benefit of the donor; and lastly, to contribute toward aids owed by the latter to his suzerain. In the two former cases all proceeds were to be equally divided, but in the third, of course, neither party profited at all. The peasant thus helped to support three sets of masters, and so far as he was concerned, the *taille* was

[36] *Ibid.*, II, 483.
[37] *Documents historiques sur l'Anjou publiés par la Société d'agriculture, sciences, et arts d'Angers*, V, 219.

entirely arbitrary. Altogether, this is a splendid example of the fundamental simplicity of all fiscal arrangements during the agricultural age.

There were, however, benefactors more generous than Robert Ivon, and their renunciations might tend indirectly to lighten the burdens of ecclesiastical tenants. In 1140 a certain Odo gave to Notre-Dame de Chartres twelve plowlands located in a forest. The canons were to divide it into portions for settlers, over whom the donor reserved only three specified rights. One of these was a *taille* every fourth year. At the proper time Odo says he will notify the canons, who shall then levy a suitable *taille*, of which they are to keep one-half. "Nor shall they levy any other *taille* for me or my heirs, unless they so desire; not even for the redemption of my body. As often, however, as they shall levy a *taille*, one-half shall belong to me." [38] If the inhabitants of this territory were oppressed by frequent exactions, it would obviously be the fault of no one but the canons themselves.

The preceding evidence has, I think, shown the futility of trying to frame one uniform theory with regard to the powers of the *avoué*. The lands of one church might have been donated by a score of lords on as many conditions, and might be scattered among regions where quite different customs prevailed. What the proprietors could enforce in one place they could not in another; everything depended on local usage. Thus in many cases the abbot of Saint-Denis succeeded in taking from the

[38] Guérard, *Cartulaire de Saint-Père*, p. xxxviii, n. 4: "Talleia supramemorata sic fiet. Quarto anno submonebo canonicos per majorem ejusdem ville, et facient talleiam convenientem, de qua habebo medietatem, et ipsi aliam. Aliam talleiam non facient pro me nec pro heredibus meis, nisi voluerint, nec etiam pro redemptione corporis mei. Quocienscumque vero ipsi talleiam fecerint, dimidia erit mea." For other such *partages* see Flach, *Origines de l'ancienne France*, II, 557, n. 1, 555, n. 2; L. Merlet, *Cartulaire de l'abbaye de la Sainte Trinité de Tiron* (Chartres, 1883), II, 94; *Gall. Christ.*, X, Instr., 337. By a compromise established about 1172 between the abbot of Saint-Corneille de Compiègne and one of his *avoués*, the two together were to levy one *taille* every year and equally divide what was collected. The result was that the men of the three vills thus concerned appealed to Pope Alexander III, who had just excommunicated the *avoué*, complaining that the abbot had violated the papal order and had extorted such a severe *taille* that many of the villagers had been forced to move to other homes. The pope commanded an investigation and the punishment of the abbot, if found guilty (Senn, *Avoueries*, pp. 236–39).

avoués exactions that he claimed were usurped;[39] but sometimes, willingly or not, he saw fit to recognize their claims to the *taille*. So, when Louis VI settled a dispute between the abbot and his *avoué* at Argenteuil in 1110, the latter was allowed, not only his regular rents of grain, but 100 *sous* for *gîte* and 100 *sous* for *taille*.[40] Later, in 1153, Baldwin IV of Hainaut arranged a similar agreement between the abbey and Vautiers, *avoué* of Solesmes, who had been accused of building a castle there against the will of the abbot, of usurping his rights of justice, forest, and *mainmorte,* and of violently extorting *taille* from the tenants three times a year. All this Vautiers agreed to surrender except the *taille;* on which score, "since the abbot was unwilling to concede him anything certain, the said *avoué* provided that he would only levy *taille* twice a year, and in such fashion that the men should not complain of it."[41] By 1233, when Solesmes received a charter of liberties, this *taille* had been fixed at 30 *livres* on the feast of Saint-Remi and 20 *livres* at Easter. Beyond these sums the *avoué* could exact nothing—not even for marrying his daughter, knighting his son, or ransom.[42]

However, it was especially when the *avoué* had done much to improve the value of the property that his claim to *taille* was considered valid by the church. Thus, by the original agreement between the abbot of Saint-Denis and the count of Beaumont, the latter was to have one-half of all custom, exaction, and *taille* from a new settlement that he was to establish on some of the abbey's waste lands.[43] And in 1156 the bishop of Cambrai decided that, since Robais, a vill of Saint-Denis, would have remained uncultivated and deserted except through the faithful efforts of the *avoué,* who had attracted colonists from Flanders, Brabant,

---

[39] Tardif, *Monuments,* pp. 235, 259 (1123–37, 1145); Flach, *Origines de l'ancienne France,* I, 392, n. 1 (1144); A. Teulet, *Layettes du Trésor des Chartes* (Paris, 1863), I, 97 (1170). These charters regularly allow *tensamentum* at a fixed rate to the *avoué.*

[40] A. Luchaire, *Louis VI le Gros* (Paris, 1890), no. 97.

[41] Duvivier, *Hainaut,* p. 577: "De tallia vero, quia nichil ei certum abbas statuere volebat, pepigit idem advocatus quod bis tantum in anno talliam faceret, eo modo quod homines de eo non conquererentur."

[42] *Analectes pour servir à l'histoire ecclésiastique de la Belgique* (Louvain and Brussels, 1864 ff.), XIII, 108.

[43] Teulet, *Layettes,* I, 71.

and other regions, he should receive half of all customs, tolls, and *tailles*, as well as "eorum denariorum assisa quod advocatus ex prima constructione ejusdem ville sibi dare constituit"—i.e. the *tensamentum*.[44]

We now logically come to the question of royal *tailles*, and the best method for approaching it will perhaps be to enumerate the provisions of some of the earlier charters and let them tell their own story.[45] For example, in 1085 Philip I gives certain lands to the Maison-Dieu d'Etampes-les-Vieilles and promises that the *hôtes* living there shall be free of all custom toward him or any person save the representative of the church; nor shall on the said land any one presume "violentiam seu toltam facere."[46] Five years later the same king bestows upon the canons of Orléans all "viaria, justicia, et tolta" held by him over certain lands at Dammartin.[47]

Under Louis VI the evidence improves both in quantity and quality. In 1114 he grants the petition of the prior of Saint-Eloi, that all persons possessing homes on the church's land outside the walls should have the same liberty as they had enjoyed when that land was inside:[48]

ab omni videlicet viatura, banno, sanguine, corveia, prepositi exactione, furis captione, incendio, tallia, seu qualibet alia mala consuetudine, quieti penitus et soluti essent.

In the next year he issues a confirmation to Saint-Paterne d'Orléans conceding[49]

[44] Tardif, *Monuments*, p. 284.

[45] The following charters have all in one way or another received the attention of Luchaire in his various books, but he nowhere gives more than passing attention to the royal *taille*. In A. Duchesne, *Histoire généalogique de la maison de Montmorency et de Laval* (Paris, 1624), Preuves, 14, is to be found a charter of Robert, king of France, confirming to the abbey of Coulombs that town "cum tota vicaria, et bannis, et incendiis, taleis, et omnibus legibus ceteris." But the "taleis" of this passage should be replaced by "tasceis," as I have been kindly informed by M. Martin-Chabot, who is now engaged in editing the acts of Robert for the Académie des Inscriptions.

[46] M. Prou, *Recueil des actes de Philippe Ier* (Paris, 1908), p. 288. In later charters *tolta* appears as an occasional substitute for *tallia*. See immediately below, and also the charter to Saint-Denis, above, n. 1.

[47] *Ibid.*, p. 310.

[48] R. de Lasteyrie, *Cartulaire général de Paris* (Paris, 1887), I, 190; Tardif, *Monuments*, p. 206.

[49] Guérard, *Cartulaire de Saint-Père*, II, 456.

totam vicariam, immo totam omnino justiciam: ita scilicet, ut intra predictos viii, aripennos nullus regie potestatis minister aliquam justiciam clamare presumat, non furem, non incendium, non raptum, non sanguinem, non rotagium, non foragium, non bannum, non talliam in hospitibus qui ibi hospitabuntur, non corveiam, non ire in nostram caballationem neque in hostem, non herbergamentum, non sacimentum, immo nichil ex toto, quod ad nostram pertinet vicariam sive justiciam.

From the same king Notre-Dame de Paris obtains a charter in 1118, relinquishing [50]

quasdam exactiones quas in terra Beate Marie apud Balneolum villam diu habueram, scilicet talliam super hospites, ammonitiones hospitum in exercitu quibus predicta terra plus justo vexabatur.

But the king reserves the annual *tensamentum,* as anciently paid by the same *hôtes* in money, wine, and grain. About the same time he also promises not to levy on any lands of Saint-Spire de Corbeil, wherever situated, "tallias, toltas et demandas vel exactiones aliquas"; [51] and in the next year he entirely remits a certain *taille* that he had been exacting at Sceaux-en-Gâtinais and gives it to be enjoyed forever by the church.[52] In 1133 he frees of *taille* a certain vill of the abbey of Saint-Magloire,[53] and in 1136 one of the priory of Juvisi, but on condition that he receive a *setier* of oats annually from each colonist.[54] Finally, a charter of 1137 exempts Frenay-l'Evêque of *tolte, taille,* and exaction, so that no one should henceforth take anything from the inhabitants except the bishop of Chartres.[55]

Recounting the acts of Louis VII and Philip Augustus similar to the foregoing would add but little to our information on the subject.[56] Like their predecessors and their vassals, they

---

[50] Guérard, *Cartulaire de N.-D. de Paris,* I, 256; Tardif, *Monuments,* p. 210.

[51] *Mémoires et documents publiés par la Société archéologique de Rambouillet,* VI, 4.

[52] Luchaire, *Louis VI,* p. 342: "quamdam talliam quam exigebamus et accipiebamus . . . ex toto dimittimus atque eidem ecclesie imperpetuum habendam concedimus."

[53] Tardif, *Monuments,* p. 226.   [54] Luchaire, *Louis VI,* p. 342.

[55] *Recueil des ordonnances des rois de France* (Paris, 1723 ff.), V, 22.

[56] See especially Luchaire, *Louis VII,* pp. 357, 368, 370, 410, 589; Delaborde, I, 155, 174, etc.

grant lands with or without justice and other customs; they reserve *tensamentum* and *taille* or issue more or less sweeping exemptions. Such documents constitute the great majority of royal charters mentioning *taille*, but there are a few minor groups that deserve passing attention. In the first place, we find occasional privileges bestowed upon an individual—usually the so-called *liber hospes* of a church, who lived in a community where *tailles* might be collected, and acted as its agent in business matters. A grant of this sort was made by Louis VI for the abbey of Tiron *c.* 1125,[57] and for that of Montmartre in 1134.[58] Secondly, there are acts of *partage*, by which the king assumes protection of certain monastic property in return for a share of the income, including *tailles*.[59] And lastly, there are the charters dealing with the perquisite known as *régale*, by which the king limits his right to *taille* from ecclesiastical tenants during a vacancy in the office of abbot or bishop.[60]

At this point it might be well to make some brief summary of the evidence thus far examined, which, though dealing for the most part with secular rights on church property, has incidentally afforded other information as well. First, as to the nature of the *taille*, it must be noticed that the word, along

[57] Merlet, *Cartulaire de Tiron*, I, 95: "hospitem illum quemcumque in domo sua de Maudonta posuerint ab omni talliata et exactione . . . liberum."

[58] *Gall. Christ.*, VII, Instr., 55. Cf. Delaborde, I, 6. Similar privileges were also frequently granted by barons.

[59] For example, the association of Louis VI by the bishop of Paris in certain property at Champeaux (Guérard, *Cartulaire de N.-D. de Paris*, I, 269); the former was to receive two-thirds "de censa illius terre, de taliis, de forisfactis," etc.

[60] So Louis VII to the bishop of Orléans (*Gall. Christ.*, VIII, Instr., 513): "quod quando episcopatus Aurelianensis in manus regias devenerit, nullam prorsus exactionem vel talliam in terra ejusdem episcopatus vel nos vel successores nostri de cetero faciemus, nisi eam quae statuto tempore debetur episcopo scilicet ad festum S. Remigii . . . Ac ne etiam talliae illius summa supra modum ad gravamen ecclesiae ullis occasionibus augeatur, certa sub assignatione statuimus, ac modis omnibus inhibemus, ne numerum LX librarum excedat." Also to the bishop of Sens (Luchaire, *Louis VII*, no. 773) and to the bishop of Paris (Guérard, *Cartulaire de N.-D. de Paris*, I, 37). Cf. the confirmation of this charter by Philip Augustus in 1206 (*Ordonnances*, XI, 292), together with assurance of no prejudice because he has just taken 240 *livres* or more, in addition to the said 60 *livres*. See the renunciation of the same right at Chartres by Henry, count of Blois, about 1105 (*Gall. Christ.*, VIII, Instr., 308), and compare the grant of the count of Champagne to Troyes in 1181 (Lalore, *Cartulaires de Troyes*, V, 45).

with its many substitutes, is used very loosely in the records; it may mean a regular or an irregular impost, a bit of violence or an unquestioned right, a limited or an unlimited obligation. We thus seem to be dealing with an institution so vague that as yet scarcely any generalizations can be made about it. This, however, can be said: whether authorized or not, it almost invariably appears in the earliest sources alongside judicial and military rights.

Secondly, with regard to the persons enjoying the exaction, we have seen in possession of it before the middle of the twelfth century kings, prelates, dukes, counts, and *châtelains*, as well as simple knights and *seigneurs*. And in respect at least to the characteristics mentioned above, the *taille* of one very much resembles the *taille* of another. One of these persons, in the capacity of *avoué*, might claim the privilege of tallaging ecclesiastical tenants within a given region. Whether the *avouerie* had been given him, whether he had reserved it over donated lands, or whether it was his by virtue of political office, he might or might not have the right to *taille*; that depended on the terms of his commission, the provisions of his grant, or the custom of the country. Some *tailles* were based on usurpation but many were not. In any case, the exaction was only incidental to the institution of *avouerie,* and not at all its creation.[61]

Thirdly, as concerns the persons liable, one cannot fail to remark that there has been little talk of serfs, though time and again the *taille* has been said to bear upon men styled *hospites*. This last point challenges our attention, and to explain it, as well as to secure further information on the previous two, it will be necessary to examine another set of charters—those dealing with *tailles* levied by the churches themselves.

Such acts, like those already studied, were issued as the result of controversy, for quarrels arose, not only between churches and *avoués*, but also between churches, and between rival authorities within a church. Thus in 1120 Notre-Dame de Paris and Saint-Martin-des-Champs ended a dispute over rights in

---

[61] For the views in this respect of Karl Zeumer see *Le Moyen Age*, XXVI, 36; and for the argument of A. Waas, above, n. 5.

Aulnay by agreeing that all rents and *pecunie questus* should be equally divided, and that no such exaction or *taille* should be made without the consent of both parties.[62] Then, about seven years later, a settlement was made between the bishop and canons of the former church, by which the chapter was accorded full disposition of its property: [63]

et in eisdem possessionibus, sive in ecclesiis, sive in hospitibus et servis, sive in domibus, sive in vineis et terris, et in ceteris, tallie et rogationes et cetera auxilia, quotienscunque opus fuerit, libere et absolute, et sine impedimento alicujus persone, a communi capitulo ubique accipiantur.

Here there is no indication of what exactions the chapter was in the habit of making, but we know from other records that in many villages it took annual *tailles*.[64]

Not long afterward the bishop of Orléans issued a charter to define the rights of the dean. The latter, he says, has been claiming, against the will of the canons, one-third "de omnibus taliis quae in terra de majoria Petri S. Crucis fierint . . . sive fierint pro papa, sive pro rege, sive pro terrarum emptione, immo quacunque fierint causa." The dean, however, has been prevailed upon to admit that his claim is unjust, since from the *tailles* mentioned the canons get nothing for their own use.[65]

---

[62] Guérard, *Cartulaire de N.-D. de Paris,* I, 40. Cf. Beyer, *Mittelrheinisches Urkundenbuch,* I, 706 (1167): "Statuimus etiam ut in omnibus curiis nostris in quibus nos vel successores nostri pro aliqua necessitate exactiones et precarias poterimus facere, tu et ecclesia tua de omnibus que ibidem possidetis liberi sitis ab omni precaria et exactione tam nostra quam successorum nostrorum aut etiam ministerialium Treverensis ecclesie."

[63] Guérard, *Cartulaire de N.-D. de Paris,* I, 338.

[64] See above; and for other examples, Guérard, *Cartulaire de N.-D. de Paris,* II, 3–36.

[65] *Mémoires de la Société archéologique et historique de l'Orléannais,* XXX, 5. Compare the agreement of 1127 between the bishop and archdeacon of Paris (Guérard, *Cartulaire de N.-D. de Paris,* I, 28): "Collectas vero episcopus, absque archidiacono, per parrochiam ipsius non faciet, nisi aut Roman veniat, aut concilium in provincia celebretur, aut forte dominum papam in ecclesia sua suscipiat; quod tamen, consulto archidiacono, faciet: in quibus quidem collectis, quia expense omnes erunt episcopi, archidiaconus nullam habet portionem. In ceteris vero communibus collectis archidiaconus, ut moris est, tertiam partem obtineat. Archidiacono autem in tota parrochia collectas sine episcopo [facere] non licebit. Quod

Presumably, though the record does not say so, he should have his third of *tailles* levied by the chapter for its own profit.

Another fruitful source of trouble was usurpation by one of the church's domanial agents. Thus the abbot of Saint-Amand repeatedly condemned his *prévôt* for levying violent *Beden* in one of the abbey's villages.[66] And in 1107 the abbot of Saint-Bertin restored to power his *minister* at Poeperinge only on condition that he should not, as his father had done, levy *coactas petitiones*.[67] In this same connection, one of the most interesting accounts is contained in an act of 1153 attesting a settlement between the dean of Sainte-Croix d'Angers and one of his mayors. "On our land he shall make no *quête*, except that of grain, which has been accustomed to be made at harvest time, and which he shall make in this way: he shall not assess it by *taille*, but shall, if he please, ask it of the men, without naming any certain amount. It shall remain in their discretion, however, either to give or not to give; and if they give nothing, or decline to give as much as he wants, he shall not on this account be permitted to use force against them, nor to summon them to court." [68]

We therefore have abundant evidence of *tailles* levied by ecclesiastics, not only in the charters just cited, but in the implications of a great many others: such as the *partages* between a church and an *avoué* or an act dealing with *régale*, where it is stipulated that the lord shall take *taille* only on such occasions

---

si quis archidiacono de suo, precibus aut ultro, donare voluerit, nequaquam debebit episcopus contradicere." And see *Gall. Christ.*, X, Instr., 214.

[66] Between 1063 and 1076 the *prévôt* had agreed to levy no "violentem precem" on the land in question (Waitz, *Urkunden*, 13), but in 1082 the abbot was forced to decree a second time (Duvivier, *Actes*, I, 47): "Violentem precem quam vulgo vocant tolpri nullo modo faciet." And this decision was confirmed in 1154 by Thierry, count of Flanders (*ibid.*, I, 71).

[67] Warnkönig, II², Urk. CLXXVIII. The same prohibition was put in the municipal charter of 1218 (*ibid.*, II², Urk. CLXXXVIII).

[68] *Mémoires de la Société archéologique et historique de l'Orléannais*, XXX, 21: "Questam nullam in terra nostra faciet, nisi eam quae tempore messis fieri solita est de frumento, quam etiam hoc modo faciet: non talliabit eam, sed quaeret ab hominibus si voluerit, non nominando eis aliqam summam. In beneplacito autem eorum erit dare vel non dare. Quod si non dederint, vel non quantum ipse voluerit dederint, nec vim facere, nec eos ad justitiam propter hoc submonere licebit."

as it had been owed the defunct prelate. Indeed, the documents regularly show that a grant to a church of exemption from secular *tailles* was equivalent to conceding the right on its part to collect the exaction.[69]

From every point of view, however, the most remarkable information on the subject is contained in the records of various controversies over *tailles* that occurred at the opening of the twelfth century. Some time before 1105 it appears that the abbot of Saint-Mesmin de Micy had had trouble with certain men of the king who were resident on his property, for in that year he requests Philip I to relieve the abbey of the injurious effects of their presumptuous action.[70] The king accordingly grants that:

ubicumque manserint homines nostri, liberi vel servi, in praefatis terris sive locis S. Maximini, terrarum debitas consuetudines, scilicet in taliis, in censu, in ceteris redditibus, quemadmodum proprii homines S. Maximini perpetuo reddant et reddendo persolvant.

Thus we are told that some of the king's men, both free and serf, had settled as *hôtes* on the lands of Saint-Mesmin; that they had objected to paying the customary *tailles* imposed by the monks on their own men, but that by the king's order they were henceforth to do so. The principle here laid down is certainly interesting, but before attempting to analyze its consequences, we should examine the extraordinary report of a

[69] See above; also Delaborde, *Actes de Philippe-Auguste*, I, 51, 68. Churches sometimes granted exemption to individuals—*ibid.*, I, 143; P. H. Goffinet, *Cartulaire de l'abbaye d'Orval* (Brussels, 1870), p. 119.

[70] Prou, *Actes de Philippe I*, p. 382: "Ubicumque locorum homines nostri in terris videlicet praefati S. Maximini habitarent seu coloni essent, ipsa loca vel terras illas ab eorum injuriosa praesumptione alleviare deberemus." A charter of Robert to Saint-Mesmin in 1022 (*Historiens*, X, 606) includes the following clause: "Concedimus etiam eis ut homines nostri liberi et servi, qui manserint vel domos habuerint in terris eorum, omnes penitus consuetudines et ex nomine taliam quemadmodum proprii, homines eorum perpetuo reddant." But this provision is tacked onto a grant of a totally different sort, and there is no explanation of it, as in the act of Philip, where the request of the abbot first appears. Furthermore, a quarrel over *hôtes* fits the early twelfth better than the early eleventh century; see immediately below. Altogether, therefore, the sentence in the confirmation of Robert looks decidedly like an interpolation in the original charter, which in the opinion of M. Martin-Chabot (see above, n. 45), was reshaped in the twelfth century.

trial held in the very next year before the king's court and in the presence of the future Louis VI.[71]

In confirming the sentence, Philip first relates the facts in the case. Some little time before, the church of Compiègne had summoned its *hôtes* to justice and had then exercised its own proper authority by taking from them for the good of the church "petitiones quasdam publicas, quas vulgo talliam vocant." Whereupon, one Nevelon de Pierrefonds, thinking to protect certain of his own men and to remove them from the law that bound other *hôtes* of the church, demanded that the money collected from such men of his be turned over to him.[72] On the other hand, the churchmen claimed that his action was entirely wrong; since on their lands he had no power, right, or justice. Then, when Nevelon had refused to submit, a day was set for trying the case at Senlis in the presence of Prince Louis.

At the trial Nevelon repeated his arguments: that whatever the church had taken as *taille* from men who, though *hôtes* of the church, were his own, should be paid to him. For this, he said, was a liberty held by him on the land of the church as if in fee of the king.[73] To all of which the churchmen entered a general denial, repeating what they had asserted before and producing their charters of immunity, by which they had secured all royal rights within their territories. It was therefore obvious, said the king, that when even his own men who settled on those lands were not free of such customs, he could have no power of granting to another the special privilege claimed by Nevelon.[74] At this point the latter, seeing the hopelessness of his case, left the court-room, and judgment was formally rendered in favor of the church: that, according to its own interest and volition,

---

[71] Prou, *Actes de Philippe I*, p. 398.

[72] "Domnus Nevelo, quosdam clientele sue suo nomine protegere nisus et ab aliorum lege segregare laborans, pecuniam que pro tallia sumpta erat sibi suisque, ut aiebat, servientibus reddi postulavit."

[73] "Clamavit namque domnus Nevelo quicquid clerici ab hospitibus ecclesie, hominibus autem ipsius Nevelonis, pro talia sumserant, sibi suisque debere reddi, hanc se in terra ecclesie libertatem habere, hoc quasi feodum a rege se tenere promulgans."

[74] "Unde cum nec etiam nostri servientes, terre illius hospites, ab hac consuetudine queant esse liberi, nos nec habere, nec alieni dare vel concedere, nec aliquem a nobis posse tenere recognovimus."

it was entitled to levy *taille*, administer justice, and exercise all power within the territories under its jurisdiction.[75]

Now, in spite of the fact that the decision went against him, Nevelon must have had some grounds for acting as he did; without some honest conviction or plausible argument he would hardly have allowed the case to go before the king's court. We must at least believe that he had good title to *tailles* from his men so long as they did not live within an immunity; his mistake lay in believing, or pretending, that such personal rights should not yield to the territorial rights of the church. The latter had from the first claimed the *taille* as sole justiciary within its lands: since Nevelon had no power of jurisdiction there, he had no power of taking *taille*. In the trial Nevelon seems to have lost confidence in his original argument and to have fallen back on the weak assertion that he really had such jurisdictional power as part of the fief held of the king—which was easily proved specious by showing that the king himself had reserved no such right within the district in question. Thus the church of Compiègne, like the abbey of Saint-Mesmin, was recognized in unmistakable terms as being entitled to tax settlers on its territory, even if they were serfs of a secular lord.

Not long afterward, in 1128, a somewhat similar case was brought before the same court, as we know from an attestation issued by John, bishop of Térouanne. "When," runs his account, "the clergy of Lille, impelled by the paramount need of their church, had demanded aid, after the fashion of other lords, from the *hôtes* of the church, the latter, with hearts hardened by the sin of avarice, went before William the Norman, count of Flanders, and by prayer or price obtained from him absolute prohibition to the clergy that they should exact anything, and to the *hôtes* that they should pay anything. Whereupon, the clergy, fearing that by this unprecedented affront the ancient liberty of their church might be impaired, sought out Louis, king of the Franks, and Renaud, archbishop of Reims, pre-

---

[75] "Ut sancte Compendiensis ecclesie clericis in omni terra illa . . . et in omnibus ejusdem terre hospitibus pro sua et ecclesie utilitate liceat talliam facere omnemque justitiam et potestatem . . . pro sua voluntate et libito liceat exercere."

senting privileges from the church of Rome and from the royal authority, and beseeching them to relieve the church of such threatened injury." [76] After the usual preliminaries, therefore, a trial was held before the barons of France, and eventually judgment was rendered to the following effect: "that the said clergy should have the same right and power over their *hôtes* as the other princes of the land had over theirs, nor should on this account any violence be done them by any prince whomsoever." [77] The count then acknowledged his wrong and received absolution.

Our record thus gives no good explanation of the count's interference with the action of the church, but in the light of the other sources just examined, it seems very probable that the *hôtes* in question were men of the count or of his vassals, and his pretext was perhaps similar to that of Nevelon de Pierrefonds. However that may be, there can be no doubt as to the position taken by the church. Saint-Pierre de Lille had been established only some seventy-three years earlier; the muniments that the clergy laid before the court must have been the charter of Baldwin V and the confirmations of it by Popes Alexander II and Gregory VII, all of which merely affirm a general immunity from secular authority.[78] Such indirect acquisition of regalian rights plainly sufficed to establish the title of the church to levy contributions from all tenants on its property—a power claimed and formally recognized, not as something unusual, but as one common to the lords of the land.

As early as the eleventh century, accordingly, the *taille* might

[76] E. Hautcoeur, *Cartulaire de l'église collégiale de Saint-Pierre de Lille* (Paris, 1894), I, 28: "Cum Insulani clerici, summa ecclesie sue necessitate constricti, ab hospitibus ecclesie, more aliorum dominorum, auxilium postulassent, illi vicio avaritie obdurati comitem Flandrie Guillelmum Normannum adierunt, et ut ipse clericis ne exigerent, et hospitibus ne clericis quicquam darent, modis omnibus prohiberet, seu prece seu precio, effecerunt; unde clerici antiquam ecclesie sue libertatem hac insolentia imminui posse formidantes, Francorum regem Ludovicum et Remorum archiepiscopum Rainaudum, privilegia Romane ecclesie et auctoritatis regie secum deferentes, expetierunt, et ut hanc injuriam ab ecclesia depellerent imploraverunt."

[77] "Communi baronum terre consensu et judicio diffinitum est, clericos illos idem potestatis jus super hospites suos quod alii principes terre super suos habere, nec ullam eis super hoc a quoquam principe violentiam inferri debere."

[78] *Ibid.*, Preface, and pp. 2–9.

be a territorial exaction which a lord imposed, not merely on his bondmen, but on all residents under his jurisdiction; and with the certainty of this fact established, we are in position to inquire how a person might or might not become subject to such a territorial *taille,* and eventually whether there may not have been at the same time a personal obligation for *taille* as well. In other words, we now have to do with what the sources call *hospites* and *hostisiae,* the importance of which for the social history of Europe can hardly be overestimated, for therein lies the key to such problems as the rise of the towns and the breakdown of the manorial system.[79]

In the first place, there is no doubt that the *hôte* of whom we have heard so frequently was a settler, a colonist, on somebody's land. He might be either serf or free, his place of origin might be known, or he might be a wanderer from nobody knew where. In any case he was made welcome by the owner of waste lands; he received a plot for his house and fields for his crops; the lord specified in advance his rent and other agricultural services; and he became liable for the common customs of the territory in which he resided. Having freely entered into this arrangement, he was presumably free to leave it when he chose to seek fortune elsewhere. Thus, with regard to the lord on whose land he settled, the *hôte* was normally free, though with regard to some other lord he might still be legally a serf. In fact, the rights of this old master sometimes had to be respected and the *hôte* would be under obligation to two men at the same time. Furthermore there were the claims of the king, count, or other suzerain to be considered—as a large number of charters bear witness.

Thus, as we learn from a confirmation by Philip I in 1065, the abbey of Saint-Pierre de Hasnon had asked, and the count of Flanders had granted [80]

ut praecinctum parrochiae totius villae Hasnoniensis, quam ipsi concambio mutaverunt, ab his quorum erat beneficium, liberum et ab

---

[79] On the class of *hôtes* see in particular L. Verriest, *Le servage dans le comté de Hainaut* (Brussels, 1910), pp. 40 ff.; H. Sée, *Les classes rurales et le régime domanial en France au Moyen-Age* (Paris, 1901), pp. 212 ff.; Pirenne, *Mediaeval Cities,* pp. 117, 130.

[80] Prou, *Actes de Philippe I,* p. 64.

omni exactione absolutum firmaremus, tam in campis quam in aqua et in silvis vel hominibus potestatis ipsius cenobii vel advenis quos albanos vocant vel servis tam sanctorum quam hominum infra praecinctum commanentibus, nulla occasione vel advocature vel fiscalis debiti ab aliqua seu magna seu parva persona nisi ab abbate supramemorati loci distringendis.

The effect of this grant was of course to establish within a certain region an immunity for the abbot of Hasnon—in that the act was nothing unusual. What distinguishes it from hundreds of earlier charters is the specific provision that it makes regarding immigrants on the abbey's land. It subjects to the abbot's authority, first, *aubains,* and secondly, serfs of outside lords, ecclesiastic or lay. The former, lordless wanderers from nowhere in particular, were everywhere considered the special *protégés* of the king or the holder of regalian rights: [81] except for this privilege at Hasnon, they would have been claimed by the count. But the abbot's immunity also gave him complete control over other men's serfs, who, as we learn from another charter of the same year,[82] were to be quit of all obligation to

[81] E. Glasson, *Histoire du droit et des institutions de France* (Paris, 1887), VII, 62. Quarrels over *aubains* were very frequent. For instance, Mabillon, *Ann. ord. S. Benedicti,* V, 649 (1090): "Contra donnum abbatem Godefridum ecclesiae Montis S. Quintini quamdam litem promovit dominus Odo castri Peronensis, abbatiae scilicet auferre volens omnes albanos, qui se se martyri praelibato pro tutela et advocatione dederant, antequam praeventi essent a suis ministris, prohibendo ne ad praedictae ecclesiae dominium ex more confugerent, neve census capitalitios exsolverent." Odo finally yielded and granted the men in question to the church, "ea videlicet conditione, ut si prius martyri manciparentur quam a suis procuratoribus praevenirentur, nullum deinceps eis jugum servitutis legaliter posset imponere." About the same time a dispute between the church of Saint-Vincent du Mans and a local lord ended in this decision (R. Charles et Menjot d'Elbenne, *Cartulaire de l'abbaye de Saint-Vincent du Mans,* Mamers, 1886–1913, p. 182): "Judicavit igitur omnis curia quod nullus alius albanius esset dicendus nisi is qui per terram ibat, et in ea nec parentem nec amicum nec hospicium ullo modo habebat, nec in illa terra aliter nisi transeundo habitabat. De talibus, ut in suo fevo, habere consuetudines sepedictus dominus debebat . . . ceteri omnes monachorum essent." Cf. *Archives historiques du Maine,* VI, 34 (c. 1100); and d'Herbomez, *Chartes de l'abbaye de Saint-Martin de Tournai* (Brussels, 1898), I, 25 (1100).

[82] Prou, *Actes de Philippe I,* p. 61: "Recuperata Hasnonia tota in terra et silvis et aqua, ut terminatur praecinctus in parochia, libera et sine advocatura et ab omni exactione remota; habitatores vero quicunque habitaverint infra praecinctum dominis suis censum tantum solvent capitum et post perpetuo sine advocato manebunt."

their masters on payment of *capitation*. This head-tax had long been and long remained an important mark of servile status, especially for men who were permitted to reside away from their birthplaces; but it was also regularly paid by men who, though born free, had commended themselves for life to the personal protection of an influential patron. So, in the charter of Robert, quoted above, the same reservation was made in favor of the lords of such *homines advocatii*.[83] In other cases, as will be seen from what immediately follows, *chevage* might be paid to the church by an *aubain*, as the formal sign of his commendation to a new superior.

Accordingly, although the institution of territorial immunity had long been a familiar one, no hard and fast rules existed to define the status of the *hôte* within it, and there were many delicate points that demanded special treatment. For instance, how soon could that status be secured by the newcomer? About the time when William of Normandy was preparing his famous expedition to England, this question was causing trouble between the abbot of Saint-Médard and the count of Soissons. For in 1066 the barons of France rendered a decision to the following effect: [84]

Item de commendatione hominum S. Medardi, de advenis etiam quos albanos vocant, quod idem clamabat comes, ita adjudicatum est, ut si infra annum quo idem advena ad terram S. Medardi applicuerit

---

[83] On the *homines advocatii* see especially Verriest, *Le servage dans le comté de Hainaut*, pp. 266 ff. With the foregoing charters compare the following. Philip I to Cluny in 1080 (Prou, *Actes de Philippe I*, p. 256): "Concedo etiam predicte ecclesie hospites omnes quicumque inibi hospitari voluerint necnon omnia quecunque nunc habet et adquirere poterit juste." Enguerrand d'Hesdin to the abbey of Anchin in 1094 (Duvivier, *Actes*, I, 295): "Omnes vero qui in terra eorum manserint, vel mansuri venerint, liberos ab omni teloneo vel redditu vel exactione facio." Robert, count of Flanders, to Saint-Donat de Bruges in 1101 (Miraeus-Foppens, II, 1148): "Ecclesiam S. Donatiani Brugensis ad statum meliorem promovens, eandem ei quam Insulana ecclesia obtinet libertatem donavi . . . ut submansores eiusdem ecclesie ab omni publica exactione liberi omnique jugo, etiam nostre dominationis, absoluti . . . nullus excepto preposito ecclesie super eos potestatem habeat." Henry, count of Champagne, to the church of Provins in 1176 (*Gall. Christ.*, XII, Instr., 54): "Adjiciens ut quicumque fuerit ecclesiae vestrae matricularius cum uxore sua et liberis ab omni talia, justitia, exactione, consuetudine, et violentia liber existat."

[84] Prou, *Actes de Philippe I*, p. 85.

capitale suum S. Medardo dederit, perpetualiter S. Medardus eum tenebit; si vero infra annum capitale suum S. Medardo non dederit, comes perpetualiter absque contradictione tenebit.

Essentially the same answer, but put in the form that was to become famous throughout western Europe, appears seventeen years later in the foundation charter of Anselm, count of Ribemont, to the local abbey, providing [85]

quod si quis utriusque sexus advena supervenerit, infra unum annum et diem praedictae ecclesiae se donare sine contradictione vel mei vel meorum successorum poterit.

Again, in 1104, this rule was applied when Aimery, viscount of Thouars, founded a church at Chaise-le-Vicomte, but now it was made to work in favor of both parties: [86]

Burgensis necnon ruricola quispiam vicecomitis seu monachorum si ad alterutrum migrare voluerit, anno uno ac die exul factus liberum iter deinceps habebit.

So, although it was not universal, the law of a year and a day became the normal standard for determining a legal residence within an immunity.[87]

It will also be noted that in such cases it was the *hôte* himself who decided his condition; he could commend himself to whom he chose, and apparently any lord was at liberty to receive him. For that reason rivalry between neighboring barons was keen, and numberless agreements were drawn up to avoid unprofitable complications. Sometimes two parties consented to abandon all men who left the land of one to settle on that of the other;

[85] *Gall. Christ.*, X, Instr., 189.

[86] P. Marchegay, *Cartulaires du Bas-Poitou* (Les Roches-Baritaud, 1877), p. 24. See the curious story told by Lambert d'Ardres (*Monum. Germ. Hist., SS.*, XXIV, 579) of the *colvekerli* of Guisnes during the eleventh century, who had to pay *capitation, formariage,* and *mainmorte:* "Concessit enim eis [Hamensibus] et in feodum confirmavit, quod quisque advena in terra Ghisnensi aliunde advolaret et annum unum et diem unum in terra sua perendinaret, vel morosius et diucius inhabitaret, simile obprobrium simul et pensionem obprobriosam incurreret et quasi de iure persolveret." On the antiquity of the law of a year and a day see Glasson, *Histoire du droit*, VII, 62.

[87] *Aubains* coming within the *bourg* of Saint-Michel de Tonnerre had to give themselves to the church inside a month or else they belonged to the count of Nevers (Quantin, *Cartulaire général de l'Yonne*, I, 298).

sometimes not to harbor each other's men at all.[88] Indeed, all sorts of conditions might be laid down with regard to migrations from territory to territory, or with regard to *hôtes* already resident on donated lands.

So in 1095, when the cathedral of Angers received the new church of Saint-Nicolas, together with two *arpents* free of all custom, it was stipulated by the donor, a certain viscount, that the canons should not admit as *hôtes* his *consuetudinarii;* but if other foreigners came, the church should have all their customs except the tolls paid in his market.[89] With this act may be compared the foundation charter for the church of Saint-Etienne de Nevers, issued by Count William II in 1097: [90]

Dono et concedo . . . totum burgum sicuti modo pro burgo habetur, aut unquam melius habebitur, qui jam ex re nomen habens Burgus S. Stephani appellatur, cum terra et hominibus inibi hospitatis seu hospitaturis, omnibusque consuetudinibus quas inibi habebam, nihil mihi penitus in ea retinens . . . Nisi quod si forte homines de terra mea pro tollenda consuetudine meas se mihi subtrahendo, hanc terram ad habitandam delegerint, prior quidem habebit in eis consuetudines et justitiam suam sicut in caeteris hominibus suis ejusdem burgi, mihi tamen serviant sicut homines mei. De alia vero terra vel provincia quicunque adveniens hanc terram ad habitandum elegerit, liber sit ab omni mea meorumque hominum justitia et consuetudine, monachisque tantum serviat et respondeat.

Within their *bourg,* therefore, the monks were to enjoy full and exclusive rights over all settlers except such as came from the count's own lands; they, it would seem, were to have double

[88] See another clause of the act of Louis VI cited above (n. 57): "Diffinitum est etiam quod hospites regis apud Balneolum stationarii et commanentes in supradicta canonicorum terra nunquam hospites fient; et similiter canonicorum hospites regis hospites nullatenus existent." See also the privileges of the chapter of Reims sworn by the archbishop (*Gall. Christ.,* X, Instr., 33): "Ut servientes nostri quos in commune seu privatim in domibus nostris habemus, etiamsi vestri capite censi fuerint, ab omni exactione tamen praeter capitalitium suum, liberi habeantur; eadem vobis de hominibus nostris servata conditione si vestri fuerint servientes." For examples of other reciprocal arrangements involving *taille* see J. Garnier, *Chartes de communes et d'affranchissements en Bourgogne* (Dijon, 1867), I, 335; Delaborde, *Actes de Philippe-Auguste,* I, 430; M. J. Wolters, *Codex diplomaticus Lossensis* (Ghent, 1849), p. 70; Miraeus-Foppens, I, 413.

[89] *Documents historiques sur l'Anjou* (Société d'agriculture, sciences, et arts d'Angers), V, 123.

[90] *Gall. Christ.,* XII, Instr., 334.

obligations, for they were to continue to serve the count as before, besides rendering all customs owed the priory. Indeed, *taille* on all *hôtes* within a village might be specifically reserved by a donor, as was done by Roger de Thony in a grant to the abbey of Conches *c.* 1150.[91] In these documents, as in most, no concern is expressed over loss of income by any lord except the princely benefactor. Nevertheless, when in 1142 Baldwin IV of Hainaut restored Broqueroie to the abbey of Saint-Denis as originally given by his father, he stipulated [92]

ut nullus deinceps comitum, principum, castellanorum, vel aliqua quelibet persona mortuam manum, vel talliam, vel aliam aliquam exactionem ab ejusdem ville incolis vel possit vel debeat exigere, salvo dumtaxat jure ecclesiarum vel quorumlibet in servis suis dominorum, si tamen jus suum per se requirunt, remota importunitate advocatorum.

In this instance, therefore, the immunity of the church was even less absolute, for any serf who became the *hôte* of the monks might still be forced to pay *mainmorte* and *taille* to his old master.

Nor is this an isolated case of the retention of such purely personal obligations. An agreement between Nicolas d'Avesnes and the abbot of Maroilles in 1151, after recognizing the former as being entitled to share the *mainmortes* of most of the abbey's men, provided that in five villages of the church [93]

91 *Ibid.*, XI, Instr., 134: "eandem libertatem et dominationem et consuetudinem habeat abbas super nostros omnes homines et advenas in terra sua habitantes quas et ego habeo super omnes nostros homines et advenas in terra mea manentes; . . . et de auxiliis mihi vel domino Normanniae pertinentibus omnes homines abbatiae insimul per manum abbatis respondeant, sicuti faciunt homines de Romeliaco vel illi de Portis per manum dominorum suorum." Cf. the charter of Jeanne, countess of Flanders, to Sainte-Pharaïlde of Ghent in 1219 (Miraeus-Foppens, II, 987): "Et sciendum quod si aliqui hospites venirent manere super Wastinam illam, ego super eos hospites haberem altam justitiam, et exercitum meum, et talliam meam, nisi per voluntatem meam remanerent. Totum aliud dominium ipsis decano et canonicis remanebit."
92 Duvivier, *Hainaut*, II, 558. Cf. d'Herbomez, *Chartes de Saint-Martin*, I, 47: "Si qui vero vel hominum Clarembaldi vel aliorum in ipsa villa manserint, in justitia quidem et districto monachorum erunt; sed et silvagium et paisnagium et alias consuetudines quas dominis suis debent persolvent."
93 Duvivier, *Hainaut*, II, 568.

nihil habet juris prorsus Nicholaus preter talliam et servitium et mortuam manum in suis propriis hominibus; et hec eadem jura, temporibus quibus requirere volet Nicholaus aut ejus minister, per abbatem aut ejus ministrum repetere debent. Homines vero S. Huberti in prefatis villis omnino liberi sunt a Nicholao et ejus ministro, et in eis nichil penitus juris habent.

And shortly afterward, in 1157, a similar right was allowed by the bishop of Auxerre to the count of Nevers, who recognized that he could levy no *taille* or *quête* in the bishop's vills, except on his own bondmen.[94]

The very next year Henry I, count of Champagne, gave a bake-oven to the church of Saint-Loup, in such liberty that the six *hôtes* who should inhabit the six houses attached to it, together with their families, should henceforth owe the count no custom and be subject only to the justice and government of the church. Even if one of them were the count's man, the count's ministers should not touch him or his within the said liberty; providing always that the count should not lose, through such residence, *taille* from any man of his; and that, when found outside the liberty, the *hôte* should be liable for the count's justice as well.[95] And in another charter of Henry I to the same church, certain land is granted, along with the *hôtes* living on it free "ab omni servicio, sive justicia, sive consuetudine michi debita, duntaxat homines mei non sint." [96]

94 *Gall. Christ.*, XII, Instr., 125: "Cognitum insuper fuit quod in burgo S. Aniani, nec etiam in aliqua terra episcopi quae sit extra munitionem Conadae, consuetudinem aliquam, nec justitiam habeo; infra munitionem nec extra talliam vel questum licet mihi facere, nisi in meis hominibus de corpore." Cf. *ibid.*, XII, Instr., 124.

95 D'Arbois de Jubainville, *Comtes de Champagne*, III, 449; Lalore, *Cartulaires de Troyes*, I, 53: "Sciendum tamen quod exactionem, que vulgo tallia dicitur, propter libertatem furni de homine meo non perdam, et quociens extra furnum inventus fuerit, libere de eo meam exercebo justiciam."

96 *Ibid.*, I, 59. See the charter of 1153 (Tardif, *Monuments*, p. 274), by which Louis VII frees his serf, Jean du Viel-Etampes: "Hic Johannes hospes est canonicorum S. Victoris, habitans in terra illa quam Thomas presbyter predictis canonicis dedit; quam terram idem Johannes in duas hostisias divisit et duas domos in ea sibi et heredibus suis extruxit, et se ipsum et heredes suos eorumdem canonicorum servientes in perpetuum esse concessit, voluntati ipsorum relinquens quem ex his ad suum servicium eligere placuerit. Quia igitur hospites et servientes canonicorum sunt, precibus domini Gelduini abbatis hoc concessimus et statuimus, ut nullus prefectorum, nullus officialium nostrorum, nec omnino aliquis in eundem

We have now seen that in the case of many ecclesiastical properties the church enjoyed the exclusive right to all so-called justiciary rights, including *taille,* over the inhabitants. If, however, the king or holder of *regalia* could grant such immunity, he could also restrict it. On occasion, a count might reserve to himself *tailles* over all *aubains,* or only over those *hôtes* who emigrated from his own lands. By his stipulation, also, a lesser lord might be allowed to recover *tailles* taken from his serfs on ecclesiastical territory; but such exceptions seem to have been rare, and where they were not made—as on the lands of Saint-Corneille de Compiègne—the church's authority was paramount. Without, for the moment, pushing this inquiry farther, we may now consider the converse side of the problem: if serfs of the church came to reside on lay property, what obligations might they have to bear?

In this connection a charter of the bishop of Cambrai lifting excommunication from Gossuin, sire d'Avesnes, gives us valuable information.[97] For he, we are told, has now—in 1111— submitted to the monks of Liessies guaranteeing them their village of the same name "ab omni advocatia liberam: videlicet tallia, exactione, hospitalitate, heribanno, fossato, equitatione, et omni prorsus inquietatione vel forisfacto." He agrees to respect the allodial holdings of the abbey and promises that serfs of the church living on them shall be free toward him of all *avouerie,* exaction, and *taille;* on their death all *mainmortes* shall be enjoyed exclusively by the church. If, however, they live at Avesnes or anywhere on his allodial properties, the lord of Avesnes is to have one-third of their *mainmortes,* and

---

Johannem aut in heredes ejus, qui in eadem terra manserint, vel in bona eorum, ubicumque fuerint, pro aliqua occasione manum mittere possit, quamdiu per predictos canonicos Stampenses in eadem terra justiciam exequi voluerint . . . Volumus etiam ut eadem terra sit de cetero imperpetuum libera ab exercitu et tallia, viaria, thelonio, et rotagio, et omni exactionis consuetudine . . . Sed ecclesie Beati Victoris jus nostrum omne et justiciam donamus." Also the grant of the lord of Termonde to the abbey of Afflighem in 1176 (E. de Marneffe, *Cartulaire d'Afflighem* (Louvain, 1894), I, 238): "Colonos ecclesie ab omni exactione liberos reddidi, ita tamen si nec servi mei nec advocatie mee subditi, nec de alia mee terre possessione ad exhibendum servitium michi fuerint obnoxij." Cf. Warnkönig, II², Urk. ccxxxvi.

[97] Duvivier, *Hainaut,* II, 496.

presumably—though the document does not say so—*taille* from them also.

With this somewhat obscure regulation may be compared a charter of Charles the Good of Flanders, issued in 1122 to settle a dispute between Baldwin of Alost and the abbey of Saint-Pierre at Ghent.[98] It too presents its difficulties, but the substance of the agreement is as follows. Serfs of the church were to be free of all custom wherever they lived, and likewise all men of Meirelbeke so long as they remained there. If, however, they moved into any portion of Baldwin's *avouerie* outside that parish, they had to pay him two *deniers* each. Inhabitants of other monastic villages were to pay each a pig or sixteen *deniers,* together with castle-guard for one week every year or a money equivalent, as Baldwin pleased. Furthermore, the men of Meirelbeke were not liable for any *taille,* no matter where they resided; and the men of other places only fixed sums—a married man twelve *deniers* and his wife six. Unmarried persons paid nothing. If a man gave himself or his serf to the church, the status of the person given should remain as specified in the grant.

This document possesses many remarkable features. The *tensamentum,* as usual, is sharply distinguished from the *taille,* though the latter, like the former, had become a fixed *cens.* Most interesting, however, is the classification of the abbey's tenants into three categories, each with its carefully stipulated obligations; and especially the information with regard to the abbey's bondmen who enjoyed to its fullest extent the privilege of extraterritoriality. That is to say, the personal right of the church to its serfs superseded all rights of the lord on whose property they might reside, and this exceptional status is specifically guaranteed to all *sainteurs,* or men who give them-

---

[98] Van Lokeren, *Chartes de Saint-Pierre,* I, 123; Warnkönig, III, Urk. xxiv: "Nullam rogationem in ea habere debet Baldwinus vel sui de his qui pertinent ad Merlebecam ubicumque habitaverint in advocatia sua; in coeteris locis habebit advocatus de homine uxorato singulis annis xii denarios, de uxore vi, de ceteris nichil usque ad copulatam . . . De servis ecclesie ubicumque habitaverint nichil habebit advocatus . . . Si vero aliquis liberorum sive servorum servum suum, sive liber se ipsum sive allodium suum S. Petro dederit, talis in aecclesia permaneat qualem se dedit."

selves in bondage to the church. If accordingly, as occurred so frequently at this time, the *sainteur* obliged himself only for *capitation, formariage,* and *mainmorte* at fixed rates, he was absolutely free of all further obligations. As serf of the church he enjoyed a greater immunity than if he merely commended himself to its protection and retained his personal freedom. And this deduction is confirmed by all the other information that I have encountered regarding this peculiar group of men.[99]

In its strict sense, therefore, extraterritorial jurisdiction was recognized primarily in the case of serfs residing on another's property. So far as freemen were concerned, change of residence normally implied change of obligations. However, when an *hôte* held land of two lords at the same time, he was naturally liable for all customary services that bore upon his holdings, and so might owe territorial *taille* to both men. For example, we find the report of a case tried before the count of Champagne in 1171 over this very question.[100] Miles de Vendeuil claimed

[99] On the *sainteurs,* or more properly *homines sancti,* see Verriest, *Servage,* pp. 171 ff., and Pirenne, *Histoire de Belgique,* I, 140. There are of course scores of acts dealing with such persons, but they usually do not mention *taille,* merely stating a general exemption from all exactions except those specified. See, however, the charter of Nicholas, bishop of Cambrai, attesting (1137–45) the self-donation of a certain Oda under his predecessor (Duvivier, *Actes,* I, 310). After stipulating the ordinary payments *de capite, pro licentia nubendi,* and *pro mortua manu,* it adds: "De petitione vero quam laica dominatio a familia ecclesiarum injuste accepit, se et suos [?quittos] et liberos, libera traditione liberoque arbitrio, prout justum et possibile erat statuit." Cf. Guérard, *Cartulaire de N.-D. de Paris,* I, 145: "Hii sunt homines Parisiensis episcopi commorantes prope Sezanniam . . . Talliam non debent." However, each owes yearly one *denariatam cere* and all must marry within the *familia* of the bishop. The donor of serfs might, of course, reserve whatever payments he chose. Thus in 1238 the lady of Boulaere freed and gave to the church of Saint-Adrien de Grammont all serfs resident at Boulaere, exempt from all *taille* and exaction, except the best chattel for *mainmorte* and aids for the marriage or knighting of her children (Miraeus-Foppens, I, 755).

[100] D'Arbois de Jubainville, *Comtes de Champagne,* III, 459. Cf. the charter of Henry I in 1177 (*ibid.,* III, 467): "Notum facio presentibus et futuris ecclesiam Beati Marie de Ulcheio talem ab antiquo optinere libertatem quod in terra ecclesie illius ubicumque sit, sive in hospites nemo manum mittere debeat absque consensu et licentia prioris vel canonicorum vel ministri ejusdem ecclesie . . . Qui si terras meas colunt, consuetudines quas terre ille debent eos reddere oportebit . . . Omnes autem homines et hospites predicte ecclesie . . . nullam etiam talliam debent, exceptis illis quos prenotavi et ea causa qua predixi." Also A. Wauters, *De l'origine . . . des libertés communales: Preuves* (Brussels, 1869), p. 73: "consuetudinem tallie quam habebat apud Vilars super homines et habitatores totius

that men removing from the estates of Saint-Médard de Soissons to cultivate lands of his should be exempt from all *tailles* of that church. To which the clerics replied that, if they wanted to retain the lands held of the church, such emigrants must continue to pay the church's *taille* wherever they went. And it was this argument that was sustained by the court, which ordained that the said men must pay *taille* to Saint-Médard twice a year, but at each time no more than four *sous*. In the same way burgesses, who were otherwise exempt from *tailles,* might have to pay them on lands held outside the town.[101]

It is therefore quite evident that the eleventh-century noble, cleric or lay, possessed an odd jumble of rights, some territorial and some personal; and in particular that alongside *tailles* which bore upon freemen as a consequence of their residence within a jurisdictional immunity, there were *tailles* which bore upon serfs because their bodies belonged to a master. Moreover, as the preceding evidence shows, it was the *hôte* who first brought these two sets of powers into conflict and thereby occasioned the scores of acts dealing with his peculiar status and the rival claims of lords and princes to share the proceeds of his labor. For the elucidation of such problems there remains, however, one large group of documents to demand our attention—namely, charters of liberties. And in this connection we should logically begin with Flanders.

When William Clito, in his famous charter of 1127 to Saint-Omer, says that he wishes the men of that town, "like the better and freer bourgeois of Flanders, to be quit of all custom," and promises to exact from them no *taille, scot,* or *Bede,*[102] he is

---

teritorii et universos qui terras in eadem villa tenent, cum alibi sint manentes . . ." Furthermore, we are told in 1232 (Garnier, *Chartes de communes,* II, 132) that it was the general custom throughout Burgundy that *homines talliabiles,* no matter where they were or whose they were, might recede from the justice and dominion of the lord who enjoyed their *tailles,* but that all property held of him remained entirely subject to his pleasure.

[101] Thus in 1136 Louis VI complains that the commune of Soissons has been doing violence to the neighboring landlords because the citizens have been refusing to pay, in outside villages, "taillias, corvadas, quas terra debebat et ceteri accolae persolvebant"—E. Martène et A. Durand, *Veterum scriptorum . . . amplissima collectio* (Paris, 1724), I, 748. Cf. the charter to Laon, below, n. 108.

[102] A. Giry, *Histoire de la ville de Saint-Omer* (Paris, 1877), p. 371; Warnkönig,

obviously confirming an established fact, rather than granting a new immunity. He implies that the greater Flemish towns, such as Saint-Omer, Bruges, Ghent, and Ypres, had already secured exemption from *tailles,* whereas his lesser subjects remained liable. But it is not till 1161 that we obtain any direct testimony as to the obligations of this latter class. In that year Count Thierry grants a special privilege for all settlers in the waste of Reninghelst, which is to be specially devoted to supplying food for his own use. Any person wishing to live there, if already held under the lordship of another, must first ask the count's permission to come; but, having that, should be admitted to complete equality with the previous inhabitants. All then, on payment of a certain annual *cens,* should enjoy the following remarkable franchise: [103]

quod legibus sive justitiis, seu etiam causis communie Furnensis, que vulgo chora dicitur, nullatenus subjacebunt; sed ab omnibus servitiis, petitionibus, talliis sive quibuslibet aliis exactionibus quibus alii incole terre nostre obligati tenentur, liberi et absoluti perpetuo habeantur, nisi forte pro communi terre defensione in exercitum evocentur.

What could be plainer? The inhabitants, immigrant and native, of this new community of Reninghelst are endowed with some of the more elementary liberties long ago obtained by the burgesses of Saint-Omer: they can be summoned to the count's army only for the defense of their *patrie,* and shall be forced to pay no *tailles, Beden,* or other exactions. These obligations, it should be noted, had not been altered by the so-called *keure* of Furnes, the law or peace which had been promulgated by the count for the government of that region, but had there as in other rural districts, remained entirely arbitrary. Indeed, as late as 1240, when the oldest extant *keure* of Furnes was issued, the only provision made regarding the *taille* was the following: [104]

I, 27: "Et sicut meliores et liberiores burgenses Flandriae ab omni consuetudine liberos deinceps esse volo; nullum scoth, nullam taliam, nullam pecunie sue petitionem ab eis requiro."

[103] Gilliodts-Van Severen, *Coutumes de la ville et châtellenie de Furnes* (Brussels, 1897), III, 20; Warnkönig, II², Urk. CLVII.

[104] *Ibid.,* II², Urk. CLX; Gilliodts-Van Severen, III, 27. Cf. the charter to Poeperinge (above, n. 67), which received the law of Furnes in 1147.

Nullus debet facere assisiam vel precariam in terra, privatam vel generalem, nisi comes; et qui inde protractus fuerit reddet quod accepit, et emendabit comiti x libras.

The count was still able to levy *tailles* at his pleasure, either from individuals or whole communities—but only he. If therefore, this statement reflects the primitive arrangement—and I think it does—we may see the count claiming as complete a monopoly of *tailles* within his demesnes as that enjoyed by a church within its territorial immunity.[105]

If now we turn back to the charter of Saint-Omer, we may be in better position to answer a question that immediately presents itself to the student of municipal liberties: when the count abandoned his right to *taille* in a town, did his act constitute entire exemption for the bourgeois? It must have done so. The count's right to take or forgo *tailles* in his communes, as in his villages, was an exclusive right. The *hôte* who settled either at Saint-Omer or at Reninghelst was exempt through residence on privileged soil, and whatever personal rights his original lord may have had were thereby put in abeyance.[106]

Now, as is well known, there was nothing peculiar in this freedom from *tailles* of the Flemish towns; it was a privilege enjoyed very generally by bourgeois communities, and one that appears quite early in Picardy. Indeed, one of the original claims set up by the communes of that region seems to have been the abolition of all *tailles* and forced exactions. Thus it was an ancient custom of Saint-Quentin, as stated in 1150, that the

[105] Compare the charter of Thierry to Berkin and Steenwerk in 1160 (Warnkönig, II², Urk. cxcix): "Sint igitur, sicut fuerunt tempore comitis Roberti, ab omni servitii opere liberrimi: videlicet, ut non eant in exercitum; ut nullus ministrorum nostrorum ab eis aliquid petat, sive sit praeco, sive forestarius, vel etiam castellanus." To judge from special exemptions granted certain groups of settlers, the men of Courtrai still owed *taille* to the count in the thirteenth century (*ibid.*, II², Urk. ccii; cf. ccxxx, cc, ccxxxii). However, the ordinance of Count Philip (*ibid.*, I, Urk. xiii), which Zeumer (*Die deutschen Städteteuern* in G. Schmoller, *Staats- und socialwissenschaftlichen Forschungen*, I, 10) understood to deal with general imposts in Flanders, plainly has to do only with municipal *tailles* levied by the local *échevins*.

[106] It should be observed that all inhabitants of Saint-Omer were free (art. 9) even from *capitation*, the charge so generally reserved to masters of serfs on privileged soil (above, n. 102).

citizens owed no *tailles*, but gave only voluntary aids to their lord; and we have ample proof that, through direct or indirect influence, this liberty became part of the unwritten law of many other towns. The charter of Lorris forbade the exaction of *tailles* by the king or any other person. At Soissons and its *filiales* the communal oath seems to have included the pledge that the members of the association should mutually aid each other in resisting all attempts to tallage them.[107] Interesting as are these sweeping prohibitions, however, they tell us little of the nature of the exactions that caused such universal opposition, and for fuller information on the subject we must look to the neighboring region of the Laonnais.

Without entering into the oft-repeated history of that troubled community, it will be worth while to recall some of the provisions of Louis VI's famous *Institutio Pacis* of 1128. According to this document, it was settled that any serf, except one of the church or of a noble who had joined in establishing the peace, should have free entrance into the new commune, and should thereby become exempt from *formariage, mainmorte,* and all payments to this master except his *capitation* or whatever other sums he might choose to give of his own free will. Thus it is evident that the ordinary lord whose men became residents of Laon could have no possible right to tallage them arbitrarily. What then of the official lords of the town? Though somewhat obscurely, it is apparently with their rights that Article 18 is intended to deal.[108]

The king there says that he has so modified the customary *tailles* that each man owing them shall pay only four *deniers* at each time when they are due, and nothing more, unless he chance to hold outside the town land subject to *taille* which he desires on that penalty to keep. From this scant notice it

---

[107] On this and what follows see *Le Moyen Age,* XXIV, 278 ff.

[108] *Ordonnances,* XI, 185: "Statuimus etiam ut homines capite censi dominis suis censum capitis sui tantum persolvant . . . nec nisi spontanei a dominis requisiti aliquid eis tribuant . . . Consuetudinarias autem tallias ita reparavimus, ut unusquisque hominum ipsas tallias debentium singulis terminis quibus tallias debet quatuor denarios solvat, ultra autem nullam aliam persolvet, nisi forte extra terminos pacis aliquam terram talliam debentem tenuerit, quam ita caram habeat ut pro ea talliam solvat."

appears that there had been *tailles* at Laon levied at well-known periods, as well as similar exactions bearing upon certain properties outside the city, but no further details are forthcoming. Fortunately, however, this same charter was subsequently issued with various amendments to several rural communities of the Laonnais and a comparison of the new articles considerably adds to our information.

By the first of these grants, to Bruyères in 1129, Louis VI provides that the commune shall pay 20 *livres* annually, one-third to him, one-third to the bishop, and one-third to Clairembaud du Marché. And the same arrangement shall hold good [109]

de placitis sive taliis que, vel ad presens ab hominibus qui in terris tallias debentibus manent persolventur, vel ab illis persolventur qui in hanc pacem venient et in terris tallias debentibus manebunt; terciam partem nobis vendicamus et terciam episcopo et terciam Clarembaldo annuimus.

It would thus appear that the customary *tailles* owed from lands in the Laonnais were also called *placita,* and whatever the previous arrangement had been, the king was thenceforth to receive a share. Later, when Philip Augustus confirmed this establishment, he repeated Article 18 of the original *paix,* amended as follows: [110]

Consuetudinarie autem tallie ita temperate sunt ut unusquisque hominum qui manet super terras tallias debentes, et qui advenerint et in terris tallias debentibus mansiones habebunt, tria placita per annum solvent, et per singula placita quatuor denarios bone monete reddent.

At last, therefore, we learn that the men of the Laonnais had been liable for three *placita* a year, and that the liberties of Laon had restricted each of these assessments to four *deniers* per man.

In the meantime, however, Louis VII had also bestowed the same law upon another group of villages in the neighborhood; [111] but in this case the commune was short-lived. Losing their

[109] Luchaire, *Louis VI,* p. 337.

[110] Delaborde, *Actes de Philippe-Auguste,* I, 235.

[111] On this and the following acts see A. Luchaire, *Les communes françaises* (Paris, 1911), pp. 79 ff.

privileged status, the inhabitants again became subject to the arbitrary *tailles* of the bishop and again trouble broke out. Finally, in 1185, Philip Augustus, finding the opportunity for intervention again favorable, imposed a complicated settlement, which may be summarized as follows. In the first place, the men of the Laonnais shall pay annually to the bishop 700 *livres parisis* "pro talliis super homines illos quas tribus de causis facere poterat, videlicet pro exercitus nostri servitio, pro domino papa, pro guerra Laudunensis ecclesie manifesta"; and 1000 measures of wine "pro tallia vini." Secondly, they shall render to the *vidame* and the *prévôt* 200 *livres* and 500 measures of wine, which form part of the fiefs held of the bishop by those officials. Thirdly, one-half of the bishop's *tailles* are owed the king, but he has forgiven these sums in return for the service of Raoul de Coucy, which the bishop has granted him. Lastly, a commission of twelve *échevins* is established to levy the said *tailles* and to settle all disputes arising therefrom.[112]

By piecing together all the information now at our disposal, we may conclude that, at the opening of the twelfth century, the bishop of Laon had the acknowledged right to tax at pleasure all inhabitants of his lands; but that, as was often the case elsewhere, part of the proceeds may have been claimed by various nobles of the vicinity. Customarily the *taille* was assessed at each of the three annual assemblies of the people, and as a result the levies were locally known as *plaids*. But in addition to them, the bishop presumably exacted also a portion of the yearly wine-crop as his *tallia vini*—an impost that sometimes appears in other regions alongside the more ordinary *tailles*.[113] On special occasions, furthermore—such as private war, a royal campaign, or a trip to Rome—he increased the customary dues. All this the *paix* changed throughout the regions that it embraced; for, compared with the obligations of the unprivileged peasantry, the *taille* allowed by that charter appears as a merely nominal survival—a sort of *capitation* that permitted no ex-

[112] Delaborde, *Actes de Philippe-Auguste*, I, 175.

[113] Above, n. 12. At Orléans, by the charter of Philip Augustus in 1183 (Delaborde, I, 108) a payment of two *deniers* on every measure of wine or grain, "que quidem collectio vulgo nuncupatur tallia panis et vini," was perpetuated in return for exemption from all other *taille* and *tolte*. Cf. *ibid.*, I, 320.

tension and needed no assessment. The settlement of 1185 for the Laonnais was by no means so generous; and yet, through the specification of the amounts of all *tailles* and the creation of a non-episcopal body of assessors, it did prevent capricious taxation by the bishop; and the help of the king, though as usual not disinterested, was decidedly favorable to the vexed tenants of the church.

Laon, however, was not the only scene of royal intervention. At Saint-Riquier Louis VI also settled a dispute by granting a communal charter, the original terms of which have not come down to us, but concerning which we may infer a few facts from a supplementary act of 1126. The men of the new commune had not, it appears, been satisfied with the exemptions that they had lawfully secured, but had again revolted, refusing to acquit various just obligations including "tallionem de exercitu regis et pastum ejusdem." In support of the abbot Louis consequently decreed that the burgesses should pay the said dues, and that no one should be free from them except military tenants and *famuli* of the church, or peasants who lived outside the town.[114]

With these provisions should be compared a similar compromise imposed in 1171 by Louis VII at Tournus. The church, it was then established, should continue to enjoy *mainmorte* from the bourgeois, but the annual *taille* was abolished, so that the abbot could thenceforth tallage his men only on stated occasions. He might make such a levy for the aid or entertainment of the king, or for the entertainment of the pope or a cardinal; and he should also be entitled to a reasonable aid—i.e. one in proportion to the expense of the undertaking—if the interests of the church demanded his presence before the pope or the king. For a like journey undertaken on private business, such as a quarrel with the monks, nothing should be demanded.[115]

Thus, although the statement cannot be made with certainty, it seems extremely probable that both at Saint-Riquier and

[114] *Ordonnances*, XI, 184. Cf. Guérard, *Cartulaire de N.-D. de Paris*, II, 3, 7, 31, 34, etc., where it appears that "tallia pro exercitu regis" was levied alongside the regular annual *tailles* in the villages of the chapter. On the lands of Saint-Germain-des-Prés *gîte* and *taille* for the king were taken in addition to annual *tailles* (Guérard, *Polyptique de l'abbé Irminon*, II, 383–91).

[115] *Ordonnances*, XI, 205.

Tournus, as in the Laonnais, occasional aids were first specified as a substitute for an annual arbitrary *taille* previously enjoyed by the church in question. At any rate, reservations of this kind become increasingly common in favor of secular lords and seem to have been tacitly understood in many cases where the charters themselves make no such stipulation.[116] Extraordinary subsidies might also exist alongside an annual *taille* which custom or enactment had rendered inelastic.[117] Indeed, all the evidence at our disposal tends to show that the aim of the newly enfranchised bourgeoisie was not so much to escape taxation, which they felt was in some fashion inevitable, as to gain control of the determination and assessment of whatever imposts they might have to pay—a project that of course called for the creation of a more or less autonomous municipal administration.

In the great communes, naturally, magistrates or councils had the power of laying rates to cover the cost of all local government.[118] The prince dealt, not with the individual citizens directly, but with their constituted authorities. When

[116] See *Le Moyen Age*, XXIV, 285, 290. In many cases the charters left a loophole for special requisitions by implying that the burgesses might still be called on for voluntary contributions. Indeed, no immunity was proof against this method of approach, as a host of later documents bear witness. In this connection, also, may be cited an interesting sequel to the foundation charter of the *bourg* of Saint-Etienne de Nevers, quoted above (n. 90). In 1171 Guy, count of Nevers, stated (*Gall. Christ.*, XII, Instr., 343) that, although his grandfather had granted the *bourg* to the church free of all custom and exaction, his brother William, "qui ultra mare obiit, et requiescit in Bethleem, in burgensibus contra prefatam libertatem novas exactiones et impositiones facere coepit, reclamantibus et egre ferentibus monachis hoc pacto dimisit: videlicet, quod pro tribus causis tantummodo; si captus se redimeret, si filiam suam nupciis traderet, si Hierosolymam pergeret; tria millia solidorum per manum prioris a burgensibus haberet." Accordingly, Guy confirms the ancient liberties of the church, saving the three aforesaid aids! And the only concession that could be got from his successor was the relinquishment of the aid for ransom and the allowance of forty days' grace on the other two (Delaborde, *Actes de Philippe-Auguste*, I, 220).

[117] *Le Moyen Age*, XXVI, 27. Cf. *Gall. Christ.*, XII, Instr., 493: an agreement of 1181 by which the burgesses of Sens are said to owe the bishop "tailliam annuatim et auxilium urgente necessitate, diligenti tamen adhibita moderatione." Cf. Delaborde, I, 34.

[118] Above, n. 105. See also the charters of Philip Augustus to Château-Neuf and to Tournai (Delaborde, I, 41, 268), and of Philip of Flanders to Aire (Warnkönig, III, Urk. CLXIV).

in sore need of money, he presented a request for a subsidy, which the town as a legal entity considered, granted, and financed by the imposition of a municipal *taille*.[119] Such an advanced type of constitution, however, could hardly be secured all at once, and many communities had to be satisfied with lesser liberties, the most rudimentary of which was the admission by the lord of certain selected burgesses to a share of the financial administration.

It is in this connection that the claims of the men of Vézelay in 1137 are worthy of special attention. Along with other grievances, they complained of the *taille* which the abbot had been accustomed annually to impose on rustics and townsmen alike. "For they said that four men, whom they should elect from among themselves, ought to be present with the dean and the *prévôt* when the said *taille* was levied, and that with their advice it should be levied and the quota of each person considered." This suggestion, however, was spurned by the abbot, who declared that he alone had the right to lay *tailles* through the agency of the dean, the *prévôt,* and other ministers of his, and without the advice or presence of the burgesses. "For so it was anciently accustomed to be done, nor could it be proved that the procedure had ever been different." Furthermore, such *tailles* bore not merely, as alleged, on bourgeois and rustics who owned their own homes, but also on those who rented their houses, whosesoever the latter might be, after they had lived one year in the town and met its other common obligations.[120]

[119] Detailed evidence of such procedure comes only from the thirteenth century, but there can be no doubt that it had been followed from an early time. See the article already cited in *Le Moyen Age,* XXIV.

[120] Quantin, *Cartulaire général de l'Yonne,* I, 319: "Item conquesti sunt de tallia que consuetudinaliter annuatim, post Natale Domini, tam de burgensibus quam de rusticis solet fieri. Dicebant enim quod quatuor, quod ipsi de se ipsis eligerent, debebant esse cum decano et preposito, quando predicta tallia fiebat et per consilium eorum debebat fieri, et mensura de unoquoque considerare . . . Item de facienda tallia in burgenses et rusticos dictum est abbatem eam licite, sine consilio et presentia burgensium, facere posse per decanum et prepositum et per alios ministros suos, quia antiquitus ita solet fieri, nec aliter factam fuisse potuit comprobari; nec tantum in burgenses et rusticos qui proprias domos habent fieri poterit tallia, sicut dictum est, sed etiam in eos qui aliorum domos conducunt, quorumcumque sint domus, postquam per annum in villa manserint, qui etiam ceteras ville consuetudines persolvent."

With this last clause we are brought back to the fact with which our consideration of the towns began: the bourgeois was from every point of view a kind of *hôte*. His status as participant of a peculiar immunity was secured by residence for a given term on privileged soil; and this status, when enjoyed to its fullest degree, made him responsible to only one superior—the patron of the community to which he belonged. In town as in country, however, quarrels arising out of conflict between personal and territorial rights were chronic, and occasional exceptions were made in favor of outside lords—particularly of ecclesiastics. Nevertheless, the general rule remains that one chief lord enjoyed, unless he chose to relax it, a complete monopoly of all rights and profits within a town.

In most communities this fact becomes apparent only on the promulgation of a charter of liberties, but we are fortunate in having one explicit statement of such customs from as early a year as 1047—the declaration of the rights of the count of Namur at Dinant.[121] There it is affirmed:

Quicumque extraneus in ville voluerit transire coloniam et ibi morari voluerit, cujuscumque antea fuerit, ad comitem pertinebit; ministeriali suo de omni forisfacto respondebit, nisi forte fuerit S. Marie aut S. Lamberti aut S. Hugberti.

Nothing is said in this document of the *taille*, but it is obvious that only the count could have had such a right over the bulk of the population, for all *hôtes* except the men of the local churches were subject to him exclusively. And when, as actually happened at Dinant, the powers of the count passed to the bishop, even a greater centralization of authority would result.

As previously remarked,[122] however, the greater episcopal communes, when we first gain detailed knowledge of their customs, seem already to have become exempt from *taille*, and so little or no information on the subject is to be gleaned from

---

[121] Wauters, *Libertés communales, Preuves,* p. 249; Waitz, *Urkunden,* p. 20. On this document see Pirenne, *Histoire de la constitution de la ville de Dinant au Moyen Age* (Ghent, 1889), p. 3. Cf. the statement of the rights of the count in Toul (Waitz, *Urkunden,* p. 15): "Alienigenae, id est warganei, qui manserint in banno, dabunt comiti IV denarios singulis annis festo S. Remigii."

[122] *Le Moyen Age,* XXIV, 281 ff.

their charters. It is rather in the acts issued for more rustic communities that we find the most interesting provisions regarding privileged *hôtes* on ecclesiastical territory. For instance, when the abbot of Stavelot reconstructed the castle of Logne in 1138, he decided to move the village of that name to the immediate neighborhood, and to provide for its colonization made the following promises. Any of the abbey's men who should come there to live was to be free, so that he should pay no *capitation, mainmorte, formariage,* toll, pannage, *gîte,* or *taille* to abbot, *avoué,* viscount, or royal emissary. But if the serf of another wanted to reside in the said place, he would still have to pay his master all custom and justice.[123] That the region here concerned was a very backward one is attested by the fact that the abbot plainly expected no settlers who were not serfs, and that he extended no immunity to those of other lords. Nevertheless, exemption from arbitrary *taille* was here as elsewhere becoming the mark of the free colonist.

Indeed, evidence to the same effect meets us on all sides. In 1141 Louis VII confirmed a grant to the churches of Saint-Martin and Notre-Dame d'Etampes of certain property formerly held by Salomon, physician to Philip I. On petition of the canons and "voto hospitum terre," furthermore, these lands were to continue to enjoy the various liberties that they had earlier had: namely, limitation of all forfeitures, restricted military service, fixed *cens,* and immunity from all *taille* by the canons.[124] It is also interesting to note that the church of Laon, which was so reluctant to emancipate its own men, was quite willing to make concessions in order to colonize its vacant lands. In 1167 the dean and chapter issued a notice to this effect: that whereas certain strangers, lacking homes of their own, had come to the church, it had been decided to settle them in the territory of Tavaux and Pontséricourt. Each should accordingly pay one *denier* for his head and another for his wife, should he have one, every year at the feast of Saint-Remi, and at the same time twelve *deniers* "de assisia" in order to be free of all *tailles* and exactions. If he built a house, he should further be liable for *cens* and

123 Halkin et Roland, *Chartes de Stavelot-Malmédy,* I, 338.
124 *Ordonnances,* XI, 192.

salvamentum.[125] And similar substitution of a fixed charge *per capita* for vague impositions is found likewise in the charters of of Saint-Germain-des-Prés to the men of the *bourg* in 1174–75, of Ferrières to the inhabitants of that *banlieue* in 1186, and of the bishop of Paris to a new town in 1199.[126]

In the meantime the kings of France, though fostering autonomous municipalities chiefly on lands not properly their own, had shown themselves quite generous in the grant of lesser privileges to agricultural communities. Thus, in the hope of attracting colonists, the customs of Lorris and Soissons were widely distributed on the royal demesnes and exemption from *taille* and *ost* was separately accorded many obscure villages.[127] It is only in the case of Etampes, however, that particulars deserving special attention are given us.

In 1120, when Louis VI took the abbey of Morigny under his protection, he decreed that the monks and their *hôtes* residing on lands surrounding the monastery should be quit of all custom toward him; but that, if they were given any *hôtes* at Etampes, the latter should continue to owe whatever obligations they had borne when in lay hands.[128] That these obligations included *taille* and *ost* clearly appears from an act thirteen years later, when the same king granted all settlers in his new market at Etampes exemption from the said burdens for a period of ten years.[129] At some subsequent time a commune was set up in the town and like immunity was indefinitely extended to all citizens; for when Philip Augustus quashed the commune in 1199, he asserted for himself the exclusive right to military service and *taille à plaisir* from all residents.[130] This, I think, is the clearest case of such royal monopoly that we possess.

With, now, the example of the king, the count of Flanders and various prelates before us, it will not be hard to see that

---

[125] Tardif, *Monuments*, p. 304.

[126] R. Poupardin, *Recueil des chartes de l'abbaye de Saint-Germain-des-Prés* (Paris, 1909), I, 231; Delaborde, *Actes de Philippe-Auguste*, I, 187; Guérard, *Cartulaire de N.-D. de Paris*, I, 78.

[127] For example, *Ordonnances*, III, 303; VI, 703; VII, 275, 444, 684; Luchaire, *Louis VI*, 341.

[128] *Ordonnances*, XI, 179.   [129] *Ibid.*, XI, 183.

[130] *Ibid.*, XI, 277. A sequel to this act in 1204 (*ibid.*, XI, 286) freed the weavers of Etampes of all custom, including *taille*, for twenty *livres* annually.

other lords, great and small, all founded towns and treated the inhabitants in much the same way. According to the liberties of Namur, any serf who resided there for a year and a day became free of all *mainmorte* and exaction toward his old master and was thenceforth subject only to the count.[131] The latter, moreover, had commuted his right of *taille,* and so the immigrant became liable only for certain fixed sums. Thus when the law of Namur was extended to Floreffe in 1151, the count provided that, in return for exemption from all *tailles* and exactions, every cultivator of the soil should pay him two *sous* annually, but a landless artisan only twelve *deniers.*[132] This is much the same institution as was established by the family of Avesnes in many outlying villages. According to the customs of Prissche every householder was yearly obliged for twelve *deniers,* a measure of oats, two loaves, and two cocks, whereas the unpropertied man paid only the money. Beyond his fixed rents the citizen owed no exaction to the lord, unless he chose to give something of his own free will.[133] At Hirson, by its charter of 1156, every head of a family rendered two *sous* to be free of all other contribution for one year, except when the lord was captured or when he married his daughter.[134] At Hereignies, a town of Saint-Amand, the *avoué* commuted his *taille* for sixteen and a half *livres* annually, a sum which was to be doubled if he married his daughter or knighted his son.[135] But as we reach

131 Martène et Durand, *Amplissima Collectio,* I, 709 (1131): "omnis servus et ancilla capitagiarii per annum et diem Bronium et S. Laurentium commorantes ab anteriore domini sui exactione et mortimanu, sicut ceteri ejusdem comitis burgenses in Namurco, penitus absolvantur, et tam in matrimoniis quam in quibuslibet occasionibus nonnisi ab abbate Broniensi amplius coerceantur." With this compare the custom of Liége, *Le Moyen Age,* XXVI, 7.

132 *Analectes,* XI, 181: "Verumtamen illi qui terram possidentes carrucis suis arabunt duos solidos tantum, sed et alii manu operarii, ut pannifices et pellifices et sutores et hujusmodi, duodecim denarios in festo S. Remigii persolvent, et sic ab omni exactione et precariis et, ut breviter concludam, sicut burgenses Namurcenses, et a coniungiis in omnibus liberi permanebunt, salvis redditibus meis, qui me jure contingunt."

133 See L. Vanderkindere, "La loi de Prisches" in *Mélanges, Paul Frédéricq* (Brussels, 1904), pp. 213 ff.; Verriest, *Servage,* pp. 41 ff.; Duvivier, *Actes,* I, 364.

134 *Ibid.,* I, 361.

135 Wauters, *Libertés communales, Preuves,* p. 55. This collection includes a characteristic set of privileges by prelates, *avoués,* and lesser lords of the thirteenth century.

the close of the twelfth century examples become too numerous to recount, and it will be more profitable to attempt some general conclusions as to the nature of the *taille* in the eleventh century—on which up to the present there has been no consensus of opinion.

Starting with the dicta of lawyers in the thirteenth and later centuries, French scholars have continued to regard the *taille* as an essentially servile obligation, and this view has reached its logical culmination in the works of M. Henri Sée, who endeavors to trace its origin back to Roman slavery.[136] On the other hand leading German authorities have insisted, with no slight exhibition of petulance at their French contemporaries, that the *taille* was always a matter *öffentliches Recht,* an institution derived from the public taxes of the Carolingian counts.[137] And yet, as earlier pointed out, there is no appreciable difference in this respect between the Western and Eastern sources. If the *taille* was in one region what it was in the other, which of these irreconcilable opinions is right?

To this question, following certain suggestions made by M. Leo Verriest in his excellent work on serfdom in Hainaut,[138] I think it should be answered that both, in so far as each lays claim to universal validity, are wrong; but that, consequently, each is in part correct. As to the first, it utterly fails—as has surely been seen in the foregoing pages—to explain the *taille* within the mediaeval town, which was never a community of serfs belonging to one master. As to the second, it not only ignores the very real fact that there was a servile *taille* in the Middle Ages, but fails to explain the universal antipathy in which the alleged public tax of the same name was held. Furthermore, labeling an institution of the feudal age public or private tells us extremely little as to its actual nature. Before any intelligent classification can be made, terms must be defined.

---

[136] *Les classes rurales,* pp. 177 ff., 308 ff., 323 ff. The oldest bit of evidence on the servile *taille* that he cites is a charter of 1205 (p. 240).

[137] Primarly Georg von Below, who gives an extensive bibliography on the subject—*Probleme der Wirtschaftsgeschichte* (Tübingen, 1920), p. 623. For further discussion of the German views and the evidence involved, see *Le Moyen Age,* XXVI, 21 ff.

[138] *Le servage dans le comté de Hainaut,* pp. 32, 120.

Now when a German historian speaks of a public right in the eleventh century, he evidently means one that originally formed part of, or was somehow derived from, the imperial authority. When a French scholar calls the same right seignorial, he merely implies that it was one held by the majority of feudal nobles. But since such persons regularly possessed many powers— judicial, military, and administrative—that might accurately be described as public under the preceding definitions, it is obvious that the terms are not mutually exclusive. One refers to the original character of the thing, the other to its actual nature in the eleventh century; and of these two matters it is the latter that demands prior determination.

First, as to the names. *Taille,* throughout the period under discussion, denoted primarily a method of taxation, and only secondarily the taxes themselves. This term, with its crude translation *incisio,* of course arose from the practice of keeping accounts by notched sticks, or tallies; but in French-speaking lands came to be applied specifically to the requisitions made by a superior, which more directly were often called *demandes quêtes,* or *prières.* In German dialects the same exactions were known as *Beden* or *Rufen,* and in Latin charters often appear disguised as *petitiones, precariae, deprecationes, rogationes,* etc. The substance of such a "prayer" was pecuniary assistance, and so we find as variants *aide* in France and *Steuer* in Germany, which likewise were Latinized in various more or less fanciful ways.[139]

Beneath this multiplicity of epithets the only stable idea that we may detect is therefore the request of a powerful person, and that obviously might vary from the dictatorial command of an absolute master to the politest expression of desire on the part of an influential friend. And if in our own day the distinction between gift and tax occasionally seems obscure, how must it have been in the Middle Ages, when one's landlord was likely to be king in fact, if not in name? If these general considerations

[139] See *Le Moyen Age,* XXVI, 10, 34, and the references there given. It will be noted that none of these expressions necessarily implied either a voluntary or a compulsory nature in the contribution—that depended entirely on local circumstances (see above, notes 18, 68). What the names do seem to indicate is that at one time or another the exactions had been somewhat informal.

are kept in mind, it will, I think, be easy to perceive why we have been dealing rather with a variable habit than with a definite institution of the eleventh century. Instead of the *taille* we have found *tailles*.

Indeed, at first sight, the diversity is decidedly puzzling; for at one time and another we have observed territorial and personal *tailles,* ordinary and extraordinary *tailles,* limited and unlimited *tailles.* However, it is plain that these distinctions were not of equal significance or antiquity. The last, in particular, was not fundamental, but arose only as the consequence of changes from primitive usage. Thus, when we first hear of fixed *tailles,* they are always compromises between the retention of an unrestrained system of exactions and its entire abolition.[140] The original *taille,* therefore, was undoubtedly arbitrary; that is to say, the amount of the imposition depended solely on the lord's will, although we may imagine that in this respect, as in so many others, custom tended to impose limits long before they were officially recognized.

In the same way, the recurrence of the *taille* would be determined in the first place by the frequency of the lord's demands, but the evidence at hand shows that, from a time to which our records scarcely reach, quite regular practices had come to be established, and that the requisition was an annual affair.[141] At harvest time, in spring and autumn, or at the three "general pleas" rustic dependents would be expected to make their contributions of money, wine, grain, or livestock. Of course there was no reason why a less importunate lord should not make his levies at rarer intervals, such as every second or third year, or restrict them to occasions of special need,[142] but the sources tend

---

140 Above, notes 30, 41.

141 For annual *tailles* by *avoués* in the eleventh century, see above, notes 16, 18. That of the abbot of Vézelay was old in 1137 (above, n. 120). But an even more interesting case appears among the charters of La Trinité de Mauléon (*Archives historiques du Poitou,* XX, 14). When, about 1120, a certain R. Gabardus departed for Jerusalem, he borrowed ten *livres* from his brother, and in return ceded him all custom from certain lands "et unam questuram convenientem in anno et pro captione corporis rectam talliatam, in borderia II solidos et dimidium."

142 Extraordinary aids and *tailles* are particularly prominent in Normandy and the adjoining regions, where they were often retained by the duke on lands given to churches in the eleventh century: see, for instance, the confirmations of Henry I

to convince us that most lords were not so kind. Extraordinary *tailles* more often appear as special obligations which rustics might have to meet in addition to their more regular payments, and which might be perpetuated after the latter had been abolished.[143] Therefore, ignoring such accidental varieties for the moment, we may concentrate our attention on the one remaining distinction, that between personal and territorial *tailles*.

For reasons explained above, I think there can be no doubt that both existed in the eleventh century. On the lands of the church, whether exercised by prelate or *avoué*, on the demesnes of king, count, *châtelain*, or plain *seigneur*, the *taille* was regularly territorial—or, if it be preferred, public; for it fell upon all inhabitants, native or immigrant, landed or landless. In other words, it was a power that mere ownership of the soil could not convey, but which was contingent upon the possession by the landlord of regalian rights, such as were everywhere claimed by immunists and feudataries. For neither the king of France within his kingdom, nor the count of Flanders within his county, enjoyed a monopoly of taxation at the opening of the twelfth century.[144] With respect to *taille*, as with respect to justice and

to Saint-Pierre-sur-Dive, Lessay, and Saint-Evroul (*Gall. Christ.*, XI, Instr., 156, 205, 235). In the same way vassals might reserve *tailles* to acquit the exactions of the suzerain—Marchegay, *Archives d'Anjou*, III, 100; Bertrand de Broussillon, *Cartulaire de l'abbaye de Saint-Aubin d'Angers* (Angers, 1903), II, pp. 284–87. Cf. L. Delisle, *Etudes sur la classe agricole en Normandie* (Paris, 1851), pp. 93–94. On the antiquity of feudal aids in Normandy, C. H. Haskins, *Norman Institutions*, p. 21. In Flanders custom in this respect seems to have remained vague somewhat longer. As late as 1176 the *échevins* of Haspres were unable to decide whether or not the count was entitled to anything for the marriage of his daughter, his ransom, or the purchase of a castle (Miraeus-Foppens, III, 347).

143 See above, after n. 114.

144 The clearest statement regarding *tailles* by lesser nobles that I have encountered is contained in a charter of a certain knight, Samson de Passavant, to Saint-Aubin d'Angers in 1138 (Bertrand de Broussillon, *Chartes de Saint-Aubin*, I, 248). By it Samson gives in free alms land for a church and cemetery, adding the following provision: "Hanc autem elemosinam cum tota dominicatione quam habebam in locis denominatis dedi et concessi liberam et quietam ab omni costuma et ab omni penitus exactione, tallia dico videlicet, corvatis pariter et bidamnis et hujusmodi violentiis, que solent milites a pauperibus extorquere." Cf. the attestation by Louis VII in 1178 (Luchaire, *Louis VII*, p. 459) that Dreu de Mello has given to Sainte-Marie de Chaage "centum solidos de roga sua in villa Mintriaci annuatim accipiendos, vel de aliis redditibus suis ibidem si roga non sufficerit."

ost, the feudal state was not a unity, but a mosaic; the pattern of which depended upon centuries of privilege and usurpation.

On certain ecclesiastical properties, it is true, men sometimes retained or secured the same right of taking *tailles* as they had on lands under their immediate jurisdiction. It is conceivable, also, that on some lay fiefs the prince may have enjoyed a similar prerogative, but if that had been the general usage, another well-known institution of the Middle Ages could hardly have arisen—that of the feudal aids. For it seems undeniable that feudal custom required the lord to demand contributions, not from the tenants of the vassal, but from the vassal himself, leaving it to the discretion of the latter to raise the sums by subsidiary aids or *tailles* of his own.[145] Thus, so far as the relations of secular lords are concerned, the *taille* passes unnoticed in the records; even when, rarely, charters were issued to deal with such matters as knight service and reliefs, there was no need for it to be mentioned. Indeed, if it had not been for the exceptional position of the *avoué* and the chronic rivalry thereby engendered, we should scarcely have heard of the *taille* before the twelfth century, when the new charters of liberties show it as a common custom on countless *seigneuries.*

In the same way, we first gain a hint of such a thing as a servile *taille* after it had probably existed for centuries. So long as serfs stayed at home, no complications would arise in connection with their peculiar status; it was only when they became *hôtes* on the soil of another that disputes called forth the settlements through which we gain our first information on the subject. Then formulated custom came to declare that, if a lord permitted his bondmen to complete a legal residence on alien territory, he must take the consequences and lose whatever revenue their

---

[145] Even on ecclesiastical territory a secular lord usually had no power of directly taxing the tenants; the aids or *tailles* due him, as may be seen from numerous acts cited above, were normally collected by officials of the church. Cf. the charter of Hugh III of Burgundy to Notre-Dame de Châtillon (Garnier, *Chartes de communes,* I, 332): "Quod si dux Hierosolymam adeat, vel filiam suam maritet, vel captus sit et redemptus, vel terram emat, unde universa terra agravetur, ipse ab abbate ecclesie beate Marie de Castellione auxilium debet petere, aut per se aut per honestas personas; et si forte abbas et canonici in auxilium denegaverint, trecentis solidis tantummodo terram ecclesie agravare poterit."

new superior refused to allow him.[146] With this the established rule touching *hôtes* on rural estates, there was nothing revolutionary in the universal practice of granting, on similar conditions, immunity to settlers in towns. But such arrangements were characteristic rather of the twelfth than of the eleventh century. In its original environment the *taille* bore upon a population that was normally stable; and it is not hard to conjecture what, under such conditions, happened on the great estate.

By the agricultural system that everywhere prevailed, the chief items in any lord's income were, first, the produce of the lands that he kept in demesne, and secondly, the rents from lands let out to peasant cultivators. These multifarious dues, however, had long been fixed by usage or agreement, and so the thrifty peasant, after meeting his annual charges, was able to put by quite a little surplus for his own consumption or for sale in the local market. It was natural that, to supplement his income, the lord should wish to dip into this surplus, and to do so was not at all difficult.

[146] The evidence cited above clearly shows, I think, that the perpetuation of private rights, such as the servile *taille*, in favor of the personal lords of *hôtes* was the exception rather than the rule—and one made more often for the benefit of the church than for that of laymen. M. Verriest seems to hold the contrary view when he affirms (*Servage dans le comté de Hainaut*, p. 125) that serfs were not freed by the charters to the *villes neuves*. In fact, such an exception was made in the case of Soignies, the charter to which from the count of Hainaut in 1142 contained the following article (Wauters, *Libertés communales, Preuves*, p. 17): "Quicumque allodium Sonegiarum infra libertatem inhabitare venerint ab omni injusta exactione, exceptis servis, liberos esse concedimus." However, the same charter also provided that serfs who refused to serve their masters could, on complaint of the latter to the minister of the church—for the town was an *avouerie* of the count—only be forced to pay a fine: "Si per eos emendaverint, sint in pace; sin autem, infra octo dies ab eorum consortio recedant. Et qui spe libertatis venerint et habitaverint, lege ville et institutionis teneantur." And, of course, refusal of admission to the serfs of the town's founder, or to those of the church, was a very common feature of municipal charters; but the door was usually left wide for the serfs of everybody else. Thus the charter of Favril, granted in 1174 by Jacques d'Avesnes and the abbot of Saint-Humbert (*Mémoires de la Société archéologique de l'arrondissement d'Avesnes*, I, 105) decreed that every immigrant should be free, but that none from the lands of the abbey or of Avesnes should be given entrance without special permission. If any ordinary lord pursued his man to the town, no heed was to be paid him, for that would disturb the burgesses in the enjoyment of their franchise; and if he became angry and caused trouble, he should be held in peace by the *avoué*.

At the appropriate season domanial agents, whose particular business it was to know each man's obligations and resources, would make the rounds of the villages, probably meeting the peasantry at one of their general courts. Perhaps clerks would be at hand with parchment rolls showing assessments of previous years; at any rate, wooden tallies would provide a rough and ready system of accounting, and each tenant would be notified of what he ought to contribute at that time toward the needs of his lord. In the case of a serf, his property was legally his master's; in the case of a *roturier,* he was subject to the lord's justice and protection. Should he refuse payment, the officials would seize his grain or drive off his pig; and against such action he had absolutely no recourse. Even when the imposition was made by sheer force, as by some rapacious *châtelain* who had usurped the functions of *avoué* on monastic property, the peasant was powerless to resist. And while the abbot was appealing to a faraway king, or imploring the bishop to launch the bolt of excommunication, the offender redoubled his pillagings. Toward his own men, of course, the prudent lord would use discretion, but he probably felt that profits over and above a bare living better befitted his estate than theirs.

Later, when marshes were being drained, forests cut down, and wastes reclaimed; when mercantile centers were springing up on every river; when lords were outbidding each other for colonists, the peasant's lot improved. He could turn his back on the penurious existence to which he had once been forced to cling, and find a new home where, thanks to immunity from arbitrary *tailles,* he could live at greater ease and perhaps lay the foundations for a tidy fortune. To every man subjection to the capricious will of a master—of which the old *taille* was a prominent feature—reeked of bondage. He bore it only until, lawfully or unlawfully, he could make his escape. So, with the increasing mobility of the population, more and more lords were compelled to meet the competition of the new centers of immunity, to emancipate their serfs and abolish or fix the *tailles* that had borne upon their territories for generations. At last, by the close of the thirteenth century, the old arbitrary *taille* had disappeared except as a vestige of serfdom in isolated regions—

and as such its memory was perpetuated by the lawyers of that age.

Consequently, if the foregoing conclusions are justified, the original *tailles* were exceedingly vague—the result of a practice developed when public and private rights were indistinguishably merged in the hands of the powerful. To the men of the eleventh century there was no necessity of meticulous legal theorizing. The mediaeval baron was a practical man, who knew what he wanted and took what he could get. With what we should call powers of taxation concentrated in his hands, he demanded and obtained regular subsidies which to him were all *aides, tailles* or *Beden;* but which to our eyes were of diverse nature, according to the status of the persons who paid. In ordinary years he could expect nothing from his noble tenants beyond their specified service and had to limit his requisitions to his peasants. On special occasions, however, custom might permit him to demand assistance from all his men. For example, when he had been captured, knights, *roturiers,* and serfs alike had to contribute toward his ransom; but, according to strict definition, the first paid feudal aids, the second public *tailles,* and the last servile *tailles.*

And was not this the case with many other rights in the Middle Ages? The same three classes might all be summoned for justice to the same hall. All three very commonly paid succession dues, whether called relief or *mainmorte.* The knights garrisoned the castle while the peasants dug the moats. Castle-guard, we may say, was a matter of contract; was the *corvée* a private right held by the lord as the master of serfs, or a fragment of one-time imperial authority exercised over the descendants of free Roman citizens? To my mind it was both.

There has been some little controversy over the origin of what mediaeval sources call *ost et chevauchée.* M. Prou has contended that the military service owed by the *roturier* of the twelfth century was derived from that owed Charlemagne by the able-bodied freeman.[147] To which it has been replied that *ost* must have been rather a sort of *corvée,* since it was also rendered by

[147] "De la nature du service militaire dû par les roturiers aux xiᵉ et xiiᵉ siècles," *La Revue Historique,* XLIV, 313 ff.

serfs to their masters.[148] That, to be sure, is an undeniable fact; but the argument of M. Prou nevertheless remains sound, for it is quite impossible to explain all the popular institutions of feudal Europe as relics of bondage. *Ost* and *taille* appear side by side in scores of documents, and this juxtaposition is more than coincidence; it is testimony that the two obligations had to a certain extent evolved along parallel courses.

With the dual nature of the *taille* now pretty well determined for the eleventh century, it should be possible in much briefer scope, and with some degree of certainty, to indicate its origins. First of all, the servile *taille* may be easily disposed of. As a phase of the personal subjection of the bondman to his master, it was potentially as old as human slavery, and further inquiry in that quarter resolves itself into a search for more or less instructive precedents reaching far back into antiquity. This task I shall leave to a more competent investigator, and turn rather to what the Frankish sources may directly or indirectly tell about that somewhat more obscure institution, the territorial *taille*.

As remarked above, when we describe this *taille* as a public impost, we imply that it was somehow founded in what had once been the *imperium,* but we do not commit ourselves to the idea that Diocletian or Charlemagne had levied such exactions. Nor do we necessarily affirm that the *taille* had ever been the monopoly of public officials in the modern sense. We merely classify it among those vague political powers that the mediaeval baron held along with, and intermingled with, such private rights as ownership of the soil or control of his *familia*. Precisely what legal title he or his ancestors had to these powers we usually cannot say, but we do know that they were wreckage of the Carolingian kingship, and it may be possible to gain some very general ideas as to when and how fragments of fiscal authority may have been picked up.

In the first place, it seems perfectly certain that the *taille* was a product of the dark age that stretched from Louis the Pious to Robert the Pious. Between it and the taxes of the Roman Empire

---

[148] Luchaire, *Manuel des institutions françaises* (Paris, 1892), p. 347, n. 2; Sée, *Les classes rurales,* p. 368.

there was no continuity; for all authorities agree that the latter, while persisting under the Merovingians, lapsed into irreparable ruin under the house of Pepin.[149] Nor was any general system of taxation developed in place of the old; the task that lay beyond the powers of a Charlemagne naturally proved too much for his successors.[150] Indeed, by the ninth century even the tradition of a universal impost had quite faded: *census* had become the ordinary name for rent; *capitatio* already denoted the *chevage* of the Middle Ages; and *tributum* was a word that might mean any kind of revenue.

The nearest approach that the age offers to a royal power of general taxation consciously exercised is the *coniectum* levied throughout considerable sections of the country to buy off the invading Northmen. [151]But although in England similar practices led to the development of a permanent Danegeld, there was no such result on the Continent. There the impost served rather to advertise the weakness of a moribund monarchy, for its efficacy depended from the first on a semi-feudal aristocracy.[152] Thus the conclusion seems to be forced upon us that the territorial *tailles* of the eleventh century could not have been vestiges of a regular governmental tax, and it remains for us to seek possible precedents among the less formal exactions of the Carolingian age.

Unfortunately, the sources of the ninth century give us little in this connection beyond a list of names, which are either so vague as to be almost meaningless or so technical as to be prac-

[149] G. Waitz, *Deutsche Verfassungsgeschichte* (Berlin, 1880–96), IV, 113; Brunner, *Deutsche Rechtsgeschichte* (Leipzig, 1892), II, 234; A. Dopsch, *Die wirtschaftsentwicklung der Karolingerzeit* (Weimar, 1921–22), I, 192 ff. The capitularies have been so exhaustively studied by these and other scholars that there is no necessity of my citing them individually. Independent examination has convinced me that Dopsch is right in interpreting *census* in most of the passages to mean rents rather than taxes.

[150] Without necessarily subscribing to the doctrine of a victorious German liberty, I prefer the views of Waitz and Brunner to those of Dopsch (*op. cit.*, II, 272 ff.), who seems to me, like Fustel de Coulanges (*Les transformations de la royauté*, Paris, 1907, pp. 501 ff.) to exaggerate the quality and extent of late Carolingian taxation. See E. Joranson, *The Danegeld in France* (Rock Island, Ill., 1924), pp. 198 ff.

[151] A. Boretius, *Capitularia Regum Francorum (Monum. Germ. Hist., Legum Sectio II)*, II, 301, 354. On the *coniectum* see Waitz, IV, 22 ff.

[152] Joranson, *Danegeld in France*, pp. 72, 84, 99, etc.

tically unintelligible. We hear of *tributa* paid by peoples along the Slavic border, presumably as the result of conquest. A few documents mention *stuofa* as annual payments of produce in German regions, but whether they were relics of military subjection, of agricultural arrangements, or of tribal offerings to the chieftain, who can say? Then too, there are the equally obscure *inferenda* of Gaul.[153] However, when we come to the annual *dona* owed the emperor by certain leading prelates, we again reach solid fact, for no less a person than Hincmar, archbishop of Reims, tells us that in his day they were really state taxes, though called gifts. And the frequent abolition or restriction of such payments by royal charter tends to confirm his statement.[154] That is the extent of our information, and we are left to guess that probably pseudo-voluntary contributions had also been taken by the kings from the secular nobility. Indeed, such a practice would fit well into the economic and political arrangements of an age when military, judicial, and administrative powers were rapidly falling into the hands of the great landlords. There is certainly no evidence that the king took such subsidies from the population at large, and we do get hints that, with or without authorization, many powerful lords were taking them.

In 787 the king writes to his *missi* in Italy that, according to what he has heard, various junior counts, public officials, and even the more influential vassals of the counts, have been in the habit of exacting contributions and collections, either for entertainment or for other purposes, under the guise of making requests. All this must stop. The king, however, by no means wishes to forbid the acceptance of presents from the more powerful and wealthy, if offered of their own free will as signs of affection.[155] Nevertheless, such abuses by royal agents apparently continued, not only in outlying districts, but on the king's own demesnes.

In the *Capitulare de Villis* Charlemagne strictly orders that

---

[153] Waitz, IV, 111–16; Brunner, II, 236.

[154] Waitz, IV, 107; G. von Maurer, *Geschichte der Fronhöfe* . . . (Erlangen, 1862–63), I, 417 ff.

[155] Boretius, *Capitularia*, I, 197. Cf. *ibid.*, I, 144.

his ministers shall not vex his *familia* with *corvées* and requisitions: "nor shall they accept any gifts from the said men—neither horse nor ox nor cow, neither hog nor sheep, neither pig nor lamb; nor any other thing except drinks, fruits, fowls, or eggs."[156] Again, half a century later, various bishops, in a letter to Louis the German, beg him not to let his officials oppress the people: [157]

Et servos regios judices non opprimant, nec ultra quod soliti fuerunt reddere tempore patris vestri ab eis exigant; neque per angarias in tempore incongruo illos affligant; neque per dolos aut per mala ingenia sive inconvenientes precationes colonos condemnent.

In these cases the taking of forced gifts was plainly a matter of usurpation, but it would be rash to conclude that it was always so. If the king could take *dona* from followers, might not they, the holders of extensive immunities, take them from their tenants? [158] Would they not in fact be expected to do so? When Charles the Bald needed tribute money for the Northmen, he deliberately abandoned the rustic population to the mercies of rapacious vassals, and there is some evidence to show that they not only passed on their own responsibilities, but made a profit for themselves as well.[159] And with the progressive enfeeblement of the monarchy, there were hundreds of state officials, lay and clerical immunists, volunteer generals and upstart princes, to make the most of whatever precedents had been given them. Under the leadership of such *potentiores* the peasantry was assembled and organized for justice and police, for war and for the construction of common defenses. Round each of them grew up a territory, inherited, bought, or stolen, to whose inhabitants he issued orders for the preceding services and—it is submitted— his customary requests for assistance. In all likelihood he bore a

---

[156] *Ibid.*, I, 83; Waitz, IV, 171.

[157] T. Gousset, *Les actes de la province ecclésiastique de Reims* (Reims, 1842), I, 259.

[158] Waitz, IV, 106; von Maurer, *Fronhöfe*, I, 423.

[159] Joranson, *Danegeld in France*, pp. 84, 102, 193. The evidence consists of a single letter of Hincmar, but we should be thankful to have so much. Mr. Joranson expresses the opinion that these *coniecta* may have had a great deal to do with the development of the *taille*. Nothing will be found in this article to contradict such a supposition, but I think the latter would probably have arisen if no "danegelds" had ever been levied.

sword instead of a royal commission, but his was the truest government of the age. This, frankly, is two-thirds conjecture, but the miserable sources of the ninth and tenth centuries will hardly, I believe, permit any other interpretation.[160] Mercenary "prayers" of the powerful may seem a decidedly indistinct notion, but it is all that the records in question bear witness to; and that, after all, was the very essence of the later *tailles*. If in the days of Charles the Fat no universal test of the legality of the exaction could possibly be formulated, what must the situation have been five generations earlier? Surely conditions then were such as could be controlled by no conceivable set of theories. Perhaps a Baldwin of Flanders wished to pose as the fountain of all political authority within his county, as the French king later claimed to be within his realm; but as a matter of historical fact, neither had ever exercised such a monopoly. Society was already feudalized when their respective fragments were detached from the Empire. If any Western prince was ever able in the eleventh century to levy an imposition more general than a feudal aid, it was rather an anticipation of the future than a survival of the past.[161]

The *taille* was normally local. It was not derived from monarchical centralization. Juristic uniformity had nothing to do with it. Born of political chaos at a time when taxation in the modern sense was impossible, it disappeared when, with the passing of feudalism, that again became an actuality. In other words, the *taille* was characteristically mediaeval.

<hr/>

[160] Aside from various words, such as *questonaria* and *rogatus,* which seem to refer to such exactions as are later called *talliae,* the tenth century charters have little to offer us. For other possible instances see von Maurer, *Fronhöfe,* I, 423; Waitz, VIII, 398; Flach, *Origines de l'ancienne France,* I, 385, n. 2. This author (*op. cit.,* II, 555, n. 2) has, I think, though with considerable vagueness, rightly explained the connection between feudal aids and *tailles.* So far as the origin of the latter is concerned, he follows, as we all must, the judicious Waitz. Furthermore, the work of Karl Zeumer, with the amendments indicated elsewhere (above, notes 61, 105), must stand as a notable contribution to our knowledge of the subject. The extension of his doctrine by Georg von Below, however, seems altogether too legalistic. Although the *taille* was a sort of tax, and although, according to strict definition, it was often a public right, the fact remains that the attribution to the eleventh century of public taxes in the modern sense is an anachronism (above, n. 137).

[161] See *Le Moyen Age,* XXVI, 44.

Taxation and Representation
in the Middle Ages[*]

HAVING, as a graduate student, been launched on a dissertation connected with English municipal history, I was counseled by my instructor—the scholar to whom this volume is presented —to begin my work with a review of parallel development on the Continent. This after a fashion I did. However, as I now know, I hardly succeeded in finding out what the books were talking about. It was not that the authors were obscure; individually they were clarity itself. It was only that they irremediably failed to agree. Particularly with regard to the taxation of the towns, which involved so many fundamental problems, the result of my reading was a growing bewilderment.

Since, for example, the commune of London could not be explained without reference to the communes of France, nor the English tallage apart from the Continental *taille*, leading writers on those subjects had naturally followed French authorities. But on examination the doctrines of the latter seemed hardly consistent either with the English evidence or with each other. And the conclusions of German scholars, based on ma-

* Reprinted from *Anniversary Essays in Mediaeval History by Students of Charles Homer Haskins* (Boston and New York, 1929), pp. 291–312.

terials from their archives, offered still another set of contradictions.

Accordingly, it was not till curiosity had led me to the documents that I began to understand what underlay the discussion. For one had only to place a few charters side by side to realize that they agreed much better than the learned commentaries which they had elicited. Whether from Languedoc, Hainaut, Cheshire, or Westphalia, they seemed to reflect much the same state of society and government. And eventually I became convinced that, when certain legalistic and nationalistic prejudices were set aside, a more sensible interpretation of the sources immediately suggested itself.

As the result of the somewhat scattering work that I have been able to do in the past dozen years, I do not flatter myself that I have made any revolutionary discoveries. I am sure only that I have gradually given up a number of ideas learned from standard books; and I hope that to state these ideas, to summarize my changes of opinion, and to present the reasons which impelled them may not be without service toward further investigation.[1]

In the latter part of the eighteenth century educated Europeans began to show a livelier interest in mediaeval institutions. This interest is commonly described as part of the Romantic Movement, but it owed at least as much to the scientific curiosity of the scholar as to Rousseau's fad of the noble savage. It was Montesquieu who penned the first famous tribute to the British constitution, making the remark heard round the world, that this admirable system of government had originated in the for-

[1] The following study is in large part based upon five articles already published; but since the conclusions of the last two considerably modify views expressed in the three earlier, I have tried to bring all into harmony. For the sake of convenience I subjoin a list of these publications, placing in brackets the abbreviations that will be used throughout the notes:
"The Aids of the English Boroughs," *The English Historical Review*, XXXIV, 457 ff. [*E.H.R.*]
"Les aides des villes françaises aux XIIe et XIIIe siècles," *Le Moyen Age*, Second Series, XXIV, 274 ff. [*M.A.*]
"La taille dans les villes d'Allemagne," *ibid.*, XXVI, 3 ff.
"The Origin and Nature of the *Taille*," *La Revue Belge de Philologie et d'Histoire*, V, 801 ff. [*R.B.*]
"The Seignorial Tallage in England," in *Mélanges d'histoire offerts à Henri Pirenne* (Brussels, 1926), II, 465 ff. [*M.H.P.*]

ests of Germany.[2] For at least a century Englishmen had already been explaining their liberties as a heritage of the Middle Ages; and henceforth the enlightened bourgeoisie of the Continent found equal inspiration in the unbroken traditions of the Mother of Parliaments. So, in the great Declaration of 1789, the principle of no taxation without representation came to be enshrined alongside that of popular sovereignty—theories, both of them, essentially mediaeval.

The effect of the French Revolution, though eventually to discredit the cosmopolitanism of the philosophers, was by no means to diminish the reawakened interest in constitutional history. For the new nationalism of the nineteenth century tended from the beginning to make the politician also a historian; to give an intensely practical bearing to the study of representative institutions. Thus, as the Napoleonic wars drew to a close, and men once more had the opportunity for leisurely research, a younger generation of students arose to test in learned books the half-imagined theses of their predecessors.

In 1818 Hallam published his *View of the State of Europe in the Middle Ages,* which included a justly famous discussion of English parliamentary origins. After a careful review of the documents, Hallam showed that the representative system had its true beginning under Edward I, who, he said, was forced by public opinion to abandon his arbitrary tallage and to recognize the right of the boroughs to grant their taxes freely. In other chapters he treated the origin of Continental assemblies, but through lack of accessible sources his discussion was necessarily meager.[3] What Hallam was to the English-speaking world Guizot

---

[2] *L'esprit des lois,* 1748. See particularly bk. XI, ch. vi: "Si l'on veut lire l'admirable ouvrage de Tacite *sur les moeurs des Germains,* on verra que c'est d'eux que les Anglois ont tiré l'idée de leur gouvernement politique. Ce beaux système a été trouvé dans les bois."

[3] H. Hallam, *View of the State of Europe in the Middle Ages,* 11th ed. (London, 1855), III, ch. viii, pt. iii. Hallam attributed the formal abolition of the tallage to the Confirmation of the Charters by Edward I, but even before that, he said, "it was a more prudent counsel to try the willingness of his people before he forced their reluctance. And the success of his innovation rendered it worth repetition." On the French estates, *ibid.,* ch. ii, pt. ii: "Nor would I deny the influence of more generous principles; the example of neighbouring countries, the respect due to the progressive civilization and opulence of the towns, and the application of that

was to the French, for by his famous lectures he did much to popularize the study of parliamentary history on the Continent. Somewhat more prone than Hallam to vague generalization, he interpreted the evolution of representative government in very much the same way.[4] And in the meantime similar opinions had been set forth by Eichhorn regarding the diets of Germany. These assemblies, he held, were necessitated by the traditional rights of the clergy, nobles, and burghers. The towns, being exempt from forced *Beden,* or taxes in place of military service, were at first negotiated with separately; then, for the sake of convenience, deputies were called to meet with the other privileged subjects of the *Landesherr.*[5]

Accordingly, by the middle of the nineteenth century, the doctrine had definitely appeared that, not only the English parliament, but similar councils all over Europe mainly owed their existence to their lords' need of funds; and that, in particular, the emergence and rapid development of the Third Estate was primarily due to the exemption of the towns from all but freely granted impositions. The theory, though combined with many decidedly romantic notions, was eminently reasonable, and it fitted what facts were then known concerning the fiscal institutions of the Middle Ages. It was only as a more critical analysis of the sources came to be made that certain investigators began to doubt the correctness of the original explanation.

Hallam's idea, well advertised in Germany by Gneist,[6] was re-examined by Riess in 1888 and found wanting. It was, he said, a mistake to suppose that Edward I had relinquished the

---

ancient maxim of the northern monarchies, that whoever was elevated to the perfect dignity of a freeman acquired a claim to participate in the imposition of public tributes."

[4] M. Guizot, *Histoire des origines du gouvernement représentatif en Europe* (Paris, 1851)—the published form of lectures given in 1820–22. Leçons xii–xiii deal with the origin of the English House of Commons. For the French estates, see his *Histoire de la civilisation en France* (Paris, 1840), IV, leçons xv–xix.

[5] K. F. Eichhorn, *Deutsche Staats- und Rechtsgeschichte,* 4th ed. (Göttingen, 1834–36), II, 471 ff.; III, 245 ff. The nobles and clergy, said Eichhorn, had to be asked for grants of *Steuer.* "In demselben Fall befand sich der Landesherr seinen Städten gegenüber, von welchen er nicht so leicht die Beisteuer erzwingen könnte, als von den Vogteipflichtigen auf dem platten Lande, wenn diese der Bitte kein Gehör geben wollten."

[6] R. Gneist, *Englische Verfassungsgeschichte* (Berlin, 1882), pp. 359 ff.

ancient right to tallage which he, like other princes, enjoyed from his domain. As a matter of fact, the king continued to tax his towns at pleasure during the very period when the House of Commons was taking form. Deputies from the boroughs, as from the counties, were summoned by the king, not through fiscal necessity, but because they were useful in connection with the judicial and administrative work of parliament. The representation of the commons was the product rather of royal ambition than of national self-assertion.[7]

However, at the time that Riess published his remarkably clear-sighted article, the ultra-nationalistic school of Freeman was in the hey-day of its glory. English opinion, taught to see in Gladstone's Reform Act a mere return to primitive democracy, was in no mood to appreciate unromantic historical criticism in a foreign periodical. So the mark theory of Maurer and Kemble long continued to flourish, and on both sides of the Atlantic champions of Anglo-Saxon liberty long continued to pour forth their eulogies.[8] Even the cautious Stubbs was to a considerable degree borne along by the enthusiasm of his contemporaries. Though holding back from the exuberance of Freeman, he still tended to interpret Edward I's policy as the result of nationalizing forces, the logical extension to the kingdom at large of principles long tried in village self-government. Since the arguments of Riess ran counter to his whole thesis, Stubbs

[7] L. Riess, "Der Ursprung des englischen Unterhauses," *Historische Zeitschrift*, Neue Folge, XXIV, 1 ff. In his argument that Edward I had the legal right to tallage his towns and other domains at pleasure, Riess was unquestionably right. But he admitted (pp. 27–28) that political considerations made advisable the request for a parliamentary grant. It is just these political considerations which I think his otherwise admirable study underestimated. Cf. Hallam's remarks, above, n. 3.

[8] G. L. von Maurer, *Einleitung zur Geschichte der Mark-, Hof-, Dorf-, und Stadtverfassung* (Munich, 1854), and other well-known works published in the next seventeen years; J. M. Kemble, *The Saxons in England* (London, 1849); E. A. Freeman, *The Growth of the English Constitution* (London, 1872). An entertaining sketch of this idea in connection with the history of parliament will be found in H. J. Ford, *Representative Government* (New York, 1924)—a book which otherwise hardly touches the subject of the present study. For further discussion of the relation of the mark theory to the question of municipal origins, see a paper on the work of Pirenne and Below in the forthcoming *Case Book* of the Social Science Research Council.

passed them over in silence and, minimizing the arbitrary character of the tallage, still cited Hallam with approval.[9] Nevertheless, since the opening of the new century, the tendency of historical criticism has been more and more to substitute sound research for the patriotic fancies of Freeman. Modern scholars, intent on correcting over-idealization in history, have drifted far even from Stubbs, and so have given proportionately greater attention to the doctrine of Riess.[10] Indeed, the reaction against the older school is now so pronounced that there is danger of its reaching another extreme. One who is quite willing to discount official altruism, and one who has no desire to resuscitate faith in the democratic mark, may still believe that taxation and representation were vitally connected in the thirteenth century. At any rate, before the matter can be settled one way or the other, prevalent ideas with regard to the fiscal obligations of the towns must be somewhat clarified.

The late Professor G. B. Adams, in the course of his admirable restatement of constitutional origins in England, was led by a clause in Magna Carta to pay some attention to the taxation of the mediaeval boroughs, particularly of London.[11] Holding the generally accepted view that the tallage was essentially servile, but knowing that it was regularly paid by burgesses who were not serfs, he sought to explain the anomaly as a result of the Norman Conquest. That event, he said, had made the towns

[9] W. Stubbs, *Constitutional History of England* (Oxford, 1873), chs. xiii, xv. In later editions Stubbs failed to give adequate recognition to the work of Riess. However, in his own book he had not insisted upon a definite right of the Third Estate to grant voluntary taxes. He clearly brought out the fact that the representative system was the culmination of previous administrative practice, not only in fiscal matters, but in others as well.

[10] See particularly G. B. Adams, *Constitutional History of England* (New York, 1921), pp. 173 ff.; A. B. White, *The Making of the English Constitution,* 2d ed. (New York, 1923), pp. 353 ff.; A. F. Pollard, *The Evolution of Parliament,* 2d ed. (London, 1926); D. Pasquet, *Essai sur les origines de la Chambre des Communes* (Paris, 1914), tr. R. G. D. Laffan (Cambridge, 1925). In general, the first three of these authors emphasize judicial and administrative matters as of greater importance in producing representative government than taxation, but with their ideas on the latter subject I cannot altogether agree. To my mind, M. Pasquet has put the question in a fairer light. See particularly his criticism of Riess (pp. 219 ff.).

[11] *The Origin of the English Constitution,* 2d ed. (New Haven, 1920), particularly pp. 385 ff.

domanial properties of the king and other lords, and so caused them to be treated as unfree communities.[12] Even London was legally tallageable at pleasure; for it was only temporarily under John that the city, given the rank of commune, was liable for feudal aids on fixed occasions.

This technical definition of commune Adams took from Luchaire,[13] but the application of it to the English evidence was part of his own rigidly legalistic system. If only communes had the right to consent to extraordinary taxation, and if even London failed to make good its claim to that status, how did it happen that within the century all the boroughs were allowed to vote subsidies in parliament? If, as Adams seemed to conclude,[14] the representation of the commons was not a matter of feudal law at all, how could he be sure that the claims of the Londoners were? The question of aid and tallage is in truth much less simple than he realized; for on analysis it is found to involve the fundamentals of feudalism, the manorial system, and urban development. It could not be settled by the mere dictum even of a great scholar like Luchaire.

As a matter of fact, French historians had by no means accepted the famous *Manuel* as the last word either on communes or on taxation. Luchaire's was but one—and not the happiest—of many arguments advanced to elucidate a very obscure subject. And for a long time these arguments had turned upon the

---

[12] *Const. Hist.*, p. 171: "As belonging to a lord, the town formed a part of his domain lands and was therefore subject to the disabilities and exactions of the serf." In this doctrine Adams has been followed by Mr. A. B. White (*Eng. Const.*, pp. 111, 122). To Adams the feudal aid was a form of service, tallage a kind of rent, "a return upon capital invested" (*Origin of Eng. Const.*, p. 254; *Const. Hist.*, p. 190). Mr. Pollard (*Evolution of Parl.*, p. 7) seems to consider both as rent. For criticisms, in my opinion justified, of Adams' technical distinction between tallage and aid, see W. S. McKechnie, *Magna Carta*, 2d ed. (Glasgow, 1914), pp. 234 ff.; C. Petit-Dutaillis, *Studies and Notes Supplementary to Stubbs' Constitutional History*, tr. Rhodes (Manchester, 1908–14), I, 91 ff. See also *E.H.R.*, XXXIV, 473 ff.

[13] A. Luchaire, *Manuel des institutions françaises* (Paris, 1892), p. 413, quoted in *Origin of Eng. Const.*, p. 385.

[14] In *Const. Hist.*, p. 172, the introduction of representative elements in parliament is described as marking a decline of feudal ideas; but compare p. 183, where the "feudal principle of an advance consent to an extraordinary tax" is said to have been extended to all forms of taxation. Mr. Pollard (*Evolution of Parl.*, p. 157) appeals to the feudal principle of suit to court in order to explain the representation of the towns.

meaning of feudal law. Augustin Thierry, taking from Guizot the task of more definitely explaining the representation of the *bonnes villes* in the estates, expressed the opinion that the privileges of the towns had made them an integral part of the feudal hierarchy, and had so entitled them to the free vote of all taxes.[15] This was an idea well calculated to appeal to a French audience. Feudalism was something that had grown up at home. If parliamentary government was but the logical extension of that system, it did not have to be regarded as essentially foreign.

The suggestion of Thierry, though supported by Boutaric,[16] was first consistently followed by Vuitry. In a noteworthy series of essays he elaborated the thesis that the royal *impôt* was only the feudal aid, somewhat extended as to the persons who paid it, the lands where it ran, and the occasions on which it was levied.[17] This theory, though vague, was at least intelligible. Its modification by Giry and his school brought little but confusion.[18] However, since being popularized by Luchaire, the notion has prevailed that only the commune was a member of the feudal hierarchy and so exempt from all impositions but the aids of the vassal. The consequence, as Adams later discovered, was to make the representation of the Third Estate inexplicable by feudal law.

Meanwhile Vuitry's system had been assailed from another quarter. Callery argued that the only taxes levied by the mediaeval kings of France were either obligatory aids on recognized occasions or commutations of owed military service. Therefore, he said, the calling of the estates must be attributed to that part

15 *Recueil des monuments inédits de l'histoire du Tiers Etat* (Paris, 1850), I, xxxv: "Par leurs privilèges . . . les villes étaient devenues . . . partie intégrante de la hiérarchie féodale, et la féodalité reconnaissait à tous ses membres le droit de consentir librement les impôts et les subsides."

16 E. Boutaric, *Les premiers Etats Généraux* (Paris, 1860), p. 5. But in his other well-known books Boutaric developed somewhat contradictory ideas. For a fuller discussion of these authors, see *M.A.*, XXIV, 322 ff.

17 A. Vuitry, *Etudes sur le régime financier de la France* (Paris, 1870), p. 532; Nouvelle série (Paris, 1883), I, 144, 150 ff.; II, 3–4.

18 A. Giry, *Les établissements de Rouen* (Paris, 1883), I, 440; J. Flammermont, *Histoire des institutions municipales de Senlis* (Paris, 1881), pp. 97 ff., and *De concessu legis et auxilii* (Paris, 1883), pp. 115 ff.; Luchaire, *Les communes françaises* (Paris, 1890). See above, n. 13.

of the feudal contract which forbade the lord to substitute money for troops without the vassal's consent—an arrangement that applied to *roturiers* as well as to noble tenants. On the destructive side the force of Callery's attack was at once recognized, but since his own proposed solution gained no favor, matters remained more obscure than ever.[19] The trouble was that no one had investigated the nature of the exactions to which the towns were liable in the twelfth and thirteenth centuries.

Now this very problem, so unaccountably neglected in France, had long attracted the attention of scholars in Germany. As early as 1878 it was treated with extraordinary thoroughness by the distinguished Karl Zeumer,[20] and from 1885 to 1920 it continued to be one of the chief concerns of another prominent mediaevalist, the late Professor Georg von Below.[21] Through their efforts, the work of the student wishing to compare the taxes of mediaeval Germany with those of France and England has been enormously facilitated.

Zeumer showed, first of all, that the *Bede* commonly paid by townsmen was originally the same exaction as that paid by peasants. Furthermore, he proved that the *Bede* was sharply distinguished from rent and was not, as Eichhorn and others had thought, a substitute for military service. It had for its base nothing more specific than the irresistible demand of a powerful person. It was essentially a tax. Originating in the requests (*Bitten = Beden*) of lords for voluntary assistance, and long considered unjustifiable, the imposition was gradually legalized and by the end of the twelfth century had become the recognized perquisite of the *Landesherr* or other holder of public authority. As such it appeared in municipal charters, by which it was com-

[19] A. Callery, *Histoire du pouvoir royal d'imposer* (Paris, 1879), and *Histoire des États Généraux* (Paris, 1881). For various reactions to Callery's doctrine, see *M.A.*, XXIV, 324–25. The most notable amendment in subsequent years was made by L. L. Borrelli de Serres, *Recherches sur divers services publics* (Paris, 1895), I, 515 ff.: that the representation of the *bonnes villes* was due only to the necessity of discussion for determining the extent of their contributions. But his thesis is based on very dubious interpretation of the charters (*M.A.*, XXIV, 310).

[20] K. Zeumer, *Die deutschen Städtesteuern*, in G. Schmoller, *Staats- und Socialwissenschaftliche Forschungen* (Leipzig, 1878), I.

[21] G. von Below, *Die landständische Verfassung in Jülich und Berg* (Düsseldorf, 1885–91); *Probleme der Wirtschaftsgeschichte* (Tübingen, 1920), pp. 622 ff.

monly restricted to fixed sums, or occasionally abolished. And this practice in turn necessitated the special treatment accorded the towns when later princes tried to levy more general subsidies and called diets to grant them.[22] To Zeumer's general argument Georg von Below gave enthusiastic support. Working back from the legal attributes of the fourteenth-century *Landesherr,* he had become independently convinced that the *Bede* was a public impost; in fact it was liability for it of the burgher estate that led him to consider the nature of the mediaeval town, and so to write his epochmaking articles on municipal origins in Germany. But in one respect he took sharp exception to Zeumer: the *Bede,* he insisted, had never been other than *landesherrschaftlich.* From the beginning it was a *Zwangsbeitrag* levied by the Carolingian count or his legal representative. If in time the exaction came into the hands of private lords, that was a later development, the result of alienation. And to all objections raised against him Below was able to bring such cogent reasoning that today the opposition has virtually collapsed. With him learned opinion in Germany sees in the *Bede* "die älteste deutsche Steuer."[23]

Now anyone who first encounters this ancient German tax in the writing of Below and his pupils will not be likely to recognize it as the *taille* of France. And yet the most cursory examination of a few pertinent charters will at once convince him of the identification; for in frontier regions, where Teutonic and Romance dialects met, *petitio* (the Latin translation of *Bede*) appears as the perfect synonym of *tallia.*[24] There, at least, what one was the other was. If the *taille* was a servile obligation, so was the *Bede;* if the *Bede* was a public tax, so was the *taille.* Could any example better prove the complete absurdity of offering a purely nationalistic explanation for an institution common to both sections of the Frankish Empire?

The mere discovery of such a glaring contradiction challenged reconciliation; and this I have made some attempt to effect, prin-

[22] For further discussion of Zeumer's argument, together with a criticism of his main points, see *M.A.,* XXVI, 21 ff., 36 ff.

[23] Heading of ch. ix in *Probleme der Wirtschaftsgeschichte.* As will appear below, I have been led somewhat to modify the view expressed in *M.A.,* XXVI, 37 ff.

[24] *Ibid.,* pp. 7-12, 20, 23.

cipally by a study of documents emanating from the Franco-German borderlands. But the fact that conclusions drawn from that evidence agree so remarkably with constitutional principles in England will perhaps excuse the broadening of my generalizations. They are presented tentatively. For though it seems to me that they must be sound, how sound they are can only be determined by much more research than I shall ever accomplish.

In the first place, there is the quarrel over public and private authority, which, without definition of terms, gets nowhere. Classification of rights in the Middle Ages based solely on juristic analysis is, in my opinion, historically worthless; for the men of that time knew nothing of it. On the other hand, insofar as the terms "public" and "private" are used to designate historical categories, to indicate whether or not a given power was originally regalian, the distinction has value, and was not altogether foreign to mediaeval thought. In eleventh-century Germany, where feudalization had only begun, such differentiation would indeed be clearer than in contemporary France, where prevalent custom allowed various political rights to the vassal. But even there did anyone suppose that merely to hold land was to possess governmental authority? Countless charters are proof to the contrary. To the best of my knowledge, the military, judicial, and fiscal powers of the baron or immunist were always recognized as coming directly or indirectly from the king.[25]

So, when French writers classify a right as *seigneurial*, they do not, or should not, deny its public character; and Below was not justified in sneering at the usage,[26] for the distinction between *Landesherr* and *Grundherr* can hardly be applied to a thoroughly feudalized country. From this point of view, also, the *régime seigneurial*, or manorial system, cannot rightly be described as wholly private, for it included many elements derived from neither landlordship nor slavery. It is my impression that, compared with economic unfreedom, legal unfreedom was of secondary account. The law of serfdom was derived from the law of slavery, but it was not that which brought the mass of the people under the will of the few. The average peasant needed

---

[25] *R.B.*, V, 856 ff.; *M.H.P.*, II, 473 ff.
[26] *Probleme der Wirtschaftsgeschichte*, p. 661, n.

the protection of a great lord in order to live, and through that necessity became subject to his jurisdiction. What came to be held marks of servitude can all be found in an early age as territorial obligations. At the same time, however, bondage did exist, and legally carried with it absolute rightlessness as against the lord. The payments and services that he exacted from the free peasant as political superior he might take from his serf as proprietary master. On which side in a given case the institution was older it is at present impossible to say.[27] Practically, the technicalities of legal status must have mattered little in an age when the average man was helpless to improve his condition and the manorial authority of the lord was distinctly arbitrary.

Whatever may be made of other peasant obligations, there can be no doubt as to the character of the early tallage, or *taille*. In the sources where it is first mentioned it appears as an exaction levied by the territorial lord upon the rustics under his jurisdiction. Like the right to hold a court or to levy military service, it was a political perquisite, in strict theory derived ultimately from the crown. Nevertheless, it was not and never had been a royal tax, Roman or Frankish. And we have no sure evidence that, as Below believed, it had ever been the count's monopoly. In eleventh-century France, at any rate, it certainly was not; for neither the count of Flanders nor the duke of Normandy, the two greatest princes of the West, had exclusive enjoyment of it. Rather it appears, like the manorial jurisdiction that it accompanied, to have been a vague power which the feudalization of society had widely dispersed before the great principalities took shape.[28]

[27] In spite of confident generalizations in many books, the subject of serfdom in the earlier Middle Ages is still very obscure. It is to be hoped that M. Marc Bloch will continue his studies in this connection; see particularly his "Transformations du servage," in *Mélanges d'histoire du moyen âge offerts à M. Ferdinand Lot* (Paris, 1925). With M. Bloch I believe that the *taille* was not purely servile, but I am not so sure as he that *mainmorte* and *chevage* were so; see the examples cited in *R.B.*, V, 832 ff., and F. Lot, *L'impôt foncier et la capitation personelle sous le Bas-Empire et à l'époque franque* (Paris, 1928), pp. 120 ff.

[28] Below was inclined to believe that the *Bede* originated in the West Frankish kingdom and spread to the east (*Probleme der Wirtschaftsgeschichte*, p. 661); but his confidence that the exaction was invented by the count seems to have been based on juristic deduction rather than actual evidence. When the miserable

In proportion as Germany remained more thoroughly Carolingian than France, such public rights as potentially went with the comital office would tend to retain their more primitive centralization.[29] However, even there political disintegration was at most only delayed, and eventually the *Bede* ended as it had in France. On the whole, I am inclined to think that Below underestimated the extent to which such fiscal authority had been feudalized in twelfth-century Germany. Perhaps, if he had not followed Zeumer in restricting his research to thoroughly Teutonic documents he would not have been so positive that most local lords had no right to tallage their dependents.[30] And in one other respect, I believe, Below's doctrine stands in need of amendment. Although many French authorities have unquestionably gone wrong in pronouncing the tallage essentially servile, it is equally incorrect to affirm that no such thing as the servile tallage existed.[31] How old it was in the twelfth century, when we first hear of it, is doubtful, but it lasted long

---

sources of the ninth and tenth centuries give us any information on the subject, they show all sorts of powerful men collecting forced gifts (*R.B.*, V, 867 ff.). Similar exactions were not unknown in Anglo-Saxon England (*M.H.P.*, II, 470, n. 1). The clearest proof that the tallage was not a princely monopoly in the eleventh century lies in the fact that the feudal tenures established in England by William the Conqueror permitted each baron to tallage his manorial dependents (*M.H.P.*, II, 471–74). Another proof may be found in the custom of the feudal aid (*R.B.*, V, 860). In his most recent work (see the previous note) M. Lot has considered the origin of the *taille* in connection with his admirable discussion of Frankish taxation. On the latter subject I of course yield to his superior knowledge. Furthermore, so far as the *taille* is concerned, I admit that his criticism (pp. 131 ff.) of a few statements that I hazarded in 1923, before making an independent examination of the sources, is quite justified. However, the article in *M.A.*, XXVI, was specifically stated to be amended by that in *R.B.*, V, 803, n. 1. If M. Lot will reread the latter, I am confident that he will find its conclusions in no essential different from his own.

29 See J. W. Thompson, *Feudal Germany* (New York, 1928), chs. ix–x.

30 In this respect municipal charters show the prevalence of identical customs on both sides of the frontier; see particularly the examples cited in *M.A.*, XXVI, 39 ff. On the failure of Zeumer and Below to appreciate the significance of extraordinary *Beden*, see *ibid.*, pp. 24, 30.

31 It is, of course, impossible to explain the origin of the servile tallage apart from that of serfdom. In the eleventh century the serf could be tallaged at pleasure by his lord so long as he was kept at home; when, however, he entered the jurisdiction of another lord, his body-master could collect only what the latter permitted (*R.B.*, V, 826 ff., 861 ff.).

after the tallage on freemen had lost its arbitrary character. Moreover, this fact greatly helps us to understand the opinion that men had of it. For if the tallage was as ancient and honorable as Below would have us believe, why was it so universally detested? With this question we are logically brought to the subject of emancipation.

The breakdown of the social system in which the tallage had developed began with the economic changes of the eleventh century. By 1100 rural and urban colonization were already well under way, and one immediate result was to place a new premium on personal liberty. The man who was legally free to move found it increasingly easy to improve his condition. Nor could serfs always be traced and brought back. For the first time in centuries opportunities for better livelihood became common and, as fast as they arose, men came from somewhere to take them. To meet the demands of a migratory population and to attract further settlers, lords began to vie with one another in guaranteeing privileged status to residents within their jurisdiction. Little by little the system was developed and extended, so that in the course of two hundred years arbitrary seignorial obligations had already disappeared throughout the more progressive regions of the West. Henceforth burdens that had once fallen upon the bulk of the rustic population tended to be characteristic only of serfs whom the emancipation movement left untouched.[32] Between them and even the humblest bourgeois lay an ever-widening gulf.

Familiar as is the subject of urban liberties, one of its fundamentals still needs emphasis—the public basis of the town's establishment. Mere ownership of the soil did not suffice for creating a privileged municipality; that necessitated the tenure of immunities which could be shared with a group of subjects. The lord of a town was the person who chartered it. As he chartered it, so it was said to stand on his domain; for that expression, in the political sense, meant the territory under his immediate jurisdiction.[33] And if under feudal custom the or-

[32] On this and what follows, see *R.B.*, V, 826 ff., 842 ff., 863 ff.

[33] Thus the well-known argument of Maitland (*Domesday Book and Beyond*, pp. 176 ff.) concerning the classification of the boroughs in Domesday is, on analysis,

dinary baron possessed the legal faculty of conferring bourgeois status, that is only added testimony to prove the public nature of his authority. Thus the typical emancipation charter to a community was not the act of a master freeing his bondmen; it was a grant of territorial franchise. It customarily restricted the exercise of the political rights—judicial, military, and fiscal —which the grantor held within the locality, and also guaranteed to all settlers freedom from the exactions of their previous lords. Moreover, this liberty, except for specified reservations, applied even to immigrant serfs. Everywhere the precedence of territorial over personal rights was advertised by the famous law of a year and a day.

In this way, and only in this way, can the taxation of the mediaeval town be satisfactorily explained. The urban settlement, because it was located within a lord's territorial immunity, was subject, unless he chose to relax it, to his exclusive and unrestrained power of tallage. But as a matter of fact the exaction, like arbitrary *corvées* and unlimited military service, was found incompatible with the interests both of the bourgeois and of their patron. So it tended to disappear. The most highly privileged towns gained complete exemption, often with the guarantee that they should be liable only for freely granted subsidies. Occasionally, though by no means regularly, special aids were reserved on definite occasions, the famous three cases of northern French custom or others. However, no separate treatment in this respect was given to towns called communes; the argument of Giry and Luchaire, in which Adams placed such confidence, was without foundation.[34]

In Germany, except for the great cities of the Rhine valley, municipal development was much more backward than in France, and most communities at the opening of the thirteenth century were still subject to arbitrary tallage. Even when that was ended, grants of complete exemption were rare. The average

---

found to be based on misapprehension. Mere ownership of the soil had nothing to do with the case. Following Maitland, I was led to erroneous conclusions in *E.H.R.*, XXXIV, 472 ff. For the views in this respect of G. B. Adams, see above, n. 12.

[34] *M.A.*, XXIV, 10, n. 3.

German town, like a French village, secured only the restriction of its *Bede* to a fixed annual sum.[35]

After 1066 English custom, as was to be expected, followed the French. Domesday Book reveals the tallage as a Norman importation intimately connected with manorial organization. It was not servile, but was levied by the baron upon all rustics, notably sokemen, subject to his jurisdiction. It was apparently an annual imposition quite distinct from ordinary rents, and a heavy one. This tallage, as is well known, long continued to be a prominent feature of seignorial exploitation, but by the thirteenth century it generally came to be only a fixed charge for the free peasant, and so in its unrestricted form a mark of servile status.[36]

So far as the boroughs were concerned, the chief peculiarity of their history was their intimate connection with the monarchy; for the dominant position of the crown in England before and after the Norman Conquest resulted in keeping most of the towns on the royal domain. However, there were notable exceptions, and in the twelfth century lay and ecclesiastical nobles, following Continental models, founded many new communities. In the charters of these seignorial boroughs tallage sometimes appears, being limited according to French precedent. But the royal boroughs had their own custom. There the Norman king seems to have been satisfied with the perquisites enjoyed by his Saxon predecessors. At least, he introduced no annual tallage comparable to that established by his vassals on their estates. Very likely the reason was that in England the king found ready-made a tax far superior to any enjoyed by his princely contemporaries. The royal geld, originally instituted to buy off the Danes, had become under Cnut a regular impost levied to maintain an army and navy, and even after 1066 it was never feudalized. So, unless specially exempted, all lands in England, whether held by king or by baron, were supposed to be taxed. With a handsome revenue thus largely supplied from the

35 *M.A.*, XXVI, 20 ff.
36 *M.H.P.*, II, 465 ff., superseding what I wrote in *E.H.R.*, XXXIV, 472 ff., when believing the tallage essentially servile.

domains of others, the Conqueror could well afford to spare his own the burden of additional exactions.

For a time no essential change was made in the ancient arrangements affecting the boroughs. Except when they had already secured special treatment, they continued to pay geld on their previous ratings. However, some time before 1130, the earlier assessments were set aside and aids at an advanced figure were substituted. The growing wealth and self-sufficiency of the towns began to assert themselves. Down to the reign of Henry II the old danegeld, together with the newer *auxilia burgorum,* continued to be levied; but that energetic ruler proceeded to evolve a new and more profitable set of taxes. From the baronage, alongside the customary feudal aids, he took scutage in place of military service. From his boroughs, and eventually from his domain manors, he exacted special subsidies variously called *dona, auxilia, assisa,* and finally *tallagia.* Taken at irregular intervals by negotiation with the separate communities, these sums mark an enormous increase over those obtained by Henry I and strikingly attest the efficiency of the Angevin's exploitation.[37]

To match this royal tallage of England contemporary princes in western Europe had little to show. It was not till the next century that the kings of France, following the example of their vassals, were able to take any decisive steps in its direction. Within each great fief custom normally permitted the lord, lay or ecclesiastic, to levy a subsidy when confronted by some special need. The aids thus taken were seignorial, rather than feudal; for they were commonly paid by both noble and non-noble tenants. Except on definitely recognized occasions, the former could be expected to pay only voluntary contributions, and the effect of municipal charters was to place many towns in somewhat the same advantageous position. But in any case the outcome was not so much a matter of law as of political strength. A weak lord was hardly able to collect even the more regular aids, while

---

[37] *Ibid.,* pp. 457 ff., 466 ff. *Donum* and *auxilium* appear in the twelfth century as equivalents for *tallagium* on seignorial estates (*M.H.P.,* II, 466–68). For the boroughs in Domesday, see "The Origin of the English Towns," *The American Historical Review,* XXXII, 10 ff. A sequel on the Anglo-Saxon borough will soon appear in *The English Historical Review.*

the mere request of a powerful prince, no matter what he asked for, could be ill refused. An autonomous city-state might dispense with all chartered privilege, but no amount of written guarantees prevented extortion from an actually dependent community. To interpret mediaeval taxation as following a set of rigid legal principles is to miss the point completely.

In order to get what money he required from an ordinary town the lord had only to negotiate for a grant, enlarging upon the urgency of his need, emphasizing the benefits secured from him in the past, and hinting the misfortune that his displeasure might occasion in the future. And if necessary, he was always willing to issue the letter of no prejudice for which his chancery kept a stock of forms on hand. It is true that auxiliary troops or money compositions were occasionally levied from towns, but such a practice could introduce no new principle; for municipal charters commonly restricted military service as well as tallage. If most taxes were levied because of wars, they were none the less taxes. The only way in which the French king, or one of his great vassals, could secure a general subsidy from all his dependents was by negotiating with each important individual or group. From that system to the calling of estates was but a step. How Philip IV and his successors used such meetings for fiscal purposes is quite familiar. And throughout the provinces from Flanders to Béarn, whether held by king or count, the same phenomenon recurred. In proportion to its wealth and power, the bourgeoisie secured place in the central councils.[38]

In Germany the situation was the same. The towns, either free of the old *Bede* or obliged to pay only fixed sums, were still solicited for extraordinary aids. And again the custom of dickering with each community was in time succeeded by the calling of representative assemblies. Even under Rudolf of Habsburg the *Reichsstädte* came to send deputies for making a grant to the king, and within another century many territorial diets had appeared in connection with similar practices on the part of the *Landesherren*.[39]

[38] *M.A.*, XXIV, 292 ff.
[39] *M.A.*, XXVI, 31 ff. On the origin of town representation in the *Landtag*, see G. von Below, *Territorium und Stadt* (Munich, 1900).

If now we turn back to England, in spite of all insular peculiarities, we find a familiar situation. The royal boroughs,
it is true, had with slight exception never been exempted from
tallage; but in the king's hands that exaction had corresponded
rather with the extraordinary aids than with the *taille* of the
Continent. That the boroughs were as legally liable for the
imposition as lawyers could make them is beyond doubt.[40]
However, this did not prevent their objecting to the tax. The
action of London, to my mind, should be interpreted, not as
an appeal to but as a protest against the law. When, during the
crisis under John, the city asked that it be exempted from
tallage and recognized as having the right to grant its aids,
it was merely echoing a demand raised by the bourgeoisie in
all quarters. Nor, in an age when mere villages were securing
such guarantees in France, could one repulse be expected to
end the Londoners' agitation. Indeed, there is plenty of evidence
to show that the tallage continued to cause bitter opposition
until it was dropped in favor of the new parliamentary grants.[41]

To explain the origin of the House of Commons as a purely
insular phenomenon is surely mistaken. Anyone who studies the
mass of relevant material on the Continent can hardly escape
the conclusion that the representation of the towns there was
the logical outcome of a new system of taxation—one forced
upon princes whose necessary expenditures were far exceeding
their ancient sources of income, and one which had grown up
with the towns themselves. To say this is not to imply that all
representative assemblies were called to grant taxes; the system
was obviously useful in many ways. But in proportion as fiscal
necessity controlled the later fortunes of the estates, so it must
have dominated their creation.

Knowing how both the earlier and later evolution of parliament turned upon matters of taxation, I find it hard to discount
that factor as determining Edward I's policy. Even in connection

[40] The towns forming the confederation of the Cinque Ports were almost alone
in being exempt from all royal tallage. In the thirteenth century the king began
levying ships from other seaports in place of tallage or as gratuitous subsidies, and
by the fourteenth century all towns were held liable for service either by sea or
land (*E.H.R.*, XXXIV, 460 ff.).

[41] *Ibid.*, pp. 473–75.

with the counties, the representation of which was the most peculiar feature of the English system, fiscal considerations can by no means be ignored. Many writers on the subject have pointed out that, thanks to the Norman perpetuation and improvement of the ancient shire court, the lesser barons and other freeholders of the kingdom had come to be grouped in legally organized communities, or communes. How useful they had been to the king in police, justice, and other local affairs is a commonplace. But was that usefulness in itself enough to account for the knights of the shire as an estate in parliament? I do not think so. By associating them with the other sections of the council, Edward was able to assure the financial support of a very important element in his state, and one which strict feudal law would have prevented his taxing. But in this respect, as in all, his policy was distinctly anti-feudal, and in following it he was not without precedent.[42]

So, too, while making allowance for the importance of judicial and administrative work, I still feel that the incorporation of the burgesses as a permanent element in the great council was due primarily to the cash which the king was thereby enabled to get. For though he was not legally forced to tax the towns with their consent through deputies, he undoubtedly found it easier to do so. It was a political necessity that faced Edward, as it faced the other princes of the age. Indeed, if any of them had been strong enough, would he not have levied his imposts despotically? We cannot doubt, as M. Pasquet has so well said, that the autocratic Plantagenet saw in the problem of parliament nothing beyond an administrative difficulty.[43] And that he dreamed of recognizing constitutional principles or of setting up national institutions is of course unthinkable.

Nevertheless, to state the king's intentions is not to exhaust

[42] The danegeld had been paid by all grades of landowners, and to supplement it Henry I had taken *dona* from the counties, apparently raised through negotiation with the shire courts. When taxes of national scope were once more levied in later reigns, it is significant that the county organization was again used to facilitate assessment and collection: Stubbs, *Const. Hist.*, I, 429; II, 223 ff.; S. K. Mitchell, *Studies in Taxation under John and Henry III* (New Haven, 1914), pp. 135, 164; Pasquet, *Origines de la Chambre des Communes*, pp. 38 ff.

[43] *Ibid.*, ch. v.

the subject. Granting that he consulted only his own interests, we may still inquire more closely how he came to act as he did; may ask what outside circumstances helped to influence his decision. It has been argued that, since many towns regarded parliamentary service as a burden and sought to avoid the expense of sending deputies, their attitude could not have availed to force the issue of representation.[44] But does this conclusion follow from the evidence? For a small community to shirk costly responsibilities was only natural—so long as it had nothing to lose. But such action always presupposed the continuance of the existing system. Though two remained at home, there would still be enough burgesses at Westminster to safeguard all; the parsimonious townsmen were not for a moment desiring a return to arbitrary taxation.

To read back into the Middle Ages the perfected constitutional practices of the nineteenth century is of course a mistake. In the thirteenth century modern ideas of parliamentary legislation and taxation by majority vote did not exist. Even the groups that later came to be called estates were still inchoate. What the king could not get from a class he might yet take from individuals. Any exaction might be solicited as an aid. And in an age when *dona* were paid by prelates, barons, merchants, villeins, and Jews, to estimate the degree of free will involved in a given grant is not easy. Names amounted to nothing and formalities to little more. Between an arbitrary imposition that could be collected only through the coöperation of the payers and a contribution levied by consent there may have been a world of difference in theory; but there was not much in practice. The force that stayed the hand of the despot was not law but the resistance, actual or potential, of the subject. Hence, however distinct their legal capacities, the measures adopted by Edward I and Philip IV were remarkably similar.

On ultimate analysis, it seems to me that in the organization of representative institutions in western Europe we encounter the necessary result of a social revolution. This revolution, the product of a commercial revival, had created a new moneyed class, the support of which proved a decisive factor in the re-

[44] *Ibid.*, pp. 179–99.

building of the European monarchies. For intelligent princes were quick to see that they stood to gain infinitely more from the good will of the rising burghers than from an outworn system of hated exactions. Accordingly, the tallage, together with other obsolete manorial arrangements, was generally abandoned in the towns, and less obnoxious payments were substituted. Especially by means of subsidies called voluntary, seignorial taxation was not only continued but enormously enhanced. Bourgeoisie and monarchy formed a famous alliance, which, breaking the political dominance of feudalism, eventually produced the modern state. That the men whose wealth had long been the chief reliance of indigent but ambitious princes should be given a voice in the reorganized central councils was quite inevitable.[45]

Thus the same statesmanship that in the twelfth century had led to the granting of liberal municipal charters gave the towns representation in the fourteenth. Though the parliamentary system was ordained by the sovereign for his own convenience, that convenience was largely dictated by his need of taxes.

[45] The object of this essay has not been to prove that taxation was the only important factor in the evolution of the representative system, but to insist that it should not be so hastily passed over as it has been in some recent books. Obviously a great deal of useful work can still be done in connection with thirteenth- and fourteenth-century taxation, and must be done before we can hope to understand the beginnings of parliament or of Estates General. It is also obvious that the evolution of similar institutions in Spain and Sicily has a direct bearing upon the subject, but the development of such comparisons I must leave to others.

The Beginnings of Representative Government in England[*]

THIS paper, as will be seen, is based upon a series of distinctions, and to some it may appear significant that my plan was drafted between lectures on Gratian and Peter Lombard. Perhaps I have devoloped a scholastic bent; but I can at least affirm that my distinctions are drawn neither from theology nor from canon law. Rather, they have been suggested by an enforced reading of English constitutional sources during the past two years. The first distinction should be familiar to anyone who has studied the political oratory of Great Britain; the others to anyone who has followed the recent discussion of parliamentary origins. Re-emphasizing these distinctions will, I hope, serve to improve our understanding of representative institutions in mediaeval England.

A Conservative argument frequently heard in the halls of parliament has been that the house of commons holds discretionary power to act for the nation as a whole. A member, no matter how many people vote for him or what may be their local

[*] Reprinted from *The Constitution Reconsidered* (New York, 1938), pp. 25–36. A paper read at the meeting of the American Historical Association in Philadelphia, December, 1937.

interests, should be regarded and should regard himself as a statesman rather than a mere delegate. The notion of a parliamentary mandate, a binding instruction laid upon either group or individual, is utterly foreign to the British constitution. Every loyal subject must fear and deplore the growing tendency to decide important issues by alleged appeals to the people—by exciting the voters to periodic states of frenzy and substituting a count of heads for political wisdom.

Such opinions—and they are by no means dead yet—rest upon a theory of representation dear to the hearts of the eighteenth-century Whigs. Writing to Sir Hercules Langrishe in 1792, Edmund Burke explained the matter as follows [1] (the *distinctio prima* of this paper):

Virtual representation is that in which there is a community of interests, and a sympathy in feelings and desires, between those who act in the name of any description of people and the people in whose name they act, though the trustees are not actually chosen by them. This is virtual representation. Such a representation I think to be, in many cases, even better than the actual. It possesses most of its advantages and is free from many of its inconveniences; it corrects the irregularities in the literal representation, when the shifting current of human affairs, or the acting of public interest in different ways, carry it obliquely from its first line of direction. The people may err in their choice; but common interest and common sentiment are rarely mistaken.

Repelling all suggestions for a change in the parliamentary franchise, he supported the thesis [2]

that neither now nor at any time is it prudent or safe to be meddling with the fundamental principles and ancient tried usages of our constitution—that our representation is as nearly perfect as the necessary imperfection of human affairs and of human creatures will suffer it to be. . . .

Similar views were continually expressed by those who opposed the Reform Bill of 1832. Even the nomination boroughs, said Peel, were a worthy feature of the ancient constitution, because they permitted the ablest representatives of the national interests

[1] *Works* (Bohn ed., London, 1855), III, 334–35.
[2] *Ibid.*, VI, 144.

to be returned as a matter of course.[3] And anyone with sufficient curiosity to search the parliamentary debates can find the same reasoning employed on many other occasions.

Much earlier, though without Burke's support, the British government had declared that the American complaint of taxation without representation was ill-founded. The colonists, it was true, elected no deputies to parliament; yet they were as adequately represented as most Englishmen. Not very long ago the women were still being told that they had no real need of the suffrage, for the men represented them better than they could hope to represent themselves. Attacking the Parliament Bill of 1911, the duke of Northumberland denounced the house of commons as a body of paid politicians and proclaimed the house of lords "the most independent assembly in the world." Said he: "We represent, my lords, in a peculiar degree the education and the intelligence of the country." [4]

Here, obviously, lies the trouble with Burke's argument. It can be used, not merely, as he used it, to defend aristocratic control of the commons, but to justify any regime that the speaker happens to like. May not Hitler assert that, by virtue of a "sympathy in feelings and desires," he represents the German people? Perhaps he has asserted it; and yet others will disagree. Indeed, any government, according to the personal attitude of the critic, may in this way be said to represent or not to represent the governed. On ultimate analysis virtual representation proves to be at its best a somewhat impractical ideal, at its worst a mere figure of speech. And in any case it is not what we normally understand as representative government. In dealing with the beginnings of the latter—as in this paper—we must keep our eyes on actual representation, that is, the practice of electing and commissioning deputies.[5]

[3] *The Speeches of Sir Robert Peel* (London, 1853), II, 276 ff.

[4] *Parliamentary Debates: House of Lords*, Fifth Series, VIII, 810.

[5] By definition of terms many books on representative institutions would have avoided considerable obscurity—among them Miss M. V. Clarke's recent work, *Medieval Representation and Consent* (London, 1936), although it contains a number of excellent chapters. Mr. Pollard, on the other hand, recognizes the ambiguity in the word representation and sensibly declares: "It is idle to seek the origin of representation in its vaguer sense." But I cannot follow him when he

Accordingly, I must differ with those who, for the present subject of inquiry, find significance in the fact that the hundred court was anciently called the hundred, and the county court the county.[6] The usage, in my opinion, hardly implies a true theory of representation. Does it not merely reflect the popular identification of a community with its government—as when we say that Russia declared war, that the church forbade the marriage of priests, or that a city regulated traffic? The language suggests at most a lawful spokesman. Nor can I, with Mr. McIlwain, perceive a germ of modern representative institutions in another practice of mediaeval courts—that of having a body of doomsmen or *scabini* to declare the customary law.[7] Since they were not elected by the suitors, they could have been representatives only in a figurative sense.

More to the point is a famous passage in the *Leges Henrici Primi*. These so-called Laws of Henry I state that the demesnes of a lord may, in either the county or the hundred court, be acquitted by the lord or his steward or, if they are of necessity absent, by the reeve, the priest, and four of the better men of the vill, on behalf of all who are not summoned by name.[8] From that dubious assertion by a private compiler of the twelfth century, the Germanist school of historians, illumined by an ardent faith in the self-governing township, once deduced a primeval English constitution based on the representative principle. Writing on the common meeting of the free Teutonic villagers, John Richard Green eloquently expressed the conviction of Freeman, Stubbs, and virtually their entire generation:[9]

Here new settlers were admitted to the freedom of the township, and bye-laws framed and headman and tithing-man chosen for its gov-

---

concludes: "It is only in this sense that parliaments were representative during the earlier periods of their existence" (*The Evolution of Parliament*, pp. 151–52).

[6] In this connection Pollock and Maitland (*History of English Law*, I, 536) speak only of a "fleeting representation." But cf. Mr. McIlwain's more positive deductions (*Cambridge Medieval History*, VII, 668).

[7] *Ibid.*, pp. 666–67.

[8] Liebermann, *Gesetze*, I, 553–54; translation in Stephenson and Marcham, *Sources of English Constitutional History* (New York, 1937), no. 26. Subsequent quotation from this book is made by permission of the publishers.

[9] *History of the English People* (New York, 1881), I, 12–13.

ernance. Here plough-land and meadow-land were shared in due lot among the villages, and field and homestead passed from man to man by the delivery of a turf cut from its soil. Here strife of farmer with farmer was settled according to the "customs" of the township as its elder men stated them, and four men were chosen to follow headman or ealdorman to hundred court or war. It is with a reverence such as is stirred by the sight of the headwaters of some mighty river that one looks back to these village moots. . . . It was here that England learned to be a "mother of parliaments."

That such an idyllic picture had to be blotted out by a new generation of scholars is indeed a pity. Even one in our own midst, Mr. Charles Beard, has shown himself especially ruthless.[10] Sympathizing with those who wish to save a corner of that once lovely fabric, I yet fear it is gone beyond hope of restoration. Mr. McIlwain would have us believe that the *Leges Henrici Primi* sketch a representative system which at least in part was Anglo-Saxon.[11] To me as to Mr. Beard, however, the passage in question does not portray a scheme of local representative government at all. In the appearance for the vill of the reeve, priest, and four select villeins, the anonymous author seems to be describing—for he is chronically inaccurate—an occasional procedure, such as that adopted for the Domesday inquest of 1086.[12] The reference, in other words, is not to an ancient routine of administering justice in shire and hundred, but to a Norman adaptation of the jury.

Here, at last, we reach something fairly solid; an opinion touching the origin of the English representative system becomes less an act of faith, as it was with Stubbs, and more a matter of real understanding. And in this connection we are all greatly indebted to Mr. A. B. White. He has convincingly shown that the characteristic self-government of the English people was due rather to the training of their Norman-French kings than

[10] "The Teutonic Origins of Representative Government," *American Political Science Review*, XXVI (1932), 28 ff.

[11] *Cambridge Medieval History*, VII, 668.

[12] Made in the hundred court, where the reeve, the priest, and six villeins attended for each vill: Stephenson and Marcham, no. 21; cf. Round, *Feudal England*, pp. 3 ff., 118 ff.

to "an urge . . . in Anglo-Saxon blood." [13] The principal stages of the development, as he sees it, are already familiar to students of English constitutional history. In the course of the twelfth century, local juries came to be used more and more frequently for a great variety of governmental business: to secure information concerning the privileges of individuals or communities; to assess persons and estates for maintenance of arms or payment of taxes; to bring charges against dishonest officials; to present the names of suspected criminals; to settle disputed titles to land or other property; to answer all sorts of questions put by the royal justices on eyre. Not uncommonly the desired results could best be obtained when the juries were popularly elected, and occasionally it was found convenient to call together a number of juries to consult with the king or his ministers. In the later thirteenth century such assemblies came to be associated with meetings of the great council; and so, we are told, the house of commons ultimately emerged.

At this point, however, I should like to interpose another distinction: that between a jury system and a system of representative government. The one does not inevitably imply the other. The essence of a jury was not that certain men were elected to represent others, but merely that certain men were put on oath to give true answers to questions. Two hundred years after the Norman Conquest the jury remained primarily a fact-finding institution. What was still demanded of the juror was particular knowledge, rather than authority to act on behalf of a community. So long as the king merely wanted information, a system of appointed juries, consulted either singly or in groups, would be entirely adequate. This may be representative government of a sort, but it is not what we recognize by that name in later England.

Sometimes, indeed, it was necessary for juries to be popularly elected—as when the counties were asked to present complaints of official maladministration. Also, when the royal justices made their great eyres through the country, they presumably wanted

13 *Self-Government at the King's Command* (Minneapolis, 1933), p. 2, and *passim*. See also *The Making of the English Constitution* (New York, 1921), pp. 353 ff.

the juries from the local communities to be free of dictation on the part of sheriffs or bailiffs, and so encouraged a form of popular choice. In any case, there can be no doubt that by 1250 elected deputies of county, hundred, borough, or manor were often being called on for help in assessing and collecting taxes.[14] And by that time the greater towns had formal rights of self-government, with elected magistrates and municipal councils.[15] It is clear, therefore, that representative institutions were more than a by-product of the jury system. They were, in fact, more than a result of convenience in royal administration. To explain their new prominence in the thirteenth century, the economic and social developments of the age must be taken into account.

From this point of view the assembly of 1254 is especially significant, and it was not a mere concentration of juries. In February of that year the king commanded the election in each county court of two lawful and discreet knights, to come before the royal council at Westminster and there represent all and several of the county in granting him an aid for his expedition to France. The sheriff was to explain to the knights and others of the county the urgency of the king's needs and was to induce them to render an efficacious aid, so that the elected knights could make a precise response to the council.[16] For the first time, so far as we can tell, knights of the shires were then summoned to attend parliament. Also for the first time, as Mr. J. G. Edwards has remarked,[17] such deputies were required to bear what amounted to powers of attorney from their respective counties.

An authorization of the sort demanded in 1254 was no empty formula; it bound the whole county to the specific action taken by its delegates. And a very similar requirement was placed in

[14] For examples of such procedure, see Stephenson and Marcham, no. 46C, D, G. The elected men, though put on oath, hardly constituted a jury or juries; rather they shared the responsibilities of the sheriffs and justices.

[15] See especially J. Tait, *The Medieval English Borough* (Manchester, 1936), chs. vi–xi; C. Stephenson, *Borough and Town* (Cambridge, Mass., 1933), ch. vi.

[16] Stephenson and Marcham, no. 46J. In addition to the books already cited, see on this assembly D. Pasquet, *An Essay on the Origins of the House of Commons* (Cambridge, 1925), pp. 33 ff.

[17] *Oxford Essays in Medieval History Presented to H. E. Salter* (Oxford, 1934), pp. 141 ff. The argument in the next two paragraphs is essentially that of Mr. Edwards.

the writs of 1268 for the election of burgesses to come before king and council—the earliest such writs of which we have the complete wording.[18] Indeed, the record contains the actual form of the letters to be sealed and attested by the electing community:

To all faithful in Christ before whom these present letters shall come, the mayor, bailiffs, and entire community of the city of York, greeting in the Lord. For the sake of the affairs concerning our lord king H[enry], illustrious king of England, his kingdom, the community of England, and us [to be considered] in the council called by the legate at London on the approaching quinzime of Easter, we have seen fit to send thither ――――, our mayor, and ――――, our bailiffs, and ――――, our citizens or fellow burgesses, so that full faith be given to them in everything which, with regard to the aforesaid matters, they shall see fit on our behalf to set forth in the council or on the occasion of the council. And we shall hold as established and accepted whatever on our behalf those men do in the aforesaid matters. In testimony whereof, etc. Given, etc.

The precedents thus set under Henry III were continuously followed under Edward I. Almost every writ that he issued for the election to parliament of burgesses or knights of the shires includes a provision that the men so chosen must have binding authority to act on behalf of their communities. For a score of years there was considerable variation in the phrases used; then the formula was invented that continued in official use for over five hundred years:[19]

. . . We command and firmly enjoin you that without delay you cause two knights, of the more discreet and more capable of labor, to be elected from the aforesaid county, and two citizens from each city of the aforesaid county, and two burgesses from each borough, and that you have them come to us on the day and at the place aforesaid; so that the said knights shall then and there have full and sufficient authority on behalf of themselves and the community of the county aforesaid, and the said citizens and burgesses on behalf of themselves and the respective communities of the cities and boroughs

18 Stephenson and Marcham, no. 48D. For the little that is known of this meeting, see the article by Mr. Sayles accompanying the original text, *The English Historical Review*, XL, 583 ff.
19 Stephenson and Marcham, p. 160.

aforesaid, to do whatever in the aforesaid matters may be ordained by common counsel; and so that, through default of such authority, the aforesaid business shall by no means remain unfinished. . . .

I heartily agree with Mr. Edwards that this is a fact deserving greater attention than it has hitherto received. Why was the king so insistent, not only upon the election of lawful men from county and borough, but also upon their being formally empowered to bind their constituents? Surely he must have wanted more than information, complaints, or requests. Within the last quarter of a century, for all the modern emphasis on economic factors in history, many writers on parliamentary origins have stressed judicial routine as the dominating influence in the development of both houses. Against that opinion I registered a mild protest in 1929.[20] Now after a wider reading of the pertinent evidence, I am prepared to strengthen it. The crux of the matter, it seems to me, lies in the distinction—the third and final one of this paper—between the original functions of parliament and the original functions of the commons in parliament.

The research of Messrs. Richardson and Sayles has proved in detail that under the three Edwards the main business of parliament continued to be judicial.[21] Most of the work that later devolved upon the privy council or the chancellor—the settlement of cases lying beyond the jurisdiction of the common law courts—was still in the fourteenth century handled by parliament. But this body, the greatest and highest of the king's courts, was the original parliament, in which burgesses and knights of the shire had no place. In 1400 the commons set forth to the newly enthroned Henry IV [22]

[20] "Taxation and Representation in the Middle Ages," *Anniversary Essays in Mediaeval History by Students of C. H. Haskins* (Boston, 1929), pp. 291 ff. Since this article was published, a number of other writers have rallied to the support of Stubbs's thesis: notably Mr. Edwards, *op. cit.*, p. 147; Miss M. V. Clarke, *Medieval Representation and Consent*, p. 315; and Miss May McKisack, *The Parliamentary Representation of the English Boroughs during the Middle Ages* (Oxford, 1932), pp. 127 ff. Even the scholars who emphasize the judicial functions of parliament give little support to Mr. Pollard's rash statement (*Evolution of Parliament*, p. 153) that the representation of the commons was merely "an unpleasant incident of feudal service."

[21] See especially their articles published in *The English Historical Review,* XLVI, XLVII, and in *The Bulletin of the Institute of Historical Research,* VIII, IX.

[22] Stephenson and Marcham, p. 256.

that, whereas the judgments of parliament pertained solely to the king and to the lords, and not to the commons except in case it pleased the king of his special grace to show them the same judgments for their satisfaction, no record should be made in parliament concerning the said commons to the effect that they are or shall be parties to any judgments henceforth to be given in parliament. To which, at the king's command, response was made by the archbishop of Canterbury, to the effect that the commons are petitioners and demandants and that the king and the lords have always had and of right shall have the [rendering of] judgments in parliament after the manner described by the same commons; except that the king especially wishes to have their advice and assent in the making of statutes, or of grants and subsidies, or [other] such matters for the common good of the realm.

The action thus taken merely confirmed the established custom of England. The commons were not and never had been judges in parliament. The fact that meetings of the parliament had come to be associated with meetings of deputies from the local communities had, so far as judicial work was concerned, no legal significance. In the words of Mr. H. L. Gray,[23]

The century of the three Edwards remains one during which the commons were practically non-existent for any one who wished to offer a petition in parliament. They stood in the same position as did the petitioner himself.

If, therefore, we take judicial functions as the determining factor in the rise of the commons, we are reduced to the contention that they were somehow invaluable as petitioners. It is, of course, undeniable that before the time of Edward I meetings of deputies were sometimes held for the specific purpose of recording popular grievances, and that in a few of the later parliaments the commons apparently did nothing but present petitions. As acutely remarked by Mr. Richardson, however,[24]

the real problem . . . is not to explain the occasional association of popular representation with a session of parliament in England or elsewhere, but to explain why popular representation became an

[23] *The Influence of the Commons on Early Legislation* (Cambridge, Mass., 1932), p. 337.
[24] *Transactions of the Royal Historical Society,* Fourth Series, XI, 170.

essential and inseparable feature of English parliaments. The explanation is not to be found by any examination of the origins of parliament, however far-reaching or ingenious.

Neither, I would add, is it to be found by tracing into earlier times any political practice that did not involve the actual election of deputies with a delegation of binding authority from the communities of England. The assembling of such communal representatives apparently began in 1254 and developed into a regular custom by the end of the century. Why a king like Edward I should have insisted on these assemblies merely to facilitate the presentation of petitions I cannot understand. But I can understand how the bringing of petitions in parliament would be encouraged by the constant election of burgesses and knights of the shires for other purposes. The principal purpose, I am convinced, was to obtain money—a conclusion that agrees with the known character of the king and the social and economic changes of the age.

The euphemistic language of the royal writs should not mislead us. In 1241 Henry III called at Worcester an assembly of the wealthier Jews from all his boroughs "ad tractandum nobiscum tam de nostra quam sua utilitate." But the matter of mutual advantage of which they were to treat was actually a tallage of 20,000 marks.[25] When Edward I notified his good men of various towns that he had commissioned John of Kirkby to explain to them and expedite through them "certain arduous and especial concerns" of his,[26] no one could have been surprised to discover that he was negotiating for a subsidy. And contemporaries were as little mystified when parliamentary representatives were summoned to consider those other "difficult and momentous affairs" to which the writs constantly refer. They knew that they would be fortunate to escape further demands for taxes.

Mr. McIlwain goes so far as to remark that, if we confine our attention to the innovations affecting parliament under Henry III, "the contemporary evidence is strongly in favour of Bishop Stubbs' view that the original motive behind the beginning of

[25] *Close Rolls, 1237–42*, pp. 281, 346–47.
[26] Stephenson and Marcham, no. 49C.

these changes was almost entirely fiscal." [27] To my mind the evidence for a similar motive on the part of Edward I is even stronger. On re-examining the records of his sixteen parliaments that included deputations of the commons, Miss M. V. Clarke has found only three in which no question of a grant was apparently raised. "The evolution of the *premunientes* clause . . . to bring the proctors of the clergy to parliament," she points out, "was frankly fiscal in intention, as there was no other reason why Edward I should require their presence." [28] And it seems idle to assert that the king had the right to tax the freeholders of shire and borough at will. As a matter of fact, the royal tallage on the towns had normally been levied through negotiation with the individual communities, and in the later thirteenth century the tallage was generally supplanted by subsidies officially styled free.[29] Meanwhile, as the burden of taxation was shifted downward from the barons to their knightly tenants, it had become practically imperative for the king to seek formal grants from the county courts according to the plan adopted in 1254.[30]

When, under Edward III, the proceedings of parliament come to be entered in the rolls, they offer continuous proof that the primary task of the commons was to vote supply. The reader almost invariably knows what to expect at the opening session. After the usual preliminaries, the lord chancellor, or some other minister, would explain the reasons for the calling of the parliament. He would set forth the great expense incurred by the king in defending the realm, in promoting worthy projects abroad, in repressing civil disorder, in maintaining the regal estate, and in otherwise assuring to the English people the blessings of a sound administration; so, in the face of the existing emergency, he would urge the commons to make generous provision for his majesty's needs, promising a gracious consideration of whatever requests they might care to make. And it is a very familiar story how the commons, by formulating joint petitions

---

[27] *Cambridge Medieval History,* VII, 678.

[28] *Medieval Representation and Consent,* pp. 315 ff.

[29] See particularly Stephenson and Marcham, nos. 46F, 49E; also my article in *Haskins Anniversary Essays.*

[30] This has been clearly demonstrated by Mr. McIlwain, *Cambridge Medieval History,* VII, 674–76.

and stipulating royal approval as the necessary condition to a grant of supply, ultimately established their control over the vital functions of the government.[31]

Accordingly, if the view here expressed is justified, the core of the English representative system has not been a vague sympathy on the part of self-appointed spokesmen, a primitive custom of deeming dooms in the name of the people, or even the selection of jurors for a sort of national inquest. Rather it has been a matter of sheer political necessity, occasioned on the one hand by the king's lack of money and on the other by the growing strength of the social groups who could supply it. Although the king might use communal delegates in a variety of ways, the compelling motive behind their incorporation as an estate of parliament was economic. Without the recurring need for general taxation, there would, I believe, have been no house of commons.

In concluding, it may also be remarked that some of the constitutional features praised by Burke as "the ancient tried usages" of England were by no means so fundamental as he imagined. It was not the original practice for members of the commons to be representatives of the nation at large. Actually, the burgesses and knights of the shires were procurators of the local communities, chosen and instructed by them, responsible to them, and legally bound to be resident within them.[32] Contemporary political thought, of course, embraced no theory of democracy founded on universal suffrage. But it did recognize the interdependence of representation and popular election, and to it the principle of the mandate was not wholly foreign— all good Tories to the contrary notwithstanding.

[31] In this respect, it seems to me, the thesis of Stubbs remains fundamentally sound (*Constitutional History*, chs. xvi, xvii).

[32] See especially the statute of 1413 (Stephenson and Marcham, no. 69D); also Pasquet, *Origins of the House of Commons*, pp. 68 ff., 194 ff.; and McKisack, *Parliamentary Representation of English Boroughs*, pp. 44 ff., 119 ff., 139 ff. How ideas of representation were affected by the social and political changes of the fifteenth century is a subject that lies beyond the scope of the present discussion.

The *Firma Noctis* and the Customs of the Hundred[*]

IN the course of several articles recently published in this Review [1] Miss E. M. Demarest has developed a new and interesting theory with regard to the beginning of royal taxation in England. The *firma noctis*, she concludes, was not a rent, as most authorities have asserted, but a tax in connexion with which the system of assessment by hide and hundred had been employed long before the danegeld was invented. To prove her contention, Miss Demarest presents various entries in Domesday as vestiges of the primitive arrangement. In the first place, many royal manors had at one time been hidated for payment of the king's *feorm*. Secondly, certain *consuetudines* in the southwestern counties had been proportioned to hidage, and they may be identified with the *firma noctis;* as may also the 'hundred pennies' of Taunton. And lastly, in the country *Inter Ripam et Mersham* the same sort of impost is found under the name of 'carucate geld.'

Now the crucial point in this argument is, I think, the iden-

[*] Reprinted from *The English Historical Review*, XXXIX (1924), 161–74. Correction of misprints and other minor changes by the author; but most peculiarities of spelling and typography have been allowed to stand as in the original.
[1] *Ante,* xxxiii. 62 f.; xxxv. 78 f.; xxxviii. 161 f.

tification of the various customs of the hundred with the food renders styled *firma noctis* or *firma diei,* for it is only the former which Domesday specifically describes as having been paid by lands outside the royal demesne and as having been collected through the machinery of the hundred. However, the survey nowhere says that these *consuetudines* were the same as the *firma noctis,* and before we insert the sign of equation, we must be sure of the value of each term. A brief examination of the farm system in general would therefore seem to be demanded by the nature of the problem.

As Mr. Round has pointed out,[2] the *firma comitatus* of the Pipe Rolls hardly appears in Domesday; in so far as it does, it seems to have been made up of various *firmae,* each the result of a separate contract with the king. For example, in Worcestershire the sheriff farmed three main sources of income: the borough, the royal manors, and the popular courts.[3] It is well known, too, that the sheriff regularly let out to sub-contractors portions of his total obligation. The royal manors were given at farm, either singly or in groups, to reeves, who bore the same relation to the sheriff as he bore to the king. With regard to the courts, there was no uniform practice, but the profits of a hundred were frequently included in the farm of the manor that served as its administrative centre.[4]

It was this farm system that underlay public finance in the eleventh century. When the commissioners of William I wished to check the royal income, they reported all increases or decreases either of the general farms owed to the king directly or of the local farms owed to his officials. Since the days of King Edward much property had been brought within the royal farm, but much likewise had been taken away from it, so that Domesday is filled with complaints of encroachment.[5] It should not be

___

[2] *The Commune of London,* pp. 12 f. See also Vinogradoff, *English Society in the Eleventh Century,* pp. 374 f.; Ballard, *The Domesday Inquest,* pp. 239 f.

[3] *Domesday Book,* i. 172. Compare Warwickshire and Leicestershire: *D.B.* i. 230, 238.

[4] Maitland, *Domesday Book and Beyond,* p. 92.

[5] Thus at Worcester, which rendered £60 annually, various barons were retaining rents and customs from their houses (*D.B.* i. 162). From Surrey comes the following

thought, however, that the farm system was peculiarly royal; it was in common use also on private estates.[6] In all such cases, then, the *firma* was an arbitrary sum determined by negotiation between the parties to the contract. It was virtually a rent and was so recognized in Domesday, where the term is often used interchangeably with *census*.[7] Furthermore, in most contexts no difficulty arises from interpreting *firma* to mean the ordinary money farm. When it is said that King Edward had held certain property 'in firma sua,' or an estate is described as having been 'de dominica firma regis,' we should naturally understand that such lands had contributed to the farm of some royal manor or, if the remark is made of a manor, that it had furnished a quota of the farm paid to the king by the sheriff. Indeed, comparison of any considerable number of Domesday descriptions will show that lands held 'in firma,' unless it was in fee-farm, were always demesne lands, and that 'de dominica firma' meant little more than 'de dominio.'[8]

Firma, however, was but a Latinization of *feorm*, the Anglo-Saxon word for food. Before it could have meant a money rent

information (*D.B.* i. 31): 'Ipse episcopus tenet Tetinges. . . . Homines de hundreto testantur quod prestitum fuit istud manerium per vicecomitem extra firmam regis Edwardi, et quod Osbernus episcopus non habuit hoc manerium T.R.E.' And see the *Clamores* of Huntingdonshire (*D.B.* i. 208) and the malversations of Henry de Ferrers in Berkshire (*D.B.* i. 57 b). Afforestation was another recurrent cause of complaint: *D.B.* i. 219 b (Corbei), 51 (Achelie), 172 (Droitwich). Throughout his numerous writings Mr. Round has repeatedly called attention to cases of the same sort.

[6] *D.B.* i. 66 b (Dobreham); i. 12 b (Platenout); ii. 110 (Breccles); i. 379 (York); i. 31, 31 b (Brunlei, Reddesolham et Fernecome). See Round, in *Domesday Studies,* i. 135.

[7] *D.B.* ii. 38 b (Wisgar); i. 247 b (Acovre); ii. 3 b (Celdeforda); ii. 180 (Sutunna). Compare the entries for Malmesbury and Hereford (*D.B.* i. 64 b, 179), and those for Torksey and Wallingford (*D.B.* i. 56, 337).

[8] The Domesday text (*D.B.* i. 190 b–192) uses the following formulae: 'Haec terra iacuit et iacet in dominio aecclesiae de Ely,' 'Haec terra iacuit semper in aecclesia,' 'Haec terra iacet et iacuit semper in aecclesia de Ely in dominica firma,' 'Totum hoc manerium fuit semper et est dominicum,' 'Hoc manerium fuit et est de dominio aecclesiae.' In the *Inquisitio Comitatus Cantabrigiensis* and the *Inquisitio Eliensis* (ed. Hamilton, London, 1876) they are constantly modified and shifted about. See particularly the cases of 'Weslai,' 'Melrede,' and 'Gratedene' (pp. 19, 104; 66, 109; 88, 111).

it must have meant a food rent, and as such the *firma noctis* has been commonly understood.[9] In fact, this peculiar render appears in the record as only an occasional variant in place of the more usual round sum of money. A manor responsible for a night's farm paid no other farm; had no other valuation.[10] Study of the relevant passages inevitably leads to the conclusion that the Domesday scribes were acquainted with two varieties of farm: one primarily reckoned in money and the other in food. *Firma* in a given instance might be used to mean either,[11] but the food farm, being archaic and exceptional, was usually differentiated by the unit in which it had been measured—the 'day' or 'night,' an arbitrary quantity of provisions that varied from region to region.[12] This was the original *firma unius noctis*, but by 1086 it was practically obsolete, and Domesday gives only enough information to warrant a guess as to how it had been superseded. In the first place, commutation had produced an intermediate stage between it and the money farm. Provender was no longer supplied as before, but the oddness of the sum substituted yet tended to keep the night's farm distinct from the ordinary money rent. Then, as the old economy had been further disturbed through detachment of the manor from the royal demesne or through change in its administration, revaluation

---

[9] Round, *Feudal England*, p. 114, n. 204. So far as Domesday is concerned, it is understood in the same way by Maitland (*Domesday Book and Beyond*, pp. 236 f., 319), Vinogradoff (*English Society*, pp. 142, 327, 384), and Liebermann (*Gesetze der Angelsachsen*, ii. 420, 'Gastung'), although these authors think that it may at least in part have originated as a tax.

[10] Those in Dorset are merely said to render a night's farm or a portion of one; the unit was so well fixed by custom that no further description of it was deemed necessary (*D.B.* i. 75). In other counties monetary values are given in a haphazard fashion; see Round, *Feudal England*, pp. 110 f., *Commune of London*, p. 71, in *Victoria History of Hampshire*, i. 401, 414, and in *Vict. Hist. Somerset*, i. 402.

[11] Note the following parallel (*D.B.* i. 75 b, iv. 31): 'Haec terra non pertinet ad firmam de Winburne'; 'Hec mansio nichil pertinet noctis firme Winburne.' There are many other passages in which the context makes us sure that *firma* refers to the *firma noctis;* see particularly the descriptions of the royal manors in Wiltshire and Somerset.

[12] For comment on the different units of assessment employed, see Ballard, *Domesday Inquest*, pp. 223 f.; Round, in *Vict. Hist. Bedford*, i. 193, *Hereford*, i. 300, *Northampton*, i. 273. Mr. Poole (*The Exchequer in the Twelfth Century*, pp. 28 f.) tries to work out a uniform monetary value in round figures for the *firma unius noctis*, but why should we suppose that such a sum existed?

had destroyed all trace of the primitive obligation.[13] The king's *feorm* had become the *firma* of the Pipe Rolls.

Thus, if the preceding explanation is sound, it is a matter of secondary importance whether the farm was paid in money or in provender; it was always rent.[14] I have failed to find in all Domesday a single instance where the word *firma* is used to mean anything else. Nor does any connexion appear to have existed between either sort of farm and hidage. One solitary entry, the description of Ewell in Surrey, seems to indicate such a relationship, but it is as obscure as it is exceptional and must, I think, be ascribed to clerical error.[15] It is true that many lands had been hidated which had never paid geld, but their 'defence'

---

[13] This evolution clearly appears in the case of Beeding in Sussex (*D.B.* i. 28). Compare 'Borne' and 'Beddingham': *D.B.* i. 20 b. In the same way the old dues from King Edward's demesne in the counties of Gloucester, Hereford, Cambridge, and Bedford had been wholly or in part commuted (*D.B.* i. 162 b, 163, 179 b, 189 b, 209). In Essex, Norfolk, and Suffolk the older farms had been changed to ordinary round sums after the Norman Conquest. So 'Celmeresfort' (*D.B.* ii. 5 b). Compare *D.B.* ii. 6, 7, 21 b, 109, 112 b, 114, 235, 282.

[14] It should be remembered that traces of food rents like those later known to have existed on many monastic estates are found in Domesday. For an example see *D.B.* i. 121 (Lanpiran) and the discussion of this question in Vinogradoff, *English Society*, p. 384, and Liebermann, *Gesetze*, ii. 420, 'Gastung.' Ballard (*Domesday Inquest,* p. 226) is inclined to translate *firma* as food where, on the whole, the ordinary meaning seems preferable. The reason why the night's farm as used on the royal demesne disappeared when the manor was infeudated was apparently that the old rent covered, not merely the income from the manor proper, but other revenue, which the king normally reserved for himself.

[15] *D.B.* i. 30 b. Except for the 'ad firmam,' only stock formulae are used. The farm of the manor, which the jury thought excessive, was £25—a sum that is no more proportionate to fifteen and three-quarter hides than the earlier valuation of £20. In the other instances cited by Miss Demarest (*ante*, xxxv. 83 f.) I can see no relation between farm and hidage. 'Cherchefelle' (*D.B.* i. 30), it is true, defended itself for thirty-four hides 'ad opus regis'; but that expression meant no more to the Domesday scribes than a dative case and was sometimes used to refer to the geld: compare 'Chingesberie' and 'Wivelescome,' *D.B.* i. 89, and see the case of 'Sclostre,' *D.B.* i. 168. Miss Demarest also reports an instance in which 'the ten hides at which Chippenham had defended itself were reduced to five because the king's ferm had pressed too heavily upon them' (*D.B.* i. 197; *Inq. Com. Cant.*, p. 2); but do not the 'eius' and the 'eum' in this entry refer to the sheriff? As a favour to him, because his farm was too burdensome, the king had cut in half the hidage of the manor. As stated lower in the same entry, five hides had been 'in firmam regis Edwardi,' two had been held by socmen, and three by the same sheriff. Therefore the latter could save whatever geld or service was laid on his own hides and possibly collect for himself what was due from those of the socmen.

was military service and not the *firma noctis*.[16] So far as our Domesday evidence goes, *fyrd* and danegeld were public responsibilities; the *feorm* was not.

With one-half of the proposed equation thus determined, we may now turn to the other half, and consider first the peculiar *consuetudines* of Somersetshire. In about a dozen instances Domesday records a custom of sheep and lambs owed from a baronial to a royal manor. In every case the former had also been in private hands *T.R.E.* and, unlike the ancient demesne of the Crown, had been hidated for geld. Six manors held of King William by his brother, the count of Mortain, are said to owe to the manor of Curry Rivel custom at the rate of one sheep and one lamb for each hide; [17] while another of the count's manors, Cricket St. Thomas, should pay at the same rate six sheep and six lambs, together with one bloom of iron for every freeman, to the manor of South Petherton.[18] On the other hand, we are told that a custom of eighteen sheep from a manor of Alfred 'de Hispania,' assessed at a hide and a half, has been added to the manor of Williton although it did not belong there *T.R.E.*[19] Here is found a different rate, which, however, was followed also in the customs rendered from Oare and Allerford at Carhampton, and in that from Brushford at Dulverton.[20] Still another scheme appears on the bishop of Salisbury's manor of Seaborough, which *T.R.E.* had been two manors, each assessed at one and a half hides, and which had customarily rendered at Crewkerne eighteen sheep with their lambs and a bloom of iron for each freeman.[21]

[16] Round, *Feudal England*, pp. 4 f., and in *Domesday Studies*, i. 120 f. The peculiar obligations of the Dorset boroughs may be explained by comparing them with the custom of Berkshire and of Malmesbury. By contributing at the rate of one mark per ten hides for the support of the house-carls, they were said to 'defend themselves and geld' for all royal service 'exceptis consuetudinibus quae pertinent ad firmam unius noctis' (*D.B.* i. 75); see the table in 'The Aids of the English Boroughs,' *ante*, xxxiv. 458. Thus they were obviously responsible for the ancient food farm, though to what extent is not stated, and besides paid merely small compositions for *fyrd*—not the usual geld.

[17] *D.B.* i. 92.   [18] *D.B.* i. 86, 91 b (Cruche).   [19] *D.B.* i. 86 b, 97 (Selvere).

[20] *D.B.* i. 86 b, 92, 96 b, 97 (Are, Alresford, Brucheford, Bridgeford).

[21] *D.B.* i. 87 b; iv. 143, 477 (Seveberge). Crewkerne was exceptional in that it had originally been a comital manor (Round, in *Vict. Hist. Somerset*, i. 398).

Concerning the nature of these customs the record says nothing; we may only be sure of the reason why they were reported by the juries. With the exception of Williton, where revenue was being enjoyed that did not belong there, the manors in question had been deprived of income that had gone towards making up the farms owed to the king. Fortunately, however, our information is not restricted to the one county. In Devonshire, as well as in Somersetshire, customs owed at royal manors had been withdrawn since the Conquest; and again one of the chief offenders was the count of Mortain. Taking advantage of the parallel entries afforded by the survey of that county, we secure the following testimony:[22]

Rex tenet Ermentone. Asgar tenebat T.R.E. et geldabat pro iii. hidis. . . . Reddit xiii. lib. et x. sol. ad pensum et arsuram. Huic manerio pertinent consuetudines istae. De Ferdendel xxx. den. et consuetudines hundreti.

Rainaldus tenet de comite [Moritoniense] Ferdendelle. Donno tenebat T.R.E. et geldabat pro i. hida. . . . De hoc manerio debentur xxx. den. per consuetudinem in Ermentone manerio regis et consuetudo placitorum, ut dicunt praepositi et homines regis.

Comes habet i. mansionem que vocatur Ferdendella. . . . De hac mansione calumpniantur hundremani et prepositus regis xxx. den. et consuetudinem placitorum ad opus firme Ermtone [*sic*] mansione regis.

Comes de Moritonio habet i. mansionem que vocatur Ferdendel . . . que T.R.E. reddebat per consuetudinem xxx. den. ad Hermentonam mansionem regis et alias consuetudines que ad hundretum pertinent, sed postquam rex Willelmus tenuit Angliam sunt ablate consuetudines predicte a mansione regis.

Evidently Fardle had contributed in two ways to make up the royal farm of £13 10s. from Ermington: through a payment of 30d. for an unnamed purpose and through other customs of the hundred, which—we are grateful to know—were the profits of justice in the hundred court. The royal reeve, who apparently farmed the hundred along with the manor of Ermington, complains that this revenue has been withheld by the count of Mortain, not only at Fardle, but at four other manors of his. No

22 *D.B.* i. 100 b, 105 b; iv. 198, 467.

further information comes from this group, except that the obligations bore no relation to hidage.[23]

However, there was another group.[24]

Rex tenet Alseminstre. Nescitur quot hidae sint ibi, quia nunquam geldavit. . . . Reddit xxvi. lib. ad pensum et arsuram. Huic manerio debentur xv. den. de Cherletone manerio episcopi Constantiensis, et de Honetone manerio comitis Moritoniensis xxx. den., et de Smaurige manerio Radulfi de Pomerei xxx. den., et de Maneberie manerio Willelmi Chevre xxx. den., et de Roverige manerio S. Mariae Rotomagensis xxx. den. Hos denarios iam per plures annos rex non habuit.

Here again appears the payment of 30d.; and finally we are given a hint as to what the sum may represent: [25]

Osbernus de Salceid tenet de rege Patford. . . . Haec terra debet per annum de consuetudine aut i. bovem aut xxx. den. in Tavetone manerio regis.

The same render is found in Cornwall, but alongside other dues, and owed to the church of St. Petrock and not to the king.[26]

Rex tenet Gudiford. Ibi est i. hida et iii. virgatae terrae et geldabat pro una virgata terrae T.R.E. . . . De hoc manerio habebat S. Petrocus T.R.E. per consuetudinem xxx. den. aut i. bovem.

Thus William had offended once, but his brother had offended seven times; for Domesday gives that number of manors, now held by the count of Mortain, from which customary dues of oxen, sheep, and money were being retained.[27]

[23] The assessment varied from one hide to one virgate. The explanation offered by Miss Demarest is that danegeld on a hidage basis had been superimposed upon an older levy of a 'ferm-tax' (ante, xxxviii. 169).

[24] D.B. i. 100. Compare Ashill in Somerset (D.B. i. 92): 'Malger tenet de comite [Moritoniense] Aiselle. . . . Hoc manerium debet reddere in Curi manerio regis xxx. den.' West Putford owed 30d. at Torrington, another royal manor in Devon (D.B. iv. 459).

[25] D.B. i. 116 b; iv. 458. The same custom is recorded as being owed at Tawton from Tawland, held by William the Usher (D.B. i. 117 b), and 10d. likewise from Shapleigh, a manor of Gerald the Chaplain (D.B. i. 117). Compare the 15d. owed at Axminster from Charton. These sums may be fractions of the value of an ox, like the famous *semibos*; but see below, n. 27.

[26] D.B. i. 120 b. We have conflicting reports about this manor. In another place its custom is set down as one ox and seven sheep (D.B. i. 121), which is repeated twice in the Exon Domesday (D.B. iv. 186, 471). A third description (D.B. iv. 104, 470) gives 30d., one ox, and seven sheep.

[27] D.B. i. 121. The payment of 15d. recurs five times; once alongside that of

It will be noticed that these *consuetudines* of Somerset, Devon, and Cornwall had many features in common, but among them was neither apportionment to hidage nor connexion with the *firma noctis*.[28] It is impossible to speak with assurance from such meagre evidence as Domesday affords, but the key to the puzzle may perhaps lie in the following entry concerning another royal manor in Devon, which had belonged to Earl Harold before the Conquest and had gelded for four hides and one furlong: [29]

Mansioni Mollande adiacet a T.R.E. tercius denarius iii. hundretorum, Normoltone et Badentone et Brantone, et tercium animal pascue morarum. Has consuetudines non habuit rex postquam ipse tenuit Angliam.

Here again, as at Ermington, we find two customs lost to the farm of a manor. If for the first we substitute *consuetudines hundreti* and for the second a number of sheep or oxen, we are confronted by a familiar situation. The one peculiarity of the entry lies in the fact that it records only the third penny and the third animal as being owed at Molland. This vill, however, had originally been a comital manor, and it was as successor of Harold that King William had got the earl's third of the revenue from the three hundred courts and of the dues paid for the agistment of animals in the neighbouring moors, a well-known institution of south-western England, traces of which have persisted down to modern times.[30] It seems likely that the customs

---

an ox. There is also one payment of 8*d.*, which reappears under 'Careurga' (*D.B.* iv. 470). Compare *D.B.* i. 120 b: 'De aecclesia S. Germani ablata est i. hida terrae quae reddebat per consuetudinem unam cupam cervisiae et xxx. den. T.R.E. eidem aecclesiae.' See also 'Ecglostudic,' *D.B.* iv. 186.

[28] Among the Somerset manors to which *consuetudines* were owing, Curry Rivel, South Petherton, Williton, and Carhampton each paid a quota of a night's farm. Crewkerne and Dulverton paid ordinary rents, and there is no evidence that either had ever belonged to a food-farm group. There is only one trace of the *firma noctis* in Devon (*D.B.* iv. 80), and none at all in Cornwall.

[29] *D.B.* i. 101; iv. 87, 462.

[30] Reichel in *Vict. Hist. Devon*, i. 398. The moors were apparently considered royal property and pasturage of animals in them, particularly overnight, had to be paid for. The same custom on a small scale existed in every manor where the lord owned a bit of pasture or woodland apart from the common fields; hence the payments for herbage and pannage that frequently occur in Domesday. See Vinogradoff, *English Society*, pp. 85, 289; Miss Neilson, *Customary Rents (Oxford Studies in Social and Legal History*, ii), ch. 3.

of live stock owed at the hundredal manors of the king were pasture rents of the same sort. And if, remembering how forest and moorland have shrunk since the eleventh century, we turn to the map, immediate support is found for that explanation. Thus of the manors under consideration, Ermington lies just south of Dartmoor, while to the north and north-west lie North Tawton and Torrington. South of Exmoor are Molland in Devon and Dulverton in Somerset; to the north Carhampton and Williton. A third group forms a semicircle south and east of the Black Down Hills and extending up into the region of Sedgemoor: Axminster in Devon, and Crewkerne, South Petherton, and Curry Rivel in Somerset. And, finally, Bodmin Moor is named after the vill that in 1086 was the central property of St. Petrock.

This theory, of course, does not admit of proof, but as a guess it seems to me much more probable than that the *consuetudines* were the vestiges of an ancient tax. The apportionment of the customs in Somerset to hidage is a remarkable fact, but one that points to a local rather than to a more general assessment, because even within the one county at least two ratios were employed,[31] and in Devon and Cornwall there was no apportionment at all. Moreover, most of the central manors to which the renders were owed had never been hidated. Thus, even if the *firma noctis* had earlier been a royal impost uniformly laid on thegnland and demesne, it is hard to see how it ever could have been reduced to such fragments as the foregoing. However, as I read the records, we have to do with a number of distinct institutions accidentally brought together by financial arrangements.[32] The royal income from the hundred, including pasture dues and the profits of justice, had been farmed along with the hundredal manor to a reeve. Originally he had perhaps been

[31] There were in particular what may be called the Exmoor rate, prevailing in Dulverton, Carhampton, and Williton, and the Sedgemoor rate used at Curry Rivel and South Petherton.

[32] It should be noticed that the render of iron appears in only three of the dozen cases in which sheep were owed at Devonshire manors. It is possible that mere carelessness led to its omission from most of the entries; or it may have been paid for a quite irrelevant purpose, such as a local iron industry. In the same county blooms of iron appear as rent from a mill at 'Lecheswrde,' from pasture at 'Stantune,' and from villeins at 'Aldedford' (*D.B.* i. 91 b, 92 b).

responsible for a *firma unius noctis,* but the oxen and sheep customarily collected from certain manors should no more be identified with that farm than the forfeitures taken in the hundred court, or any other source of income that he may have had. The proposed equation of the night's farm and the customs of the hundred proves unacceptable.

If we now turn to the other region where, as Miss Demarest has shown, customs similar to those of the south-western counties existed, we find descriptions even more mystifying than those just considered.[33] In proportion to its length, no portion of Domesday offers a greater number of obscure and contradictory passages than that of the strange country *Inter Ripam et Mersham.* Indeed, even the men who condensed the returns seem only partially to have understood them, and to have been quite at a loss for conventional forms under which to organize the materials. Thus, in the survey of the first hundred, it is said that King Edward held the manor of West Derby with six berewicks and then that Ughtred held six manors, but neither group is fully described.[34] Instead, a haphazard list of manors with their owners and renders *T.R.E.* is followed by a very confusing summary of the king's income from the hundred. In the other five hundreds, as if the first attempt at complete analysis had been despaired of, the Domesday account is restricted to much briefer, but scarcely more satisfactory, statements. The holders of land are sometimes called thegns, sometimes drengs, and sometimes freemen.[35] The manors which they held are, in a very faltering way, classified as berewicks of the king's hundredal manor, and no report is made of their respective assessments or values.[36]

---

[33] Miss Demarest, 'Inter Ripam et Mersham,' *ante,* xxxviii. 161 f. Similar units of payment, as Mr. Round has indicated (*Vict. Hist. Hereford,* i. 269), are found along the Welsh border, but there the dues were paid by tenants to their direct lords.

[34] *D.B.* i. 269 b.

[35] Farrer, in *Vict. Hist. Lancashire,* i. 286, n. 2.

[36] For example, Newton hundred; but compare the next hundred (Walintune). It looks as if the scribes had started out with one scheme of classification, but had abandoned it because it entailed too many complications. To the end they seem to have been in doubt whether payment of regular *consuetudines* to the king's manors made berewicks out of the thegns' manors or not.

We thus have an outline of the financial system employed in all six hundreds, together with a detailed description of its working in one of the six. It is made quite clear that the royal revenue from each hundred was farmed, as in many other parts of the kingdom, along with the central manor after which it was named.[37] The constituent elements of each farm, therefore, were principally two: the income from the manor proper, and certain *consuetudines* paid by various thegns who held land within the hundred. Here then are encountered customs of the hundred which may profitably be compared with those of Somerset, Devon, and Cornwall. Unfortunately, however, the explanation of them attempted in the survey of the first hundred is such as almost to defy comprehension.

'All these thegns,' says our record, 'were accustomed to render two ores of pence from each carucate of land,' to perform various duties in connexion with the king's demesne properties, and to pay certain forfeitures and a relief.[38] In the preceding list of lands held in the hundred, moreover, each manor is said to be worth or to render—the expressions are equivalent—a comparatively small sum of money, obviously what it paid into the farm of the central manor. Now, as Miss Demarest shows,[39] in more than half of these cases the payment was at the rate of just two ores, or 32*d.*, the carucate, which Domesday tells us was here the sixth of a hide. This cannot be mere coincidence; the render must have been that described as one of the *consuetudines* of the region.

There were, however, many exceptions; Miss Demarest counts thirteen.[40] In those manors the rate of payment is found, after a little calculation, to have been less than 32*d.* in only three cases; in the rest to be considerably higher. These discrepancies have

[37] Thus: 'Totum manerium Salford cum hundreto reddebat xxxvi. lib. et iv. sol.' 'Totum manerium Lailand cum hundreto reddebat de firma regi xix. lib. et xviii. sol. et ii. den.' *Firma* is used in the same way in four of the six descriptions. It can mean nothing more than an ordinary rent, unless one accepts Miss Demarest's idea that every manor of the royal demesne 'gave its share, either the whole ferm of a day or night or some aliquot part of it' (*ante*, xxxviii. 168).

[38] *D.B.* i. 269 b.   [39] *Ante*, xxxviii. 166.

[40] This number does not include 'Uvetone,' which Domesday rates at one carucate worth 30*d.* As Mr. Farrer suggests, comparison with the other entries would seem to show that this is a clerical error for 32*d.*

caused Mr. Farrer, as an expert on Lancashire antiquities, and Miss Demarest to carry out intricate calculations intended to corroborate their respective explanations of the custom of the two ores.[41] Such complications may, I think, be avoided by understanding the desultory remarks of the Domesday compilers in a slightly different way.

The following entry, which stands first among the descriptions of the thegns' holding, may serve as introduction: 'Dot tenebat Hitune et Torboc. Ibi i. hida quieta est ab omni consuetudine praeter geldum. . . . Valebat xx. sol.' This hide in Huyton and Tarbock, then, is one of those which did not pay the ordinary rate of 16s., and it was quit of all custom except geld, a statement which ought to mean that it was exempt from all the *consuetudines* normally owed by a thegn in the hundred of West Derby. The same comment reappears under Kirkdale; and under Agarmeols is another that must mean the same thing: 'Haec terra quieta fuit praeter geldum.'

At the end of the list then comes this significant passage: 'Omnis haec terra geldabat et xv. maneria nil reddebant nisi geldum regi Edwardo.' But where are all these manors that were quit of all custom save geld? Mr. Farrer thinks that they are those enumerated in the last ten paragraphs, but the latter are at most only eleven.[42] Even if we add to them Huyton and Kirkdale, we get only thirteen—a group, furthermore, that lacks all homogeneity. But Miss Demarest has counted thirteen manors that are alike in not being valued at the normal rate, and examination of her list shows that it includes Formby, which, says Domesday, had been held *T.R.E.* by three thegns for three manors. Here, therefore, are fifteen manors distinct from the rest because

41 Mr. Farrer (p. 277) decides that the custom of 32d. on the carucate was paid in addition to the render recorded in Domesday. He is consequently led to the remarkable conclusion that in most of the manors of the hundred a rent was levied alongside the *consuetudo* at the very same rate. Miss Demarest's theory is that the exceptional renders were the result of a reduction in carucage which, however, had not effected any change in the amounts paid, or at least in the amounts reported in Domesday.

42 Mr. Farrer (pp. 284, n. 11, 285, n. 1) interprets the last sentence in the description of Agarmeols, quoted above, to apply to the rest of the list, but it is plainly a mere variation of the comment made on Kirkdale and on Huyton, placed after instead of before the valuation. Miss Demarest follows Mr. Farrer.

of their unusual renders, six of which are specifically stated to have been exempt from *consuetudines*.[43] Can we hesitate to believe that with characteristic caprice the Domesday scribes omitted similar comments from the other nine?

Putting together the facts thus ascertained, we find that the thegns of West Derby hundred had owed King Edward, in addition to the geld, a custom of two ores from each carucate in their possession; but that in a number of cases this custom, together with others, had been compounded for by the payment of a rent usually assessed at a higher rate than 16s. on the hide. Either the customs, accordingly, or the rents that took their place went towards making up the farm of £26 2s. owed to the king from West Derby. But three hides, adds Domesday, were free, 'quarum census perdonavit teinis qui eas tenebant. Istae reddebant iv. lib. et xiv. sol. et viii. den.' This is a different matter. Not merely customs, but the entire rent from three hides—which three is not said—had been pardoned, so that the farm had lost £4 14s. 8d.[44]

Then ensue other complications. After making certain generalizations about the exempted manors, Domesday adds, by way of postscript, two restrictive paragraphs. Ughtred held Little Crosby and Kirkdale quit of all customs except six, which are now enumerated: 'geldum vero regis sicut homines patriae solvebat.'[45] That is to say, these lands were not free of all custom, as had earlier been implied, but of nearly all; and their liability for geld is reiterated. Lastly comes this passage:

[43] Three of these have already been cited; see the previous note. The other three (North Meols, Halsall, and Hurleton) are supplied by an entry quoted below.

[44] These three hides were taken by Mr. Farrer, and after him by Miss Demarest, to be the three hides included in the last eleven manors in the preceding list, and as a consequence both have difficulty in accounting for the fact that the stated sum corresponds neither with the custom of the two ores, which would come to 48s., nor with the Domesday valuations, the sum of which is £3 7s. 4d. Since, however, no particular three hides are specified, there is no reason why the rent should correspond with either.

[45] Little Crosby is previously stated to be one of six manors held by Ughtred, but is not further described. Kirkdale, however, is one of the fifteen exempted manors that are described. There is no reason for doubting that the geld here mentioned is the ordinary danegeld.

In Otringemele et Herleshala et Hiretun erant iii. hidae quietae a geldo carucatarum terrae et a forisfactura sanguinis et femine violentia. Alias vero consuetudines reddidit omnes.

Another amendment is made. These hides were free of the custom of the two ores, here called 'carucate geld,' and of two forfeitures, but not of the others.[46]

To develop one consistent theory out of such isolated scraps of information as those given us by Domesday seems to me to be out of the question. The glimpses that we obtain of the working of the hundredal organization are sufficient only to show that it embraced much of which we know almost nothing. Danegeld, *fyrd,* justice, and a great deal else seem to have been administered in connexion with the hundred court. Hidation of the country was but one phase of this administration, and it is interesting to see that it could be adopted for local assessments as well as for more general levies. Just what the custom of the two ores may have been is impossible to say, but it seems to have been as peculiar to the country *Inter Ripam et Mersham* as the six-carucate hide, and as distinct from the *firma noctis* as a relief or a burgage rent.

In all England, so far as we know, there was only one other instance of similar dues. The customary payments of sheep in Somerset were likewise proportioned to hidage and made through the hundred organization, but it seems probable that they were pasture rents. The carucate geld may in fact have been something of the same sort. It is well known that cornage or neat-geld was a common incident of drengage tenure in the border counties of the north, but in view of the silence of Domesday with regard to those regions, the original nature of all such customs must probably remain an unsolved mystery.[47]

---

[46] Either the 'three hides' in this entry are a mistake or other lands besides those mentioned were included in the liberty; but this is a matter of no importance. What is significant is the fact that the carucate geld is here clearly differentiated from the ordinary geld; for all three of these manors are set down in the preceding list of lands, all of which are said to have gelded.

[47] See J. Wilson, in *Vict. Hist. Cumberland,* i. 314 f.; G. T. Lapsley, 'Cornage and Drengage,' in *Amer. Hist. Rev.* ix. 670 f.; Miss Neilson, *Customary Rents,* pp. 120 f. If the *consuetudines* of the south-western counties may be connected with cornage,

Finally, if the food farm cannot be detected either in the *consuetudines* of Somerset or in those of Lancashire, there can be no reason for seeing it in the 'hundred pennies,' a phrase that occurs only in the description of Taunton.[48] The well-known list of customs belonging to the bishop includes first the obscure 'borough-right,' then three pleas usually reserved to the Crown, after them the hundred pennies, and lastly the ecclesiastical dues of Peter's pence and church-scot, suit to the episcopal court, and military service.[49]

Since one-third of the *consuetudines hundreti* was regularly called *tertius denarius hundreti,* the hundred pennies enjoyed by the bishop may well have been only the ordinary revenue of the hundred of Taunton. This may have included dues of animals such as were paid to the church of St. Petrock at Bodmin, but evidence in that respect is lacking. On the other hand, there is the possibility that the man who held the hundred, even at this early time, had a prescriptive right to the collection of an aid or private geld. The hundred pennies or hundred silver of the later extents were plainly the same as the *auxilium hundredarii,* information concerning which is quite explicit.[50] In either case the identification of the hundred pennies with the *firma noctis* remains without corroboration.

The evidence at our disposal therefore fails to admit of a definitive theory to explain all the anomalies of Anglo-Saxon finance. The carucate geld of the north-west may have been

---

they would seem to support Mr. Lapsley's contention that the latter was related to pasturage privileges, but the fact that both, as well as the carucate geld, are found in lands where there must have been a considerable substratum of Celtic custom is very striking.

[48] *D.B.* i. 87 b. The hundred pennies seem to be referred to twice in the Exon Domesday (*D.B.* iv. 162). See Round, in *Vict. Hist. Somerset,* i. 404.

[49] *Ibid.* i. 420.

[50] *Domesday of St. Paul's* (Camden Society, 1857), p. 143; *Ramsay Cartulary* (Rolls Series), i. 267. See Miss Neilson, *Customary Rents,* p. 129. Miss Demarest cites as analogous payments certain isolated examples of *census* or *consuetudo* said to be paid into hundreds in the East Anglian counties. It is impossible to determine the exact meaning of these passages without becoming involved in the complex question of the socman in that region. *Census,* however, regularly means rent; payment into the hundred should mean that it was contributed towards the farm paid for some hundred. *Consuetudo,* on the other hand, very commonly refers to forfeitures, and they would naturally be collected in the hundred court.

fundamentally the same as the hundred pennies or the *consuetudines* of the south-west. But whatever they may have been, they were farmed out like other royal revenues, and the rent covering them could be reckoned either in pence or in produce. Connexion between the night's farm and the customs of the hundred was quite fortuitous.

Commendation and Related Problems in Domesday [*]

ON the subject of commendation in pre-Norman England the recognized authority for well over forty years has been Frederick William Maitland. In his classic discussion of the sokemen and *liberi homines* of Domesday [1] he expressed the opinion that 'commendation seems put before us as the slightest bond that there can be between lord and man.' Along with *commendatio*, however, many passages in the survey mention *consuetudo*, *servitium,* and *soca* as other ties that may bind a man to his lord. Thus, 'if the man "withdraws," or gives or sells his land, we often read of the soke "remaining"; we sometimes read of the commendation, the custom, the service "remaining." ' In the 'tangled skein' of such relationships 'the thread that looks as if it would be the easiest to unravel is that which is styled "mere commendation. " ' This act, whatever the words used to describe it, seems not of necessity to have involved any rights over land, although 'Domesday Book seems to assume that in general every owner or holder of land must have had a lord.' True, the ancient law had compelled only landless men to commend themselves, but it had supplied landed men with 'motives for so doing.' In

* Reprinted from *The English Historical Review*, LIX (1944), 289–310. See the note appended to the previous essay. Much the same comment applies here.
1 *Domesday Book and Beyond* (1897), pp. 66–74.

particular, the lord became the warrantor of his man's title to real property. Thus the 'nexus between man and lord' eventually came to involve the matter of landholding. As reported by Domesday, 'the usual practice certainly is that a man who submits or commits himself for "defence" or "protection" shall take his land with him; he "goes with his land" to a lord. Very curious are some of the instances which show how large a liberty men may have enjoyed of taking land wherever they please.'

Passing over for the moment the instances here cited by Maitland, we may note merely his principal conclusions. Freedom of commendation, the right to seek a lord where one chooses, is often associated with freedom of alienation, the right to go with one's land wherever one pleases. 'How large a liberty these phrases accord to lord and man it were hard to tell. . . . At any rate, in one way and another "the commendation" is considered as capable of binding the land. The commended man will be spoken of as holding the land under (*sub*) his lord, if not of (*de*) his lord. In many cases if he sells the land "the commendation will remain to his lord"—by which is meant, not that the vendor will continue to be the man of that lord (for the purpose of the Domesday Inquest this would be a matter of indifference), but that the lord's rights over the land are not destroyed. The purchaser comes to the land and finds the commendation inhering in it.'

Maitland's conclusions, despite the scholarly caution with which they were stated, must appear very remarkable to one who has studied the development of feudal and manorial institutions on the Continent.[2] *Commendatio* was one of many words that came into England with the Norman Conquest—words whose meaning had been well established by long usage among the peoples of the Carolingian Empire. To the Frenchman of the eleventh century, so far as we can tell, commendation was always a personal relationship.[3] Such continued to be vassalage, the

---

[2] See the works referred to in my article, 'The Origin and Significance of Feudalism,' *American Historical Review*, xlvi. (1941), 788 ff.; also Bloch in *The Cambridge Economic History*, i. (1941), ch. vi.

[3] This, of course, is true of the word only when it denotes the reciprocal side of patronage (*patrocinium*). *Commendare* could still be used in the less technical sense of 'entrust,' as when a man placed something in the care of another.

peculiar form of commendation that had come to be associated with the holding of military benefices, or fiefs. Such, too, had ever been the commendation of lesser men, the poverty-stricken or defenceless who, in return for sustenance and protection, had put themselves under the *mund* of a powerful lord. And whatever the ceremony by which the act was accomplished, commendation was regularly for life. More than that, in practice if not in theory, it everywhere tended to become hereditary. The factor that determined whether, in a given case, the law formulated a doctrine of status rather than of contract was likely to depend upon the economic condition of the persons involved. As acutely observed by M. Marc Bloch in this connexion, 'the little man almost always gives away his posterity.'[4]

Our chief concern, however, is not with the Continental institution that might be called *commendatio* but with the English institution that was so described by the Domesday clerks. With regard to that institution we are well informed. The entire body of Anglo-Saxon literature, not merely the great collection of the dooms, testifies to the antiquity of the personal relationship between lord and man.[5] In England, as on the Continent, it appears under two main aspects: the honourable bond between the *hlaford* and his military retainer (*gesið* or *þegn*) and the very different bond between him and his more humble follower (*folgere*), his peasant or household servant. In either case the man's commendation—to adopt the later terminology—could by no means be rescinded at his pleasure. Beginning in the seventh century, royal dooms imposed heavy penalties on those who deserted their lords without leave and carefully defined the conditions under which such leave might be obtained. A drastic law of treason, betrayal of one's lord, was promulgated by Alfred and his successors. By the end of the tenth century, official enactments took for granted that every subject of the king, by compulsion or otherwise, would have a lord. And even contemporaries realized the fact that compulsion could be economic

<hr/>

[4] *Ibid.* i. 255.

[5] Stephenson, 'Feudalism and Its Antecedents in England,' *American Historical Review*, xlviii. (1943), 245 ff. For references to the dooms, see Liebermann, *Gesetze der Angelsachsen*, ii. 410 ff. ('Freizügigkeit'), 423 ff. ('Gefolge'), 427 ff. ('Gefolgschaft'), 506 ff. ('Herrensuche'), 507 ff. ('Herrenverrat'), 577 ff. ('Mannschaftseid').

as well as legal. Thus we find in the *Dialogue of Salomon and Saturn* the remarkable statement that 'a wealthy *eorl* may, according to his own inclination, easily choose a mild lord, perhaps a prince; the poor man has no such choice.' [6]

Maitland, of course, was thoroughly familiar with the Anglo-Saxon law; his conclusions quoted above were drawn solely from the evidence of Domesday. What, precisely, is the character of that evidence? The inquiry is well worth making because Maitland's opinion, through constant reassertion, has tended to become a sort of historical dogma with important bearings upon the subject of manorial organization in pre-Norman England. Vinogradoff, especially, was led to declare that 'the practice of voluntary and personal commendation was not kept up' after the Conquest. 'The lawyers of William the Conqueror started from the principle that mere personal commendation did not amount to a dependence of the land, and that a tenant who could go with his land where he pleased was not part and parcel of the manor in which he paid his dues to a lord.' [7] Similar views have been expressed, not only by Vinogradoff's many disciples, but even by the sceptically inclined William John Corbett: 'In particular they [the new French landlords] were hostile to the system of commendation under which some of the cultivating classes had been free to select and change their lords. As a result commendation was entirely swept away, and the men in every manor, whatsoever their social status, became bound to their lords by an hereditary tie.' [8] So too, in a more recent book, Mr. Jolliffe confidently describes 'the brittleness of Saxon lordship,' which implied only a 'loose bond of commendation,' a connexion between lord and man that in the Confessor's reign was 'personal, revocable, dependent upon the mere right of patronage. . . .' [9]

On venturing into the field of Domesday interpretation one can do no more than follow the trail of John Horace Round. In his original essay on the nature of the great survey [10] that master

---

[6] Lines 389–91 (Grein, *Bibliothek*, iii. pt. 2); quoted by Liebermann, ii. 506.

[7] *English Society in the Eleventh Century* (1908), p. 347; cf. p. 224.

[8] *Cambridge Medieval History*, v. (1929), 513.

[9] *The Constitutional History of Medieval England* (1937), pp. 142–3.

[10] *Feudal England* (1895), pp. 1–146.

of historical criticism gave particular attention to the personal, tenurial, and jurisdictional relationships of men in Cambridge-shire and the neighbouring counties. For such relationships, as he was the first to prove, are brilliantly illuminated by parallel descriptions in the *Inquisitio Comitatus Cantabrigiensis* and the *Inquisitio Eliensis,* as well as in Domesday Book itself. Round's words, however familiar to the student of English constitutional history, must once more be quoted because some of their implications seem to have been generally ignored. After citing two pages of extracts from the pertinent documents, he declared it obvious 'that *dare, vendere,* and *recedere* are all interchangeably used, and that even any two of them (whether they have the conjunction "et" or the disjunction "vel" between them) are identical with any one. . . . Further, the insertion or omission of the phrase "sine" (or "absque") "ejus licentia" is immaterial, it being understood where not expressed. So, too, with the words "cui voluit." ' Thus he clinched an argument that enunciated our recognized canons of Domesday criticism: 'it is neither safe nor legitimate to make general inferences from a single entry'; 'if we find that a rule of interpretation can be established in an overwhelming majority of the cases examined, we are justified, conversely, in claiming that the apparent exceptions may be due to errors in the text.' [11]

In the light of subsequent commentary on Round's deductions, it may be well to emphasize what they originally meant to him. First, Round definitely stated that wherever Domesday attributes to a man the freedom of 'giving,' 'selling,' or 'receding' we must take for granted the phrase 'without his lord's permission.' Secondly, Round must have believed that such formulas had to do with the alienation of land, for he cited as an 'equivalent tenure' the privilege of unrestricted sale guaranteed to the citizens of Bayonne by William of Poitiers.[12] Thirdly, in his ensuing discussion of thegnland and sokeland, Round referred to the *saca et soca et commendatio* reserved by the abbot of Ely with respect to men *qui vendere potuerunt* as rights 'over the holder of land.' [13] In this last connexion it should be par-

[11] *Ibid.* pp. 20–6.   [12] *Ibid.* p. 22, n. 39.   [13] *Ibid.* p. 30.

ticularly noted that no less than four of the passages quoted by Round specifically report the soke as being over men, not land.[14] Besides, I should like to point out a fact which Round failed to mention: that the *potuerunt recedere sine licentia* of one formula is replaced in another by *potuerunt recedere cum terra ad quem dominum voluerunt.*[15]

Maitland, who had of course read and profited by Round's essay, might well have thought it advisable to consider the two following questions. If, in the oft-repeated Domesday formula, the soke remaining to a lord was over the seller of the land, would not, *a fortiori,* the commendation be over him too? And if the Domesday scribe considered it a matter of indifference whether he wrote *vendere terram suam* or *recedere cum terra sua,* and whether he added *cui voluit* or *ad quem dominum voluit,* why should we suppose that any of these phrases implied freedom of commendation? Maitland, it may at once be replied, based his conclusions on the evidence of Domesday as a whole, not merely on the few sections with which Round was particularly concerned. And the latter, strangely enough, appears to have adopted Maitland's opinion in preference to his own when he contributed various chapters on the Domesday survey to *The Victoria History of the Counties of England.* Thus in the series of volumes published between 1900 and 1904 Round,[16] without intimating that he had changed his mind, quoted his previous remarks about *dare, vendere, recedere,* and the like, only to cite with approval the later work of Maitland. The subject, he said, remained obscure—one that 'even the genius of Prof. Maitland' had not entirely elucidated. Yet such phrases as *potuit recedere ad quem dominum voluit* and *potuit ire quo voluit* apparently referred to 'the liberty of personal movement' and implied the act of commendation which occasionally involved rights over land. And in his own translations of Domesday [17] Round care-

---

[14] Namely, 'socha eius' (*I.E.* p. 106); 'socham eorum' (*I.C.C.* p. 3); 'socha de VIII sochemannis' (*D.B.* i. 200); 'saca eorum' (*I.E.* p. 109). The page references for the *I.C.C.* and the *I.E.* are to Hamilton's edition (1876).

[15] *Feudal England,* p. 25; citing *D.B.* i. 195*b,* and *I.C.C.* p. 7.

[16] *V.C.H. Hampshire,* i. 440 ff.; *V.C.H. Surrey,* i. 288; *V.C.H. Hertford,* i. 269; *V.C.H. Essex,* i. 358 ff.; *V.C.H. Bedford,* i. 207–9.

[17] E.g. for Hampshire, Worcestershire, and Essex. The Domesday translations

fully set forth the same interpretation by means of footnotes. Perhaps, therefore, we should not blame Adolphus Ballard for discovering liberty of commendation in what Domesday plainly calls a liberty of sale.[18]

Re-examination of the phraseology employed throughout Domesday and the related documents nevertheless tends, I believe, to justify Round's original contention; the true meaning of the passages in question is freedom of alienation, not freedom of commendation. First of all, let us summarize the facts with regard to the formulas that constantly recur. So far as Cambridgeshire is concerned, Round's essay stated the case admirably, with the single exception that has been noted above. Sometimes, in place of the *cui* (or *quo*) *voluit* after *dare, vendere,* or *recedere,* we find *ad quem voluit* or *ad quem dominum voluit.* That this is merely another instance of variation in language is made clear by parallel entries in Domesday Book and the *Inquisitio Comitatus Cantabrigiensis.* There are at least two good examples in addition to the one quoted by Round:

D.B.	*I.C.C.*
(i. 197*b*—Dullingham) Hanc terram tenuerunt xvi sochemanni et dare et vendere terram suam potuerunt.	(p. 17) De hac terra [unam hidam] tenuerunt viii sochemanni regis Edwardi; potuerunt dare cui voluerunt. . . . Et alii viii tenuerunt unam hidam de comite Algaro; potuerunt dare atque recedere ad alium dominum.
(i. 200—Harlton) De hac terra tenuit Orgar iiii hidas de Heraldo comite et recedere potuit.	(p. 46) De hac terra tenuit Orgarus homo comitis Haraldi iiii hidas; potuit recedere ad quemlibet dominum cum terra sua T.R.E.

---

by other persons in the *V.C.H.* generally lack explanatory footnotes and are often unreliable.

[18] *The Domesday Inquest* (1906), pp. 113, 123–8. Yet Ballard found it impossible to be consistent. On page 124 he translated three consecutive passages from the Hertfordshire Domesday: the first, 'vendere poterat,' as 'had liberty of commendation'; the second, 'vendere poterant,' as 'with liberty of commendation'; the third, 'vendere terram suam poterant,' as 'could sell'!

The same formulas frequently appear in the surveys of the East Anglian counties, together with such obvious equivalents as *potuit ire quo voluit* [*cum terra sua*] and *potuit abire* [*sine licentia*].[19] The surveys of the adjoining counties to the west provide innumerable examples of similar usage. Those of Bedfordshire and Middlesex prefer [*terram suam*] *cui voluit* [*dare et*] *vendere potuit* [*sine licentia*] [*domini sui*], together with the variant [*de terra sua*] *quod voluit facere potuit*. In Hertfordshire and Buckinghamshire the abbreviated form *vendere potuit* is almost always used; while in Gloucestershire, Worcestershire, and Herefordshire the favourite is [*cum terra sua*] *poterat ire quo volebat*. By way of negation we also find in these counties *non poterat separare* (or *vendere* or *mittere*) *ab ecclesia* (or *extra ecclesiam* or *extra manerium*), *nusquam cum ea terra se vertere poterat,* and *non poterat recedere a domino suo* (or *a domino manerii*). Except for Huntingdonshire, Nottinghamshire, Derbyshire, Lincolnshire, and Yorkshire—where all such information is regularly omitted—the surveys of the remaining counties often repeat the formulas that have already been mentioned. But the alternative expression *libere tenuit* was commonly used by the Domesday clerks for three groups of counties: (1) Northamptonshire, Oxfordshire, Warwickshire, and Leicestershire; (2) Staffordshire, Shropshire, and Cheshire; (3) Devon, Somerset, and Dorset. The second of these groups was further characterized by the frequent substitution of [*cum hac terra*] *fuit liber* [*homo*]; [20] the third by the frequent substitution of *pariter* for *libere*.[21] Finally, we have the surveys of Hampshire, Wiltshire, Berkshire, Surrey, Sussex, and Kent, which again

---

[19] The bracketed phrases in these and the following excerpts were optional with the scribe. There are many other variations besides those noted.

[20] But every man described as a *liber homo* did not have the right of 'going with his land where he chose' (Round, *Feudal England*, pp. 34–5; Maitland, *Domesday Book and Beyond*, pp. 104–5; Ballard, *Domesday Inquest*, pp. 112–46).

[21] It would seem that *pariter* and *in paragio* were not exact equivalents of *libere* and *in alodio;* but that tenure in parage was merely one variety of Anglo-Saxon free tenure—one that regularly implied liberty of alienation for a group of co-heirs. The frequency of holdings in parage by numbers of thegns running up to twenty-two in the southern counties makes it probable that holdings by considerable groups of *liberi homines* elsewhere were also in parage, though not so called. See Round, in *V.C.H. Hampshire*, i. 441–2; Vinogradoff, *English Society*, pp. 245–50.

employ the formulas of East Anglia and the adjoining counties, but favour *potuit ire quo voluit,* with the noteworthy variant *tenuit in alodio* (or *alodium*).

The Domesday *alodiarii* have a peculiar interest for one who seeks to understand seignorial arrangements in Saxon England. *Alodium,* we may agree with Vinogradoff,[22] was 'land in the full and free disposition of its owner, the *terra testamentalis* of the charters, the *terra quam vendere potuit cui voluit* of the Domesday Survey.' How, then, could it be held of anybody? Vinogradoff, believing that all such land was properly 'under the direct supremacy of the king,' attributed the phrase *tenuit in alodio de rege Edwardo* to unjustifiable assumption by the 'feudalists of the Survey.' But he had to admit that *alodia* were also recorded as held of 'private persons.' The difficulty is removed, I think, by regarding the *alodiarius* as a proprietor bound to a lord, whether the king or another man, by commendation—a personal tie that did not affect his legal title to the land.[23] In this connexion we have the well-known case of a disputed holding in Hampshire.[24] Chardford, we read, is held of the king by Hugh de Port, and of Hugh by William. Two freemen held it as two manors of King Edward *in alodium*. William also holds of Hugh one and a half virgates in another vill, which were held of Alwin by two freemen, 'sed non fuit alodium.' There, too, Picot holds two and a half virgates of the king. Phitelet held them as a manor of King Edward *in alodium*. This land is claimed by William as belonging to his manor of Chardford, being part of Hugh's fief 'per hereditatem sui antecessoris,' and he supports his claim by the testimony of the better and elder men of the hundred and shire. Picot, to the contrary, presents the testimony of 'villeins, mean people, and reeves,' who are willing to prove by oath or ordeal 'that he who held the land was a freeman and could go with his land where he

[22] *Ibid.* p. 237. Cf. Ballard, *Domesday Inquest,* pp. 140–3; Maitland, *Domesday Book and Beyond,* pp. 153–4.

[23] As Maitland pointed out, the better description of such a tenure was *tenuit sub* rather than *tenuit de,* but consistency can never be expected in Domesday.

[24] *D.B.* i. 44*b.* Cf. Round, in *V.C.H. Hampshire,* i. 439–41. The single instance of *alodiarii* who could not 'recede' (*D.B.* i. 52*b,* 'Cauborne') may properly be regarded as a scribal error.

pleased.' According to my interpretation, the latter phrase means simply that the holder had the right of alienation and so was none other than the Phitelet who held the land *in alodium*— presumably by the allegation of Picot who, whatever the validity of his claim or the character of his witnesses, was in possession of the disputed property when the survey was made.

In the case just described Domesday gives only a few of the pertinent facts and we have no record of the final settlement. It should, however, be remarked that William of Chardford based his claim on a title secured by his lord Hugh from a Saxon predecessor. Similar claims are very common throughout the survey and many of them involve the matter of commendation. For example, let us consider the entry under the manor of Easton in Bedfordshire.[25] There, we are told, one virgate is held by William de Warenne. It was held by Avigi, a man of Aschil, the predecessor of Hugh Beauchamp; and Avigi could sell to whom he pleased. Hugh accordingly claims this land from William and all the jurors of the county testify that the said land does not belong to William. In the same vill Avigi also held a hide and a virgate which he could alienate (*donare*). This land was subsequently granted to him by King William, who by writ commended (*commendavit*)[26] him to Ralph Taillebosc so that he should serve the latter as long as he lived. But on the day of his death he declared himself the man of William de Warenne, and 'therefore William took possession of this land.' Both instances show that, at least from the Norman point of view, a man's commendation might determine the allocation of his land to a particular manor.

Without attempting to answer all the questions raised by these entries, we may profitably glance at the greatest of the early Norman records inspired by seignorial interest—the *Inquisitio Eliensis*. That famous document lists not only the lands of which the abbey enjoyed actual possession *T.R.W.* but also those to

---

[25] *D.B.* i. 211*b*.

[26] This is one of the few instances in Domesday when the word is used in its less technical sense. Cf. *ibid.* i. 163, 'Berchelai': 'Hos Willelmus comes commendavit preposito de Berchelai ut eorum haberet servitium.' Also i. 160*b*, 'Otendone': 'Has duas terras habet uxor Rogerii de rege in commendatione'—i.e. in custody by royal grant.

which, even if they were possessed by other tenants-in-chief, it laid claim. Within the latter category we may distinguish three varieties of holdings: (1) demesne lands of the monks *T.R.E.;* (2) lands which, though granted to various persons *T.R.E.*, could not lawfully be alienated from the Church; and (3) lands held *T.R.E.* by the abbot's men with power of alienation. So far as the present inquiry is concerned, the first two varieties are of no especial importance.[27] To illustrate the third it may be well to quote a few examples:

(Harlton, Cambridgeshire.) [28] In Herlestona tenet Picotus vicecomes unam hidam et dimidiam sub abbate Ely iussu regis, et quidam sochemanus tenuit eam de predicto abbate et in tempore regis Aedwardi potuit recedere cum terra sua absque eius licentia, sed semper remansit socha eius in ecclesia sancte Aedeldrede, ut hundredum testantur.

(Shelford.) [29] Ipse Hardwinus adhuc tenet in ista villa 1 hidam et dimidiam et vi acras quas tenuerunt vi sochemani de socha abbatis Ely, de quibus non potuerunt dare nec recedere nisi iii virgas absque eius licentia. Et si alias vendidissent iii virgas, predictus abbas semper socham habuit T.R.E.

(Eversden.) [30] Hugo de Berners 1 hidam. . . . Hanc terram tenuit Aedwi sub abbate Ely; [potuit dare vel vendere sine licentia eius, sed socam habuit Algarus comes].

(Hanningfield, Essex.) [31] Episcopus Baiocensis tenet ii hidas terre. . . . Has hidas preocupavit Turoldus de Rouecestre et abbacia de Ely calumpniatur. Hanc terram tenuerunt duo liberi homines et hundredum testatur quod ipsi libere tenebant terram suam, et tantummodo erant commendati abbati de Ely.

[27] Brief mention may be made of the fact that the second variety of holdings, as shown by Round (*Feudal England,* pp. 28–35), was for some reason called thegnland in the Ely records. Elsewhere the word seems regularly to have designated land that had been granted to thegns, as by the famous charters of the bishop of Worcester. The Ely thegnlands, on the contrary, were often held by sokemen. Whatever the explanation of the local usage, we may be sure that the legal title to the properties in question lay with the Church and not with the actual possessors. See Ballard, *Domesday Inquest,* pp. 129–30; Vinogradoff, *English Society,* pp. 370–2.

[28] *I.E.* p. 106. Parallel passages in Round, *Feudal England,* p. 22.

[29] *I.E.* p. 107. Parallel passages in Round, *Feudal England,* p. 18.

[30] *I.E.* p. 110. Cf. *D.B.* i. 199; *I.C.C.* pp. 84–5. The bracketed passage, like those below, follows the superior Domesday text.

[31] *I.E.* p. 128. Cf. *D.B.* ii. 25.

(Banham, Norfolk.) [32] Et in eadem villa III liberi homines de dimidia carucata terre et v acris, de quibus abbas non habebat nisi commendationem. Soca in Kanincghala regis. . . . [Hos liberos homines tenuit Rafridus, post Willelmus de Scohies, et abbas saisivit eos propter commendationem suam.]

(Soham, Suffolk.) [33] In Saham unus liber homo commendatus Sancte Aedeldrede. . . . Soca in Hoxa. [Hoc tenuit Robertus Malet de rege; abbas derationavit et eam Robertus de eo tenet.]

The first two of the foregoing excerpts are typical of many which the *Inquisitio Eliensis* summarizes as follows: 'Illi qui hanc terram tenuerunt de soca T.R.E. vendere potuerunt, sed saca et soca et commendatio et servitium semper remanebant ecclesie Ely.' [34] The holders of what the record thus terms sokeland as distinguished from thegnland [35] enjoyed the legal power of alienation, but the abbot continued to have their commendation, soke, and service. Of these which was the decisive factor in determining manorial allegiance *T.R.W.*? The last four excerpts provide a positive answer; it was commendation. We should not be misled by such phrases as *tantummodo commendati* and *non habebat nisi commendationem*.[36] They obviously mean that the men in question were bound to the abbot by mere commendation—*commendatio sine soca,* as the survey often puts it. Round clearly stated the case in his original essay: as a seignorial right, *commendatio* 'took precedence' over *soca,* and *servitium* of some kind went with the former as a matter of course.[37] At Banham, 'by virtue of his commendation,' the abbot took possession of

[32] *I.E.* p. 133. Cf. *D.B.* ii. 213*b*.
[33] *I.E.* p. 156. Cf. *D.B.* ii. 385. Hoxne was the chief manor of the bishop of Thetford.
[34] *I.E.* pp. 121–2. The same statement is repeated several times in the following pages.
[35] See below, after n. 75.
[36] As, presumably, Maitland was when he declared that commendation was at most a slight bond—a verdict in which he has been followed by practically all subsequent writers. Occasional entries (*D.B.* i. 142*b*, 'Standone'; ii. 40*b*, 'Roinges'; ii. 59, 'Cingehala') to the effect that some man 'was so free that he could go where he pleased with his sake and soke,' or 'could sell his land with sake and soke,' hardly imply what Maitland supposed (*Domesday Book and Beyond*, p. 100). The meaning is probably that the soke did not 'remain' to his lord. See the remarks of Mr. Salzman in *V.C.H. Cambridge*, i. 348.
[37] *Feudal England*, pp. 30–4.

three freemen whose soke belonged to the king. He proved that
the freeman of Soham, whose soke lay in the bishop's hundred,
was his *commendatus* and so forced Robert Malet to hold the
freeman's property of the abbey. Numerous instances of the
same principle enforced against other barons occur throughout
the *Inquisitio Eliensis*.[38]

Analogous evidence may, indeed, be readily found in many
sections of Domesday. Thus, with regard to Count Alan's manors
of Ingham and Stalham in Norfolk, we are told that 'Robert
Malet claims these two manors because Edric his predecessor had
the mere commendation of those who held them *T.R.E.*; he says
that his father was seized of them, and this is attested by Roger
Bigot.'[39] At Stalham Roger is himself reported as holding a
freeman, together with one at Horsey, of whom 'Ailwin his
predecessor did not have even the commendation *T.R.E.*; and
yet he claims them as of his fief by the king's gift because the
said Ailwin had the commendation of them *T.R.W.*'[40] The
entries just cited bring out another point of considerable importance in Domesday criticism: the fact that a baron's predecessor had the commendation of certain men was in itself no proof
of the baron's legal title. He also had to adduce a royal grant to
the men in question; for it often happened that the holdings of
a particular thegn would be distributed by the Conqueror
among several of his vassals.

We are thus logically brought to the lists of *invasiones* appended to the surveys of Essex, Norfolk, and Suffolk. Although
in two of the three cases the *invasiones* are specifically described
as *super regem,* the comments of many well-known scholars
would lead us to suppose that they were *super liberos homines
patriae*.[41] The Domesday description of East Anglia, we are told,
reveals manors in the making—new seignorial organizations to

[38] E.g. pp. 109 ff., 141 ff.

[39] *D.B.* ii. 148*b*. Cf. ii. 153*b* (Kilverstone, held by Robert Malet): 'Hic iacet I
sochemannus regis, LX acrarum terrae, unde suus antecessor habuit commendationem tantum, et terram clamat de dono regis.'

[40] *Ibid.*, ii. 187*b*.

[41] This, of course, is the thesis defended by the many disciples of Vinogradoff.
See, for example, D. C. Douglas, in *Oxford Studies in Social and Legal History*, ix.
(1927), 110–11: 'A comparison between the *T.R.E.* and the *T.R.W.* entries of

which Norman conquerors ruthlessly annexed groups of freemen and so brought about their legal and economic degradation.
Such activities there may have been in the years following 1066,
but I fail to detect any evidence of them in the Domesday
invasiones. Let us turn, for example, to the record for Suffolk.[42]
In all, nineteen cases are listed, with a supplement concerning
three disputes between the bishop of Bayeux and the mother of
Robert Malet. Of the nineteen the first six deal with encroach-
ments by Richard son of Count Gilbert. He holds four freemen
in Bradley 'of whom his predecessor [Wisgar] never had the
commendation.' He holds a freeman in Groton who had been
seized by one of his men and who, the hundred testifies, never
belonged to Wisgar. He holds three properties to which Wisgar's
title was at least doubtful.[43] He has taken a freeman in Cavendish
who was commended to Earl Harold (and who should therefore
be in the royal demesne). The next three entries are concerned
with a free woman and certain other holdings of St. Edmund's,
of which the abbey has been despoiled by William de Partenai.
Then come reports about four properties that for one reason or
another are in the king's hands. And lastly, we hear of five *invasiones* much like those attributed to Richard son of Count
Gilbert.[44]

In only one case are we left to speculate about the reason for
the entry: 'In Lauen Albericus de Ver tenet III liberos Ulwini
antecessoris Alberici de Ver commendatos tantum, in soca
Sancti Edmundi. . . .' Perhaps Aubrey was withholding the
abbot's soke; perhaps he had never obtained the king's grant of

Domesday itself shows everywhere the encroachment upon the liberties of the
peasant class. The possession of the vague superiorities involved in commendation
is, for instance, very frequently made the starting-point for an assertion of the
full rights involved in complete lordship. Men are everywhere making manors
by the simple process of creating a few acres of demesne land and arranging round
it the obligations of the free peasantry.' Cf. the remarks of Charles Johnson and
J. H. Round in *V.C.H. Norfolk,* ii. (1906), 30.

42 *D.B.* ii. 447*b* ff.

43 Note especially that Richard took over two *invasiones* from his predecessor:
one by Wisgar himself and one by a man of his.

44 These include one by a man of St. Edmund's who is now in the king's mercy,
and four by royal barons who have taken freemen commended to Earl Harold or
to others not their predecessors.

these particular freemen. To argue that he had no right to them because they had been 'only commended' to his predecessor is to ignore the clear testimony of countless Domesday entries—not merely those cited above but those relating to virtually every fief in East Anglia. Nor are we justified in supposing that the king's interest in the native population was that of a benevolent protector. A dispassionate reading of Domesday Book must lead to the conclusion that William regarded the land and its cultivators like any other Norman-French *seigneur*. In my opinion, there is no evidence to warrant Ballard's contention that 'a man who held freely, or was at liberty to commend himself, *T.R.E.*, was said to hold of the king'—i.e. to enjoy the mere dependence of subject upon sovereign.[45] As Maitland declared, the manors of Edward the Confessor do not 'stand out in bold relief'; they resembled other manors before the Conquest.[46] And I would add that, according to Domesday, the king's *commendati* were quite like those of other lords; there was nothing peculiarly royal in the relationship of Edward, Harold, and William to their own men.

It is hardly necessary to take up in detail the lists of *invasiones* for Essex and Norfolk. Like the list for Suffolk, they report numerous seizures by barons of what rightfully belonged either to the fiefs of others or to the king's demesne.[47] And not infrequently, as in the case of Aubrey quoted above, they neglect to state why the baronial occupation was illegal. Little care, obviously, was taken in the composition of the lists. The entries are often jumbled or incomplete, and a good many *clamores* like

[45] *Domesday Inquest*, p. 120.

[46] *Domesday Book and Beyond*, p. 65.

[47] It is worth remarking that in Norfolk three *invasiones* are attributed to St. Edmund's abbey (*D.B.* ii. 275*b*): land at Runcton held by five freemen *T.R.E.*, which the abbot claims by the king's gift; twelve acres at Shelfanger held *T.R.E.* by a freeman commended to Algar, concerning which the abbot's steward offers proof that he acted in ignorance; and one freeman at Winfarthing who was annexed to the land of St. Edmund's by permission of the abbot's reeve. Cf. the Essex complaint (*ibid*. ii. 103) that the monks of Canterbury have added to their manor of Lawling a hide that was held by three freemen *T.R.E.*; also the interesting statement (*ibid*. ii. 100) that a freeman with forty acres who belonged to Havering *T.R.E.* is now held by St. Peter of Westminster 'because of his own will he came to the abbey and did not render customary service at Havering.'

those included are left scattered throughout the preceding folios. We hear, for example, that Roger of Poitou, succeeding Norman son of Tancred, has added to the manor of Buxhall in Suffolk three freemen whose commendation and soke *T.R.E.* belonged to the king. Furthermore, Roger holds one of King Edward's freemen whom Norman took without warrant from the manor of Thorney.[48] In Norfolk the same Roger holds the manor of Tunstead, to which *T.R.W.* were added six freemen of whom St. Benet had enjoyed the soke, and of one commendation also.[49] To at least this one, as I understand the record, the Church must therefore have a just claim. Finally, in this connexion, we may note the entry for the royal manor of Bergholt in Suffolk. *T.R.E.* it was held by Earl Harold while two other manors, Bentley and Shotley, were held by his brother Guert. But *T.R.W.* these two manors were financially subordinated to Bergholt, and with them considerable property that had belonged neither to Harold nor to Guert. At Shotley *T.R.E.* there were 210 sokemen; now there are 119. And of the latter Harold had the commendation of four, Guert of two; 'all the others were commended to other barons *T.R.E.*,' including the predecessors of Robert Malet and Robert son of Wimarc.[50] Even the king, it appears, could encroach upon the rights of his honourable vassals.

The Domesday evidence thus far examined, if my interpretation is correct, fails to support the belief that commendation in Saxon England was a slight and fragile bond, which could be made and unmade by a lord's men at will but which could some-

---

[48] *D.B.* ii. 350b.

[49] *Ibid.* ii. 244.

[50] *Ibid.* ii. 287. The first volume of Domesday, with its greater condensation, provides fewer examples; but here are two from Hertfordshire (*ibid.* i. 137, 137b). Count Eustace holds Tring, which was held by Engelric *T.R.E.* After the Conquest he attached to this manor three sokemen: two who had been the men of Osulf and one who had been the man of the abbot of Ramsey. Robert d'Ouilly, and of him Ralph Basset, holds Tiscote, which was held *T.R.E.* by five sokemen with power of alienation: two men of Brictric, two men of Osulf, and one man of Edmer. None of them belonged to Wigot, predecessor of Robert; but 'one of them redeemed his land from King William for eight ounces of gold and afterwards turned for protection to Wigot, as the men of the hundred testify.' The later commendation of the one was thus used as an excuse for securing the land of all five. Cf. Round in *V.C.H. Hertford,* i. 268–9; Maitland, *Domesday Book and Beyond,* pp. 137–8.

how become inherent in land.[51] And the rest of the evidence that
has been adduced in this connexion by Maitland and others is
of much the same kind.[52] Occasionally, of course, Domesday does
refer to some Englishman as having sought a new lord 'after
William arrived in the country.' Three instances of such action
have already been noted—all of them allegations by tenants-in-
chief who wished to justify their claims to particular properties.[53] In the first Avigi seems to have violated a royal precept by
commending himself to William de Warenne rather than to
Ralph Taillebosc; in the second the anonymous holder is said
to have come voluntarily to Westminster Abbey instead of serving at the royal manor of Havering where he belonged *T.R.E.;*
in the third a certain sokeman, after redeeming his land from the
Conqueror, turned for protection to Wigot the predecessor of
Robert d'Ouilly. Out of many similar instances two may be
given here. In Surrey Walter of Douai holds two hides of the
king, he says. But the men of the hundred testify that they have
seen no proof of such royal grant, declaring merely 'that a certain freeman who held this land with power of alienation placed

[51] It is a well-known fact that the right to a man's commendation *T.R.E.* could
not only be transferred from one lord to another but could even be partitioned
among co-heirs (Maitland, *Domesday Book and Beyond,* p. 74; Ballard, *Domesday
Inquest,* pp. 126–8). How could this have been true unless commendation was considered both valuable and permanent? By a fraction of a man's commendation
Domesday of course means a fraction of the rent or service derived from him; for
a man was not supposed to have more than one lord. A single instance has indeed
been cited to the contrary (*D.B.* i. 133, 'Daceworde'): 'Hanc terram tenuit Aluric
Blac de abbate Westmonasteriensi T.R.E. nec poterat eam ab aecclesia separare,
ut hundredum testatur, sed pro aliis terris homo Stigandi archiepiscopi fuit.' But
the point is merely that the abbey claims Datchworth as its own property, although it was previously held by a man of Archbishop Stigand and is now held
by a man of Archbishop Lanfranc. See Maitland, *Domesday Book and Beyond,*
p. 74.

[52] The passage chiefly relied on by Maitland (*ibid.* p. 72) to prove his thesis with
regard to liberty of commendation is the one following (*D.B.* i. 72, 'Hiwi'): 'Toti
emit eam T.R.E. de aecclesia Malmesberiensi ad etatem trium hominum et infra
hoc terminum poterat ire cum ea ad quem vellet dominum.' This, however, I take
to mean simply that within the given term Toti could alienate the property. Maitland and Vinogradoff (*English Society,* pp. 347–8) also cite various entries dealing
with commendation T.R.W. (see the accompanying discussion) and with commendation in certain boroughs (see immediately below).

[53] See above, p. 165; n. 47; n. 50.

himself in the hands of Walter for the sake of defence.'[54] In Berkshire *T.R.E.* the sons of Eliert held Linford of the abbot of Abingdon and had no right to alienate it from the Church. Nevertheless, they commended themselves to Walter Gifford and he now holds the manor of the abbot—apparently because the latter has made good his claim to the land.[55]

Throughout these entries the presumption is strong that, even when the Norman Conquest brought new lords to most of the native population, the small proprietor was not allowed to be the man of whomsoever he pleased. Together with his land, he was assigned to a particular baron, or else he was adjudged to be a demesne tenant of the king. There is no denying that William's seizure and regrant of English estates constituted a political and social revolution of far-reaching importance; it is not so certain that all his acts marked a radical departure from the established law of the old monarchy. A noteworthy story in the description of Suffolk indicates that, with respect to commendation, King William may well have accepted a precedent from King Edward. The latter, we read, first outlawed Edric of Laxfield; then became reconciled with him, restoring his lands and granting by writ and seal that he might again receive any of the freemen previously commended to him. And so the problem of which men actually returned caused trouble for the

[54] *D.B.* i. 36: 'Hoc autem testantur quod quidam liber homo hanc terram tenens et quo vellet abire valens sumisit se in manu Walterii pro defensione sui.' The difficulties encountered by Round and others in understanding entries like this are largely removed, I think, by distinguishing between commendation and the right of alienation. In each of the following cases a reference can thus be seen to a *commendatus* who still retained title to his land. *D.B.* ii. 40b: 'Brumleiam tenuit Alwinus libere pro uno manerio et . . . erat commendatus Wisgaro potens terram suam vendere.' *Ibid.* ii. 47, 'Eiland': '. . . quidam liber homo erat commendatus Roberto . . . et poterat ire quo vellet.' *Ibid.* ii. 71b, 'Phenge': '. . . tenuit liber homo pro manerio . . . qui T.R.W. effectus est homo antecessoris Ranulfi Piperelli sed terram suam sibi non dedit.' *Ibid.* ii. 74b, 'Peresteda': '. . . 1 liber homo semper tenet v acras et fuit commendatus antecessori Ranulfi sed cum terra sua posset ire quo vellet.'

[55] *Ibid.* i. 59: 'Walterius Gifard tenet de abbate Linford. T.R.E. tenuerunt filii Eliert de abbate nec poterant alias abire absque licentia, et tamen commendaverunt se Walterio sine abbatis precepto.' The record is plainly intended to show that Walter's possession depends on the unlawful commendation of Eliert's sons, who seem to have disappeared from the scene.

Domesday commissioners when they had to adjudicate the claims of Robert Malet, Edric's successor.[56]

Before attempting further comment on seignorial organization in pre-Norman England, however, let us see what Domesday has to report about some of the boroughs. In an earlier work [57] I have advanced the thesis that most Anglo-Saxon burgesses were not sharply distinguished, either economically or legally, from the population of the surrounding countryside. Re-examination of the evidence regarding commendation in the boroughs tends, I think, to strengthen that thesis. In most cases Domesday merely lists the properties that were held *T.R.E.* by the king, the earl, and other persons, with a few desultory remarks about special privileges enjoyed by the holders. Such properties—normally stated to be so many *burgenses, hagae, domus,* or *mansiones*—are sometimes recorded under the borough, sometimes under the particular manors to which they were attached.[58] It is only occasionally that the Domesday formulas mention or imply the commendation of the tenants. For example, we are told that at Hertford 146 burgesses were in the soke of King Edward. Of them various 'houses' are now held by barons; but 'King William has eighteen other burgesses who were the men of Earl Harold and Earl Lewin.' [59] So, too, at Buckingham the bishop of Coutances is said to have three burgesses whom Wulfward held; but eight other barons are said to have burgesses who were the men of six lords *T.R.E.*[60]

Casual statements of this kind would lead us to believe that Anglo-Saxon burgesses, like rural tenants, were regularly commended to the manorial lords who got their rents and other services. There may have been exceptions to the rule. Already

---

[56] *D.B.* ii. 310b: 'Postea conciliatus est regi Edwardo et concessit ei terram suam; dedit etiam brevem et sigillum ut quicumque de suis liberis commendatis hominibus ad eum vellent redire suo concessu redirent.' Cf. the entry for Peasenhall, *ibid.* ii. 313.

[57] *Borough and Town* (1933), ch. iv.

[58] See Ballard's complete enumeration in his *Domesday Boroughs* (1904), ch. ii.

[59] *D.B.* i. 132.

[60] *Ibid.* i. 143. Cf. Guildford (i. 30): 'Si homo eius in villa delinquit,' etc.; also Ballard, 'An Eleventh-Century Inquisition of St. Augustine's, Canterbury,' in *British Academy Records of Social and Economic History*, iv. (1920), 9: '. . . isti habuerunt in civitate consuetudines suas de suis hominibus.'

under King Edward a few boroughs were beginning to feel the influence of commercial revival; a few groups of burgesses were enjoying a foretaste of the new municipal liberty that rejected all claims based on commendation.[61] But with regard to that relationship the descriptions of the Cinque Ports, York, and the recently founded French boroughs have nothing to tell us. And the carelessly phrased entries for Norwich, Thetford, and Stamford do not, in my opinion, prove that the local burgesses had any peculiar freedom of commendation. I quote the three passages in question:

(Norwich.) [62] In Noruic erant T.R.E. MCCCXX burgenses. Quorum unus erat ita dominicus regis ut non posset recedere nec homagium facere sine licentia ipsius. . . . De MCCXXXVIII habebant rex et comes socam et sacam et consuetudinem, et super L habebat Stigandus socam et sacam et comendationem, et super XXXII habebat Heroldus socam et sacam et comendationem. Quorum unus erat ita ei dominicus ut non posset recedere nec homagium facere sine licentia ipsius.

(Thetford.) [63] In burgo autem erant DCCCCXLIII burgenses T.R.E.; de his habebat rex omnem consuetudinem. De istis hominibus erant XXXVI ita dominice regis Edwardi ut non possent esse homines cuiuslibet sine licentia regis. Alii omnes poterant esse homines cuiuslibet, sed semper tamen consuetudo regis remanebat praeter herigete.

(Stamford.) [64] In his custodiis sunt LXXVII mansiones sochemanorum qui habent terras suas in dominio et qui petunt dominos ubi volunt; super quos rex nichil aliud habet nisi emendationem forisfacturae eorum et heriete et theloneum.

The first of these passages, it seems to me, contains a typical Domesday error. The three items, being obviously intended to

---

[61] Hemmeon, *Burgage Tenure in England* (1914), pp. 45–50; Stephenson, *Borough and Town*, pp. 88–96, 107–19.

[62] *D.B.* ii. 116.

[63] *Ibid.* ii. 118b. Cf. the bit of information about Ipswich that happened to be included in the description of a Suffolk fief (*ibid.* ii. 402). Robert, father of Sweyn, had forty-one burgesses there with sake and soke and commendation. Fifteen of them are now dead; so he has lost their commendation, but has kept the sake and soke (presumably over their tenements). Other customs belong to the king.

[64] *Ibid.* i. 336b. Cf. the freedom of sale and departure enjoyed by the men of Torksey, who were more highly privileged than those of Lincoln in being exempt from toll (*ibid.* i. 337). Note, too, that the burgesses of York were not liable for heriot (*ibid.* i. 298b).

account for the 1320 burgesses, should all read 'socam et sacam et consuetudinem.' Thus corrected, the statement can be taken to mean that only one of the Norwich burgesses was the king's own man, and only one was Earl Harold's. As to who held the rest of the burgesses Domesday is silent; presumably, as in other such cases, they belonged to various magnates of the shire. The Thetford entry can be interpreted in the same way: 36 of the 943 burgesses were men of the king; 907 were men of other lords, to whom as a matter of course their heriots had to be paid. Nor do we have to find a contradiction in the custom of the Stamford sokemen. The allegation that they held their lands in demesne and sought lords where they wished looks like a clumsy variation of the familiar 'they could go with their lands where they pleased.' That is to say, they had liberty of alienation, but were commended to the king who was therefore entitled to their heriots.[65]

The third of the passages just quoted may also serve to introduce what little has to be said here of soke, sokemen, and sokeland. Except in a few particulars, Maitland's fine exposition of the subject remains authoritative. As he pointed out, we must ordinarily take the *soca* of Domesday to be the precise equivalent of *saca et soca*.[66] Either expression could be used to designate the judicial power of one man over another—if not the right to

[65] For citation of the principal sources dealing with the Anglo-Saxon heriot, see Liebermann, *Gesetze*, ii. 500–2 ('Heergewäte'). In spite of certain ambiguous passages in Domesday, I think we must agree with Liebermann that the heriot was essentially a payment, often of horses and arms, due to a lord on the death of his man. Canute's doom says as much and then proceeds to specify the amounts owed by earls, king's thegns, and other thegns (II Canute, 70–1). The same conclusion is supported by the Domesday entry for Berkshire (*D.B.* i. 56b): 'Tainus vel miles regis dominicus moriens pro relevamento dimittebat regi omnia arma sua et equum 1 cum sella, alium sine sella.' Cf. the entries for Herefordshire (*ibid.* i. 179, 181) compared with that for Shrewsbury (*ibid.* i. 252): 'Burgensis qui in dominio erat regis cum moriebatur habebat rex x solidos de relevamento.' The remarks about thegns in Derbyshire, Nottinghamshire, Yorkshire, and Lincolnshire (*ibid.* i. 280b, 298b, 376), and about *alodiarii* in Kent (*ibid.* i. 1), should probably be interpreted as referring to the king's own men.

[66] *Domesday Book and Beyond*, p. 84; Vinogradoff, *English Society*, p. 122; Stenton, in *Publications of the Lincoln Record Society*, xix. (1924), introd. p. xxxvii. Ballard's denial of this equation (*Domesday Inquest*, pp. 84, 117–9) cannot be sustained, though he was right in holding that the sokeman should not be defined as a man subject to sake and soke; see immediately below.

hold a separate court, at least the right to appropriate various profits of justice. Soke, as we find it in the charters of the Anglo-Saxon kings, could normally be exercised by the grantee 'over his own lands and over his own men.' [67] In other words, he could claim particular fines and forfeitures from a culprit either because the latter was commended to him or because the offence took place on his property. Through exceptional privilege, furthermore, a great ecclesiastic or high official might obtain soke over a considerable territory, such as a hundred, that would otherwise be within the king's jurisdiction. The endless complications arising from the grant and regrant of such authority are familiar to all students of Domesday and call for no lengthy discussion in these pages. A few words, however, should be said about the constant association in Domesday of soke and commendation.

The *Inquisitio Eliensis* declares that the abbey, aside from portions of its demesne, has been despoiled of two kinds of land: 'thegnland,' which could not lawfully be alienated from the Church, and 'sokeland,' which could lawfully be alienated by the holders on condition that their soke, commendation, and service remained to the Church. [68] The terminology can hardly be explained as more than the vagary of a local scribe. The holders of either thegnland or sokeland could be either sokemen or freemen (*liberi homines*); and while the latter term could refer to thegns, the former could not. Parallel entries prove that the same person might be called first a sokeman and then a freeman. [69] In the East Anglian counties the landholder who

[67] Vinogradoff, *English Society*, p. 129.
[68] See above, pp. 165-8. Note also the distinction in the *placitum* of 1072-5 quoted by Round, *Feudal England*, pp. 30 ff. The holders of 'thegnland' owed a variety of agricultural services 'et ubicunque forsfecerint abbas forsfacturam habebit, et de illis similiter qui in eorum terram forsfecerint.' That is to say—though the text is somewhat corrupt—the abbot had soke over the land as well as over the men. In the case of 'sokeland,' on the contrary, it was the soke over the holder, together with his commendation and service, that remained to the Church. Mr. Salzman (in *V.C.H.* Cambridge, i. 348) has noted this fact and finds it hard to understand; for, he believes, commendation was only a 'slight bond' and jurisdictional rights were usually 'bound up with tenures.'
[69] Round, *Feudal England*, p. 32, and in *V.C.H. Essex*, i. 351-8, 460; Johnson, in *V.C.H. Norfolk*, ii. 28; Salzman, in *V.C.H. Cambridge*, i. 347.

does not have the right of alienation is almost invariably styled a sokeman rather than a freeman; in Cambridgeshire, on the contrary, most sokemen are said to have that right.[70] What, then, are we to conclude regarding a sokeman when nothing is said of his tenure, as in Lincolnshire? Shall we agree with Vinogradoff that he was a man 'who could not recede with his land' and therefore a sort of '*colonus* ascribed to the glebe'?[71] Or shall we agree with Mr. Stenton that he was essentially a small proprietor characterized by an independence inherited from Danish conquerors?[72]

We may, at any rate, agree with both scholars in describing the sokeman as a peasant, a two-hundred man rather than a thegn.[73] Besides, it seems to me, we must definitely reject the idea that the sokeman was thus named because of some peculiar status with regard to judicial soke. Maitland long ago indicated the great objection to that argument.[74] 'Very often the lord has not the soke over his sokemen. This may seem a paradox, but it is true. We make it clearer by saying that you may have a man who is your man and who is a sokeman, but yet you have no soke over him; his soke "lies" or "is rendered" elsewhere.' And more recently Mr. Stenton has re-emphasized the same fact. As he points out, the word 'sokeman' is not a Danish importation. It is pure English, meaning by derivation a man bound to 'seek' some one else, especially a man bound to do suit and service to a lord.[75] Inevitably, therefore, we are reminded of Aethelstan's doom about *hlafordsocn* and wonder whether a freeman who sought a lord might not at one time have been called his sokeman.[76] Whatever may be thought of that, *sochemannus* in

[70] See especially the figures given by Ballard, *Domesday Inquest*, pp. 113–22.
[71] *English Society*, p. 435.
[72] *Lincoln Record Society*, xix. introd. pp. xx–xxvi. But cf. his earlier essay, 'Types of Manorial Structure in the Northern Danelaw,' *Oxford Studies in Social and Legal History*, ii. (1910), 43, where the view expressed resembles that of Vinogradoff.
[73] On these two classes, see my article in *The American Historical Review*, xlviii. 245 ff.
[74] *Domesday Book and Beyond*, p. 105.
[75] *Lincoln Record Society*, xix. introd. p. xxvi.
[76] III Aethelstan, 4; cf. Liebermann, *Gesetze*, ii. 506 ('Herrensuche'). Maitland (*Domesday Book and Beyond*, pp. 85–6) noted this obvious connexion, only to re-

Domesday is plainly a term based on long usage and devoid of technical import. William's clerks, for all they knew, might just as well have written *geneat,* with or without a Latin ending.[77]

The sokeland of Domesday (*terra de soca* or merely *soca*) was defined by Maitland as a 'territory in which the lord's rights are, or have been, of a judiciary rather than of a proprietary kind.' [78] And this idea was developed by Vinogradoff into one of his favourite theses. 'The opposition between the manor, as the economic unit of an estate, and the soke, as the jurisdictional union encircling the manor and often consisting of places scattered around it, is one of the important results of the different modes by which lords acquired rights of superiority over their dependents.' The sokeland, it is true, appears only in 'the Scandinavian north'; but 'the Saxon south,' he believed, had earlier 'gone through approximately the same stages,' 'had already arrived in the eleventh century at the goal reached by the northern districts only in the twelfth and thirteenth centuries.'[79] The manorialization of England had thus been largely effected through seignorial exploitation of delegated authority from the king, of the royal rights that came to be known as sake and soke. However convincing Vinogradoff's thesis has seemed to many historians, it contains a serious flaw. The flaw lies, not in the statement that a territory placed under seignorial sake and soke was 'a piece of public administration broken off from the hundred,' but in the assumption that the sokeland of Domesday was such a territory. The fact is that the lord of the manor to which a particular sokeland was attached might not have soke (i.e. judicial rights) over it at all.[80]

---

mark that, 'although we do not know what English word was represented by *commendatio,* still there is no distinction more emphatically drawn by Domesday Book than that between *commendatio* and *soca.*' The ordinary Domesday *soca,* however, is not the *socn* in which we are here interested. Mr. Stenton has shown (*ante,* xxxvii. 230 ff.) that the Anglo-Saxon equivalent of *commendatio* was probably *manraeden,* Latinized as *manreda.*

[77] As has frequently been remarked, Bracton's derivation of *sochemannus* from *socus,* a ploughshare, was reasonable enough though quite erroneous.

[78] *Domesday Book and Beyond,* p. 115.

[79] *English Society,* pp. 130–1, 134, 320–2.

[80] Since the clerks who drew up the survey of Lincolnshire and the neighbouring counties constantly used *soca* in two different senses (to denote either sokeland

We must therefore, it seems to me, prefer Ballard's definition of the manorial sokeland as 'a tenement having no demesne and inhabited by sokemen'[81]—a definition that has received good support from the careful research of Mr. Stenton.[82] The tie that bound the sokeland to the manor was hardly the judicial authority of the lord; nor was it necessarily his ownership of the soil.[83] What could it have been except the commendation of the sokemen? Once that relationship is acknowledged to have been firm and lasting rather than slight and temporary, seignorial organization under the Anglo-Saxon monarchy appears in a new light. In particular, it becomes easier to understand how a cluster of sokelands could constitute a great estate in north-eastern England throughout the whole period from the tenth to the

---

or sake and soke), the exact meaning of a good many passages remains obscure. But in some cases there can be no doubt. For example, *D.B.* i. 288*b*: 'Terra Walterii de Aincurt. . . . Manerium. In Horingeham . . . Walterius habet in dominio ii carucatas. . . . Soca. In Fiscartune habet Walterius dimidiam carucatam terrae ad geldum, unde soca pertinet ad Sudwelle. . . . Soca. In Mortune habet Walterius dimidiam carucatam terrae ad geldum, de qua soca pertinet ad Sudwelle. . . . Soca. In Farnesfeld habet Walterius ii bovatas terrae ad geldum. Una est in soca de Sudwelle et alia regis sed tamen ad hundredum de Sudwelle pertinet.' Note that the customary service owed from sokeland included labour (*ibid.* i. 280*b*): 'Super socam quae iacet ad Cliftune debet habere comes terciam partem omnium consuetudinum et operum.' Southwell was a manor belonging to the archbishop of York.

[81] *Domesday Inquest*, p. 60. The true import of Ballard's argument seems not to have been appreciated by Vinogradoff (*English Society*, p. 122, n. 1).

[82] 'Types of Manorial Structure,' pp. 17–20; though he still insists (p. 21) that 'by derivation the essential feature of sokeland consists in its subjection to the judiciary power of its lord.' Cf. his remarks in *V.C.H. Derby*, i. (1905), 312–3: '. . . it is clear that the power of jurisdiction was no inseparable part of the lord's rights over his sokeland, which included labour services and the payment of customary dues, and a number of vague rights comprised under the Domesday formula of "commendation." '

[83] I do not see how, in the absence of positive information, we can be sure that the Lincolnshire sokeman's land was regularly his own. Mr. Stenton's argument in support of that hypothesis, it seems to me, rests on somewhat dubious evidence. Although the Ely sokelands, according to the *Inquisitio Eliensis*, were lands which the holders could alienate from the Church, the services of typical sokemen in the Danelaw appear to have resembled those of the men who held the Ely thegnlands. But for reasons stated herewith the distinction need not be considered of prime importance.

fourteenth century.[84] And with less emphasis placed on an alleged depression of the agricultural class, there is less need of proving that sokemen were commonly descended from Danish warriors.[85] But how, it will at once be asked, could the mere commendation of a free proprietor permanently affect the tenure of his land? To give a just answer to this question is to understand the dominant economy of the age.

We are so used to buying and selling all commodities in a cash market it is hard for us to imagine a society that lacked any such market, except for a few articles of small value. In Saxon England, assuredly, there was no flourishing real-estate business. Throughout western Europe, for at least five hundred years, land had been thought of as a means of subsistence, not as a source of profit. Why should the owner of a few acres wish to sell them? If a man had no land, his immediate concern was to obtain some on the best possible terms. If he was fortunate enough to have land, he would above all else want to keep it and hand it on to his children. In those days, however, protection was almost as essential to the little man as food; so, unless he was already taken care of, he would commend himself to a neighbouring magnate. To secure what he needed he might be compelled to cede his property to the lord and henceforth to hold it as a benefice. Or he might be able to retain the legal title by agreeing to perform specific service. Practically, the difference to him would be slight; for in either case he would be assured of livelihood, and his descendants would normally expect the continuance of the same arrangement. We are thus led to conclude that, although a common freeman of the year 1066 might legally alienate his land, he would hardly dream of doing so. To all

---

[84] *Ibid.* pp. 67–86.

[85] In this connexion I should like to see some good evidence cited as to prevalent social conditions among the Vikings of the ninth century, and as to how those conditions were affected by settlement in conquered lands. I am impressed, not so much by Mr. Stenton's acceptance of the traditional theory, as by his frank acknowledgement that the Scandinavian place-names of the Danelaw tend to prove the opposite (*ibid.* pp. 90–1). Since conjecture is in order, I may ask: What is to prevent our supposing that the Danish chieftains who seized eastern England brought over tribal followers and conferred on them portions of the occupied territory?

intents and purposes his mode of life was determined by status rather than by contract.[86]

If the foregoing argument is well founded, the distinction between manorial tenants who could sell and those who could not was a matter of secondary importance in the eleventh century. Both kinds of men are listed in Domesday, along with lands and domestic animals, as so much seignorial property. The chief concern of William's commissioners was to determine where every acre of his kingdom lay—to whose fief it belonged unless it was actually in the king's hands.[87] The uniform system of feudal tenures, together with the Norman-French aristocracy, was of course new. Yet, according to Domesday, the holdings of the Conqueror's barons were aggregations of manors that had earlier been possessed by thegns of King Edward. In spite of all that has been written to the contrary, I believe that Domesday gives an essentially true picture of society and institutions under the Anglo-Saxon monarchy. I cannot see that the jurors of 1086 were guilty of falsification when they described pre-Norman England as covered with *maneria,* however the latter were then designated. This is not to suppose a manorial system that remained unchanged from the days of Alfred to those of Henry III and without varying as between East Anglia and Wessex. It is merely to register the conviction that, so far as we may judge from Domesday, the agrarian organization of the English countryside was not materially affected by the introduction of feudalism properly so called.[88]

The Norman Conquest, to be sure, brought a stricter definition of the seignorial holding. Being construed as a component unit in a fief, the manor became, if it had not already been so, a centre of judicial administration through a hallmoot. The

[86] That eleventh-century society was dominated by a money economy, as suggested by Mr. Stenton and developed by Mr. Douglas (see their works cited above), seems to me an exaggeration. I prefer Mr. Stenton's later thesis that the truly revolutionary change came only towards the end of the twelfth century; see *The American Historical Review,* xlviii. 264-5, commenting on *The First Century of English Feudalism* (1932).

[87] I accept, of course, Mr. Galbraith's convincing demonstration (*ante,* lvii. 161 ff.).

[88] For my own ideas on the subject, see *The American Historical Review,* xlviii. 245 ff.

lesser men attached to it were generally called villeins and eventually declared unfree. Peasants of a higher order were commonly described as sokemen, whether free or bond.[89] All tenants who were not members of the feudal aristocracy were permanently subjected to manorial control, unless they could prove their title to an exceptional variety of freeholding. Yet all such definition, in my opinion, was only the legal expression of long-established facts.[90] Precisely how they had come to be determined we shall never know. A good deal, however, may yet be learned about the twelfth-century manor and its relation to that of Domesday. Let us hope that someone with access to the relevant sources will give the problem the attention it deserves. If the present study has contributed to that end, its purpose will have been fully attained.

[89] Until the subject of socage tenure under the Norman kings has been more thoroughly studied, there can be little profit in speculation as to how it was developed from the tenures of the sokemen described in Domesday. Vinogradoff's explanation of villein socage as something peculiar to the ancient demesne of the Crown is not convincing; as he admits, bond sokemen are often found on manors outside the ancient demesne (*Villainage in England*, pp. 113–25, 196–203). Glanvill and Bracton tell us almost nothing about free socage except that it differed in certain respects from military tenure. The problem that remains unsolved is how land held in free socage might be alienated. Could it be sold? If B holding of A enfeoffed C, would the latter hold of B or of A, and under what conditions? On the labour service and other obligations of sokemen in the twelfth century, see the essays of Stenton and Douglas, *Oxford Studies in Social and Legal History*, ii. 22–7; ix. 88–9; also Ballard, *Domesday Inquest*, pp. 157–64. What I wrote in 1926 about sokemen and their obligations for tallage (*Mélanges d'histoire offerts à Henri Pirenne*, ii. 472–3) should be amended in the light of the facts presented above.

[90] No attempt can be made here to discuss the continuity of seignorial arrangements in general. It may, however, be pointed out that commendation was by no means 'swept away' by the Norman Conquest. On the contrary, it was retained as an essential feature of the manorial system. Any peasant, on being admitted to a tenement, was normally required to swear fealty to the lord of the manor and according to an ancient formula. Such *fidelitas*—or *homagium* as it was sometimes improperly called—not only resembled but actually was the *manraeden* or *commendatio* of the earlier period.

Notes on the Composition

and Interpretation of

Domesday Book *

AMONG the statistical records of the Middle Ages Domesday
Book is outstanding. Its very name testifies to the fact that,
concerning the tenure of land and appurtenant rights, it was
long recognized as authoritative—as providing what amounted
to final judgments.[1] Even after Domesday Book had lost its original value for the decision of cases in the courts of law, it remained
very famous. Like Magna Carta and Westminster Abbey, it
was a great national monument, acclaimed in exuberant language by generation after generation of scholars. Within the
last half-century or so, to be sure, all such opinions have come to
be reconsidered by historians trained in more exacting schools.
Yet we of today, while preferring sound appraisal to mere
eulogy, continue to regard Domesday Book as a marvelous
record—in many respects the finest of the mediaeval period.

It is not my intention to sketch here, in any detail, the development of Domesday criticism; but only to introduce a few notes,
of a rather technical character, as a supplement to what has most
recently been published on the subject. All students of Domes-

* Reprinted from *Speculum*, XXII (1947), 1–15.
[1] *Dialogus de Scaccario,* I, xvi.

day Book will already know that modern re-examination of it began with Round's essay of 1895.[2] He showed that, to understand Domesday Book, we must compare it with various contemporary, or nearly contemporary, documents—especially the *Inquisitio Comitatus Cantabrigiensis*,[3] which gives us in a corrupt manuscript of the twelfth century the original returns from the one county of Cambridge. From this document, together with the related *Inquisitio Eliensis,* we may see that Domesday Book was made by condensing and rearranging, tenant by tenant, the verdicts of local juries that had first been set down, hundred by hundred, in each shire. So great a task, Round declared, could not have been completed within the year 1086—though Volume II of Domesday Book, as we now have it, seems to reveal a first effort of condensation made at an early date. Volume I was actually a later and better compilation; yet even it is filled with mistakes, as collation with the *Inquisitio Comitatus Cantabrigiensis* and *Inquisitio Eliensis* clearly proves. For the scholarly historian, accordingly, there can be no alternative to impugning "the sacrosanct status of the Great Survey." [4]

In the main, I am convinced, Round's criticism of Domesday Book can never be superseded; for it resulted from a masterly study of the only evidence we are ever likely to have. Until recently, indeed, scarcely any amendment to it had been proposed by leading authorities on the institutional history of England. Then, in 1942, Mr. V. H. Galbraith published an article that suggested a major change in Round's thesis.[5] Domesday Book, Mr. Galbraith believes, was immediately based, not on the original returns of 1086, but on a series of local surveys drawn up by the royal commissioners within their respective jurisdictions. Such local surveys, now represented by the Exeter Book and Little Domesday,[6] systematically rearranged the material of the returns for each county in order to describe, first, the royal demesne and then, one after the other, the baronial

---

[2] *Feudal England,* pp. 1–146.

[3] Edited, together with the *Inquisitio Eliensis,* by N. E. S. A. Hamilton (London, 1876); referred to in the following notes as *I.C.C.*

[4] *Feudal England,* p. 20.

[5] *English Historical Review,* LVII (1942), 161–77.

[6] See below, notes 14–15.

fiefs. The principal object of the Domesday inquest could not therefore have been, as Round and his many followers supposed, to provide a basis for the reassessment of the royal geld or to record other items of Anglo-Saxon custom. That Domesday Book had an essentially feudal character was no accident resulting from some kind of official afterthought. On the contrary, it was the logical product of the Conqueror's inquest, and there is no good reason for doubting that it was actually written, even as we now have it, in the year 1086.

Differing from Mr. Galbraith, Mr. D. C. Douglas has re-affirmed his belief that "the investigations made in 1086" were of a "multifarious nature." The king "desired to know all that men could tell him about his new kingdom, its inhabitants, its wealth, its provincial customs, its tax-paying ability." Mr. Douglas admits that the Domesday inquest resulted in the composition of "feudal summaries" for various groups of counties, but considers it "hazardous to assert" that the original returns were not also used for Domesday Book, as they were for a number of local compilations.[7] The issue thus drawn is quite plain, and has to do, not merely with the way in which Domesday Book was composed, but with the governing motive behind the inquest of 1086. My own opinion, as already stated,[8] is that Mr. Galbraith has the better of the argument. In what follows I hope to show how considerable independent study has tended to support his thesis, and how acceptance of that thesis may lead to certain changes of Domesday interpretation.

It is remarkable that the question of the Domesday circuits has remained about as vague as Eyton left it nearly seventy years ago.[9] From internal evidence, almost none of which he thought needful to specify, he decided in favor of nine circuits. The groups of counties thus distinguished held to the order of the Domesday descriptions except in two cases, each apparently the result of later displacement. Naturally enough from the geo-

---

[7] *The Domesday Monachorum of Christ Church Canterbury* (Royal Historical Society, 1944), pp. 19 ff.

[8] *American Historical Review*, LI (1945), 104–5; cf. *Eng. Hist. Rev.*, LIX (1944), 309, n. 2.

[9] R. W. Eyton, "Notes on Domesday," *Transactions of the Shropshire Archaeological and Natural History Society*, I (1878), 99 ff.

graphical point of view, he said, Oxfordshire had come to be put
between Buckinghamshire and Gloucestershire, though it really
belonged with Northamptonshire, Leicestershire, and Warwickshire; Huntingdonshire between Cambridgeshire and
Bedfordshire, though it really belonged with Derbyshire, Nottinghamshire, Yorkshire, and Lincolnshire.[10] Eyton, for one
writing in the pre-Round era, had a good knowledge of Domesday Book, and his hint on the circuits of 1086 deserved to be
more thoroughly followed up than it was.

Adolphus Ballard had only this to say on the subject: [11]

There can be no doubt about the south-eastern and south-western
circuits: the language of the Shropshire and Cheshire Commissioners
is almost the same as that of the Commissioners for Gloucester,
Worcester, and Hereford, and it would seem better to group these
five shires in a western circuit, extending along the Welsh border;
Stafford appears to fall naturally with Warwick, Northampton,
Leicester, and Oxford, into a West-Midland circuit, also of five
counties. There is a marked similarity between the Hertford and
Cambridge and Bedford surveys, and an East-Midland circuit could
be formed by grouping these three shires with Middlesex and Buckingham. In this way Mr. Eyton's nine circuits could be reduced to
seven.

But what are the marked similarities of language to which
Ballard referred—whether or not we attribute them to the
Domesday commissioners? In that connection something more
definite can surely be said about the internal evidence of Domesday Book.

Leaving to one side the question of the Domesday circuits,
which is only a matter of inference, let us concentrate on the
language of the record itself, which is a matter of direct
observation.[12] By that test alone, whatever the basis of Eyton's

[10] For Eyton's groups see below, n. 13.

[11] *The Domesday Inquest* (London, 1906), pp. 12–13. The few remarks made by
other historians about the Domesday circuits add little if anything to what was
said by Eyton and Ballard; e.g., J. Tait, *Victoria County History of Shropshire,*
I (1908), 304.

[12] Comparison of the Domesday entries dealing with Anglo-Saxon tenure, and
supposedly with commendation, first led me to make a tentative classification of
the county surveys (see *Eng. Hist. Rev.,* LIX, 294 ff.). It was only later that I read
Mr. Galbraith's article, and still later that I looked up Eyton's essay of 1878. To

or Ballard's classification, the county surveys seem to fall into at least seven groups, as indicated in the following table.[13]

Group   Counties

   I.   Kent (1), Sussex (2), Surrey (3), Hampshire (4), Berkshire (5)

  II.   Wiltshire (6), Dorsetshire (7), Somersetshire (8), Devonshire (9), Cornwall (10)

 III.   Middlesex (11), Hertford (12), Buckingham (13), Cambridge (18), Bedford (20)

 IV.   Oxford (14), Northampton (21), Leicester (22), Warwick (23)

  V.   Gloucester (15), Worcester (16), Hereford (17), Stafford (24), Shropshire (25), Cheshire (26)

 VI.   Huntingdon (19), Derby (27), Nottingham (28), Rutland (29), York (30), Lincoln (31)

VII.   Essex (32), Norfolk (33), Suffolk (34)

Group VII may be quickly disposed of. It is determined by the so-called Little Domesday, the peculiar survey of the three East Anglian counties published as Volume II of Domesday Book.[14] Group II is also easy to identify; for its content is the same as that of the famous Exeter Book, from which the Domesday description of the southwestern counties was unquestionably derived.[15] Precisely what sort of revision was thus involved, however, remains uncertain even in Mr. Galbraith's article. How were the entries in the Exeter Book "systematically altered to the standard Winchester *formulae*"?[16] Did such alteration bring them into complete agreement with Domesday entries for the adjoining regions, or was some of the old technical language allowed to

---

me, as presumably to many others, the assertion that Domesday Book was composed with a view to reassessing the geld never seemed convincing; for no such reassessment was ever made.

13 The numbers in parentheses indicate the order of the county surveys in Domesday Book. I add a concordance to show how Eyton's groups (small Roman numerals) differ from those cited here: I = i; II = ii; III = iii + v (Cambridgeshire and Bedfordshire); IV = vi; V = iv + vii (Staffordshire, Shropshire, and Cheshire); VI = viii; VII = ix.

14 See especially Round, *Feudal England*, pp. 98 ff., 139 ff. Certain characteristics of this group, along with those of other groups, are shown in the accompanying table below.

15 This was definitely proved, as Mr. Galbraith reminds us, by F. H. Baring, *Eng. Hist. Rev.*, XXVII (1912), 309 ff.

16 *Ibid.*, LVII, 165–66.

stand? An answer can best be given by citing specific examples, and for the present purpose a fairly literal translation should be quite adequate.

First, a typical entry in the Exeter Book for Somersetshire:[17]

Serlo has a manor (*mansionem*) which is called Lovington and which three thegns, Aelmarus and Siricus and a woman Alfilla, held in parage (*pariter*) on the day King Edward was alive and dead. It rendered geld (*reddidit gildum*) for 6 hides. Those can be cultivated by (*possunt arare*) 8 plows. Of the aforesaid hides Aelmarus had 4 hides and Siricus 1 and Alfilla another hide. These lands Serlo holds as a manor. Of them Serlo has 3 hides minus 5 acres, and 2 plows in demesne; and the villeins [have] 2 hides and 5 acres, and 6 plows. And [there are] 8 villeins and 9 bordars and 2 slaves; and 16 beasts (*animalia*) and 1 riding-horse and 11 swine and 80 sheep; and a mill that renders 10s. annually; and a wood 4 furlongs in length and 2 in breadth; and 40 acres of meadow. And it is worth 100s. annually, and when Serlo received it 6l.

Second, the description of the same manor in Domesday Book:[18]

Serlo himself holds Lovington. Three thegns held it *T.R.E.* as three manors and it gelded (*geldabat*) for 6 hides. There is land for 8 plows. In demesne there are 2 plows, and [there are] 2 slaves and 8 villeins and 9 bordars with 6 plows. In it a mill renders 10s., and [there are] 40 acres of meadow; [also] a wood 4 furlongs in length and 2 furlongs in breadth. Previously [it was worth] 6l.; now 100s.

Third, a typical Domesday entry for Sussex:[19]

The same Reinbert holds Mountfield of the count. Goda held it *T.R.E.* and could go where she pleased (*quo voluit ire potuit*). Then as now it acquitted itself (*se defendebat*) for 1 hide. There is land for 8 plows; in demesne there are 2, and 9 villeins with 2 cotters have 6 plows. In it [there are] 8 acres of meadow, and woods [producing] 10 swine. *T.R.E.* it was worth 3l., and afterwards 20s.; now 4l.

Comparison of the second with the first description of Loving-ton clearly shows how the Domesday compilers obtained the condensation upon which they were obviously intent. They discarded some of the older formulas in favor of briefer ones and they omitted not only repetitious phrases but also a considerable

[17] *Domesday Book*, IV, 419.   [18] *Ibid.*, I, 98.   [19] *Ibid.*, I, 18b.

189

amount of detailed information. Within the last category may be noted (1) the names of the "three thegns"; (2) the statement that their tenure was in parage; (3) the distribution among them of the six hides; (4) the division of the six hides between Serlo and his villeins; and (5) the statistics regarding livestock. These omissions are not without significance. Although we, as students of eleventh-century England, might gladly dispense with estimated numbers of pigs, sheep, and cows for the year 1086, we should like to know infinitely more about institutions, customs, and persons *T.R.E.* than even the Exeter Book gives us. To the Domesday compilers, apparently, such information was of minor importance, for they deleted large sections of it. The broader problem of interpretation thus suggested, however, must be left for discussion below; in the meantime let us return to a comparison of the quoted texts.

As the Domesday entry for Lovington may be taken to exemplify those in our Group II of the county surveys, that for Mountfield may be taken to exemplify those in Group I. Comparing the two, we readily see that they resemble each other in specifying (1) the present holder (. . . *tenet* . . .); (2) the holder *T.R.E.;* [20] (3) the estimate of plowlands; (4) the division of plowteams between the lord and his manorial tenants; (5) the classification of such tenants; (6) the acreage of meadow; and (7) the annual income from the manor earlier and now (1086). The entries for Mountfield and Lovington, however, have at least two outstanding differences: the use, with regard to hidage, of the formula *se defendebat* instead of *geldabat;* [21] and, with regard to woodland, of the formula *silva . . . porcis* [22] instead of an estimated size by length and breadth. In the one case, it is worth noting, the formula *geldabat* was substituted for *reddidit gildum* by the Domesday compilers; in the other they held to the

[20] The position of this statement towards the beginning of the entry, with or without further comment on the nature of the tenure, deserves special attention.

[21] In the present case, as in many of those cited below, allowance must be made for exceptions. Thus, *se defendebat* can occasionally be found in the surveys of the southwestern counties, and *geldabat* in those of the southeastern counties, especially in that of Hampshire.

[22] The extension *silva de . . . porcis de pasnagio* proves that the formula was intended to estimate annual income in terms of pigs.

formula of the Exeter Book. In neither did they follow the example set, if it had been set, in Group I. The "Winchester standard" thus seems to have permitted considerable variation of language. But before attempting further generalization, we might do well to examine other groups of county surveys.

Beginning with Eyton, all authorities have agreed that in 1086 a particular circuit was established for the northern counties of York, Lincoln, Rutland, Derby, Nottingham, and Huntingdon. Anyone who looks through Domesday Book can, indeed, hardly escape the conclusion that the surveys of these six counties have common peculiarities. Our Group VI is characterized, first, by a series of marginal notations (M for *manerium*, B for *berewicha*, and S for *socha*);[23] secondly, by the introductory formula *In . . . habet . . . . . . car' ad geldum;*[24] thirdly, by the consistent omission of all data regarding tenure *T.R.E.*, even when the name of the Anglo-Saxon tenant is given. Besides, most of the surveys in this group are preceded by a rather peculiar statement of local customs, and three of them are followed by a list of *clamores*.[25] As in Group II, manorial woodland is regularly described by giving its dimensions. In other matters of routine Group VI agrees with the common practice of the southern counties, except that it includes the only estimates of seignorial tallage to be found in Domesday Book.[26]

Turning back to the south, we encounter what Ballard described as the East Midland circuit—our Group III, which embraces the counties of Middlesex, Hertford, Buckingham, Cambridge, and Bedford. Like Group VI, it has marginal notations, though much less frequent;[27] like Group I, it uses

[23] See the references provided by my article, *Eng. Hist. Rev.*, LIX, 305 ff.

[24] The prevalence in Huntingdonshire of a different system of assessment led to the substitution of *hid'* for *car'*; see Round, *Feudal England*, pp. 44 ff., 69 ff.

[25] *D.B.*, I, 208, 375 (Huntingdon, York, and Lincoln). Similar lists in the Exeter Book were omitted from the final compilation; so the only comparable entries are the *invasiones* for Essex, Norfolk, and Suffolk (*ibid.*, II, 99b, 273b, 447b).

[26] Such estimates, though regular in Lincolnshire, appear outside it only once in Yorkshire and once in Nottinghamshire; see my paper, "The Seignorial Tallage in England," *Mélanges d'histoire offerts à Henri Pirenne* (Brussels, 1926), pp. 6 ff. It may also be noted that for estimating plowlands the formula *hanc terram possunt arare . . .* of the Exeter Book constantly reappears in the survey of Yorkshire.

[27] Only an occasional M or, more rarely, a T (for *terra*).

the formulas *se defendebat* and *silva . . . porcis;* unlike both, it records the holder of the manor *T.R.E.* at the close of the entry, along with some one of many remarks about his tenure.[28] More or less peculiar to this group are also the following expressions: *et adhuc . . . carucae possunt esse* (or *fieri*),[29] *pratum . . . car'*,[30] *pastura ad pecuniam villae,* and *in totis valentiis valet. . . .*

For no definite reason, except that he wanted a West Midland circuit of five counties, Ballard added Stafford to the four chosen by Eyton.[31] But the language of the surveys, I think, rather justifies the inclusion in our Group IV of merely Oxford, Northampton, Warwick, and Leicester. This group, on comparison with Group III, will be found to have in common with it only one of the features mentioned in the preceding paragraph—the designation of the holder *T.R.E.* at the end of the manorial description. Further remarks about the nature of his tenure are almost invariably reduced to the simple formula *libere tenuit.*[32] Woodland is estimated by giving its length and breadth, and assessment to the royal geld is regularly indicated by the statement that in the manor (*ibi*) are so many hides.[33]

[28] The surveys of Cambridgeshire and Bedfordshire are remarkable for the meaningless variation of formulas involving *vendere, donare, recedere,* etc., that was long ago described by Round. On the other hand, the surveys of Middlesex, Hertfordshire, and Bedfordshire tend to prefer the simpler *vendere potuit;* see *Eng. Hist. Rev.,* LIX, 292 ff., and the citations there made. Eyton's separation of the two former from the three latter counties was presumably based on no more than the order given in Domesday Book.

[29] A similar modification of the standard formula concerning plowlands occasionally reappears in the surveys of Gloucestershire and other western counties.

[30] I.e., meadow enough to provide hay for so many plowteams.

[31] Perhaps Ballard was acquainted with Eyton's amendment to his former statement, in *Domesday Studies: Staffordshire Survey* (London, 1881). There he asserted that Staffordshire, Warwickshire, and Oxfordshire belonged in the same circuit because the surveys of those three counties differed in certain respects from the surveys of the adjacent counties. But to support his opinion Eyton presented only a few superficial observations, largely vitiated by the fact that he misunderstood the Domesday system of assessment in hides.

[32] That a man did not thus hold, however, was stated in a variety of ways.

[33] This is the ordinary usage; other formulas were also used, particularly . . . *tenet . . . hid' in. . . .* On the frequent appearance of the carucate in the Leicestershire formulas see Round, *Feudal England,* pp. 82 ff. And cf. his remarks about the "intruding manors" of the Northamptonshire survey in *The Victoria County*

We are thus left with the counties of Gloucester, Worcester, Hereford, Stafford, Shropshire, and Cheshire, whose surveys may be combined to form Group v because they all differed from those of Group iv in two outstanding respects: the designation of the Anglo-Saxon holder towards the beginning of the entry rather than at its end and the use of peculiar language to describe his tenure. For the counties of Gloucester, Worcester, and Hereford, as for those of the southeast, the common formula is *potuit ire quo voluit;* for Staffordshire, Shropshire, and Cheshire it is *liber erat cum hac terra, tenuit ut liber homo,* or some such phrase.[34] Otherwise, in spite of numerous local variations, Groups v and iv resemble each other closely—especially in the formulas dealing with woodland[35] and with assessment to the geld.

Our comparative study, summarized in the accompanying table, thus shows how, by the test of language alone, the county surveys of Domesday Book tend to fall into distinct groups. Despite the general acceptance of a central plan, no major formula is consistently used even throughout Volume I, nor is any single order of such formulas. This is a striking fact, which naturally leads us to indulge in speculation as to how it came about. We may be sure that in 1086 royal commissioners went from county to county and there interrogated juries from each hundred. Yet before we, with Ballard, ascribe the linguistic variations of Domesday Book to the commissioners, we ought to know (1) what questions were put by them; (2) what sort of answers were given by the jurors; (3) how and by whom such answers were recorded; (4) what other materials were used in drawing up the so-called original returns; and (5) how these returns were affected by the work of compilation. In all five cases we sadly lack positive evidence.

With regard to the questions put by the commissioners, it

History of Northampton, I (1902), 269 ff. For reasons already given, local differences of geld assessment do not affect our classification of the surveys in seven groups.

[34] In separating the three former counties from the three latter, Eyton implied that he was influenced merely by the grouping of the surveys in Domesday Book.

[35] By way of exception, we find in Shropshire the regular use of the formula *silva . . . porcis incrassandis;* cf. n. 22 above.

CHARACTERISTICS OF DOMESDAY SURVEYS	GROUPS						
	I	II	III	IV	V	VI	VII
M, S, etc. in margin			x			x	
Se defendit pro . . . hid'	x		x				
Geldat pro . . . hid'		x					
Ibi . . . hid' [ad geldum]				x	x		
In . . . . . . tenet . . . *car' ad geldum*						x	
Silva . . . porcis	x		x				x
Silva . . . . . . long' *et . . . . . . lat'*		x		x	x	x	
Holder *T.R.E.* towards beginning	x	x			x	x	x
Holder *T.R.E.* at end				x	x		
Data on tenure *T.R.E.**	2, 5	2, 3, 6	1	3	2, 4		1

* 1. *Potuit vendere, dare, recedere,* etc.
  2. *Potuit ire quo voluit* (or *facere quod voluit*)
  3. *Libere tenuit*
  4. *Tenuit ut liber homo,* etc.
  5. *Tenuit in alodio*
  6. *Tenuit in paragio*

is at least a shrewd guess that they have been preserved in the introduction to the *Inquisitio Eliensis*.[36] The list is very famous, but because we shall have occasion to refer to it later, its contents may once more be described. These are the subjects on which the king there asks for specific information: (1) the name of the manor; (2) its tenant *T.R.E.* and *T.R.W.*; (3) its assessment to the geld; (4) its division of plowteams between the lord and his tenants; (5) the classification of the latter; (6) the manorial woodland, meadow, pasture, mills, and fish-ponds; and (7) the appraisal of the whole *T.R.E.* and *T.R.W.*, with account taken of whatever has been removed or added, how much each freeman or sokeman held at either time, and whether more income could be got from it.[37] We do not know how faithfully

[36] Round, *Feudal England*, pp. 130 ff. See also the recent and excellent discussion in F. M. Stenton, *Anglo-Saxon England* (Oxford, 1943), pp. 644 ff.

[37] The exact relationship of these last clauses to one another is by no means clear in the statement that has come down to us; but, as will be seen, the corresponding portions of the final compilation were characterized by similar vagueness.

the king's instructions were carried out by the commissioners, precisely what information they obtained, or how they obtained it.[38] Such testimony as was presented by the local juries would be written down by the commissioners' clerks, and they would presumably be Frenchmen with little if any knowledge of Anglo-Saxon. Besides, a considerable amount of material probably came to the commissioners in the form of briefs (*breves*) prepared by the greater barons for their fiefs or by the king's officials for his demesne.[39]

Of the returns that somehow came to be made from the Domesday inquest one fragment has been saved for us in the so-called *Inquisitio Comitatus Cantabrigiensis*.[40] We should not, of course, trust a poor copy for such details as numerals and proper names, or even for the careful inclusion of words and phrases. Yet we can hardly doubt that in the main it reproduces the language of the original. If, accordingly, we glance through the collation of the *Inquisitio Comitatus Cantabrigiensis* with Domesday Book,[41] we are logically brought to the following conclusions. As noted above, Group III of the county surveys is characterized by a number of formulas: not only those tabulated but also those dealing with plowlands, meadow, pasture, and annual income. The *Inquisitio Comitatus Cantabrigiensis* regularly includes these same formulas and in the same order. To a later compiler we can attribute only (1) the insertion of hundredal rubrics, marginal letters, and the like; (2) the omission of statistics concerning livestock; and (3) a number of verbal

---

[38] Cf. Round's comment in *V. C. H. Buckingham*, I (1905), 207: "It is possible that the Domesday Commissioners themselves varied, on their several circuits, in the amount of detail they asked for, but it was clearly the compiler who was chiefly responsible for cutting down the information supplied on certain points in the inquiry."

[39] See Galbraith, *Eng. Hist. Rev.*, LVII, 174–76. R. Lennard, *ibid.*, LVIII (1943), 38–39, agrees that the "neglected satellite" from Bath may be understood as the abbot's *breve*. Douglas, *Domesday Monachorum*, pp. 19 ff., rejects a similar explanation for the similar document which he has edited; but something more remains to be said on the subject. Until the character of these and other local surveys has been more positively determined, their significance for the problem under discussion remains doubtful.

[40] Round, *Feudal England*, pp. 3 ff.; Galbraith, *Eng. Hist. Rev.*, LVII, 170.

[41] *I.C.C.*, pp. 1 ff.

changes, especially about landholding *T.R.E.*[42] Comparison of the four Hertfordshire entries preserved in the *Inquisitio Eliensis* with the corresponding portions of Domesday Book leads to similar conclusions.[43]

It might therefore be supposed that Domesday Book faithfully reproduced all prominent features of the original returns because it was directly compiled from them. But Mr. Galbraith is right, I think, in deciding that Domesday Book was not thus composed. The resemblance between it and the *Inquisitio Comitatus Cantabrigiensis* does not rule out the possibility of earlier drafts prepared by the commissioners for the regions which they visited. As Mr. Galbraith has pointed out,[44] the *Inquisitio Eliensis* apparently took from one such regional survey the description of the abbot's manors in Norfolk and Suffolk and from another the description of those in Huntingdonshire. The former case has little to offer us in the present connection,[45] for the second volume of Domesday Book was left unrevised. The latter case is more interesting, for it seems to show how the writing of Domesday Book involved the condensation of a preliminary survey of the northern counties. The final compiler left out not only the enumerations of domestic animals but also various other details.[46] Unhappily, we cannot tell whether he was likewise responsible for the omission of all data concerning Anglo-Saxon tenures—a peculiarity of our Group VI—because the four manors described were all held by the abbot *T.R.E.* For better information in this respect we must turn to the Exeter Book.

How in Domesday Book certain peculiarities of the Exeter Book were eliminated, while others were generally preserved,

[42] The variety of the changes made in this respect by the compilers, whether of Domesday Book or of the *Inquisitio Eliensis,* was even greater than Round indicated (*Feudal England,* pp. 18 ff.). It did not result in marked condensation and was obviously dictated by sheer caprice.

[43] *I.C.C.,* pp. 124–25; *D.B.,* I, 135.

[44] *Eng. Hist. Rev.,* LVII, 166 ff.

[45] For minor differences see the footnotes to the translations of Domesday Book in *V. C. H. Norfolk,* II (1906), and *V. C. H. Suffolk,* I (1911).

[46] *I.C.C.,* pp. 166–67; *D.B.,* I, 204. Domesday Book omitted the dimensions of lands other than woods and substituted *terra . . . car'* for longer formulas about plowlands. See above, notes 28–29.

has been illustrated by the entries quoted above. Then, too, it was remarked that the final compiler made numerous omissions, including the word *pariter*. A rapid check of similar instances furnished by the two books leads to some curious results. In about 36 per cent of the fifty-odd cases for Devonshire Domesday Book either retains *pariter* or substitutes *in paragio*,[47] very often by means of marginal or interlinear insertion; in about 36 per cent it substitutes *libere;* in about 28 per cent it omits *pariter* without substitution of any kind.[48] Only fragments of the Dorsetshire survey remain in the Exeter Book, but they indicate very much the same practice for that county.[49] On the other hand, examination of the Somersetshire survey produces the following statistics. In about 88 per cent of some 125 cases Domesday Book omits *pariter* without substitution; in about 5 per cent it substitutes *libere;* in about 7 per cent it keeps *pariter* or substitutes *in paragio*.[50] For Wiltshire and Cornwall the Exeter Book gives us virtually nothing; all we can say is that neither *pariter* nor *in paragio* is to be found in the Domesday survey of either county, and that *libere* appears only seven times—by interlineation in the survey of Wiltshire.

As if these complications were not enough to obscure the record, Domesday Book gives us a number of others, which must be taken into account before we attempt to draw any general conclusions. The Exeter Book often tells us that men holding in parage *T.R.E.* as well as others, could go with their lands to whatever lords they pleased, where they would, or the like. Domesday Book sometimes keeps the statement, at least in abbreviated

[47] Occasionally Domesday Book inserts *libere* before *in paragio*. Such a rough estimate as that made here is facilitated by the parallel versions of *The Devonshire Domesday,* published by The Devonshire Association for the Advancement of Science, Literature, and Art (1884–92). For this purpose, O. J. Reichel's translation in *V. C. H. Devonshire,* I (1906), is useless because it fails to indicate the omissions of Domesday Book.

[48] The appearance in this context of *pro manerio* and the like seems to result from the transposition of an earlier phrase, or one in part imagined.

[49] We here find the same equation of *libere* and *pariter* (or *in paragio*), marked by frequent interlineation.

[50] Interlineation of such words in the Domesday survey of Somersetshire is very rare. My checklist, it should be noted, has been greatly facilitated by the translation in *V. C. H. Somersetshire,* I (1906), by E. H. Bates, which faithfully indicates omissions from the Exeter Book made by Domesday Book.

form.[51] Occasionally it substitutes *libere tenebat*.[52] More frequently than not, however, it leaves out the formula altogether.[53] Likely to be omitted also is the contrary statement: that so-and-so could not detach himself, or be separated, from a particular manor. In matters such as these, obviously, the compilers of Domesday Book followed no definite rule of procedure, and we are left to wonder why they failed to adopt one.

To say that Domesday Book is never consistent in anything would be quite wrong. After studying the substance of Volume I, at any rate, we can hardly escape a very different conclusion. Not only the classification of manors according to who held them in 1066 but also their internal structure is set forth with impressive uniformity. Despite innumerable errors of detail, the plan of the book as a whole was admirably carried out; and, as we have seen, the variation in the major formulas serves to classify the county surveys in a number of groups without affecting the quality of the information there given. For example, assessment to the royal geld was honestly reported, no matter what verb happened to be used in a particular entry. Manorial woodland was regularly estimated, whether in terms of area or of porcine income. Although the compilers invariably left out enumerations of domestic animals, they invariably included, as best they could, other manorial statistics—concerning plowteams, agricultural tenants, meadow, pasture, mills, fish-ponds, etc. And, together with comment of one sort or another,[54] they always gave a state-

[51] E.g., *D.B.*, IV, 358 ("Cadberie"): ". . . poterat sibi eligere dominum secundum voluntatem suam cum terra sua." *Ibid.*, I, 97*b*: ". . . poterat ire quo volebat." For other variations of this formula see *Eng. Hist. Rev.*, LIX, 293 ff.

[52] E.g., *D.B.*, IV, 46 ("Ragintone"), 115 ("Raweberga"), 116 ("Colrige"); I, 82*b*, 102, 102*b*.

[53] For Devonshire the percentage of omission as against retention is almost ten to one.

[54] As remarked by Salzman, *V. C. H. Cambridge*, I (1938), 339, the list in the *Inquisitio Eliensis* does not include a question about plowlands. But one way of stating whether more could be got from a manor would be to set down how many additional plowteams could be used on it; see Stenton, *Anglo-Saxon England*, p. 646.

ment of what the manor was worth to the holder. Why did they faithfully list all important Anglo-Saxon tenants while omitting so much about Anglo-Saxon tenures?

A possible solution to our problem is suggested by the *Inquisitio Eliensis.* It can hardly be mere coincidence that the matters there specified were precisely those which the compilers of Domesday Book carefully retained. The clerks who composed the final surveys must have been instructed to set down that particular information according to a prescribed plan, but to save space by omitting whatever additional information seemed unnecessary. Perhaps the compiler was definitely told not to enumerate domestic animals; with regard to a good deal else, at any rate, he was left to use his discretion—and that proved to be a variable quantity. For example, let us try to imagine what happened to the formulas concerning parage and liberty of alienation in the Exeter Book. From the facts cited above it seems likely that the compilers started with the surveys of Devonshire and Dorsetshire. There, after naming the tenant of a manor *T.R.E.,* they began to delete additional statements about his tenure, though haphazard revision occasionally brought the writing-in of a deleted phrase. As the compilers reached the Somersetshire survey, however, omission of all such details, with little or no correction, became the rule; so that the surveys of Wiltshire and Cornwall were virtually stripped of all information about the nature of Anglo-Saxon landholding. Similar conjecture applied to our Group III would lead us to conclude that for Middlesex, Hertfordshire, and Buckinghamshire somebody was sensible enough to substitute *vendere potuit* for the incredible variety of formulas that had been used for Cambridgeshire and Bedfordshire. And it is at least possible that, in somewhat the same way, relatively simple formulas came to be used throughout Groups IV and V, while similar entries were altogether eliminated from Group VI.

Fundamentally, of course, Domesday Book was only a digest of material provided by the original returns, and so to a considerable degree had to reproduce their language. When, for instance, the record gave estimates of land in terms of area, no compiler could readily substitute others in terms of yield.[55] We may thus be sure that a group of county surveys in Domesday Book was sometimes characterized by a certain formula because it had been adopted by the royal commissioners, or their clerks, within a particular region.[56] But we may be equally sure that this was not always the case. Several formulas of the Exeter Book, whether or not they had been taken from the original returns, were systematically changed by the compilers of Domesday Book. For the *reddidit gildum* of the older survey the compilers substituted *geldabat,* though the *se defendebat* of the southeastern counties would have been quite as useful.[57] From these facts the only possible conclusion is that the distinguishing features of our seven groups can in part be attributed to some phase of the Domesday inquest itself, in part to some later work of compilation. How many stages there were in that compilation remains, for the present study, a matter of secondary importance.

Essentially Domesday Book is therefore a description of landed estates, well planned and well executed to accord with what are recognized as the Conqueror's own instructions. Materials not specifically demanded, such as information about the tenure of land *T.R.E.,* might be deleted at the discretion of the compilers. Apparently it was also left to them, if they pleased, to draw up lists of current disputes over the possession of certain properties; but enumerations of this kind were eventually retained for only three counties in Volume I.[58] To what extent the compilers were likewise responsible for Domesday's inchoate and incomplete description of local custom in counties and boroughs we

[55] Examples of the latter usage may be seen in the *pratum* . . . *car'* of Group III, as well as in the *silva de* . . . *porcis de pasnagio* of Group I or the *silva* . . . *porcis incrassandis* of Shropshire.

[56] E.g., especially, the formulas of the *I.C.C.* already noted.

[57] The fact that, for Group III, this formula was derived by Domesday Book from the original returns (*I.C.C.*) would lead us to suppose that the same procedure had been followed for Group I. Cf. *Domesday Monachorum,* ed. Douglas, pp. 81 ff.

[58] See above, n. 25; and on the *invasiones* of Little Domesday, *Eng. Hist. Rev.,* LIX, 299 ff. Such lists, obviously, could be prepared only by the compilers, who summarized information obtained from the original inquest. If that information had already been recorded in separate manorial entries, no supplementary list would be necessary. But absolute consistency in this respect should not be expected of the Domesday clerks.

have no way of deciding. We know merely the appalling result. With regard to the boroughs, in particular, the record is so generally characterized by errors, obscurities, and omissions as to madden the would-be historian of municipal institutions in early England. Happily for the reader, no review of controversial essays on the Domesday borough [59] is here contemplated; it will suffice to offer, as of some possible significance, the following considerations.

The placing of boroughs at the head of a county survey, we may well believe, was no more than a scribal device inconsistently used by the compilers of Domesday Book. The original returns were presumably expected to include statistics about the boroughs; for they, no less than manors, were units of seignorial income. So a borough over which the king had no direct control was regularly described as part of the fief of the baron who held it. The king's revenues from a borough of his own, like whatever he got from a shire court, could properly be described as part of the royal demesne; [60] yet the compilers hesitated to list such perquisites under the heading *Terra Regis*. And what were they to do with the supplementary material provided by at least some of the local juries? The easiest way out would be to include what they had and not to worry about the rest. This, I imagine, they did. For some groups of counties we therefore have lengthy statements, for others meager statements, and for a few none at all. [61] Perhaps Mr. Galbraith's suggestion, that the inquest of 1086 involved the drawing-up of a separate *breve* for the royal demesne in each county, may eventually throw more light on the subject.

---

[59] See J. Tait, *The Medieval English Borough* (Manchester, 1936); C. Stephenson, *Borough and Town* (Cambridge, Mass., 1933); A. Ballard, *The Domesday Boroughs* (Oxford, 1904); F. W. Maitland, *Domesday Book and Beyond* (Cambridge, 1897), pp. 172 ff.; and the references given in these books.

[60] So, in the Exeter Book, they were described under the heading *Dominicatus Regis*. For the views of Maitland and Ballard on this subject see the books cited in the preceding note.

[61] Many details of local custom are given in Groups v, vi, and vii; at least estimates of the *firma noctis* from the counties in Group iv; but only a few random statements in Groups i and ii. The surveys of the East Anglian counties (Group vii) contain even more detail than the rest and are even less intelligible—because, perhaps, the compilers of Little Domesday despaired of revising them.

Scanty as it is, the evidence just reviewed tends to encourage further generalization. The compilers of Domesday Book, we may conclude, knew little about Anglo-Saxon institutions and cared less. Nor should we imagine that the clerks who wrote the original returns had a radically different attitude. Those records, if we had them, might give us a good many more details; but I doubt that they would greatly clarify the picture of pre-Norman England which we gain from Domesday Book. The example of tenure in parage is again illuminating. The term was obviously French, translated into Latin and used to designate an English custom. From what we know about the revision of the Exeter Book we may be positive that the failure of Domesday Book to describe a particular tenure as having been in parage is of no significance; in all probability it was actually prevalent throughout many shires in whose surveys Domesday Book does not mention it.[62] We may even suspect that the French word *parage,* however exact its meaning in Normandy, was applied by the Conqueror's clerks to an Anglo-Saxon tenure which they did not fully understand. To rely upon the Domesday record for accurate information in such a case is plainly foolish.

Heeding this lesson, which is logically derived from the one taught by Round, we should not expect Domesday Book to be more trustworthy in what it tells us about commendation, soke, or proprietary right in pre-Norman England. With regard to such relatively superior persons as thegns, *cnihtas,* moneyers, lawmen, and *alodiarii* the language of Domesday Book is hopelessly confused, the substance of its entries vague and fragmentary. For the same reason the problem of the Domesday *burgenses* remains notoriously difficult. Nor is the record consistent when it comes to the manorial population. Is it credible that there were *servi* in all the English counties but four northern ones; that, with two or three exceptions, neither *radchenistres* nor *ancillae* were to be found outside the western counties; or that, with similar exceptions, sokemen lived only in the eastern counties? Although the king's writ apparently distinguished *sochemanni* and *liberi homines* from other manorial tenants, the Domesday clerks utterly failed to make a clear

[62] See *Eng. Hist. Rev.,* LIX, 295, n. 2.

distinction even between those two groups. Whether or not *villanus* was regarded as a technical term we can only wonder. And who, besides the *cotarii* officially asked for, were the nominally Anglo-Saxon *cotsets* or the nominally French *bordiers,* Latinized as *bordarii?* [63] In this connection we seem to be sure of only one fact: that Domesday Book was primarily concerned, not with varieties of Anglo-Saxon status, but with the agrarian unit that had come to be called a manor—who and what were attached to it, who had held it, who now held it, and what it was worth.

If the opinions expressed above are well founded, there can be no doubt as to the purpose either of Domesday Book or of the inquest that led to its composition. The whole project was thoroughly feudal. Mr. Galbraith's conclusion to this effect, I believe, is entirely justified. In reply to Mr. Douglas's objections I can only say that the results of the Domesday inquest, if interpreted as he interprets it, were signally poor. Domesday Book, I would add, did not include a report about the service owed by the barons because the king, presumably not needing one, did not ask for one. Nor, according to my view of feudalism,[64] does the fact that Domesday Book included reports about the geld and other sources of royal income make the great survey any the less feudal. It could, indeed, have remained essentially feudal and been more of a judicial record than it obviously was. As Mr. Douglas remarks,[65] Domesday Book frequently mentions disputes over land and occasionally tells how one of them has been settled by the royal commissioners. Yet, as legal reports, such entries are distinctly bad throughout Volume I, and with the *invasiones* of Volume II they sink to an even lower level.

Discussing the juridical value of Domesday Book inevitably leads to asking when it was written. It is significant that the compilers, after describing a certain property as held by one man though claimed by another, always left the matter undecided if, in fact, it still remained so in 1086. Are we to believe that the

---

[63] See especially the statistical tables in Henry Ellis, *General Introduction to Domesday* (London, 1833), II, 422 ff., which have formed the basis of famous comments by Seebohm, Round, Maitland, Vinogradoff, and many other scholars.

[64] Presented in *Am. Hist. Rev.,* XLVI (1941), 788 ff.; XLVIII (1943), 245 ff.

[65] *Domesday Monachorum,* pp. 26 ff.; *History,* XXI, 256–57.

writing of Domesday Book could take some fifteen years,[66] and that in the meantime its tentative allocation of contested lands would remain unaltered or that it would fail to record any change of tenant? Much more sensible, it seems to me, is Mr. Stenton's opinion, that Domesday Book must have been completed by the year 1088.[67] But in that case we might as well agree with Mr. Galbraith that the famous colophon "means what it says," and therefore ascribe both volumes to the year 1086. I do not see how anyone who studies Domesday Book as a whole can escape the conclusion that it was hastily thrown together and never systematically revised. As it stands, Domesday Book is wonderful enough. We should not expect it to be other than the Conqueror himself planned it.

[66] *Ibid.*, XXI, 254–55.

[67] *Anglo-Saxon England*, p. 647, n. 3: "On general grounds, there is an overwhelming probability that the volumes were written before the information which they contain was seriously out of date; that is, before, at latest, the confiscations after the revolt of 1088."

The Origin and Significance of Feudalism [*1]

IN 1850 Paul Roth, professor of law at Marburg, published a remarkable book on the beginnings of what we are accustomed to call the feudal system.[2] This subject, the author remarks in his introduction, is of prime importance and has already received much attention. But those who have treated it, he is convinced, have all too often ignored the clear evidence of the sources for the sake of theses dictated by national or social prejudice. Thus Montesquieu, as a loyal member of the French nobility, has ably presented the argument that the Frankish state was never without a feudal nobility, for feudal institutions

[*1] Reprinted from *The American Historical Review*, XLVI (1941), 788–812. Here appended is the first note in the original printing.

To introduce a discussion on this subject, parts of the following article were read at the meeting of the Mediaeval Academy in April, 1940; and I welcome the opportunity of thanking those who participated in the discussion for a number of very useful criticisms. At the same time I wish to express my indebtedness to Dr. E. K. Graham's dissertation on Anglo-Saxon Vassalage (Cornell University, 1938), for a better understanding of the early literature that constitutes his principal source. It is also fair to state that the members of my seminar during the year 1939–40 have had no small share in the study here presented. By reading many books and documents together we all, I am sure, learned much more than any of us would have learned alone.

[2] *Geschichte des Beneficialwesens von den ältesten Zeiten bis ins zehnte Jahrhundert* (Erlangen, 1850).

were implicit in the custom of the conquering Germans. Later writers, though inspired by opposite sentiments, have used the same reasoning to justify the Revolution of 1789—to condemn the pretensions of the nobility as a vestige of the feudal anarchy created by barbarian invaders. Even the more recent school of French historians, led by François Guizot and Benjamin Guérard, continues to depict the Germans as destroyers of civilization, who substituted for the orderly government of Rome the chaotic relationships of vassals and lords. And German scholars, notably Karl Friedrich Eichhorn, have tended meekly to accept the conclusions of the French. Georg Waitz, it is true, has now given a masterly description of the ancient Germans, proving that they were organized in true states, not in mere bands under chieftains; yet, when he comes to the establishment of the Frankish kingdom, he abandons his original position and portrays vassalage as fundamental to the Merovingian constitution. This, declares Roth, is fatal to an understanding of the most important subject in the entire history of German law—the destruction of the royal authority.

How did it come about, Roth asks, that so great a people, at one time the dominant power and the cultural leader of Europe, was plunged from its high estate, to lose piecemeal in a four-hundred-year agony all that it had hitherto gained? The pitiful allegation of Niebuhr and other misguided historians that the Germans are by nature devoid of political sense, of all talent for state building as even for national union, he indignantly rejects. The true cause of the German misfortunes is to be seen in the vicious constitution of the feudal state, a sham monarchy that was actually the denial of all public authority.[3] Roth undertakes to prove that originally "the basis of the German state was not vassalage, not the dependence of a band upon a chieftain, but the simple relationship of subject to sovereign (*Unterthanverband*), the dependence of every freeman upon the common ruler of the state."[4] And through this demonstration the comforting certainty may be perceived that the anarchy of the Middle Ages,

[3] See especially Roth's introduction to his *Feudalität und Unterthanverband* (Weimar, 1863), which was written in reply to the criticism of Waitz (below, n. 22).

[4] *Geschichte des Beneficialwesens,* p. vii.

"eine mit etwas Kultur bedeckte Barbarei der schlimmsten Art," was the direct opposite of all that Germans had anciently stood for; that the constitutional changes in their modern states have marked a return, essentially, to the primitive Germanic system.[5] Whatever may be thought of Roth's conclusion—in which, itself, a certain tinge of nationalistic prejudice may be detected— his criticism of his predecessors was not without justification. Montesquieu's famous chapters "Des lois féodales," [6] a scholarly piece of work for the age in which it was produced, established the basis for all future discussion of feudal origins. According to Montesquieu the essence of feudalism lay in the custom of vassalage, which can be traced back to the *comitatus* described by Tacitus. To vassalage the fief was entirely subordinate, being a form of pay for loyal service. The earliest fiefs were horses, arms, and food; for it was the Frankish conquest of Gaul that first provided lands wherewith chieftains could reward their followers. On Roman soil, Montesquieu holds, the Franks still maintained their ancient customs. The *comites* of Tacitus reappear in the later documents as *antrustions, leudes, fidèles,* or *vassaux;* the properties bestowed on them as *biens fiscaux, bénéfices, honneurs,* or *fiefs.* And from the beginning these grants included not only economic control of the peasant population but also what was to become known as seignorial justice.[7]

Since, Montesquieu continues, the fiefs originally created through the distribution of conquered lands were revocable at will, neither the royal vassals nor the subvassals to whom they gave estates could enjoy more than a precarious title. The introduction of tenure for a term of years, or even for life, made no radical change in the situation. It was not until fiefs were permitted to become hereditary that subinfeudation attained a dangerous growth—encouraging the mass of freemen to commend themselves with their lands to the more powerful nobles and so, eventually, to remove themselves from the direct control of the royal government. The formulation of a policy tending in this direction can be attributed to Charles Martel, who

[5] *Feudalität und Unterthanverband,* pp. 34–35.

[6] *De l'esprit des lois* (first published at Geneva in 1748), bks. xxx–xxxi.

[7] *Ibid.,* bk. xxx, chs. iii, xvi ff.

despoiled the church in order to obtain lands for a second distribution of fiefs. Thereby the Carolingian monarchy was committed to a ruinous policy that reached its culmination under the sons of Louis the Pious. The kings, defied by the few great vassals upon whom the multitude depended, lost all effective power. "L'arbre étendit trop loin ses branches, et la tête se sécha. Le royaume se trouva sans domaine, comme est aujourd'hui l'Empire. On donna la couronne à un des plus puissants vassaux." Here, with the rise of the Capetian house, Montesquieu brings his acute analysis to a close.[8]

As remarked by Roth, Montesquieu's opinion came to be generally adopted by succeeding writers, most of whom agreed that feudalism was by origin Germanic and that it was thoroughly bad. So Eichhorn, in the first volume of his pioneer work on the legal history of Germany,[9] describes Frankish vassalage as derived from the German *comitatus* and coming to be associated with the benefice system through grants made by the Merovingian kings to their *antrustiones* and *leudes*. In subsequent chapters he passes rapidly over the increasing power of the greater vassals, their alliance with the Austrasian mayors, Charles Martel's secularization of church estates, the growth of subinfeudation, and the tendency of fiefs to become hereditary. The final result, declares Eichhorn, was the feudalism that proved the bane of his country—a system under which functions of government were combined with the holding of particular lands, under which the nation, split into fragments with conflicting interests, existed only by virtue of a common culture.[10]

The argument was one that could be readily turned to political advantage by a clever Frenchman. Thus Guizot, in his famous lectures of 1829,[11] describes the feudal system as at best "a first step out of barbarism." Although the primitive freedom of the barbarian—the right to do what one pleases at one's own risk— came to be limited through the influence of hereditary fiefs,

---

[8] *Ibid.*, bk. xxxi, chs. ix–xxxii.

[9] *Deutsche Staats- und Rechtsgeschichte* (4th ed., Göttingen, 1834). The first volume originally appeared in 1808.

[10] *Ibid.*, §§ 26, 27, 120 ff., 141, 167, 205, 286.

[11] Published in 1830 under the title, *Histoire de la civilisation en France* (2d ed., Paris, 1840), onzième leçon.

vassalage always permitted an excessive individualism. Political and social progress became possible only when feudalism, itself incapable of development, yielded to the rejuvenated monarchy in alliance with the Third Estate. But even so qualified a recognition of Germanic freedom is repudiated by Guérard, the scholarly editor of the *Polyptyque de l'abbé Irminon*. He refuses to admit that the savage invaders of his country knew any form of liberty, individual or public. Barbarism and destruction, he asserts, were the sole contribution of "the people that Germany vomited upon Gaul." Under their domination society lacked all feeling of common interest. Force ruled. The weak, in order to live, commended themselves to the strong.[12] "Alors il n'eut plus de patrie; et ce nom, tout-puissant dans l'antiquité, fut sans vertu et sans signification."

Opinions of this sort could not long go unchallenged by the rising school of German historians, and first in the field was Waitz—though Roth considered him but a feeble champion. Waitz, it must be admitted, was somewhat cautious; he left his eight volumes of *Deutsche Verfassungsgeschichte* [13] to stand without introduction, summary, or conclusion. Yet he evidently shared the current opinion that feudalism implied political disintegration and sought to clear the German name of responsibility for the evil institution.[14] So, in his first volume, Waitz offers proof that the primitive Germans were no mere savages. Rightly interpreted, the famous description by Tacitus shows that they had true political organizations headed by kings and princes and that only such elected rulers were surrounded by sworn bands of warlike companions. The personal fidelity of the latter, far from being incompatible with the existence of public authority, was closely subordinated to it. But among the early Germans, declares Waitz, the *comitatus* was at most an exceptional arrangement, which hardly survived the Frankish occupation of Gaul. Except for the Merovingian *antrustiones*, the armed guards of the king, the *comitatus* appears in the later

[12] *Polyptyque de l'abbé Irminon,* ed. Guérard, I (Paris, 1844), 199 ff.
[13] First ed., Kiel, 1844–78.
[14] Waitz more clearly expressed his view in an article of 1861, reprinted in *Abhandlungen zur deutschen Verfassungs- und Rechtsgeschichte von G. Waitz* (Göttingen, 1896), pp. 314 ff.

period solely as a literary tradition, preserved in *Beowulf* and in other epics celebrating the deeds of ancient heroes.[15] The vassalage of the later Frankish kingdom was not derived from the German *comitatus* but from the Gallo-Roman *patrocinium*— a relationship by which, for the sake of protection, lesser freemen often bound themselves to the powerful. At the same time, through a process that may be obscurely traced under the Merovingian kings, the Roman *precarium* (or *precaria*), land held by a tenant at the will of a donor, was developed into the benefice or fief, an estate conferred on a vassal in return for specified service.[16] Thus reduced to its constituent elements, the feudal system must be recognized as quite alien to the Germanic polity.

To appreciate the force of Waitz's argument, we have to read between the lines. In the case of Roth, as already remarked, that is not necessary; he never leaves us to guess at his purpose in writing. After an excellent beginning, he says, Waitz has failed to do full justice to the national cause. The Frankish monarchy, as a soundly Germanic state, was never to the slightest degree feudalized until the eighth century.[17] Vassalage, Roth was willing to concede, was derived from the ancient *comitatus;* for the *vassi dominici* of the Carolingians were only the *antrustiones* under another name. But this, he insists, is by no means to admit that the promiscuous vassalage of the feudal age was a Merovingian institution. The old Frankish law permitted no *Privatgefolgschaften*—no subordination of freemen to any persons except the king and the officials whom he appointed and dismissed at pleasure. Vassalage, even in the more primitive stage of the *comitatus,* was essentially a public relationship: the followers swore fealty to their leader, gave him warlike service, and were subject to his judicial control. The source of vassalage could not therefore be the *patrocinium,* which had never been more than a private relationship under the Romans and so remained under

[15] *Deutsche Verfassungsgeschichte,* I (3d ed., Kiel, 1880), 236 ff., 371 ff.

[16] *Ibid.,* II ¹ (3d ed., Kiel, 1882), 330 ff.; IV (2d ed., Berlin, 1885), 176 ff., 234 ff., 287 ff. In mediaeval Latin *precarium* was generally supplanted by the feminine *precaria.*

[17] See especially *Feudalität und Unterthanverband,* pp. 1, 31.

the Merovingians.[18] The original Frankish constitution, further-more, recognized no such thing as a fief, even under the name of *beneficium*. When the Merovingian kings conferred estates upon their retainers, the grants were in full ownership; the *precariae* held of churches or other private donors carried with them no political privilege and specified no military service.[19] The all-important question, therefore, is how the right to have vassals came to be enjoyed by a horde of *seniores*, who at the same time secured possession of fiefs that implied governmental authority over masses of free inhabitants.

It was the secularization of ecclesiastical estates, Roth declares, that "provided the means for transforming the kingdom of the Franks into the feudal state." [20] Charles Martel, confronted by need of a more efficient army and having no domains of the crown at his disposal, took the drastic step of distributing various lands of the church among his vassals in return for quotas of troops. And since the legal title remained with the despoiled abbeys and bishoprics, these lands could be granted to the actual holders only as *precariae verbo regis*, as benefices to be enjoyed on condition that the specified service was regularly performed. Systematized by Pepin and Charlemagne, the new form of tenure was quickly extended to other properties—to those obtained by vassals from private lords as well as to those obtained from the king. For the recipient of a royal benefice was authorized to bestow similar benefices upon other tenants in order that they might equip themselves as part of his contingent. The feudaliz-ing process, thus launched, soon gained irresistible headway. For a while the Carolingians were able to maintain the old German tradition of a centralized state; then the unscrupulous aris-tocracy, turning upon the power that had so blindly fostered

[18] *Geschichte des Beneficialwesens*, pp. 1 ff., 105 ff., 146 ff., 276 ff., 367 ff.; *Feu-dalität und Unterthanverband*, pp. 205 ff., 231 ff. More specifically, Roth declares that the *leudes* of the Merovingian period were identical with *fideles*, merely the faithful subjects of the king; that the *pueri, satellites, gasindi*, and similar members of private households, who performed duties like those of the later vassals, were unfree servants.

[19] *Geschichte des Beneficialwesens*, pp. 203 ff.; *Feudalität und Unterthanverband*, pp. 37 ff.

[20] *Ibid.*, p. 128.

it, reduced the monarchy to impotence. By the tenth century public offices, royal revenues, military command, judicial authority—the general control of the free population—had alike become mere appurtenances to fiefs and so, according to what was already the established custom, hereditary possessions of the new-grown feudal nobility.[21]

The great originality of Roth's thesis lay in its exposition of the feudal system as an innovation of the eighth century. To most of his predecessors, headed by Montesquieu, the essence of feudalism had been the Germanic custom of vassalage, to which fief holding with all its implications was a natural supplement. Even Waitz, although he denied the attribution of feudalism to German influence, explained the system as a gradual development out of institutions already prevalent in the Merovingian kingdom. And this opinion he resolutely maintained despite all that Roth could aver to the contrary.[22] In particular, he declared, Roth could produce no evidence to account for the deliberate feudalization of the state by the early Carolingians. They were, in fact, quite as German as the Merovingians. Why should the younger house, with all its genius for war and politics, have abandoned the time-honored principles of the Frankish monarchy? Under pressure of what necessity could Charles Martel, the restorer of the kingdom, have been induced to create a system of military benefices and thereby to inaugurate the fatal extension of vassalage? The best solution Roth had to offer was that the impoverishment of the ordinary freemen came to preclude their fighting distant campaigns without pay. An unconvincing argument Waitz called it—and in this opinion he was followed by Heinrich Brunner.[23]

Thanks to the careful research and eminent good sense of

[21] *Geschichte des Beneficialwesens*, pp. 313 ff., 392 ff., 416 ff.; *Feudalität und Unterthanverband*, pp. 71 ff., 244 ff., 315 ff., 322 ff.

[22] *Über die Anfänge der Vassalität* (Göttingen, 1856), which includes criticism that Waitz repeated and amplified in the later editions of his *Deutsche Verfassungsgeschichte*.

[23] *Deutsche Rechtsgeschichte* (1st ed., Leipzig, 1887–92). The second edition (Vol. I, Leipzig, 1906; Vol. II, Leipzig, 1928, ed. Claudius von Schwerin) incorporates Brunner's later work on the origins of the feudal system. More detailed treatment of particular topics is to be found in his collection of special articles, *Forschungen zur Geschichte des deutschen und französischen Rechts* (Stuttgart, 1894), pp. 1–87.

that fine scholar, our understanding of the whole controversial subject has been greatly improved. Roth's thesis, Brunner concludes, is sound insofar as it derives the feudal state from the union of two distinct institutions, vassalage and the benefice, brought about in the eighth century.[24] Besides, Roth has correctly insisted upon the military *Gefolgschaft* of the primitive Germans as the source of mediaeval vassalage, which was based on warlike service. To deny, with Waitz, this elementary fact is utterly to misconceive the problem under discussion.[25] In the main Brunner also agrees with Roth's explanation of the military benefice as a legal result of the Carolingian secularizations.[26] But Roth, in Brunner's judgment, has failed to appreciate the ultimate significance of the new policy. The rapid extension of vassalage, henceforth associated with benefice holding, was the inevitable consequence of a military revolution— a change from infantry to cavalry as the dominating element in the Frankish army. The Merovingian *antrustiones*, like the members of the ancient *comitatus*, had generally served on horseback; but until the eighth century the mass of the royal forces had consisted of foot soldiers. The experience of warfare, especially with the Saracens, now demanded a reversal of the situation; hence the lavish bestowal upon vassals of estates to be held on condition of furnishing mounted troops.[27] Hence also the anxiety of the government to defend and increase the liberties of the holders; for the military benefice was no mere source of private income to the fortunate possessor. The capitularies show that, as indicated by Waitz, land held by a royal vassal

[24] *Deutsche Rechtsgeschichte,* II, 329.
[25] *Ibid.,* I, 186 ff., II, 134 ff., 349 ff., 360: "Sowohl der rechtsgeschichtliche als der politische Schwerpunkt der Vassalität liegt in der kriegerischen Dienstpflicht der Vasallen. Wer sie bestreitet, bemüht sich vergebens, die Ausbildung und Verbreitung der ganzen Institution zu erklären." As will be shown below, Brunner does not exclude the possibility of a certain Gallo-Roman influence.
[26] *Ibid.,* I, 289 ff., II, 329 ff. But in this connection Brunner follows a suggestion of Waitz in holding that the charters of the Merovingian kings, despite the traditional Roman forms, often gave the recipient no more than a restricted title to his land. Conditional tenures for the benefit of royal retainers had thus actually existed long before the eighth century (*Forschungen zur Geschichte des deutschen und französischen Rechts,* pp. 1 ff.).
[27] *Ibid.,* pp. 39 ff.

in return for military service was officially considered a sort of immunity—a privileged territory within which the lord exercised fiscal, judicial, and other political functions.[28]

According to Brunner, therefore, what we know as feudalism was based on a new tenurial system developed by the Frankish rulers of the eighth century—a system of military benefices held by vassals on condition of regularly owed service. Before the end of the Carolingian period it was already the rule for a vassal to obtain such a benefice and for his title to be *de facto* hereditary. By that time, too, the major offices in church and state were coming to be regarded as benefices.[29] But throughout this whole new development the "impelling factor" was vassalage,[30] and the source of vassalage was the primitive *comitatus*. Here, it is worth noting, Brunner renders no moral or patriotic judgment upon feudalism—as to whether it was good or bad, was or was not Germanic. Tacitly reverting to the opinion of Montesquieu, he simply concludes that, as a matter of historical fact, vassalage can be traced back to the custom of the early Germans which permitted any freeman to have an armed *Gefolgschaft*.[31]

Much remains to be said of Brunner's views on particular questions, but for the moment attention must be turned to a monograph published between the dates of the first and second editions of the *Deutsche Rechtsgeschichte*. In his brilliant *Essai* of 1902 Paul Guilhiermoz re-examines the writings of the late Roman Empire and there discovers what he takes to be convincing evidence for the origin of mediaeval vassalage. During the fourth, fifth, and sixth centuries, he points out, not only the emperors but also the masters of troops were accustomed to surround themselves with bands of household guards usually called *scholares* or *buccellarii*. In spite of the fact that the members of such a band were often of German birth, the organization itself was utterly different from the Germanic *comitatus*. The latter was fundamentally aristocratic in that it was made up of

[28] *Deutsche Rechtsgeschichte*, II, 344, 383 ff. Cf. Waitz, *Deutsche Verfassungsgeschichte*, IV, 294 ff.
[29] *Deutsche Rechtsgeschichte*, II, 344 ff.   [30] *Ibid.*, p. 368.
[31] *Ibid.*, I, 187, n. 32, II, 351 ff. See below, n. 46.

free tribesmen who considered the bearing of arms a mark of distinction and companionship with a famous warrior a source of honor. The Roman *scholares*, on the contrary, were mercenaries selected only for their soldierly prowess; though many of them were legally free, their social rank was hardly above that of the armed slaves who were frequently employed in the same capacity.[32] The *buccellarii* of the Visigoths and Ostrogoths settled within the imperial provinces differed in no way from the rest. The Gothic leaders, evidently, continued a Roman practice that had already been adopted by such barbarian generals as Stilicho and Ricimer. And the Merovingian *antrustiones* were nothing else than *scholares* or *buccellarii* under a Frankish name—royal bodyguards, free or unfree, whose legal status was merely that enjoyed by all menials in the king's palace.[33] Through an elaborate argument—of which more below—Guilhiermoz then proceeds to show how the *antrustiones* formed the nucleus from which sprang the Carolingian *vassi* and so, ultimately, the French nobility.

Here, in brief, are the principal theories which were offered by earlier writers to explain the development of feudalism and which are still influential; for lively debate on the subject has been continued in a number of recent books.[34] The present

[32] Guilhiermoz, *Essai sur l'origine de la noblesse en France au moyen âge* (Paris, 1902), pp. 5–37. Although Guilhiermoz has been accused of exaggerating the aristocratic character of the *comitatus*, his main point, that the profession of arms was essentially honorable among the Germans but not at all so among the Romans, can hardly be denied.

[33] *Ibid.*, pp. 38–70. The inclusion of the Lombard *gasindi* in the same category raises a number of questions which Guilhiermoz tends to ignore (see below, n. 45).

[34] At this point it will be convenient to list various modern works to which reference can henceforth be made by citing a brief title or merely the author's name: Alfons Dopsch, *Wirtschaftliche und soziale Grundlagen der europäischen Kulturentwicklung* (2d ed., Vienna, 1923–24); G. von Below, *Der deutsche Staat des Mittelalters* (2d ed., Leipzig, 1925); Ferdinand Lot, in Gustave Glotz, *Histoire générale: Histoire du moyen âge*, I (Paris, 1928–35), ch. xxv; Heinrich Mitteis, *Lehnrecht und Staatsgewalt* (Weimar, 1933); Hermann Krawinkel, *Untersuchungen zum fränkischen Benefizialrecht* (Weimar, 1937); J. Calmette, *La société féodale* (Paris, 1938); Marc Bloch, *La société féodale* (Paris, 1939). Dopsch has supplemented his *Wirtschaftliche und soziale Grundlagen* with a number of articles, notably two: "Die leudes und das Lehenswesen" and "Beneficialwesen und Feudalität," *Mitteilungen des österreichischen Instituts für Geschichtsforschung* (henceforth *M.Ö.I.G.*), XLI (1926), 35 ff., and XLVI (1932), 1 ff. Two of the many excellent articles by F. L.

trend of the discussion, however, can hardly be understood until the main question at issue is clearly defined. What precisely do we mean when we talk of "feudalism"? The concept, it would seem, is a wholly modern one; neither the English word nor its equivalent in any other language was apparently invented much before the nineteenth century.[35] Although men in the Middle Ages were quite familiar with vassals and fiefs and with vassalage and feudal tenure, they apparently did not think in terms of a broad feudal theory—a set of feudal principles by which to construct a social and political framework. To have any validity, therefore, whatever generalization we make must be squarely based on our knowledge of actual institutions. And those institutions must be of the region where the custom properly called feudal was first developed—that is to say, mediaeval Gaul. A sociology of feudalism there may be, but only comparison with the original feudalism can rightly determine the feudal character of some other custom, wherever it may have existed.[36]

Turning then to the native land of feudalism, we have no trouble in finding the central institution from which our word is derived. It was the *feudum* or fief. Yet this is not the primary element to be examined. Feudalism, as acutely remarked by Lot, presupposes vassalage; for a fief could not exist apart from a

---

Ganshof may also be mentioned here: "Note sur les origines de l'union du bénéfice avec la vassalité," in *Etudes d'histoire dédiées à la mémoire de Henri Pirenne, par ses anciens élèves* (Brussels, 1937), pp. 173 ff.; "Benefice and Vassalage in the Age of Charlemagne," *Cambridge Historical Journal*, VI (1939), 147 ff. Among the older books that remain particularly useful because of recent editions are A. Esmein, *Cours élémentaire d'histoire du droit français*, ed. R. Généstal (15th ed., Paris, 1925), and Richard Schröder, *Lehrbuch der deutschen Rechtsgeschichte*, ed. Eberhard von Künssberg (7th ed., Berlin, 1932). Additional titles in great number will be found in the bibliographies and notes of the works here cited.

[35] No example of "feudalism" earlier than that is given in the *New Oxford Dictionary*, though the expression "feudal system" is cited from Adam Smith's *Wealth of Nations*. *Féodalité*, used in the same sense, does not appear in French writings until the eighteenth century (Bloch, pp. 1–3). Montesquieu, as already remarked, entitled his famous chapters "Des lois féodales."

[36] I am inclined to agree with those scholars who find the ordinary remarks about feudalism in the abstract either so vague as to be historically useless or so inaccurate as to be historically dangerous: Lot, p. 641; Calmette, p. 1; Below, pp. 332 ff.; Mitteis, p. 3.

vassal to hold it.[37] "On est convenu de parler de 'féodalité' et non de 'vassalité' à partir du moment où il n'y a plus en fait, sauf de rares exceptions, de vassal sans fief." The status of vassal, we know from countless documents of the eleventh and twelfth centuries, could always be acquired, with or without the prospect of a fief, merely by performing homage and swearing fealty.[38] And solely in this way could one become a vassal. Although fiefs might be declared hereditary, vassalage was never inherited. When a vassal died, his fief legally reverted to the lord, in whose hands it remained until such time as the heir performed homage and so qualified himself to receive investiture.[39] Only a vassal could properly be a fief holder, and there can be no doubt that, in the feudal age proper, vassalage was restricted to mature men. The reason is clear: a vassal was supposed to be a warrior. Clergymen, it is true, often held fiefs while debarred from bloodshed by canon law. But the qualifications that came to be put on their homage and fealty were plainly the result of compromise. At one time ecclesiastical vassals had fought like the rest; it was the Hildebrandine papacy that finally compelled the making of exceptions in their favor.[40] Feudal tenure, whatever its minor adaptations, was essentially military because the original vassalage was a military relationship.

Here, if I am not mistaken, is the key to the whole develop-

[37] Lot, p. 676, n. 188; cf. Guilhiermoz, p. 236. On the introduction of the vernacular "fief" see Lot, p. 675; Mitteis, pp. 108 ff.; Bloch, pp. 254 ff.

[38] Vassals without fiefs were by no means unheard of in the later Middle Ages. Guilhiermoz, pp. 242 ff.; Bloch, pp. 260 ff.; Mitteis, pp. 519 ff. On homage and fealty see particularly Esmein, pp. 189 ff.; Calmette, pp. 30 ff.; Bloch, pp. 224 ff.; Mitteis, pp. 479 ff. The primary and decisive element in the ceremony was homage, for in the twelfth century, as in the Frankish period, it was always possible for one man to swear fealty to another without becoming his vassal. In other words, although any vassal could properly be styled a *fidelis*, all *fideles* were not vassals. This fact, which has been obscured in too many standard books, is a familiar one in Anglo-Norman law; for Continental evidence see Guilhiermoz, p. 255. The earlier history of homage and fealty will be discussed below.

[39] This was the generally recognized custom (described especially well by Esmein, pp. 195 ff.), though a powerless lord—e.g., the French king in the eleventh century —was unable to enforce it. See below, n. 86.

[40] A. Pöschl, "Die Entstehung des geistlichen Benefiziums," *Archiv für Katholisches Kirchenrecht*, CVI (1926), 25 ff., 89 ff.; Mitteis, pp. 74 ff., 179 ff.

ment of feudalism—the justification for the emphasis long placed on the problem of its origin. No amount of legalistic reasoning can obscure the fact that the feudal aristocracy of the eleventh century differed radically from the Roman aristocracy of the fourth in being thoroughly warlike. And this character, beyond all question, was a barbarian inheritance. Is it mere coincidence that the vassalage glorified in the *chansons de geste* is so close in spirit to the primitive *comitatus?* [41] To derive vassalage from the Gallo-Roman *patrocinium,* one must somewhere, in the course of a devious argument, introduce a revolutionizing factor.[42]

Historians who have no passionate interest in disproving the Germanic origin of feudalism might well be expected, like Brunner, to prefer the simpler theory of Montesquieu. But to most it has seemed possible to accept that theory only with various qualifications; for the alleged persistence of the *comitatus* among the Franks has been found hard to prove, especially in the face of telling criticism by Guilhiermoz.[43] His thesis, it

[41] This fact is well brought out, in the midst of much fanciful speculation, by Jacques Flach, *Les origines de l'ancienne France,* II (Paris, 1893), 431 ff. Guilhiermoz also makes constant use of the *chansons de geste* in his splendid chapters on the relation between the later vassalage and chivalry; cf. Bloch, pp. 354 ff.

[42] For example, George Burton Adams attributes the change to the influence of the *comitatus* itself. *Civilization during the Middle Ages* (revised ed., New York, 1922), p. 202. His article, "Feudalism," in the eleventh edition of the *Encyclopædia Britannica* suggests that the *patrocinium* was adopted by the Franks mainly because, unlike the *comitatus,* "it was not confined to king or tribal chief" (see above, n. 31). The disconnected writings of Fustel de Coulanges positively affirm the Roman origin of feudalism and admirably describe the nonmilitary patronage and the nonmilitary benefice in Frankish Gaul but lapse into vague conjecture when approaching the question of how these institutions became militarized. *Histoire des institutions politiques de l'ancienne France: Les origines du système féodal,* ed. Camille Jullian (Paris, 1890), especially pp. 12, 152, 247, 280, 316; cf. Lot, pp. 643–57 and n. 95. Waitz, denying that vassalage as such implied any military obligations, seeks to explain the latter as arising out of the benefices acquired by vassals, in spite of the fact that the original benefices were nonmilitary *precariae.* In this respect, as concluded by Brunner (above, n. 25), the criticism of Roth is unanswerable; cf. Mitteis, p. 177.

[43] Brunner, though inclined (*Deutsche Rechtsgeschichte,* I, 60) to agree with Seeck as against Guilhiermoz that the imperial guard of *scholares* was an adaptation of the Germanic *comitatus* on Roman soil, admits (*ibid.,* II, 354) that the Gallo-Roman custom of maintaining unfree household troops may have influenced the development of vassalage in Neustria. Cf. Dopsch, *Wirtschaftliche und soziale Grundlagen,* II, 304 ff.; Mitteis, p. 20; Schröder, pp. 168 ff.; Calmette, p. 16; Bloch,

will be remembered, depends on two identifications: that of the Merovingian *antrustiones* with the Roman *scholares* and that of the Carolingian *vassi* with the *antrustiones*. By reviewing the evidence for each of these identifications we may test not only them but the Montesquieu-Brunner theory as well.

First we have the familiar account of the *comitatus* in the *Germania* of Tacitus, supplemented by other literature that indicates a widespread existence of the custom among later invaders of the imperial lands.[44] The German word represented by the *comes* of Tacitus was presumably one related to the Anglo-Saxon *gesið*, which literally means "a companion on a journey"—one eventually turned into *gasindus* by less scrupulous Latinists.[45] As described by Tacitus, at any rate, the *comes* was a free warrior who voluntarily, by a solemn obligation (*sacramentum*), agreed to become the devoted follower of a military chief (*princeps*), sharing his fortunes even to the death in return for sustenance, equipment, and a share of the booty gained in war. The companion might or might not be of a family reputed noble; within the chosen band no such distinction could equal that of valor and loyalty on the field of battle. The chief, as held by Brunner, might be any freeman who could afford the expense of having armed retainers; for Waitz's read-

---

p. 233. Lot, after agreeing with Brunner that the Roman *scholares* resembled the *comites* of Tacitus and without referring to the fact that the armed *pueri* of great persons in the Merovingian kingdom were usually slaves, concludes (p. 661, n. 117) that "les seules vues satisfaisantes sur l'origine de la vassalité privée sont celles de Guilhiermoz."

44 Brunner, *Deutsche Rechtsgeschichte*, I, 186–95. See also the notes to the more recent editions of the *Germania*, especially that of Rudolf Much (Heidelberg, 1937).

45 *Ibid.*, p. 156; Brunner, *Deutsche Rechtsgeschichte*, II, 350 ff.; Bloch, p. 237; F. Liebermann, *Die Gesetze der Angelsachsen* (Halle, 1903–16), II, 427 ff. (*Gefolgsadel*). Briefly, the Anglo-Saxon sources indicate that the *gesið* (translated as *comes* by Bede and other Latin writers) was always a freeman; that in addition he was the warlike follower of a chief with whom he lived and for whom, if necessary, he died; that any man of wealth and distinction might be expected to have *gesiðas;* that it was presumably those of the king who acquired hereditary noble rank with a wergeld three times that of the *ceorl*. Even Guilhiermoz cannot explain away this evidence, though he continues to regard the *gasindi* of the Lombards as a variety of *buccellarii* (pp. 47 ff., 92 ff.). The sources, I believe, tend rather to support Brunner's view that the Continental *gasindi* were free *Gefolgsleute*—a matter of some interest, because in the eighth century *vassus* and *gasindus* were sometimes used as synonymous terms.

ing of *princeps* as "prince" in the political sense, though still repeated in a number of books,[46] is hardly supported either by the context of the *Germania* or by any other source.

Following Montesquieu, all nineteenth century historians regarded the Merovingian *antrustiones* as a royal *comitatus*. Then Guilhiermoz advanced the thesis that they were merely imperial *scholares* under another name, and his reasoning is hard to set aside. Our principal source for the Frankish institution is a document preserved in the formulary of Marculf (seventh century).[47] This is a royal notification to the effect that so-and-so, "coming with his arms into our palace, has been seen to swear to us *trustem et fidelitatem in manu nostra*" and is therefore to be reckoned among the *antrustiones* and is to enjoy a special wergeld. The entire formality, as Guilhiermoz has shown, appears Roman rather than Germanic.[48] The *Lex Salica*, furthermore, makes it clear that the king could choose whomsoever he pleased for his *trust*—Frank or Roman, free or unfree— and that the higher wergeld, three times whatever it would normally have been, was a form of protection shared by all royal servants.[49] The *antrustiones*, it must be admitted, no more resemble the *comites* of Tacitus than do the armed *pueri*, usually slaves, whom Gregory of Tours and other writers describe as guarding all prominent persons in Merovingian society.[50]

[46] E.g., Schröder, p. 39; Below, p. 220; and, strangely enough, Lot, p. 660.

[47] *Monumenta Germaniae Historica: Legum Sectio V, Formulae,* ed. Karl Zeumer (Hanover, 1886), p. 55.

[48] Guilhiermoz (pp. 77 ff.) is in this particular supported by Mitteis, who (pp. 24 ff.) concludes that whatever connection there had been between the *Antrustionat* and the old *Gefolgschaft* left no trace in the formula of Marculf. The oath sworn by the new *antrustio* was presumably derived from that commonly taken by Roman soldiers (Brunner, *Deutsche Rechtsgeschichte*, II, 78 ff.). The Frankish word *trust* meant simply protection, here specifically the defense of the king's person (*ibid.*, pp. 34 ff.). And historians have generally ceased to understand the vague phrase *in manu nostra* as hiding a reference to homage (see below, n. 56).

[49] Guilhiermoz, p. 67; Brunner, *Deutsche Rechtsgeschichte*, I, 375, and II, 137.

[50] Guilhiermoz, pp. 19, 49 ff.; Roth, *Geschichte des Beneficialwesens*, pp. 152 ff.; Brunner, *Deutsche Rechtsgeschichte*, I, 373 ff. Gregory of Tours, it should be noted, does not mention *antrustiones* but evidently includes them among the *pueri regis* (see below, n. 68). The word *trustis* reappears in the Carolingian capitularies to designate either a band of evildoers (like the Anglo-Saxon *hloð*) or a posse for the pursuit of thieves (Brunner, *Deutsche Rechtsgeschichte*, II, 647, 745). Such usage

To accept the first identification made by Guilhiermoz involves no serious embarrassment; the second is a very different matter. Since, in his opinion, mediaeval vassalage was derived from the ignoble status of mercenary troops in the late empire, it always retained a certain "quasi-servile" character, as did the ceremony of homage, which implied a sort of bodily subjection. Nevertheless, by the ninth century vassalage had actually lost all taint of unfreedom, for only an honorable relationship could become the basis of feudal nobility. So Guilhiermoz has to introduce a revolutionizing factor of his own—a mysterious influence exerted upon the Franks by the Anglo-Saxons of the eighth century, who had preserved the aristocratic *comitatus* of the ancient Germans in their institution of thegnage. And the social transformation thus wrought made possible the formal establishment of military benefices, which were somehow developed out of the peasant holdings earlier assigned to armed slaves and other lowborn retainers.[51] All this is ingenious but quite unconvincing. The suggestions of Guilhiermoz with regard to Anglo-Saxon influence in the Frankish kingdom and the consequent emergence of the fief have met with general skepticism. His explanation of homage as a reminiscence of serfdom, though supported by various writers, is hardly more than a juristic fancy inspired by belief in the quasi-servile character of vassalage.[52] Upon what, aside from the wish to identify the original vassals with the *antrustiones,* does that belief rest?

There is, of course, the derivation of the word *vassus* (or *vassallus*). In the *Lex Salica,* and occasionally in other documents, *vassus* is used to designate an unfree servant.[53] Does this prove that the later *vassi* were the descendants or the successors

would hardly have been possible if the word had been commonly applied to an honorable *Gefolgschaft.*

[51] Guilhiermoz accepts the Roth-Brunner thesis as fundamentally true but amends it as here stated (pp. 86 ff., 92 ff., 102 ff., 140 ff., 322 ff.).

[52] See the excellent summary of the question by Lot (p. 667, n. 144), whose remarks apply with equal force to the argument of Mitteis (pp. 31 ff.). It may also be pointed out that the ceremony of homage regularly included not merely the submission of the vassal but likewise his recognition by the lord as a social equal— usually through a kiss, or perhaps a present.

[53] Brunner, *Deutsche Rechtsgeschichte,* I, 372.

of slaves? Not at all. *Vassus,* the Latinized form of the Celtic *gwas,* is merely one of many common words for "boy"—such as the Latin *puer* and the Germanic *degan* (thegn), as well as *knecht* (*cniht,* knight).[54] Like their modern counterparts, they might be applied to persons of either high or low degree; and whatever technical meaning one of them might acquire cannot be taken for granted at all times and in all regions. Throughout the Middle Ages the men (*homines*) of a lord (*senior* or *dominus*) could be serfs, free peasants, vassals, or other dependents; while common usage gave the title of lord to the head of a household, the owner of an estate, the ruler of a territory, a prelate of the church, or indeed any person of authority.[55] And as there were various kinds of such superiority, there were various ways of recognizing it. We should always remember that the *commendatio* of Latin writers was an extremely vague term; when we read that somebody thus placed himself under a lord's patronage, protection, or *mund,* we must not suppose that he necessarily became that lord's vassal. Although the ceremony that established vassalage was a form of commendation, it was not the only one.[56] The meaning of *vassus* in the eighth century

[54] *Ibid.,* p. 188; Guilhiermoz, pp. 52 ff. In later sources *pueri* occasionally appears as the equivalent of *vassalli* or *milites;* cf. the Bayeux Tapestry: "Hic Odo baculum tenens confortat pueros." In the older Anglo-Saxon poetry either a servant or a *gesið* may be called a *þegn;* modifying words show which implication is intended. Eventually, as the honorable implication is taken for granted, *þegn* altogether supplants *gesið.* The verbal change hardly proves the growth of a new nobility based on domestic service: Liebermann, II, 680 ff. (Thegn); Guilhiermoz, pp. 92 ff.; Graham, as cited above, n. 1.

[55] Bloch, pp. 223 ff.; Ganshof, in *Cam. Hist. Jour.,* VI, 171, n. 114.

[56] Bloch, pp. 227 ff., 247 ff.; Lot, pp. 643 ff., 648 ff., 666 ff.; Brunner, *Deutsche Rechtsgeschichte,* II, 67 ff.; and especially Mitteis, p. 72: "So ist insbesondere die Kommendation bis ins Hochmittelalter hinein immer zu allen möglichen Rechtsgeschäften verwendet worden, die mit dem Vasallenverhältnis gar nichts zu tun hatten. . . . Es ist daher . . . stets auf die Intention zu achten, in der die Kommendationsform gebraucht wird . . . erst der Dativ des Zwecks gibt ein vollständiges Bild des erstrebten rechtsgeschäftlichen Erfolges." How then can Mitteis (pp. 27 ff.) find the "root of vassalage" in the commendation described by the formula of Tours no. 43 (Zeumer, p. 158)? That celebrated document tells of a man with insufficient food and clothing, who commends himself for life *in potestate vel mundoburdo* of a magnificent lord. To make a vassal of this poor fellow, who presumably became a peasant, is to perpetuate the confusion of Waitz, so ably criticized

must therefore be determined through a careful reading of contemporary documents rather than from an alleged implication of the word itself.

So far as royal vassals are concerned, all authorities agree that, from the time we first hear of them, they were persons of great distinction. The capitularies constantly refer to *vassi dominici* as exercising political functions alongside counts and bishops, as enjoying special privilege and honor, as frequently possessing rich estates, and in any case as forming the elite of the Frankish army.[57] But the vassals of persons other than the king, it is said, were likely to be men of base condition—dependents whose vassalage, lacking the glory of a royal connection, retained its primitive character.[58] To justify such a view there is, in my opinion, little positive evidence. Texts that impute an inferior status to mere *homines* or *commendati* of a lord need not be interpreted as referring to vassals at all.[59] Whenever vassals are

---

by Roth over seventy-five years ago (*Über die Anfänge der Vassalität,* pp. 267 ff.). Carolingian writers who tried to be accurate described the ceremony later called homage by such a phrase as *commendatio in vassatico.* See below, n. 65.

[57] Lot, pp. 668 ff.; Guilhiermoz, pp. 130 ff.; Dopsch, in *M.Ö.I.G.,* XLVI, 19 ff.; and especially Ganshof, in *Cam. Hist. Jour.,* VI, 148 ff.

[58] For example, Mitteis, pp. 46 ff.; Ganshof, in *Cam. Hist. Jour.,* VI, 152 ff.; Bloch, pp. 241 ff. The idea goes back to a phase of Roth's *Senioratstheorie (Geschichte des Beneficialwesens,* pp. 369 ff.; *Über die Anfänge der Vassalität,* pp. 246 ff.)—the building of *Privatgefolgschaften* by the newly endowed aristocracy of the eighth century—which was adopted with modifications by Guilhiermoz. But there is no good reason for believing that such *Gefolgschaften* had not existed from the beginning (see above, notes 31, 46). The very first vassal to be mentioned in the capitularies is the one who follows his lord, a *homo frankus,* to the benefice obtained by the latter and who, after the death of the lord and the acquisition of the benefice by another man, returns to his original lord's family. *Monumenta Germaniae Historica: Legum Sectio II, Capitularia,* ed. Alfred Boretius, I (Hanover, 1883), 38. See Ganshof, in *Etudes . . . Henri Pirenne,* p. 187. Why Krawinkel (p. 56) should suppose that the vassal in question was unfree I cannot understand.

[59] As is done by Ganshof (in *Cam. Hist. Jour.,* VI, notes 37-38), when he reads a "bond of vassalage" into the formula of Tours (above, n. 56) and into the Capitulary of Aachen (Boretius, p. 172). The other capitularies that he cites include the one discussed immediately below and two others which, in my opinion, hardly bear out his contention that the vassal's position "can have been little better than that of a servant liable to be punished and dishonored by his master." It is, of course, undeniable that many *vassi non casati* were comparatively poor; but why must we consider them as servile?

mentioned, no matter whose they are, they regularly appear as fighting men, sharply distinguished by their superior equipment from armed peasants in the royal host.[60] Even the capitulary most frequently cited to prove that Carolingian vassalage still had a servile connection can be interpreted to prove the opposite.

The document in question is Charlemagne's *Capitulare Missorum*, which gives instructions for the swearing of fealty to the king and his sons.[61] On the list of those required to take the oath stand bishops, abbots, counts, and royal vassals; subordinate officials, clerical and lay; the generality of free suitors to the courts, whether mere peasants or the men of the great persons named above; and a variety of lesser people, including at the end serfs who have been honored (*honorati*) with benefices and offices or who have been honored in vassalage (*in bassalatico*), so that they may have horses and bear lance, shield, and sword. In the Carolingian age, as later, it was thus possible for a man of unfree birth to become a vassal, but such procedure appears always to have been exceptional.[62] The clear implication of the capitulary is that the serf so honored has been raised out of his original class; since he is now a mounted warrior, he must, as such, swear fealty to the king.

The conclusion that Carolingian vassalage from first to last was essentially honorable finds support, I believe, in all the pertinent sources. Indirectly the capitularies tell us a good deal about the mutual obligations of lords and vassals. The vassal was bound by oath to maintain unswerving loyalty to his lord; to refuse to follow one's lord on a lawful expedition was to break one's plighted faith.[63] In return the lord owed his vassal protection and respect; if he failed in such duty, the vassal was

---

[60] Brunner, *Deutsche Rechtsgeschichte*, II, 282 ff.; and above all Guilhiermoz, who cites a wealth of evidence in his second and third chapters.

[61] Boretius, p. 66. The following interpretation is based on the text as it stands, which is from a single and very corrupt manuscript.

[62] Brunner, *Deutsche Rechtsgeschichte*, II, 283; Lot, p. 667, n. 144.

[63] Boretius, p. 41: Pepin's *Decretum Vermeriense*, which declares that if a wife refuses to go with her husband when he follows his lord, *cui fidem mentiri non poterit*, she may not remarry during the man's lifetime, though he may. The fealty binding the husband indicates that he was a vassal. See below, n. 71; Mitteis, pp. 44 ff.

justified in renouncing him.[64] This relationship was established by the ceremony of homage, the earliest clear reference to which is found in the familiar story of Tassilo, duke of Bavaria.[65] Whether written in 757 or some thirty years later, the account in the royal annals is good evidence that "commendation in vassalage" was a well-known Frankish custom by the second half of the eighth century and one in which contemporaries saw no ignominy. For here, as in the long series of like episodes that followed, the ruler employed vassalage for the purpose not of disgracing a rival but of securing his fidelity. The policy was quite similar to that adopted with a view to controlling officials of church or state and even members of the royal family.[66]

On the whole, I find it incredible that the vassalage which suddenly appears in the records of the eighth century was in any respect a new development. Nor can I believe that the resemblance between this traditional vassalage and the Germanic *comitatus* was a matter of sheer coincidence. Yet, if the connection between the two is not provided by the *antrustiones,* where is it to be found? By reviving an older view with regard to the Merovingian *leudes* (or *leodes*), Alfons Dopsch has suggested a possible answer.[67] Here, briefly, is the evidence. Gregory of Tours, who almost never uses a Germanic word, mentions *leudes* (i.e., *leute*) three times—clearly implying that such "people" of a king were his, not in the general sense of political subjects but in the special sense of military followers.[68] Men of

---

[64] Boretius, p. 215.

[65] It has been told in all the books on early feudal institutions—most recently by Mitteis, pp. 65 ff., and Krawinkel, pp. 48 ff. Cf. Ganshof, in *Cam. Hist. Jour.,* VI, 155 ff.

[66] Guilhiermoz, pp. 127–28.

[67] In *M.Ö.I.G.,* XLI, 35 ff. Dopsch rejects the entire argument of Roth (above, n. 18), hitherto accepted by virtually all authorities (e.g., Guilhiermoz, p. 52, n. 3), and in so doing necessarily goes back to the views of Eichhorn and Montesquieu. Dopsch's chief concern (as in his *Wirtschaftliche und soziale Grundlagen,* II, ch. iv) is to prove an intimate connection between vassalage and benefice holding throughout the Merovingian period—a thesis for which, it seems to me, he produces quite insufficient evidence.

[68] *Historia Francorum,* ii, 42; iii, 23; viii, 9. In the first of these instances Gregory tells us that Clovis seduced King Ragnachar's *leudes* with golden bracelets and sword belts (a reminiscence, as Dopsch points out, of the lordly ring-giver in Anglo-Saxon poetry); in the second that King Theudebert, when attacked, was successfully

this kind seem also to be thought of in the peace of Guntram and Childebert II (587), who agree not to entice or to receive each other's *leudes*.[69] And the vaguer references in other sources at least indicate that the persons styled *leudes* belonged to the warrior class, were likely to be politically and socially prominent, and often received grants of land from the royal fisc.[70] Accordingly, the Merovingian oath of *fidelitas et leudesamio* [71] may well be understood as having anticipated the oath demanded by Charlemagne of every free subject, that he would be faithful to the emperor "as a man rightly should be to his lord."

We now realize that the Merovingian state, far from being the noble Germanic structure imagined by Roth, was a pseudo-Roman sham that utterly collapsed under the degenerate successors of Clovis. With it disappeared many vestiges of the old imperial government, including apparently the Frankish imitation of the Roman *scholares*. Much more vigorous than any such vestiges was the native custom of the barbarian conquerors, especially that governing the life of the warlike aristocracy. Within this sphere the persistence of what we call vassalage must be considered a strong probability. Guilhiermoz, I think, has rightly insisted that the chivalrous *adoubement* of the Middle

---

defended by his *leudes;* in the third that King Guntram suspected one of his *leudes* as the father of Prince Lothair.

[69] Boretius, p. 14.

[70] The pertinent writings, some of which have dubious value, are cited by Dopsch and Roth to support opposite opinions. Neither extreme has to be accepted. As Brunner remarks (*Deutsche Rechtsgeschichte*, II, 14, n. 16), it is quite possible that the word *leudes* might sometimes have the broader meaning of people in general; cf. the familiar uses of the Latin *homines*.

[71] We have only this vague description in a document preserved by Marculf (Zeumer, p. 68). The sources are meager, but they definitely indicate that, contrary to Roth's belief, both the Merovingians and the Carolingians sought to bind all subjects to the king by the same oath of fealty as traditionally bound a man to his lord. Dopsch, as cited above; Mitteis, pp. 25 ff., 47 ff.; Ganshof, in *Cam. Hist. Jour.*, VI, 171 ff.; Boretius, pp. 63, 92, 101 ff., 124. Cf. the doom of King Edmund; Liebermann, I, 190, II, 556 (*Königstreue*), 577 (*Mannschaftseid*). If this view is correct, the mediaeval oath of fealty had its origin in the personal relationship that became known as vassalage. The *sacramentum* referred to by Tacitus in describing the bond between *comes* and *princeps* may well have been a formal act of some kind (see *Germania*, ed. Much, p. 163 and the following note); fealty can then be understood as a superimposed Christian ritual (Esmein, p. 190; Calmette, pp. 38 ff.; Bloch, p. 225).

Ages, despite the utter silence of the Merovingian records, must be traced back to the formal arming of the German youth as described by Tacitus. He even suggests that the substitution of homage for the Roman exchange of documents in commendation was a consequence "of the recrudescence of Germanism that accompanied the rise to power of the Austrasian family of the Arnulfings." [72] Why may we not attribute the whole Carolingian development of vassalage to this same factor, rather than to juristic necessity or to an imaginary Anglo-Saxon influence? At any rate, the little information to be gained from the wretched sources of the early Frankish age points to the military retainers styled *leudes,* in preference to the palace guards styled *antrustiones,* as the precursors of the Carolingian *vassi.*[73]

If the foregoing argument is well grounded, there is no reason for supposing any great change in the institution of vassalage under the Carolingians except that now produced by close association with fief holding. Whether the military benefice was or was not an eighth-century invention is a matter of secondary importance.[74] Our chief interest is rather the wide extension of feudal tenure that came in the ensuing period. To account for this extension we must, in my opinion, consider the following

[72] Guilhiermoz, pp. 79, 393 ff. It is worth noting that in the latter connection Mitteis (pp. 480–81) finds a strong Germanic tradition in the ceremony of homage, quite apart from the doubtful element of the handclasp (p. 31).

[73] Lack of evidence makes it futile to inquire what relationship, if any, existed between *leudes* and *gasindi,* or why these terms came to be superseded by *vassi.*

[74] The ideas of Waitz, Roth, and Brunner have been sketched in the preceding pages; for those of Dopsch see above, n. 67, and below, n. 77. Ganshof, defending the "classic theory" of Brunner, admits that benefices held by vassals are not unknown before the time of Charles Martel but contends that they were generally established only in the eighth century (*Etudes . . . Henri Pirenne,* pp. 175 ff.; cf. Mitteis, pp. 107 ff.). Lot, on the other hand, refuses to accept the Roth-Brunner thesis, which he calls that of "explosive vassalage" (pp. 664 ff.). The sudden appearance of military benefices in the eighth century is due, he believes, merely to the fact that they were not commonly recorded in charters; if the Merovingian capitularies had been preserved, we should hear more about such grants in the earlier period. In this argument he has the support of Krawinkel (pp. 137, 163 ff.)—and, I think, rightly; for I cannot believe that so useful an institution as the military benefice was primarily the result of legal difficulty arising from the confiscation of church property. The objections of Lot (p. 662) and Krawinkel (pp. 80 ff.) to Brunner's peculiar interpretation of the Germanic land grant (above, n. 30) are, in my opinion, likewise sound. A good review of the whole controversy has recently been given by H. A. Cronne, "The Origins of Feudalism," *History,* XXIV (1939–40), 251 ff.

points. The basis of the new system, assuredly, was military need. The king gave fiefs to his vassals and encouraged subinfeudation on the part of the latter for the primary purpose of securing a better army; and, no matter what may be made of the Saracen danger,[75] there was an increasing demand for mounted troops. The rapid introduction of heavy-armed cavalry, as Guilhiermoz has admirably shown, was of profound social significance. As the *miles* became exclusively a *caballarius*, the gulf between his status and that of the peasant grew wider. The profession of arms came to be governed by an aristocratic code of chivalry—a set of rules that had meaning only for the highborn. Thus in the later Middle Ages knight and noble were virtually synonymous terms. Land held for agrarian rent or service, whatever the nature of the original contract, was no fief; the tenant, however free in law, was no vassal.[76]

The vassal's obligation, being military, was *ipso facto* political; so, according to Carolingian standards, it was proper for him to receive political privilege in return. The truth should never be overlooked that a fief brought to the holder not merely the rights of a landlord but also those of an immunist.[77] Leading authorities are today agreed that the personal relationship of lord to vassal carried with it no power of jurisdiction.[78] What we know as feudal justice could not be separated from the territorial immunity which every fief was construed to imply. And insofar as the feudal lord had the right to hold courts, to levy tolls and other imposts, to requisition labor and materials, to raise fortifications, and to muster the population for local defense, he was

[75] Lot, p. 665; Mitteis, pp. 124 ff.; Dopsch, in *M.Ö.I.G.*, XLVI, 9 ff.; and especially Krawinkel, pp. 11 ff.

[76] Guilhiermoz, ch. iii, particularly pp. 450 ff.; Lot, pp. 656–57, 673; Bloch, pp. 267 ff.

[77] Brunner, *Deutsche Rechtsgeschichte*, II, 344, 383 ff.; Below, pp. 243 ff. This idea has been well developed by Dopsch (in *M.Ö.I.G.*, XLVI, 19 ff.), though he tends, I think, to exaggerate the administrative usefulness of the *vassi* in order to minimize the significance of any military or economic change during the Carolingian period. Krawinkel seems also to be carrying the argument too far when he concludes (pp. 134 ff.) that, even in the Merovingian period, immunity was the essence of every benefice.

[78] See the excellent discussion in Mitteis, pp. 164 ff., 296 ff., and the literature there cited, especially the various articles of Ganshof. Cf. Lot, p. 670; Helen M. Cam, "Suitors and *Scabini*," *Speculum*, X (1935), 189 ff.

obviously a public official.[79] It is, indeed, no mere form of words to assert that every fief was an office; for the rule of primogeniture evidently came to be incorporated in feudal law through recognition of this principle.[80] Another phase of the same development may be seen in the fact that by the end of the ninth century the more important agents of the state had been brought within the category of royal vassals. The transition was an informal one, of which the capitularies tell us little, but that the result was quite in accord with Carolingian policy seems clear. If every feudal tenant was to some degree a count within his own territory, when a count became a vassal, would not the county be his fief? [81]

The conclusion thus seems inevitable that to talk of "political feudalism," as distinguished from "economic feudalism," is misleading.[82] All feudalism was political; and if we wish to refer to the agrarian economy presupposed by feudal tenure, we have the accurate and familiar expression, "manorial system." The original feudalism, as I understand the term, was a phase of government developed by the Frankish kings on the basis of a pre-existing barbarian custom of vassalage. It was not, therefore, an inevitable stage in economic evolution. Although it involved a system of rewarding soldiers with grants of land, it was by no means that alone. Nor was it the mere equivalent of provincial autonomy under a failing empire. To appraise its historical

---

[79] Esmein (pp. 171 ff.), it seems to me, is entirely justified in his criticism of those historians who seek to derive the *seigneurie* of the Middle Ages from the ownership of either land or serfs. In this connection, however, a remark of Mitteis (p. 295, n. 109) is worth repeating: that, so far as France is concerned, the distinction between *régime seigneurial* and *régime féodal* is only a bit of modern theorizing; they are "two different aspects of the same thing, in practice hardly to be separated." Thus any single power held by a mediaeval baron may be called feudal in that it was part of his fief, seignorial in that it was exercised over men who were not vassals. And no matter what phase of seignorial government we examine, the responsibility of individual subjects will be found to vary according to their social rank, not according to some feudal or nonfeudal quality in the governmental function. Cf. Bloch, pp. 373 ff.

[80] Mitteis, pp. 657 ff.; Calmette, pp. 53 ff.; Bloch, pp. 313 ff.

[81] Brunner, *Deutsche Rechtsgeschichte,* II, 344; Below, pp. 243 ff.; Mitteis, pp. 198 ff.; Ganshof, in *Cam. Hist. Jour.,* VI, 167 ff.

[82] These phrases have been popularized especially by Adams; see, for example, *The Origin of the English Constitution* (New Haven, 1912), pp. 44 ff.

significance is, to say the least, not easy; for, as feudal custom was inherited and further developed by the states of later Europe, it became increasingly complex and variable. What follows is intended as a mere preliminary statement—mainly an attempt to dispose of a few troublesome misconceptions.[83]

As already remarked, many famous scholars have believed that feudalism was politically baneful—have considered it a sort of cancerous growth within the state. Yet as long ago as 1818 Henry Hallam expressed the opinion that the feudal system had much to be said in its favor.[84] Despite its shortcomings it must be valued, he says, as "a school of moral discipline," which nourished a spirit of honorable obligation, a noble sentiment of personal loyalty. Although under that system private war and its attendant disorders flourished everywhere, the "inefficiency of the feudal militia" tended to save Europe from the "danger of universal monarchy." "To the feudal law it is owing that the very names of right and privilege were not swept away, as in Asia, by the desolating hand of power." These sentiments, most of us will agree, are a trifle exuberant. But Hallam makes a good point when he adds:

It is the previous state of society under the grandchildren of Charlemagne we must always keep in mind if we would appreciate the effects of the feudal system upon the welfare of mankind. The institutions of the eleventh century must be compared with those of the ninth, not with the advanced civilization of modern times. If the view that I have taken of those dark ages is correct, the state of anarchy which we term feudal was the natural result of a vast and barbarous empire feebly administered, and the cause rather than the result of the general establishment of feudal tenures.

Too few historians, it seems to me, have followed the lead offered by the eloquent Hallam. Too many have repeated vague generalizations to the effect that feudalism was virtually synonymous with political disintegration.[85] The meaning of such

[83] Although Mitteis deals admirably with various phases of the problem, he pays little attention to the one that seems to me most important—the working of feudal government in the principalities of the tenth and eleventh centuries.

[84] *View of the State of Europe during the Middle Ages* (London, 1818), ch. ii, pts. 1–2.

[85] See in particular the definition of Adams, *Civilization during the Middle Ages,*

remarks depends altogether on what state they refer to. Will they hold good, in the first place, for the Carolingian Empire? The capitularies of the eighth and ninth centuries reveal on the part of the kings a definite policy of using traditional vassalage to buttress the monarchical authority. Royal vassals, serving as heavy-armed cavalry and leading similar contingents of their own men, formed the principal strength of the army. They were increasingly employed in routine administration as well as for special missions. They came to be placed in many prominent offices of church and state. To enable them to meet their costly obligations, they were commonly endowed with rich benefices that included rights of immunity. But this glorification of vassalage for governmental purposes often tended to weaken and discredit the primitive bond. Vassals living on distant fiefs lost respect for a lord with whom they had little contact. Disloyal officials, in spite of enforced homage, continued to be disloyal. No amount of legal enactment could prevent usurpation or deter men from supporting the immediate lord who gave them sustenance and protection. And the establishment of hereditary tenure, though encouraged by the emperors, perpetuated more abuses than benefits.[86] In other words, the feudalizing policy of the Carolingians failed, not because it was in itself evil, but because it sought to accomplish the impossible.

The empire of Charlemagne was indeed too "vast and barbarous" and too "feebly administered" to be held together in the troubled period that ensued upon his death. The entire

---

p. 221: "Feudalism is a form of political organization which allows the state to separate into as minute fragments as it will, virtually independent of one another and of the state, without the total destruction of its own life with which such an experience would seem to threaten every general government." Even James Westfall Thompson, for all his sympathetic treatment of the subject, can assert that "feudalism destroyed the empire of Charlemagne"—*The Middle Ages* (2d ed., New York, 1932), I, xv. And many French historians (e.g., Calmette, pp. 2, 22 ff., 56 ff.) have expressed similar opinions. Good criticism of the old view will be found in Below, pp. 43 ff., 231 ff., and Mitteis, pp. 3 ff.

[86] Bloch (pp. 293 ff.) cites with approval the judgment of Montesquieu that fiefs tended to endanger the state when they became hereditary. To be exact, however, feudal law recognized no absolute inheritance of fiefs; the heir had the right to investiture, as he kept the right to possession, only on certain conditions. It was when vassals got completely out of hand that political disruption ensued (Mitteis, pp. 205, 640 ff.).

political experience of western Europe for the next three hundred years, down to the new age of economic recovery, demonstrated at least one fact: that a state, in order to survive, had to be relatively small.[87] Even the kingdom of Charles the Bald had ceased to have any reality long before it was acquired by Hugh Capet. Its territory had now been divided among a dozen or more principalities, one of which—a remnant of the old Neustrian march—was held by the king. If we examine these principalities, the true states of the eleventh century, what do we learn of feudalism and its political significance? A cursory glance shows that feudal custom was generally prevalent in those where the central authority was strong as well as in those where it was weak. The difference between typical members of the two groups is found to lie not in any theoretical powers of the ruler but in his ability to enforce them. As has often been pointed out, the feudal contract allowed each party to denounce the other for stated cause, primarily default of aid or protection; it was the absence of a common superior to render effective justice that resulted in the chronic warfare called private.[88] Within any well-organized state whose military and civil administration depended largely on feudal relationships, the regulation of the latter was imperative—was, in fact, an essential part of the system under which they were supposed to exist. And it is a mistake to consider feudal decentralization an unmitigated evil. The construction of every fief as a restricted sphere of seignorial government may well be compared with the modern establishment of partial autonomy in cities, townships, and other local units.[89] Feudal anarchy there was in many regions of mediaeval Europe, but feudalism was not of necessity anarchical.

The proof of this statement is very familiar. It lies in the fact that the feudalism of northern France, derived from the later

[87] Unappreciated by most writers on mediaeval institutions, this truth has been clearly stated by Below (pp. 345 ff.). It is a great misfortune that he did not live to complete his second volume, which would have dealt with the German principalities.

[88] The discussion of this subject by A. Luchaire is justly famous. *Manuel des institutions françaises* (Paris, 1892), pp. 219 ff. Cf. Mitteis, pp. 534 ff.; Esmein, pp. 247 ff.

[89] Rightly emphasized by Below, pp. 302 ff.

custom of the Carolingian Empire, was taken over and developed with remarkable success by the Normans, first in their own duchy and then in England. The Norman dukes—like the marquises of Flanders, the counts of Anjou, and various other French princes, including Louis VI as ruler of the Capetian domain—made feudal tenure the basis of the most efficient government then possible in western Europe. So, to my mind, their little territories were feudal states par excellence; for it is an academic question whether the organization of an actual state could be reduced to feudal relationship alone. The French kingdom of the eleventh century was no more of a state than the Holy Roman Empire of the eighteenth; and the kingdom described in the Assizes of Jerusalem seems to have been equally theoretical.[90] Nor is much profit to be derived from argument about the ideal feudal state— a matter that resolves itself into arbitrary definition.[91] What needs rather to be studied is the practical working of feudal institutions in the Middle Ages. Politics were politics, and statesmanship was statesmanship, even then.

[90] It will be readily understood that, in this respect, I agree with Mitteis, pp. 534 ff., rather than with John L. LaMonte, *Feudal Monarchy in the Latin Kingdom of Jerusalem* (Cambridge, Mass., 1932), pp. 87 ff., 243 ff. The principalities established by the crusaders were, in my opinion, the true Latin states of Syria; the kingdom of Jerusalem was at most an afterthought.

[91] Thus Adams, ignoring his original definition (above, n. 85), comes to describe the twelfth-century feudalism of England as ideal (*Origin of the English Constitution*, pp. 186 ff.). But he himself points out that such a discussion depends on what we mean by "feudalism" and what we mean by "ideal." No feudal state, of course, could seem ideal to everybody; what pleased the Angevin Henry II could never please all his vassals or his Capetian lord either.

Feudalism and Its Antecedents
in England *

IN a previous article I reviewed the opinions of various historians on the origin and significance of feudalism and ventured to state some of my own.[1] Feudalism proper, I concluded, was essentially political, being a phase of government developed by the Frankish kings through the granting of benefices to their vassals. Originally the fief was not any benefice, but a military benefice; the vassal was not any man of a lord, but a military retainer. Vassalage, whatever the derivation of the word, was directly descended from the Germanic custom that Tacitus called the *comitatus.* Although the benefice was the outgrowth of the Roman *precarium,* feudal tenure was wholly mediaeval in that the fief was a benefice held by a vassal. By rewarding their vassals with fiefs, the Carolingians sought to provide themselves with a force of heavy-armed cavalry; by insisting that all great officials should be their vassals, they hoped to strengthen the royal administration; and by extending the privilege of immunity to all fief-holders, they deliberately gave numerous powers of local government to the feudal aristocracy. The dis-

* Reprinted from *The American Historical Review,* XLVIII (1943), 245–65.

[1] *Ibid.,* XLVI (1941), 788–812. For a more popular presentation on a broader scale see my *Mediaeval Feudalism,* recently published by the Cornell University Press. In particulars this book anticipated conclusions here made.

integration of the Carolingian Empire resulted from its inherent weakness, not from the feudalizing policy of its rulers. Feudal institutions worked effectively in many of the small states that had emerged by the middle of the tenth century. The usefulness of feudal tenures, feudal armies, feudal castles, and the like is evinced by the fact that they came to be adopted throughout mediaeval Europe. To misunderstand feudalism is to misunderstand the political life of the Middle Ages.

The purpose of the present article [2] is to apply these conclusions to the feudalism of England, a subject on which a formidable mass of writing has already accumulated. Happily for the reviewer, however, a good part of the mass may be disregarded as too antiquated to require discussion. None of the old constitutional histories of England need even be mentioned except that by William Stubbs.[3] His views on the feudal development of England may be cited because they show how confused the whole matter remained until J. H. Round had clearly stated and effectively solved the central problem.[4] On taking up the subject of feudalism, Stubbs flatly states that "by its historic origin and growth" it was "distinctly Frank." "Feudalism in both tenure and government was, so far as it existed in England, brought full-grown from France."[5] William, however, was both wise and strong. He merely substituted "the Frankish system of tenure . . . for the Anglo-Saxon"; he did not introduce "the feudal principles of government," which in every state where they were logically carried out reduced the central monarchy to "a mere shadow of a name."[6] Even with regard to tenure there was after 1066 a very gradual transformation of Anglo-Saxon forms into Norman. Presumably "the actual obligation of military service was much the same in both systems, and . . .

[2] I wish to thank the members of my graduate seminar during the academic year 1941–42 for contributing to this article as their predecessors did to its predecessor.

[3] The following references are to the sixth edition (Oxford, 1903), which was but slightly changed from the first edition of 1873.

[4] In his famous essay, "The Introduction of Knight Service into England," *Feudal England* (London, 1895), pp. 225–314; first published in *The English Historical Review*, VI–VII (1891–92).

[5] *Constitutional History of England*, I, 273, and n. 2.

[6] *Ibid.*, I, 274, 279.

even the amount of land which was bound to furnish a mounted warrior was the same, however the conformity may have been produced." The change was essentially one "from confusion to order." "The complicated and unintelligible irregularities of the Anglo-Saxon tenures were exchanged for the simple and uniform feudal theory." [7]

Stubbs, it may be noted, never uses the term "Anglo-Saxon feudalism"; all that he will admit is that on the eve of the Norman Conquest "Anglo-Saxon institutions were already approaching the feudal model." [8] For Stubbs, as an ardent disciple of Georg Waitz, refuses to see any connection between Gallo-Roman vassalage and the Germanic *comitatus*. The latter, since it had preserved "a more distinct existence" among the invaders of Britain, was perhaps "one of the causes that distinguished the later Anglo-Saxon system most definitely from the feudalism of the Frank empire." [9] Being by origin a sort of *gesið*, who was none other than the *comes* of Tacitus, the thegn could not really be a vassal. "Frank vassalage was based on the practice of commendation and the beneficiary system." "Each of these practices had its parallel in England"—as had also the Continental grant of immunity.[10] But a peculiar combination of the elements differentiated the Frankish from the Anglo-Saxon custom. Under the first the benefice and the *comitatus* remained unconnected; under the second they were "in the closest connexion." [11] Throughout all this discussion, despite its conscientious and learned character, one feels that Stubbs is somehow managing to argue in circles. He is sure only of his conclusion: that English institutional development has been continuous since Anglo-Saxon times, uninterrupted by the feudalizing policy of the Norman conquerors.

To the broad theory of feudalism thus presented Round, of course, paid little attention. His article on the introduction of knight service into England dealt solely with that one problem, but it was of crucial importance. The establishment of feudal

---

[7] *Ibid.*, pp. 282–83.　　　　[8] *Ibid.*, pp. 283 ff.
[9] *Ibid.*, pp. 273–77. On Waitz see *Am. Hist. Rev.*, XLVI, 791 ff.
[10] Stubbs, I, 170–75, 275–76.　　　　[11] *Ibid.*, p. 170, n. 2.

tenure in the Norman kingdom, Round conclusively proved, was not a matter of gradual change. On the contrary, it came about through the revolutionary action of the Conqueror himself, who gave much of England as fiefs to his vassals without the least regard to the military, social, or tenurial customs of the Anglo-Saxons. In the arrangements made by each vassal to provide his owed service the king would have no interest as long as that service was duly rendered, and it was defined in terms of contemporary Norman-French feudalism. As the direct result of Round's work, most scholars have long since abandoned the idea that the feudalization of England was of slight constitutional significance and now agree that, from almost every point of view, the year 1066 marks the beginning of a new epoch in the history of the kingdom.[12]

Nevertheless, the school of which Stubbs was a prominent member still had much to say on the subject of feudal institutions. Maitland, in particular, devoted a considerable portion of his eloquent *Domesday Book and Beyond* to the matter of Anglo-Saxon precedent for Norman feudalism. Without depreciating Round's work, Maitland questions whether the Conqueror really "introduced any very new principle." To follow up this query he offers his entire second essay, there discussing the development of seignorial justice, the gradual subjection of the free population to aristocratic control, and the increasing importance of subordinate land tenure, especially that involving military service.[13] All these factors, in Maitland's opinion, must be regarded as having contributed to the growth of feudalism, which "is and always will be an inexact term"—one that may be rightly used to denote all the more characteristic phases of mediaeval

---

[12] See especially the fine tribute to Round in F. M. Stenton, *The First Century of English Feudalism, 1066–1166* (Oxford, 1932), Introduction. Cf. R. R. Darlington, in *History*, XXII (1937), 1–13, and D. C. Douglas, in the *Economic History Review*, IX (1938–39), 128–43. At this point a reference may also be given to C. Petit-Dutaillis, *Studies and Notes Supplementary to Stubbs' Constitutional History*, trans. by W. E. Rhodes (Manchester, 1908)—a well-known volume which is now itself in need of much supplementary criticism.

[13] F. W. Maitland, *Domesday Book and Beyond* (Cambridge, 1897), pp. 160, 220–356.

life. According to this view, England had been feudal long before William of Normandy defined the service to be owed by his barons. As early as the tenth century we find something very like feudal tenure in the *beneficia* conferred on his thegns by Oswald, bishop of Worcester. By that time the manorial system was already old throughout most of England. And seignorial justice can be traced back not only to the first grants of immunity but even, by implication, to the first land books of the Anglo-Saxon kings. As Maitland states in his preface, he has tried to "abandon as little as may be of what we learnt from Dr Konrad von Maurer and Dr Stubbs."

In these opinions Maitland received the warm support of Paul Vinogradoff, whose third important work was dedicated to his lamented friend.[14] Meanwhile, however, George Burton Adams had re-examined the subject of "Anglo-Saxon Feudalism" and had arrived at wholly different conclusions.[15] Maitland's argument for pre-Norman feudalism in England, Adams declares, "rests upon the existence before the Conquest of three groups of institutional facts: dependent tenures, private jurisdictions, and military service as an element in land tenure." But "if we grant the existence of these facts in Saxon England have we admitted the existence there of the feudal system proper?" The answer, he says, must be no; for "those characteristics of feudalism in the wider sense . . . are not in the line of the ancestry of feudalism proper." Only one form of dependent tenure may be rightly designated as feudal—the one distinguished by the *"patrocinium* contract," which specified honorable service, essentially political rather than economic. Since that form of tenure did not exist in Saxon England, neither did a truly feudal jurisdiction or a truly feudal military system, both of which were based on the feudal contract.

Maitland apparently never answered this criticism by Adams, who reaffirmed and amplified his opinions in 1912 with reference

---

[14] *English Society in the Eleventh Century* (Oxford, 1908); this was preceded by *Villainage in England* (Oxford, 1892) and *The Growth of the Manor* (London, 1905).

[15] *Am. Hist. Rev.*, VII (1901), 11–35. The following quotations are from pages 12, 14, and 17.

only to certain objections that he had received in private letters.[16] Yet a telling rejoinder could easily have been made by any upholder of the Stubbsian tradition who had thought to proceed somewhat as follows. The keystone in the logical structure of Adams is the *"patrocinium* contract," the best example of which is the well-known formula of Tours.[17] By it a man who lacks both food and clothing yields and commends himself into the power, defense, or *mundoburdum* of such and such a magnificent lord, agreeing, in return for a means of subsistence, to give him lifelong service *ingenuili ordine.* To turn this agreement into a feudal contract Adams by his own definition must read into it the idea of honorable service and make it wholly different from all varieties of personal dependence in Saxon England. But how can he do this when the earliest of the dooms establish penalties for the breach of the *mundbyrd* enjoyed by *eorl* and *ceorl,* as well as by king and ecclesiastic, and when the records of the later kingdom constantly tell of commended freemen who, as such, owe service "of a free order" to their lords? [18] In my opinion, at least, Adams made his fundamental mistake in accepting the views of Waitz and Fustel de Coulanges with regard to the origin of feudalism. Having done so, he was logically obliged to admit that something very like feudalism did exist in Saxon England. He would have done better to follow Paul Roth and Heinrich Brunner.[19]

More recently the historical student has been provided with a splendid supplement to Round's work by Mr. Stenton. In order to explain the title of his book, *The First Century of English Feudalism, 1066-1166,* he states what is unquestionably the judgment of most scholars today: [20] "The more clearly the Anglo-Norman aristocracy of barons and knights is seen in the

[16] *The Origin of the English Constitution* (New Haven, 1912), pp. 44 ff. On the supplement concerning "Political and Economic Feudalism" see *Am. Hist. Rev.,* XLVI, 808.

[17] Quoted by Adams, *ibid.,* VII, 31; cf. XLVI, 802, n. 56.

[18] Aethelberht, 2, 6, 8, 10, 13–15; Wihtraed, 2: F. Liebermann, *Die Gesetze der Angelsachsen* (Halle, 1903–16), I, 3–4, 12. For other references see below.

[19] Their views are sketched in *Am. Hist. Rev.,* XLVI, 792 ff.

[20] P. v.

light of records written from its own standpoint, the more widely it seems to differ from the native aristocracy which preceded it, and the more misleading it seems to apply the adjective 'feudal' to any aspect of English society before the Norman Conquest." Mr. Stenton's comment, however, is restricted to one or two phases of later Anglo-Saxon history; he is not led to consider the comprehensive theories of institutional growth presented by Adams and Maitland. So it may still be worth while to review, as briefly as possible, the entire question of the alleged Anglo-Saxon feudalism. Although we may be convinced that the phrase is unjustifiable, we may try to understand what institutions were actually developed in pre-Norman England and how, if at all, they were related to those properly termed feudal.

At the beginning of our investigation we are confronted by a famous problem of social history. Twelfth-century England was characterized by the sharp differentiation of two classes: the landlords, who constituted a political and military aristocracy, and the cultivators of the soil, who constituted an economically dependent peasantry. Had this differentiation resulted from the feudalizing policy of the Norman kings, and perhaps of their immediate predecessors, or had it formed part of the original Anglo-Saxon system? Many distinguished historians have taught that the Germanic invaders of Britain, like those of Gaul, commonly settled in free villages, where as peasant-warriors they long maintained a sort of primitive democracy.[21] Widespread belief in this doctrine has tended to obscure the fact that it involves not an easy interpretation of history but a difficult one. Any member of the Germanist school, following Stubbs, has to show how his cherished democracy was first derived from the warrior aristocracy pictured by Tacitus and was then changed back into much the same kind of aristocracy.[22] The institutional

[21] Cf. H. Brunner, *Deutsche Rechtsgeschichte,* I (2d ed., Leipzig, 1906), 341: "Als Krieger und Bauer war der freie Germane in die fränkische Geschichte eingetreten. Allmählich steigerten sich die Ansprüche, die der Landbau einerseits, der Heerdienst anderseits an ihn stellten. Zwar führt er noch abwechselnd den Pflug und die Waffe; aber immer lästiger wird es ihm, jenen mit dieser zu vertauschen. . . ." Although it must be realized that the present study deals with only one phase of a European problem, tentative conclusions may, nevertheless, be drawn on the basis of the English evidence; and such procedure may eventually help us to understand the somewhat inferior sources of the Frankish monarchy.

history of England would be greatly simplified if we could accept the view of Frederic Seebohm [23] that English society was from the first dominated by the manorial system, which had long prevailed throughout the Roman provinces and which accorded very well with the established custom of the Anglo-Saxon invaders themselves.

Seebohm, however, has been repeatedly convicted of rash generalization. Few scholars of today would commit themselves to his central thesis, that English history "begins with the serfdom of the masses . . . a serfdom from which it has taken 1000 years of . . . economic evolution to set them free." [24] As has been clearly proved by Vinogradoff,[25] the serfdom, or villeinage, of the common law was the product of arbitrary definition by Norman lawyers. For the sake of a practical rule to govern judicial action, they declared that the typical villager (*villanus*) was a serf and therefore devoid of civil rights in the king's court. Their doctrine was in flat contradiction of Domesday Book; in

[22] The description of early Germanic society by Tacitus, whatever may be thought of its general validity, is the best we have, and its meaning is beyond dispute. The typical warrior of Tacitus was certainly no peasant.

[23] The book that profoundly shocked the learned world of the day was *The English Village Community* (London, 1883). It was followed by *The Tribal System in Wales* (London, 1895) and *Tribal Custom in Anglo-Saxon Law* (London, 1902). From the remarks of Petit-Dutaillis (pp. 1 ff.) and of most later writers on English constitutional history, one might suppose that Seebohm's argument lacks all justification. Yet it has been strongly supported by W. J. Ashley, *Surveys Historic and Economic* (London, 1900), pp. 39 ff.; H. M. Chadwick, *Studies on Anglo-Saxon Institutions* (Cambridge, 1905); and W. J. Corbett, in the *Cambridge Medieval History*, II (Cambridge, 1926), ch. xvii. To what extent I am indebted to these three authors for many of the views expressed below should be fairly obvious.

[24] *English Village Community*, p. ix.

[25] In his *Villainage in England*, which, like Maitland's *Domesday Book and Beyond*, was inspired by the desire to refute Seebohm. The development of serfdom is too large a subject for discussion in the following pages. I may, however, express the opinion that throughout the Middle Ages legal unfreedom was much less important than economic unfreedom. Under the Roman law the *colonus* was personally free, as was the villein under the common law of England except in respect of his subordination to a single manorial lord. The persistence of a Germanic vernacular among the Anglo-Saxon peoples perhaps indicates that they outnumbered the conquered Celts and Latins, but not that they were all descended from invading warriors. We may well believe that the Anglo-Saxons, like the Danes of the ninth century, resettled whole regions by bringing over their women, children, and economic dependents—Chadwick, *The Origin of the English Nation* (Cambridge, 1907), pp. 181 ff.; below, n. 35.

1066 the bulk of the English population was not legally unfree and, so far as we can tell, never had been. Yet, granting the soundness of Vinogradoff's argument, must we admit that Seebohm was entirely wrong? Since he had undertaken "a strictly economic inquiry," he really meant by "serfdom" not a legal theory but a form of agrarian subjection. In defining a new law of serfdom did not the Norman lawyers merely recognize the fact that the average peasant, at least in relation to his lord, was actually unfree? If we look for that kind of unfreedom, we find plenty of it—in the Anglo-Saxon records as well as in Domesday Book.

In other words, this part of Vinogradoff's work by no means refuted Seebohm's major contention. Nor did Vinogradoff believe otherwise; for he later published a second volume, *The Origin of the Manor,* in which he vigorously defended the orthodox view. Whatever may be thought of his opinions, he presented them with force and clarity. His conclusion can best be stated in his own words: "firstly, that the manorial system arises at the end of the Old English period mainly in consequence of the subjection of a labouring population of free descent to a military and capitalistic class, and, secondly, that the personal authority of the lord of the manor is gradually gaining the mastery over a rural community of ancient and independent growth." [26] Under "the manorial system" Vinogradoff thus includes most of what Maitland preferred to call "feudalism." The terminology is a matter of slight consequence. Our primary interest is in the origin of particular institutions: especially, to adopt a Continental classification, the villa, immunity, commendation, and the benefice.

No historian, so far as I am aware, has denied that the villa of the later Roman Empire, at least from the standpoint of economic administration, anticipated what the English came to call a manor. Such a villa seems plainly indicated by the dooms of Aethelberht, which prescribe penalties for homicide within the *tun* of the king or of an *eorl* and for unlawful entry into a *mannes tun.*[27] From first to last the Anglo-Saxon charters are mainly

[26] P. 235.

[27] Aethelberht, 5, 13, 17 (Liebermann, I, 3–4). The penalties in the three cases

concerned with the alienation of landed estates which obviously include a large resident population of cultivators, whether free or unfree. Maitland, it is true, develops an elaborate argument to the effect that such grants imply the concession of political rather than of proprietary rights.[28] But this argument, as he frankly admits, is inspired by the consideration that otherwise "there will be small room left for any landowners in England save the kings, the churches, and perhaps a few great nobles," under whom the tillers of the soil will be "merely . . . slaves or *coloni*." Agreeing with Chadwick,[29] I ask "Why not?" We have authentic charters of immunity from as early a time as the seventh century.[30] If a king of that age wished to establish a governmental exemption for the benefit of a church or some other grantee, was there any need of his resorting to legal subterfuge?

No historian, so far as I am aware, has asserted that early Saxon England never contained a free village; yet actual proof of any such village is hard to adduce. Complete lack of evidence forced Stubbs to the reluctant conclusion that the Anglo-Saxons had not "brought with them" the *mark* system of the primitive Germans. He firmly believed, however, in the self-governing township, with its democratic assembly, popular trials, by-laws, elected officials, and definite representation in the hundred and the shire court.[31] Vinogradoff, too, continued to have faith in the village community of Germanist tradition, though Maitland refused to allow it other than economic functions.[32] Emphasizing the undoubted fact that the lowest political unit known to the dooms is the hundred, he thought it incredible that, if the township had ever had its own court and officials, they would have received no mention in the many enactments dealing with police and other local affairs. Maitland's argument, it seems

are 50*s.*, 12*s.*, and 6*s.*; but the third involves no bloodshed. I therefore see no reason why the "man" in that instance must have been a *ceorl*, who could not have possessed a villa. It was this consideration that led Liebermann to vary his translation of *tun* from "Ortsbezirk" to "Hofbezirk."

[28] Maitland, pp. 230 ff.
[29] *Studies on Anglo-Saxon Institutions*, pp. 372–74.
[30] Maitland, pp. 270 ff.   [31] Stubbs, I, 89–99, 115, 128.
[32] Maitland, pp. 147 ff.; criticized by Vinogradoff in his *Growth of the Manor*, pp. 145 ff. Cf. Ashley, pp. 61 ff.

to me, is conclusive, and is supported by all we know of parallel institutions on the Continent.[33] The self-governing village community of early mediaeval Europe, I suspect, has never been more than a figment of the romantic imagination.

The economically independent village that Maitland accepted cannot be ruled out of account as equally improbable. But what are the proofs of its existence? It does not, of course, appear in the charters. According to Liebermann, it is indicated only once in all the dooms, and I retain a doubt as to that one indication.[34] Maitland's strongest argument for the free agrarian community is based on the Domesday inquest. Within the old Danelaw, as he points out, we find villages that were shared in the time of King Edward by a considerable number of proprietors, often styled freemen or sokemen.[35] This fact, however,

[33] For additional discussion and references see my paper in *The Constitution Reconsidered*, ed. Conyers Read (New York, 1938), p. 38; also my *Borough and Town* (Cambridge, Mass., 1933), pp. 5, 18.

[34] Ine, 42 (Liebermann, I, 106); explained, *ibid.*, II, 297–98 ("Bauer," 3–4). This is the famous provision that, if certain *ceorlas* fail to build their shares of a fence about a field used in common, and if animals get in and destroy anything, those guilty of the neglect shall be liable for damages to the rest. Liebermann's interpretation depends on the fact that no lord is mentioned. But if there was as yet no manorial court, the suit for damages would lie in the folkmoot; and under such conditions would the lord need to be mentioned? As to the undoubted reference in the doom to the open-field system, I agree with Seebohm that the latter presupposes seignorial management rather than its absence. In the present connection, however, I merely insist that we cannot be too sure of what the passage implies.

[35] Maitland, pp. 129 ff.; cf. Vinogradoff, *English Society*, pp. 332 ff., 414 ff., 431 ff. The latter seems to regard the petty freeman of the Danish regions as a warrior in reduced circumstances; but it is very significant that in Alfred and Guthrum, 2 (Liebermann, I, 126), the Danish freedman is equated with the rent-paying *ceorl* of Wessex: Chadwick, *Studies on Anglo-Saxon Institutions*, pp. 397 ff. That the Danish conquests involved the migration of countless peasants has been made clear by Stenton, "The Danes in England," *Proceedings of the British Academy*, XIII (1927), 219 ff., 232 ff. On the peculiarity of agrarian organization in the shires colonized by the Danes see also Stenton, "Types of Manorial Structure in the Northern Danelaw," *Oxford Studies in Social and Legal History*, II (1910), 1–96; and Douglas, "The Social Structure of Mediaeval East Anglia," *ibid.*, IX (1927). Both of these writers tend to consider the typical sokeman a wholly free peasant; yet even Vinogradoff (*English Society*, p. 435) was led to observe that "when we hear of a socman, without further qualification, we ought primarily to think of one who could not recede with his land, and thus, notwithstanding his personally free condition and his public rights, was nevertheless actually a '*colonus* ascribed to the glebe,' to use the Roman term."

leaves many questions unanswered. What sort of people were these proprietors? Did they till the soil with their own hands? Were their holdings restricted to a single village or scattered in many villages? Were they the descendants of Danish conquerors who had abandoned the profession of arms or of Danish peasants who had improved their condition? Had the Danes created these villages, or had they in some fashion resettled them? And to what extent did their agricultural system resemble that of the Saxon invaders some four centuries earlier? Until we have answers to many such questions, we must withhold judgment concerning the relevance of the Domesday statistics to the subject under discussion. And we must not wholly rely on the imaginative reconstruction of primitive institutions from alleged vestiges in a later age—a dangerous procedure against which the historian has long been warned.[36]

A prominent feature of the twelfth-century manorial system was the political authority exercised by the lord over his rural tenants, both free and servile. One school of writers, which included G. B. Adams,[37] has explained this authority as being ultimately derived from the *dominium* of the Roman proprietor over his estates and slaves. Another school, which I believe to have the better of the argument,[38] has contended that public authority could hardly arise out of private ownership and must therefore have resulted from a delegation by the state—i.e., a formal grant of immunity. As to the antiquity of such grants in England there is no dispute. From the seventh century on they were regularly made by the Anglo-Saxon kings in favor of churches; somewhat later they seem to have been acquired also by prominent laymen. The controversial question is whether immunists did or did not have the right to administer justice in a seignorial court. Maitland was inclined to allow the right even to the first of them; [39] quite recently Mr. Goebel has declared that seignorial courts were unknown in Saxon England.[40] So far as the present inquiry is concerned, the matter is of secondary

[36] See especially Ashley, pp. 45, 79. [37] *Am. Hist. Rev.*, VII, 23 ff.
[38] *Ibid.*, XLVI, 808, n. 79. [39] Maitland, pp. 258–90.
[40] J. Goebel, *Felony and Misdemeanor*, I (New York, 1937), 336 ff. See Miss Cam's criticism, *Am. Hist. Rev.*, XLIII, 583 ff.; Stenton, *First Century of English Feudalism*, p. 42; Corbett, *Cam. Med. Hist.*, III (Cambridge, 1936), 405 ff.

importance. I need only express tentative agreement with the view that the original immunity, in England or on the Continent, established a merely fiscal privilege, the power of taking or sharing the public revenues collected from certain persons or from certain districts; but that courts of one sort or another were assuredly being held under seignorial franchise long before the Norman Conquest.

Throughout the preceding discussion it should not be forgotten that our chief concern is with a social problem—the differentiation of a landed aristocracy from an economically dependent peasantry. The evidence thus far reviewed fails to show that such differentiation was a comparatively late development among the Anglo-Saxons. On the contrary, the principal sources of the seventh century indicate that "from the earliest Anglo-Saxon times the peasant's obligation for rent, and therefore the village on the soil of a landlord, must have been the rule." [41] The *ceorl*, though personally free and perhaps having servants of his own, commonly appears as an agricultural tenant, from whom his lord was apt to receive labor service as well as a heavy *gafol* paid in kind.[42] More remains to be said about the legal and economic position of the *ceorl*, but for the moment let us merely agree that he seems to have been a peasant. As such, the dooms regularly contrast him with some person called *eorl, gesiðcund man, twelfhynde man,* or *þegn*. What do these terms imply?

One of them may be quickly disposed of. The "twelve-hundred man" of Wessex was thus styled because he enjoyed a wergeld of 1200s., whereas the *ceorl* was only a "two-hundred man." The West Saxon thegn's wergeld was 1200s. and so, evidently, was that of the earlier West Saxon *gesiðcund man*.[43] It would therefore be a logical deduction that all three words

[41] Liebermann, II, 298 ("Bauer," 5).

[42] Ine, 67 (Liebermann, I, 118). See Chadwick, *Studies on Anglo-Saxon Institutions,* pp. 100 ff., 404; Corbett, *Cam. Med. Hist.,* II, 568.

[43] The numerous references to the dooms will be found in Liebermann, II, 731 ff. ("Wergeld," 3-4). As to the main facts there is no controversy, though attempts to equate the monetary systems and to explain the social distinctions thus made have led to very complicated and often unconvincing arguments: e.g., Chadwick, *Studies on Anglo-Saxon Institutions,* pp. 12 ff., 105 ff., 400 ff.; Corbett, *Cam. Med. Hist.,* II, 567. On the peculiarity of Kentish custom see also R. H. Hodgkin, *A History of the*

designated members of a single class—men who were noble at least insofar as they were protected by a sixfold wergeld. And since *eorl* is later replaced in the Kentish dooms by *gesiðcund man,* it might even be supposed that all four terms were essentially synonymous despite the local variation of wergeld. Many writers, however, have insisted on a much more elaborate classification. The *eorl,* they say, was a representative of the old Continental nobility described by Tacitus.[44] The *gesiðcund* men of the dooms were descended from the warlike companions of a king, the members of his *comitatus,* whom he usually rewarded with estates and so made into a landed aristocracy. The thegns were more properly royal servants whose families, acquiring wealth and power, gradually supplanted or absorbed the *gesiðcund* nobility in the course of the tenth century.[45] This elaborate theory has nothing to support it but the consecutive appearance in the dooms of the three terms just mentioned, together with a number of doubtful interpretations to be commented on below.

Gesið occasions little trouble; all agree that it denoted an honorable companion, especially one who shared a military expedition. A man who enjoyed the status of *gesið,* whatever that might imply, would be called *gesiðcund.* And since *eorl* was a vague word that hardly meant more than "distinguished man," there is no reason why an *eorl* could not be a *gesið,* or vice versa.[46] Could not either be also a *þegn?* Although by derivation this term is now admitted to have meant "boy" and not "servant," the common opinion seems to be that its "early his-

Anglo-Saxons (Oxford, 1935), I, 205 ff.; J. E. A. Jolliffe, *The Constitutional History of Medieval England* (London, 1937), pp. 11 ff.

44 So, for example, Stubbs, I, 168 ff.; Liebermann, II, 268 ("Adel," 1).

45 A. G. Little, in *Eng. Hist. Rev.,* VI (1889), 723 ff.; L. M. Larson, *The King's Household in England before the Norman Conquest* (Madison, 1904), chs. ii–iii; Liebermann, II, 427 ff. ("Gefolgsadel"), 680 ff. ("Thegn"). Stubbs (I, 172 ff.) had found it hard to distinguish the thegn from the *gesið.*

46 Chadwick, *Studies on Anglo-Saxon Institutions,* pp. 111 ff., 379 ff.—a discussion that takes up in detail the pertinent references of Bede. Corbett (*Cam. Med. Hist.,* II, 566) proposes "warrior" as the best translation of *eorl* and thinks that *gesiðcund* has the same implication, that of one "suited by birth and training" to be a military companion. This is merely a clearer statement of what Chadwick had already suggested.

tory . . . is one of service." [47] No such conclusion can be fairly drawn from Anglo-Saxon literature. In only three of some thirty passages in *Beowulf* can *þegn* mean other than a man of high rank, a warrior. [48] And before we condemn to servitude the youths who poured the ale at the lord's table or cared for the hero's arms, we should remember how, in the days of chivalry, highborn squires performed much the same duties. Our standard Anglo-Saxon dictionary [49] gives the primary meaning of *þegn* as "a servant, one who does service for another"; but this definition appears to be based on little more than the fact that the word was often used to translate the Latin *minister,* and usually if not always with an honorable implication. A reference to *þegn* as the equivalent of "disciple" leads us to *Andreas*—that marvelous tale in which the Twelve are described as glorious heroes, bold warriors, *þeodnes þegnas;* in which the cannibalistic Mermedonians are called devil's thegns; in which God and two of His angels pose as boatmen, brave thegns ready for a voyage. [50] Throughout the Anglo-Saxon period nothing finer could be said of a man than that he was a true thegn—witness, finally, the magnificent tribute to Offa in the *Song of Maldon.* [51]

In *Beowulf* the same persons are often referred to as *eorlas, gesiðas,* and *þegnas;* whatever the peculiar implications of the three words, they were all used to designate men of honorable position—seafarers and fighters. So it is in the other poems and also, I believe, in the dooms. Although the usage varied from age to age, it served to indicate a single aristocracy, the "dearborn" class of warriors. The law cared not at all whether *ceorlisc* was contrasted with *eorlcund, gesiðcund,* or *þegnboren;* the social distinction was the same. And we must conclude, from the

[47] Larson, p. 90.

[48] Ll. 494, 673, 1794. The second of these references is to an *ombiht þegn,* i.e., one who performs a special office. The same term is used in line 229 to indicate a coast guard, *Hroðgares þegn* who rides to the seashore on Beowulf's arrival.

[49] That of Bosworth, ed. T. N. Toller (Oxford, 1882–98). There are many compounds (e.g., *burþegn, discþegn, horsþegn*), some of which may have been used to denote lowborn servants; but note the equivalence of the three mentioned to "chamberlain," "steward," and "constable."

[50] Ll. 3, 40 ff., 245 ff., 323 ff., 344 ff., etc. Similar instances abound in *Elene, Judith, Genesis,* and other Anglo-Saxon poems. See Chadwick, *Studies on Anglo-Saxon Institutions,* pp. 348–50; Hodgkin, II, 457 ff.

[51] Ll. 281 ff.

adjectives commonly employed and from much corroborative evidence, that both ranks were hereditary.[52] Acquisition of royal or ecclesiastical office could of course be expected to increase a man's wergeld; a king's thegn was worth more than an ordinary thegn, and every honest priest came to enjoy thegnly status. But the dooms do not justify the idea that the status ever depended on wealth.[53] The *ceorl* and the merchant who "throve to thegnright" appear solely in a private compilation of the eleventh century. The author, as Liebermann has shown, added certain of his own remarks to introduce a few documents that he had collected.[54] For this introduction he used only sources known to us and sometimes misunderstood them. A sermon about good old days that never existed should not be preferred to the testimony of official records.

The foregoing interpretation of the sources naturally leads to the question: What were the relations, political and economic, between the warrior and peasant classes? The typical thegn, as portrayed in the dooms, was a landed proprietor who lived in a fortified dwelling, or *burh*,[55] and was supported by agricultural tenants, either slaves (*þeowas*) or freemen (*ceorlas*). The latter, as we have seen, would normally owe both rent and labor in return for the land which they occupied. Being legally free, they might be supposed to have had the right to leave the estate whenever they chose to do so. But could they? Aside from their obligations to the lord as proprietor or immunist,[56] they might

[52] Liebermann, II, 269 ("Adel," 4), 731 ("Wergeld," 2). Throughout the Anglo-Saxon period, as later, all freemen could be called on for military service whenever the occasion demanded. But it was only the warriors proper who counted for anything on the field of battle: Liebermann, II, 499 ff. ("Heer"); Chadwick, *Origin of the English Nation,* pp. 158 ff.; Hodgkin, I, 206 ff., and II, 590 ff.; below, n. 62.

[53] Ine, 23, 24, 32 (Liebermann, I, 100–02) have been interpreted by Chadwick (*Studies on Anglo-Saxon Institutions,* pp. 91 ff.) to imply a West Saxon gradation of wergelds based on property; but the dooms cited refer only to Welshmen, and Chadwick's opinion is rejected by Liebermann, II, 646 ("Sechshunderter"). On the king's thegn and the priest see Liebermann, II, 680 ("Thegn," 3), 662 ("Stand," 5).

[54] *Ibid.,* III, 256–57, 259. The passages in question are Gepyncðo and Norðleod, 7–12 (*ibid.,* I, 456–60).

[55] *Ibid.,* II, 330 ("Burg," 1); Stephenson, *Borough and Town,* pp. 53–54.

[56] Such a person clearly appears in Ine, 50 (Liebermann, I, 110–11), as the gesiðcund landholder who may be the lord of freemen and may himself have a

be bound to him by the tie of commendation. Our records of
the seventh century show that one freeman was often under the
protection (*mundbyrd*) of another; that any man—whether slave
or free, whether peasant or warrior—could have a lord; and that
such a lord, however illegally, might compel his *ceorl* to work
on Sunday.[57] From the same age comes our first doom to the
effect that "if any one goes without leave from his lord or steals
away into another shire, and if he is there found, he shall go
back to where he was and pay his lord 60s." [58]

This doom, with additional penalties, is repeated over and
over in the following centuries.[59] And in the meantime we have
another significant regulation: the relatives of a lordless (and
landless) man must "settle him to folkright" by finding him a
lord at the local court.[60] Beginning with Aethelstan, the state
constantly tries to enforce the rule that every man who cannot
otherwise be held to justice must have a lord to be responsible
for him. Is this relationship vassalage, as so many writers would
have us believe,[61] or is it a form of seignorial bondage? The
answer, in my opinion, depends upon the class to which the
folgere, or *commendatus*, belonged. A thegn who fought for his
lord and, if necessary, died with him on the field of battle may
well be called a vassal in the proper sense of that French word.
A vagabond *ceorl* who by compulsion was attached to a lord—
and would the latter accept him for love?—must have been a
peasant, and a very unfree one. A man like this, commended
for life and put to work on another's land, could have been
little better off than a Roman *colonus*. Unless we clearly dis-

lord other than the king. In the later dooms an immunist of this sort is regularly
described as *landrica* or *landhlaford* (*ibid.*, II, 131).

[57] See especially Wihtraed, 5, 9, 10; Ine, 3, 50, 70, 74 (*ibid.*, I, 12, 13, 90, 110, 119, 120).

[58] Ine, 39 (*ibid.*, I, 106).   [59] *Ibid.*, II, 427 ("Gefolge," 26).

[60] II Aethelstan, 2 (*ibid.*, I, 150); see also II, 425 ("Gefolge," 9).

[61] So, for example, Liebermann in much of the comment cited above and
throughout his notes generally. As I have tried to make clear in my previous
article (*Am. Hist. Rev.*, XLVI, 802 ff.), this confusion is inevitable unless we restrict the term "vassalage" to an honorable relationship between members of the
warrior class. Even Adams (*Origin of the English Constitution*, pp. 44–45) had to
admit that the Anglo-Saxon oath of a man to his lord (Liebermann, I, 396) is much
the same as a feudal oath of fealty. The man in question was presumably one of
honorable status.

tinguish between the churlish and thegnly classes and regard them as essentially hereditary groups, we can expect to have no real understanding of the Anglo-Saxon system.

Even those historians who believe the thegn originally to have been a servant agree that he was pre-eminently a fighting man in the eleventh century.[62] By that time it had long been customary for kings, ecclesiastics, and other wealthy men to grant estates as "loans," or benefices, to all sorts of presumably deserving persons. Such grants, in England as on the Continent, were regularly made for no more than three lives and on condition of specified rent or service.[63] Land thus held by a thegn might conceivably resemble what the French then called a fief. Maitland was of the opinion that, in particular, Bishop Oswald's loans to various friends and retainers definitely anticipated the feudal tenure of the Norman monarchy. But Mr. Stenton's reply to this well-known argument, it seems to me, is decisive. "None of all the documents which have come from Bishop Oswald offers any anticipation of the feudal principle by which a man will take land from a lord in return for a definite amount of military service to be rendered in respect of his tenure." [64] The bishop's memorandum, so greatly relied on by Maitland, describes "a very incoherent series of obligations," which "range from hunting service to bridge-building." His "famous 'law of riding' meant not military service but the duty of escorting a lord from place to place." [65] Those of the grantees who were thegns would doubtless have to fight because of the personal liability attaching to their status. They would not, however, owe service by virtue of a territorial assessment in five-hide units; for that rule applied solely to the mustering of the peasant population for the *fyrd*.[66]

[62] Maitland, pp. 161 ff.; Vinogradoff, *English Society*, pp. 403 ff.; Liebermann, II, 680 ("Thegn," 2).

[63] Maitland, pp. 299 ff.   [64] *First Century of English Feudalism*, p. 128.

[65] *Ibid.*, p. 124.

[66] *Ibid.*, pp. 115–19, 127–28. This, I think, is an important consideration. The older view, well presented by Vinogradoff (*English Society*, pp. 22 ff.), owed much of its confusion to the belief in the *ceorl* who acquired thegnly status along with the title to five hides of land, etc. (above, notes 53–54). Once that legend is discarded, it becomes unnecessary, with Mr. Stenton, to minimize the significance of the five-hide unit (on which see Round, *Feudal England*, pp. 44 ff.).

In Saxon England we therefore discover the manorial system, a dependent peasantry, a military aristocracy, grants of immunity, benefices, and various forms of commendation, including one that resembled vassalage. Yet, for lack of the fief, we discover no feudal tenure. What was the all-important element which, introduced by the Frankish rulers, transformed and recombined these common institutions of western Europe to produce, ultimately, the feudal state and feudal society? Careful analysis of the whole problem tends only to confirm the thesis of Brunner: that the revolutionary factor was the Carolingian development of heavy-armed cavalry.[67] In this connection, however, review of the English sources leads to a very natural query. As far back as our information extends, the Anglo-Saxon warrior was equipped with helmet, coat of mail, shield, spear, and sword; and he often had a horse also. In the tenth and eleventh centuries, if not earlier, all better-class persons were expected to ride on any expedition, whether peaceful or warlike.[68] A thegn without a mount would be an absurdity. Why, then, was there no heavy-armed cavalry in pre-Norman England?

It is no adequate reply, though an undoubted fact, that Anglo-Saxon warriors merely rode to the battlefield and then dismounted to fight on foot—like the thegns of Byrhtnoth at Maldon or those of Harold at Hastings. The Franks had at one time done the selfsame thing. What had induced them to change their traditional tactics? The solution to the problem, I suggest, will be found by studying the introduction of the thoroughbred charger or *destrier,* whose size and strength permitted the mailed warrior to fight on horseback. I have, unfortunately, no positive evidence to offer and can only hope that some such evidence may be found by a better-qualified investigator. Over thirty-five years ago William Ridgeway threw out a hint to the effect that "the history of Teutonic chivalry is closely bound up with

---

[67] See *Am. Hist. Rev.,* XLVI, 794 ff., 807. When that article was written I had not realized that we must distinguish between great horses and ordinary horses.

[68] For the early use of the arms mentioned and also of the horse, our best source is *Beowulf;* see Chadwick, *Origin of the English Nation,* pp. 186 ff. References to the later sources will be found in Liebermann, II, 614 ff. ("Pferd").

that of . . . great horses." [69] He had little to say about the perfection of the breed except that it was presumably a cross between the Libyan horse, long famous for its speed, and the stockier horse of Europe. But Mr. Tarn has now shown that it was the Nesean horse of Media, probably of mixed Asiatic and Libyan blood, that made possible the heavy-armed cavalry of the Parthians and so, eventually, the *cataphracti* of the Byzantine Empire.[70] Since neither the Romans, the Gauls, the Germans, the Huns, the Moors, nor the later invaders of western Europe had such a cavalry force, it seems necessary to conclude that the Franks learned the new military system from the east. How they did so is a subject that richly deserves consideration by a competent scholar.

In whatever fashion the great war horse may have been imported into Frankish Gaul, I am convinced that the importation was of prime significance. According to the *Iudiciae Civitatis Lundoniae*,[71] an English horse under Aethelstan was worth as much as four oxen; but the *Lex Ribuaria* [72] proves that, as early as the first half of the eighth century, the equipment of a Frankish warrior—including horse, shirt of mail, leggings, helmet, shield, lance, sword, and sheath—was valued at over twenty-two oxen. If the mounted thegn of England was an aristocrat, how much greater an aristocrat was the contemporary knight of France! [73] The average peasant, whose movable wealth

[69] *The Origin and Influence of the Thoroughbred Horse* (Cambridge, 1905), p. 331. I have looked in vain for any further consideration of this matter in all the standard histories of warfare, including the last edition of C. W. C. Oman's *Art of War in the Middle Ages* (London, 1924).

[70] W. W. Tarn, *Hellenistic Military and Naval Developments* (Cambridge, 1930), pp. 73 ff.

[71] VI Aethelstan, 6 (Liebermann, I, 176).

[72] *Monumenta Germaniae Historica, Leges,* V (Hanover, 1889), 231.

[73] Mr. Stenton (*First Century of English Feudalism,* pp. 132 ff.) has raised the interesting question of why popular usage continued to favor the English *cniht* instead of adopting the French *chevalier*. His explanation, that the old word primarily denoted a servant in a great household and so could be applied to the Norman vassal, is not wholly convincing. I suggest, rather, that in 1066 the thegn was essentially a twelve-hundred man, a member of the aristocracy that suffered irretrievable defeat at Hastings, whereas the *cniht* was a man who, though not of thegnly rank, had come to be a mounted retainer. What I earlier wrote (*Borough and Town,* see index) about thegns and *cnihtas* may stand in some need of revision; but I still hold to my principal contention, that such persons seem to have

fell far short of a plow team, could no more hope to be a warrior of this sort than to wear the papal tiara. Even if, in time of emergency, someone provided him with the necessary arms and mount, he would be only a peasant on horseback—and hardly that, we may be sure, as soon as he encountered the enemy. It would, indeed, be very difficult for the ordinary gentleman, however proud his ancestry, to maintain his social superiority unless he could obtain a fief in return for knightly service.

That the Norman Conquest produced a military revolution in England has never been disputed. Yet it was once the fashion to interpret the change as primarily one of tactics. Stubbs evidently believed that knighthood was "a translation into Norman forms of the thegnage of the old Anglo-Saxon law"; that knights' fees were "gradually introduced"; and that Norman castle-building was a matter of relative insignificance.[74] These beliefs now seem impossible. The battle of Hastings, we have learned, resulted in vastly more than the substitution of a mounted for a dismounted army in the field. The military system of the Conqueror necessitated the deliberate establishment of feudal tenure with all its far-reaching implications. Among the latter was the immediate dominance of England by a French aristocracy whose life was governed by the code of chivalry. And chivalry, to the knight of that age, meant the completion of a long and arduous professional training, rather than a web of romantic fancy.[75] The castle, too, was a military innovation of first importance, constituting an indispensable center not only of local defense but likewise of routine administration, whether royal or seignorial.[76]

------

been much the same whether they lived in a borough or not. That a merchant could acquire thegnright, as alleged in *Geþyncðo* (above, n. 54), I greatly doubt. Liebermann, II, 681 ("Thegn," 8–9), states that a gildsman in an Anglo-Saxon borough, though styled a thegn, enjoyed only an ordinary man's wergeld. But the eight pounds to be collected for the killing of a thegnly gild-brother at Cambridge was obviously a compensation to the gild, not to the kindred—B. Thorpe, *Diplomatarium Anglicum Aevi Saxonici* (London, 1865), pp. 611–12.

[74] Stubbs, I, 283, 285; and see index under "Castles."

[75] S. Painter, *French Chivalry* (Baltimore, 1940); Stephenson, *Mediaeval Feudalism*, ch. iii.

[76] Pioneer work in this connection too was done by Round: *Quarterly Review*, CLXXIX (1894), 27 ff.; *Archaeologia*, LVIII (1902), 332 ff. See also E. S. Armitage,

To summarize the social results of the Norman Conquest is a much harder task, because so much depends on our understanding of historical developments in the previous centuries. To me, at any rate, the belief in a primitive democracy of warrior-peasants seems to rest on little more than faith. If the *ceorl* was likely to be an economic dependent in the seventh century, we need no elaborate argument to account for his later depression through the king's alienation of fiscal and judicial rights.[77] And if the Anglo-Saxon nations were from the first dominated by a dear-born class of fighting men, we do not have to worry about the origin among them of a landed aristocracy. From the making of this fundamental distinction it does not, of course, follow that during all these troubled years there were no intermediate

Early Norman Castles of the British Isles (London, 1912); Stenton, *First Century of English Feudalism*, ch. vi; Painter, in *Speculum*, X (1935), 321 ff., and in *Am. Hist. Rev.*, XL (1935), 450 ff. Although Mrs. Armitage's work is an invaluable guide for the student of early castles, I have objected (*Borough and Town*, pp. 53 ff.) to her interpretation of the word *burh* and to her use, shared with Mr. Stenton and many others, of the phrase "private castle." Her suggestion (p. 74) that the separate fortification of the motte indicated the lord's fear of his own garrison shows no lively appreciation of vassalage. And the view, so often expressed elsewhere, that castles were built all over England to keep down the conquered population, seems a little far-fetched. Were castles any less plentiful on the other side of the Channel?

77 Maitland's argument for the gradual depression of the *ceorl*—and to the best of my knowledge no one has improved on it—ascribes decisive influence to the acquisition by great lords of the king's *feorm* together with various powers of justice and police (Maitland, pp. 318 ff.). In this connection it is significant that Liebermann, who accepts Maitland's central thesis, agrees with Seebohm, Chadwick, and Corbett that the *feorm* or *fostre* of the dooms and land books was not a royal tax but an ordinary rent in produce: Liebermann, II, 264 ("Abgabe"); Chadwick, *Studies on Anglo-Saxon Institutions*, pp. 100 ff.; Corbett, *Cam. Med. Hist.*, II, 568. As to governmental subjection of the peasantry, it was undoubtedly important; yet one might suppose that, on the whole, it was the result rather than the cause of economic subjection. There is, finally, the alleged reduction of the average family holding from 120 to 30 acres—the solution given to the puzzle of the hide by Maitland's third essay. The puzzle, nevertheless, remains; for what Bede and the early records meant by *terra unius familiae*, or any of its equivalents, is still an unknown quantity. The hides of even our oldest sources may very well have been fiscal or military units like those of Domesday—Corbett, "The Tribal Hidage," in *Transactions of the Royal Historical Society*, New Series, XIV (1900), 187 ff.; Chadwick, *Studies on Anglo-Saxon Institutions*, pp. 363 ff.; Hodgkin, II, 401. The problem is not one peculiar to England; see the very suggestive remarks of Marc Bloch in the *Cambridge Economic History*, I (Cambridge, 1941), 230 ff., 265 ff.

groups and no shifts of personal status. We must not ignore the independent freeman, the legal owner of a few acres, who commended himself to a powerful lord and still retained control of his land; or the superior peasant, such as a *geneat* or *radcniht*, who might hope to attain high rank in the service of a wealthy patron.[78]

Whatever the minor differences of legal and economic condition in Saxon England, they did not long survive the Norman Conquest, which established the rule that a gentleman must have had a chivalrous education and that a rustic, unless he could offer acceptable proof to the contrary, was an unfree villein. The precise fate of the old aristocracy we do not know.[79] Domesday shows that by 1086 it had all but disappeared from the scene, and there is no profit in speculating on how many thegns were able to escape degradation by adopting a knightly career. Such a person would be quickly absorbed into the Norman-French baronage. As to the agricultural population we are better informed. The merging of all *servi* and *villani* in a single class, though it abolished Anglo-Saxon slavery, legally debased thousands of agrarian tenants. Many a sokeman or small farmer, on being attached to the manor of an unscrupulous adventurer, must have suffered real hardship.[80] Yet, for reasons already stated, the arbitrary formulation of a comprehensive law could have made little change in the life of the average peasant. What the courts now recognized as serfdom was actually no new thing in England.

Stubbs, as we have seen, held that feudalism "when applied to governmental machinery" had a "disruptive tendency." "The great feature of the Conqueror's policy is his defeat of that tendency." [81] William tried "to reign as an English king." [82] At Salisbury in 1086 he demanded from all freeholders "little more than . . . the oath of allegiance which had been taken by the Anglo-Saxon kings." Wishing to preserve the national customs

[78] Stenton, *First Century of English Feudalism*, pp. 124 ff.; Corbett, *Cam. Med. Hist.*, III, 402 ff.; Vinogradoff, *English Society*, pp. 69 ff.

[79] Stenton, *First Century of English Feudalism*, p. 115.

[80] Vinogradoff, *English Society*, pp. 410–30.

[81] Stubbs, I, 277–78, 290.   [82] *Ibid.*, p. 280.

and laws, "he kept up the popular institutions of the hundred court and the shire court." He maintained the ancient *fyrd* and the ancient *witenagemot.* By amalgamating the offices of earl and *comes,* of sheriff and *vicecomes,* he avoided the proved evils in both the English and the Continental systems. He prevented the growth of "hereditary jurisdictions" and, by scattering the lands in baronial fiefs, of "contiguous territorial accumulations." "In the department of finance . . . he retained the revenues of his predecessors and added new imposts of his own"—such as the feudal reliefs, aids, and tallages.[83] Now that Round, Adams, Stenton, and others have so thoroughly criticized these opinions in the light of an improved knowledge of the sources, all I have to say on the subject can be reduced to a few supplementary notes.

In any appraisal of feudal institutions, it seems to me, we must hold to a realistic standard. The truly important question is not whether the feudalism of England was "ideal," [84] but how it worked; and how, as a practical system of government, it did or did not resemble the feudalism of the Continent. As long as historians continue to compare the English monarchy of about 1100 with the fictitious French monarchy of the same period, so long will they misunderstand the significance of feudalism. It is only by considering the actual states known to William the Conqueror that we can hope to appreciate his policy. His model of government was assuredly Norman rather than English, and the fact that he had not previously borne a royal title was unimportant. Within his principality he was a true successor of the Carolingians, for he there enforced the regal authority which they had long abandoned. To say this is to imply much more than that one of his ancestors had been recognized as duke by Charles the Simple in 911. Neither the legal concept

[83] *Ibid.,* pp. 289–303.
[84] See the interesting thesis of Adams (*Origin of the English Constitution,* pp. 186 ff.), which I find much preferable to the one he originally supported (*Am. Hist. Rev.,* XLVI, 810–12). I should take exception only to his definition of feudal justice and to his overemphasis of theory. The substance of his argument is a description of feudal practice rather than of feudal ideals. And was it not out of such practice that the English constitution developed? To find the "germ of the constitution" in any theory of feudalism is, I believe, to place undue reliance on a preconception.

of a duchy nor familiarity with feudal custom had been brought by the Vikings to the coast of France. Whatever they came to know of such matters they must have learned from their neighbors. Back of the Norman monarchy in England lay centuries of Frankish tradition. Before we attribute any remarkable peculiarity to the new structure, we should do well to compare it with Flanders and Anjou, as well as with Normandy.[85]

Much of what Stubbs believed has been so thoroughly disproved that there is no need of referring to it again. His argument that William preserved the old *fyrd* and the old oath of allegiance is essentially correct, but is so because the *arrière-ban* and the general obligation of fealty to the ruler of the state was included in Frankish custom. The duke of Normandy, like the count of Flanders, always maintained the principle that formal war, as distinguished from the prosecution of a lawful feud, could only be waged in his name; that every fortress within his territory must be opened to him on demand; and that, in case of necessity, all able-bodied men were liable for military service.[86] It was likewise established practice that certain taxes were reserved to the prince, such as those levied on trade by sea. In England William was fortunate enough to inherit the danegeld, together with a system of royal tolls; and to them he added not merely the feudal aids but also the *monetagium*.[87] So it

[85] For such an undertaking we have available three splendid books: H. Pirenne, *Histoire de Belgique*, Vol. I (5th ed., Brussels, 1929); L. Halphen, *Le comté d'Anjou au XIe siècle* (Paris, 1906); C. H. Haskins, *Norman Institutions* (Cambridge, Mass., 1918). On the other principalities of feudal France only too little work has been done, although there are numerous brief sketches; see especially the chapters of Halphen in *Cam. Med. Hist.*, Vol. III. Mr. Stenton (*First Century of English Feudalism*, ch. i) has shown how Norman and English custom varied in certain respects; yet such differences, when compared with the body of common custom, appear very small indeed. Until Mr. Douglas has produced more cogent evidence, I cannot accept his conclusion (*Ec. Hist. Rev.*, IX, 129) that "it must . . . always remain difficult to regard English feudalism as in any exact sense a Norman creation."

[86] Haskins, pp. 22 ff., 38; Pirenne, I, 119–26; Adams, *Origin of the English Constitution*, pp. 186–91.

[87] The princely control of commerce is best shown by the charters later issued to the great towns: e.g., Saint-Omer and Rouen (Stephenson, *Borough and Town*, pp. 35 ff., 40 ff.); cf. the works of Pirenne cited *ibid.*, p. 11. The *monetagium*, a well-known tax on the Continent, was introduced into England by William I, as we know from Henry I's Coronation Charter, as well as from obscure references in

was in the field of adjudication. The English pleas of the crown generally corresponded to the Norman pleas of the sword, which had their parallels elsewhere in France. We know much less about the ducal courts of Normandy than about the hundred and shire courts of England. If our information were more complete, the alleged difference between feudal and territorial justice might not be so clear-cut. In Flanders the earliest sources reveal a well-organized judicial system, under which the count's *châtelains* (or *vicomtes*) administered his justice in district courts, assisted by groups of *échevins*.[88] Even the local government of England takes on a French aspect after 1066, if we give it more than a superficial glance. To the Conqueror his "earls" were *comtes* in fact as well as in name, and his "sheriffs" were *vicomtes*—quite like the Flemish *châtelains* as soon as castles had been erected to serve as administrative centers in all the counties.[89]

To object that such a state as I have described was not truly feudal is, in my opinion, to beg the whole question. If the greater principalities of eleventh-century France were not feudal states, where shall we ever find one? A region in which a theoretical ruler permitted chronic anarchy—like the Burgundian duchy—was not a state at all. Mr. Stenton has given us a splendid picture of the Conqueror's administration, showing how it altogether depended on the loyalty of his vassals.[90] This, as I see it, was the essence of feudal government. Under feudalism the prince who could enforce his rights had, on the whole, to deserve the fealty of his liegemen. Whether a particular baron held a royal office by hereditary title, or whether that office was

Domesday (*ibid.*, pp. 100 ff.). On Continental imposts resembling the English danegeld see E. Joranson, *The Danegeld in France* (Rock Island, 1924).

[88] Pirenne, I, 126–30; W. Blommaert, *Les châtelains de Flandre* (Ghent, 1915); Haskins, pp. 24 ff., 45 ff., 88 ff.; cf. Halphen, *Le comté d'Anjou*, pp. 98 ff. On the nature of feudal justice see my *Mediaeval Feudalism*, ch. ii; also the references in *Am. Hist. Rev.*, XLVI, 808. A closely related subject is the ecclesiastical authority of the prince, to which the books of Pirenne, Haskins, and Halphen all devote considerable space.

[89] See the references in the previous note; Stenton, *First Century of English Feudalism*, pp. 222 ff.; W. A. Morris, *The Mediaeval English Sheriff to 1300* (Manchester, 1927), chs. ii–iii; Painter, in *Speculum*, X, 321 ff.

[90] *First Century of English Feudalism*, ch. vii.

a legal portion of his fief, was politically of minor significance. The all-important thing was the mutual faith of lord and man, as is graphically proved by the contrast between the reigns of William I and Stephen. When, thanks to the economic changes of the twelfth century, the king was able to base his government on the employment of mercenary troops and professional ministers, England was already ceasing to be feudal.

The Problem of
the Common Man in
Early Mediaeval Europe *

FOR over a hundred years no subject of historical research has
attracted greater interest or has been more passionately discussed than the ordinary inhabitant of the Western countryside
during the early Middle Ages. Of what descent was he, and of
what fundamental character? Was he free or unfree? Was he a
peasant proprietor or an economic dependent? Did he live by
fighting, by working, or by combining the two occupations? Did
he have any political power? If so, what was it; and how and
where was it exercised? Such questions as these must indeed be
answered by one who hopes to understand the development of
European civilization. We should, as so many generations of
scholars have insisted, give thought to the beginnings of our
nations, our states, and our societies. But the task of finding good
answers to the questions is not easy; for the curious student who
works back of the glib statements in most popular histories is
confronted by a mass of abstruse writing that inevitably tends
to discourage him. He will not know that the substratum of
actual evidence is much less bulky and, as it seems to me, much
more intelligible. At any rate, let us see whether something

* Reprinted from *The American Historical Review*, LI (1946), 419–38.

cannot be done to simplify what the historian of mediaeval Europe has long considered a fundamental problem.

Once we have attacked this problem, we can hardly escape the *Markgenossenschaft,* a topic which the reader of current historical journals is not likely to find exciting. A century or so ago, the situation was very different—as we soon discover if, with Alfons Dopsch,[1] we trace the various theories of the *Markgenossenschaft* to their earliest formulation. It was in 1768 that Justus Möser published the first edition of his *Osnabrückische Geschichte.*[2] Here he depicted his native land, the old Saxony of pre-Carolingian times, as having been populated by free German peasants who, within the confines of local territories (*Marken*), were joined in voluntary associations for the sake of common economic and political interests. Through direct assemblies these associates (*Markgenossen*) regulated their pastoral and agricultural pursuits, electing headmen to enforce their decisions and to lead them in war. Theirs was a golden age of liberty and equality—one which, being dictated by nature, could dispense with an elaborately organized state, and which ineluctably ended with Charlemagne's conquest of Saxony.[3] Can anyone doubt that this idyllic society, so appealingly sketched in Möser's frontispiece,[4] was inspired by the sentimental Jean-

---

[1] *Wirtschaftliche und soziale Grundlagen der europäischen Kulturentwicklung* (Vienna, 1918). Translated and condensed by Erna Patzelt (New York, 1937). The following references are to the original edition.

[2] *Ibid.,* I, 8 ff. For the sake of comparison it may be remarked that Montesquieu's *De l'esprit des lois* was first published in 1748; Rousseau's *Discours sur les arts et sciences* in 1750; his *Contrat social* in 1762; and Herder's *Ideen zur Philosophie der Menschheit* in 1784–91.

[3] See especially Möser (2d ed., Berlin, 1780), I, 11 ff., 83 ff. Note also the division, in his preface, of German history into four periods. "In der ersten und güldnen war noch mehrentheils jeder deutscher Ackerhof mit einem Eigenthümer oder Wehren besetzt; . . . nichts als hohe und gemeine Ehre in der Nation bekannt; niemand, ausser dem Leut oder Knechte einem Herrn zu folgen verbunden; und der gemeine Vorsteher ein erwählter Richter, welcher blos die Urtheile bestätigte, so ihm von seinen Rechtsgenossen zugewiesen wurden."

[4] See the accompanying plate, which has been reproduced from Möser's second edition because no copy of the first seems to be available in America. Here may be admired the warrior-peasant of primitive Germany in a romantic setting that includes his wife and child (and presumably the wife and children of a neighbor). His spear and shield, ready to hand, recline in the foreground, while he strives to

The original *Markgenosse*

(frontispiece of Möser's *Osnabrückische Geschichte*, 1780)

Jacques? Thus to conclude, as a matter of fact, is not to rely on mere surmise. Möser himself declared that, after reading Voltaire and other authors, he was finally enthralled by Rousseau.[5] How, in turn, Möser's work captivated the rising school of German historians has been admirably shown by Dopsch,[6] and with such a wealth of detail that only the salient features of this famous literary development need be mentioned here. Möser, we should note, attributed to the ancient *Markgenossenschaft* both economic and political functions, the latter being necessitated by the former. To Möser the typical German was the possessor of an individual homestead (*Einzelhof*), who shared with his *Markgenossen* the use of adjacent woods, streams, pastures, and the like.[7] It was left for Möser's followers in the next century—particularly Eichhorn, Grimm, Beseler, Landau, and Georg von Maurer—to transform his thesis of original private ownership into one of original communism. In doing so the later writers were undoubtedly influenced by their better appreciation of the open-field system and the accompanying allotment of peasant holdings within the mediaeval villa, or manor. Thus the village, rather than a group of *Einzelhofen,* came to be recognized as the primitive *Mark*—the natural settlement of free warrior-peasants with an innate passion for equal justice, the true cell of Germanic society.[8] And since Germanic society had to be based on the sacred principle of consanguinity, numerous scholars arose to show how the *Markgenossenschaft* was

---

till his recalcitrant soil. We notice that his hair—in a hardly successful attempt to illustrate the coiffure of the Suevi, as described by Tacitus—is tied in a topknot, and that his plow is distinctly crude. But how are we to explain his team of long-tailed horses, his greyhound, and—God save the mark—his shorts?

[5] "Zuletzt zog mich Rousseau ganz an sich." Quoted from one of Möser's letters by Georg Kass, *Möser und Goethe* (Berlin, 1909), p. 21.

[6] I, 10 ff. His work should be consulted for all references not given in the pages immediately following.

[7] Note that Möser, while restricting his book to a consideration of ancient Saxony, devoted his preface mainly to determining periods in *die Geschichte von Deutschland,* and that his disciples, led by Eichhorn, applied his conclusions to Germany as a whole.

[8] Hence August Meitzen's *Siedlung und Agrarwesen,* which set forth the persuasive theory that the nucleated village was essentially Germanic, the *Einzelhof* essentially Celtic.

in some way derived from the *uralt* institution of the family.[9] Meanwhile Möser's exposition of the *Markgenossenschaft* as the primeval form of political organization among the Germans had likewise met with enthusiastic reception. Such influential writers as Rogge and Dönniges went even beyond Eichhorn in arguing that the German state was originally democratic. Its later domination by a feudal aristocracy was the result of degeneration—marked the triumph of greed and violence over the liberty, equality, and pure self-government of ancient Germany. Several scholars,[10] it is true, refused to accept what they denounced as an obvious exaggeration; and their demand for more positive evidence received strong support from Georg Waitz, one of the great historians of all time.[11] Yet Waitz remained firmly convinced that the *Markgenossenschaft* was the basic institution of Germanic society, an agrarian association that might well have had political functions of a local character. The debate then became more intricate as well as more acrimonious. Thudicum defended Maurer's thesis by presenting further alleged proofs from late sources. Roth, Gierke, and Sohm upheld Waitz in some particulars only to differ with him in others—while by no means agreeing among themselves.[12]

For the present study these disputes have relatively slight importance. Our interest in the *Markgenossenschaft* lies not in its probable significance for state-building but in its presumed existence. If there never was any such thing, why bother with an estimate of its potential influence? To Fustel de Coulanges goes the honor of having first appreciated the underlying problem and of having boldly attacked it. In his essay "De la marche

[9] Hence the thesis of W. Arnold and others (following Kemble, below, n. 31), that place names reflect the primitive settlement of families or clans.

[10] Notably W. E. Wilda and H. von Sybel.

[11] In this verdict I heartily agree with Dopsch. Waitz proved himself a fine historical scholar by basing his conclusions on the study of authentic sources. Whenever we disagree with him, we must present equally good reasons for doing so. Most of his contemporaries, like too many of ours, seem to have thought that historical truth could be found through juristic theorizing. In my *Borough and Town* (Cambridge, Mass., 1933), pp. 5, 11, I have explained why I prefer Waitz to Maurer on the subject of urban origins.

[12] For a discussion of the controversy between Waitz and Roth over the development of feudalism, see my earlier article, *Am. Hist. Rev.*, XLVI (1941), 788 ff.

germanique"[13] he briefly stated the thesis of the Germanist school,[14] examined the relevant sources, and gave his own conclusions. So far as it went, in my opinion, his judgment was decisive. Throughout the extant documents of the earlier Middle Ages the word "mark" (*marca*) invariably means a boundary. It is only in the land grants of the twelfth and following centuries that it sometimes designates a particular property, such as a villa; and descriptions of these properties often include the term *communia*. But the latter does not imply communal ownership by villagers. It denotes merely a piece of land, e.g. a wood, which, at least to some extent, is jointly used by various persons and which can only be alienated subject to their rights of common. To accept the current doctrine of the *Markgenossenschaft,* accordingly, one must first read into comparatively late sources a meaning which they never had and then apply that misinterpretation to an imaginary society of a thousand years earlier.[15]

Fustel's argument, however cogent it may appear to us, had surprisingly little effect upon the learned world of his day. French historians, angered by his delineation of the early Germans as rather better than savages, seemed more inclined to attack than to support anything he said.[16] German historians, to whom the works of the French school had long been anathema, generally disregarded him. And English historians, with few

[13] *Recherches sur quelques problèmes d'histoire* (Paris, 1885), pp. 319 ff. These were studies which Fustel had earlier written to supplement the first volume of his *Histoire des institutions de l'ancienne France* (Paris, 1874), but which he had not separately published. It is greatly to be regretted that the writing of so brilliant a scholar never caught up with his research.

[14] The authorities referred to by Fustel are principally such German historians as Maurer, Waitz, and Sohm, together with the French historian, E. L. V. de Laveleye, whose *Histoire des formes primitives de la propriété* had been published in 1874. On the contemporary work of Seebohm (unnoticed by Fustel), see below, n. 33.

[15] The words are my own; Fustel was much less emphatic.

[16] Dopsch has shown (I, 46) how both Glasson and Viollet, avoiding Fustel's main argument, continued to defend the juristic thesis that primitive communism must have preceded individual ownership of land. For the works of other French historians, as well as for those of various German and English historians, see immediately below. It should be noted that at this point Dopsch, after an enthusiastic tribute to Fustel de Coulanges, diverts his chief attention to the broader subject of Germanic *Kulturentwicklung* upon Roman soil. So what follows is essentially my own criticism of the books cited.

exceptions, refused to be perturbed by the criticism of any foreigner. It must, indeed, have been very gratifying to the many exponents of nationalistic history that Fustel could be said to have proved merely the inadequacy of the word "mark." So, to escape the rigor of his logic, all one had to do was to substitute *commune rurale, Landgemeinde,* "village community," or "township." Yet the question remains whether such substitution really adds to our knowledge. To give the *Markgenossenschaft* a new name is not to demonstrate its existence. Although Fustel died prematurely, and without adequate recognition, no student can do better than take his work as a model of historical criticism. Let us see, more precisely, what a few typical writers of the next generation were able to advance in favor of the good old Germanist doctrine.

Beginning in 1886, Jacques Flach published a history which, by virtue of its pleasing style rather than of its scholarship, has had considerable influence.[17] Flach's first volume, dealing with the emergence of *le régime seigneurial,* is devoted to a romantic portrayal of the family as the governing factor in primitive French society. His second volume (1893) attempts to show how the same thesis can be developed to explain the institutions of the eleventh and twelfth centuries—especially *la commune* and *la féodalité.* Ignoring Flach's description of feudalism as being irrelevant to the present study, we need only remark that he finds the origin of the urban commune in the rural commune, which he manages to derive from Frankish institutions in Gaul and so, presumably, from earlier Germanic custom. To state Flach's argument more positively is quite impossible, as anybody who reads his book will quickly realize. His one sure conclusion would seem to be that Fustel de Coulanges was wrong; Germanic society had been characterized by the free self-governing community. Yet, to justify his faith in that institution,

---

[17] *Les origines de l'ancienne France* (4 vols., Paris, 1886–1917). By way of contrast C. Pfister's admirable chapters in E. Lavisse, *Histoire de France,* II, pt. 1 (Paris, 1903), not only accept Fustel's conclusions regarding the *Markgenossenschaft* but decline to imagine a substitute called *commune rurale* or anything else (see especially p. 204, n. 2). On the continued support to Maurer's theory of urban origins by Petit-Dutaillis, Bourgin, and others, see my *Borough and Town,* pp. 15, 18.

Flach could refer to nothing earlier than the seignorially organized villas of the Carolingian period. To one who begins his inquiry without such faith, Flach's volumes, whatever their literary merit, remain wholly unconvincing.

In Germany, meanwhile, it had been Fustel's misfortune to have his work cited with approval by Richard Hildebrand, a professor of political economy who in 1896 published a sociological essay on the early stages of human culture.[18] According to Hildebrand, men were first hunters and fishers, secondly herdsmen, thirdly peasants and landlords. Had the Germans, as pictured by Tacitus, approached the third stage? Assuredly not, for their agrarian system was still quite primitive. Even the most famous of German historians had failed to recognize that fact and had therefore imposed upon the scholarly world an opinion compounded of romantic imagination and a misreading of the sources.[19] More especially, the sacred doctrine of the *Markgenossenschaft* was no better than a myth![20] Hildebrand was obviously inviting Jovian thunderbolts, and they descended in due course. Prominent historians joined in ridiculing not only his interpretation of Caesar and Tacitus but also his application of the sociologists' comparative method to the study of early German society.[21] And since a good deal of

18 *Recht und Sitte auf den verschiedenen wirtschaftlichen Kulturstufen* (Jena, 1896). Likewise appreciated by Hildebrand was the pioneer work of Denman Ross, *The Early History of Landholding among the Germans* (Boston, 1883), which had denied the whole theory of communism in the primitive *Markgenossenschaft*. See Dopsch, I, 44–45.

19 "Die Zusammenstellung von 'liberté,' 'fraternité' und 'égalité,' von welcher sich humoristischer Weise auch deutsche Historiker haben anstecken lassen, um auf dieser Trias die 'germanische Urzeit' oder die 'älteste deutsche Agrarverfassung' aufzubauen, beruht auf reiner Ideologie und Phantasterei" (Hildebrand, p. 125).

20 "Von der 'geläufigen Vorstellung der alten deutschen Markgenossenschaft' bleibt gar nichts übrig: Das Ganze ist ein Hirngespinnst" (*ibid.*, p. 180).

21 Together with the works cited immediately below, see R. Kötzschke, "Die Gliederung der Gesellschaft bei den alten Deutschen," *Deutsche Zeitschrift für Geschichtswissenschaft*, Neue Folge, II (1897–98), 269 ff. And for a good review of the whole question by a supporter of the orthodox position, see G. von Below, *Probleme der Wirtschaftsgeschichte* (Tübingen, 1926), chs. i–ii. Below's restatement of Maurer's theory of urban origins, including the substitution of *Landgemeinde* for *Markgenossenschaft*, has been summarized in my *Borough and Town*, pp. 3 ff.

this criticism was not without justification, the arguments of Fustel de Coulanges tended to be discredited along with those of Hildebrand.

Long before Hildebrand's particular heresy could be refuted, however, a more insidious attack was launched against the dogma of the *Markgenossenschaft* by Werner Wittich, a pupil of the specialist on agrarian history, Georg Friedrich Knapp.[22] Under the inspiration of his distinguished master, rather than of Fustel de Coulanges, Wittich in 1896 published a book on the development of great landed estates in northwestern Germany.[23] The bulk of his work, consisting of a dozen chapters, dealt with the landlords and peasants of the old Saxony from the later Middle Ages down to the nineteenth century. It was only in an appendix that Wittich raised the question whether the *Grundherrschaft* of that period had resulted from a mediaeval deterioration of society or had prevailed among the primitive Germans. The latter supposition Wittich declared to be the much more probable. As delineated by Caesar and Tacitus, German society was plainly an aristocracy, in which the warrior did not himself guide a plow. Although his income was primarily derived from agriculture, he was supported by the labor of servile dependents (*Knechten*). He was, in other words, a petty *Grundherr*. And if we turn to the *leges barbarorum*, said Wittich, we find additional evidence for the same conclusion. The *liberi homines*, who appear so prominently in those compilations, were not peasants but small landlords, some of whom had only to expand their holdings to become the great landlords of the subsequent age.

It was, of course, against Wittich that the thunderbolts were thenceforth directed. Recognized authorities on the legal and

[22] Knapp's first book, on the emancipation of the German peasantry, was published in 1887. His second, *Grundherrschaft und Rittergut* (Leipzig, 1897), incorporated a series of earlier lectures and was in turn incorporated in his *Einführung in einige Hauptgebiete der Nationalökonomie* (Munich, 1925).

[23] *Die Grundherrschaft in Nordwestdeutschland* (Leipzig, 1896), especially Anlage VI. During these same years P. Heck complicated the problem under discussion by advancing, with little success, the thesis that in the *leges barbarorum* of the Frankish period the men described as *liberi* or *ingenuiles* were really dependents, that the true *Gemeinfreie* were the *nobiles*. Anyone interested will find specific references to Heck's publications in the articles herewith cited.

institutional history of Germany, led by Heinrich Brunner [24] and Richard Schröder,[25] proceeded to demolish as best they could the work of Knapp and all his school. The writings of Caesar and Tacitus, as well as the barbarian codes, were once more subjected to laborious analysis and commentary. The triumphant result, according to these same authorities, was that Wittich had utterly failed to prove his unorthodox thesis. The typical German, they insisted, had always been the common freeman, a warrior-peasant who customarily tilled his own soil when not actually engaged in fighting. Such *Gemeinfreien* truly constituted the primitive German nation; for the nobles and serfs mentioned by Tacitus were but minor groups, relatively unimportant either politically or economically. Insofar as Germanic custom continued to prevail in the many barbarian states of the following centuries, the same social condition came to be reflected by the legal compilations then made. The common man was still a warrior-peasant of the old type; it was not until the Carolingian period that "feudalizing tendencies" began to bring about his long degradation.

Wittich, nevertheless, remained unconvinced. In an article of 1901, though hard-pressed to meet all the arguments of his many antagonists, he stoutly maintained his original thesis.[26] Ultimately, he declared, the upholders of the traditional doctrine

[24] The first edition of Brunner's *Deutsche Rechtsgeschichte* (Leipzig, 1887–92) in general supported Waitz with regard to the *Markgenossenschaft*. Brunner's article on "Nobiles und Gemeinfreie der karolingischen Volksrechte," *Zeitschrift der Savigny-Stiftung für Rechtsgeschichte,* Germanistische Abteilung, XIX (1898), 76 ff., presented a detailed refutation of Heck, Knapp, and Wittich. And in a second article, *ibid.,* XXIII (1902), 193 ff., he replied to Wittich's rebuttal (see below, n. 26). A final summary of his argument then appeared in the second edition of the *Deutsche Rechtsgeschichte* (Leipzig, 1906–28). That Brunner must be regarded as one of the dozen best historians of the early twentieth century is, I think, beyond dispute (see *Am. Hist. Rev.,* XLVI, 794 ff.)—but not because he continued to believe in the *Markgenossenschaft* and its typical member, the warrior-peasant (see my quotation, *ibid.,* XLVIII, 249, n. 21).

[25] The many editions of Schröder's *Lehrbuch der deutschen Rechtsgeschichte,* ending with the fifteenth (Berlin, 1932), have continued to defend the theory of the *Markgenossenschaft.* See also Schröder's criticism of Wittich in the *Zeitschrift der Savigny-Stiftung für Rechtsgeschichte,* Germanistische Abteilung, XXIV (1903), 347 ff.

[26] *Ibid.,* XXII (1901), 245 ff.

had little to fall back on but an unjustifiable interpretation of Tacitus. It was ingrained habit of thought that led them to read into the records of a primitive age such modern ideas as democracy and the nobility of toil.[27] When dealing with the meager sources of the early Middle Ages, nobody should pretend to arrive at more than hypothetical conclusions; he submitted merely that his opinion was better supported by the available evidence than that of his opponents. "Jedoch habe ich eingesehen, dass die Annahme von der alten Bauernfreiheit der Germanen nicht eigentlich auf einer wissenschaftlich begründeten Einsicht sondern auf einem nationalen und liberalen Glauben an ein 'güldenes' Zeitalter im Sinne Mösers beruht." [28] Wittich's challenge, it seems to me, deserves a fairer answer than it has ever received. Before extending our criticism in that direction, however, we must see what had meanwhile become the accepted belief of English historians.

How the theory of the *Markgenossenschaft* was popularized by Kemble, Freeman, and Stubbs, together with their many disciples in England and America, is so familiar a story that detailed recapitulation of their work is hardly needed here.[29] Kemble's enthusiasm for Anglo-Saxon literature naturally led him, after studying at Göttingen, to accept the confident assertions of German historians with regard to the antiquities of his

[27] "Ein Schluss aus diesen zahlreichen übereinstimmenden Angaben des Schriftstellers auf die wirtschaftliche Thätigkeit oder besser Unthätigkeit der freien Männer scheint mir nicht nur erlaubt sondern geboten; dass der freie deutsche Mann, den Tacitus schildert, nicht selbst regelmässig den Pflug führte, wird wohl jeder Unbefangene zugeben. Brunner scheint es für etwas Unerhörtes zu halten, wenn man einer Volksklasse die eigene wirtschaftliche Thätigkeit abspricht. Auch hier sind wieder ganz moderne Anschauungen wirksam, ich meine die ungemessene Hochschätzung der wirtschaftlichen besonders der Handarbeit. Die ganz antike und mittelalterliche Welt ist nur verständlich, wenn man sich von der Anschauung, dass 'wirtschaftliche Arbeit adelt,' frei macht. Alle Erwerbsthätigkeit war ein schmutziges Geschäft, das der anständige Mensch nur nothgedrungen ergriff" (*ibid.*, XXII, 253–54).

[28] *Ibid.*, XXII, 264.

[29] In addition to what Dopsch has to say on the subject, see especially W. J. Ashley, *Surveys Historic and Economic* (London, 1900), pp. 39 ff. For my own opinions the reader is referred to my previous articles: *Am. Hist. Rev.*, XLVIII, 245 ff., and "The Beginnings of Representative Government in England," in *The Constitution Reconsidered*, ed. Conyers Read (New York, 1938), pp. 25 ff.

country as well as theirs.[30] So in his famous work, *The Saxons in England*,[31] he sought to impress his compatriots with the significance of the *Markgenossenschaft* throughout their national history. The measure of his success can still be discerned in almost every book that deals with early England. Stubbs, it is true, was too good a scholar to accept Kemble's thesis without grave reservation. Yet even Stubbs was so captivated by the Germanist doctrine that he tended to interpret all English history as having been dominated by the primitive institution of the township, which he described as the logical development of the *Markgenossenschaft*. It seems never to have troubled him that positive evidence for any such primitive institution was as completely lacking under the second name as under the first.[32]

Once again the adherents of the orthodox school were aided by the fact that their principal antagonist exposed himself to assault from the flank as well as from the front. Unlike Fustel de Coulanges, Frederic Seebohm adopted the method of arguing back "from the known to the unknown"—a method which had been continuously used to justify the theory of the *Markgenossenschaft*, and which Seebohm now used in an effort to

[30] Kemble should be gratefully remembered not only for his pioneer work in editing the Anglo-Saxon charters but also for his fine appreciation of the Anglo-Saxon poems—wonderful sources which have been neglected by too many English historians of later generations.

[31] 1st ed., London, 1848; 2d ed., London, 1876. Kemble's work was based on the thesis (p. 35) that the mark was "the original principle of settlement, prevalent either in England or on the continent of Europe, among the nations of Germanic blood." But to prove the existence of the mark in Britain he had to rely on the theoretical arguments of Eichhorn, Grimm, and Dönniges (cited above), together with a fanciful derivation of place names which has now been thoroughly discredited. See, among the more recent works, Dopsch, I, 265; *The Cambridge Economic History*, I (Cambridge, 1941), 35, 177; and F. M. Stenton, *Anglo-Saxon England* (Oxford, 1943), p. 23, n. 3, and p. 314, n. 1, together with the articles there cited.

[32] *The Constitutional History of England* (Oxford, 1903), I, 33 ff., 53 ff. This sixth edition made no essential change in the thesis presented by the first in 1873. Like Brunner, with whom he had so much in common, Stubbs naturally accepted Waitz as the greatest of the earlier authorities on Germanic institutions. He frequently referred also to the works of Georg von Maurer, Sohm, and others of the orthodox school; but never, one notes with regret, to those of Fustel de Coulanges. In my opinion, the remarks made over fifty years ago by Ashley (pp. 61 ff.) still remain valid.

refute it.[33] On the whole, it must be granted, Seebohm's argument was the more scholarly of the two; yet, because he cited a spurious charter and misinterpreted a few authentic documents, he could be said to have presented an utterly false thesis. Besides, by adducing Welsh and Scandinavian records of the later Middle Ages to explain the character of ancient tribal organization, he made himself still more vulnerable to the attack of historians suddenly grown conscientious. Vinogradoff and Maitland, though by no means agreeing on the nature of the early village community, heartily joined in denying Seebohm's major allegations.[34] And despite all that has been written to support his opinion in preference to Kemble's, most writers on early English institutions, consciously or unconsciously, hold an abiding faith in the *Markgenossenschaft*.[35]

[33] *The English Village Community* (London, 1883). References to Seebohm's later work, as well as to that of Chadwick, Corbett, and numerous other historians, will be found in *Am. Hist. Rev.*, XLVIII, 250 ff.

[34] *Ibid.*, XLVIII, 247 ff. Utter lack of evidence, Maitland concluded, must force us to reject the alleged self-governing township of the Anglo-Saxons; to hold that the primitive Germanic village was a purely agrarian community, which somehow operated without moot or elected officials. This concession to the heretical enemy Vinogradoff refused to make. He steadfastly reaffirmed his faith in Georg von Maurer's thesis and like him, of course, could adduce as proof nothing earlier than manorial records of the fourteenth century. Vinogradoff, it should be noted, was already a convinced believer in the *Markgenossenschaft* when he published his *Villainage in England* (1892). And in 1902, before establishing residence in Britain, he collaborated with Brunner and Schröder in their attack upon Wittich (*Zeitschrift der Savigny-Stiftung für Rechtsgeschichte*, Germanistische Abteilung, XXIII, 123 ff.).

[35] For the most entrancing picture of primitive Germanic society one should turn, not to the pages of Freeman and Stubbs, but to those of their disciple, John Richard Green, whose *History of the English People* was published in 1881. In the villages of the early Germans, he declared (I, 8, 12–13), "lay ready formed the social and political life which is round us in the England of to-day. A belt of forest or waste parted each from its fellow villages, and within this boundary or mark the 'township,' as the village was then called . . . formed a complete and independent body, though linked by ties which were strengthening every day to the townships about it and the tribe of which it formed a part." The "sovereignty of the settlement" resided in its moot, the assembly of its component freemen. "Here new settlers were admitted to the freedom of the township, and bye-laws framed and headman and tithing-man chosen for its governance. Here plough-land and meadow-land were shared in due lot among the villagers, and field and homestead passed from man to man by the delivery of a turf cut from its soil. Here strife of farmer with farmer was settled according to the 'customs' of the

For example, let us glance at what may justly be considered the last word on the subject—Mr. F. M. Stenton's *Anglo-Saxon England*.[36] "The starting-point of English social history" he declares to have been, "not the manor, but the community of free peasants."[37] In all the Anglo-Saxon kingdoms the *ceorl* was originally a rural freeholder.[38] The importance of the open-field system in "Old English agrarian life" may have been somewhat exaggerated; yet it was the village that "throughout Old English history . . . formed the basis of social organization."[39] Within the village the free *ceorlas* constituted not only an "economic association" but also some kind of political unit, because we have "a definite reason for believing in a primitive township-moot."[40] Nor was the *ceorl* a mere peasant; although "in all the recorded fighting of Anglo-Saxon history the typical warrior is the man of noble birth, . . . there are facts which suggest that the ceorl may have been by no means negligible as a fighting-man."[41] And the "urgent necessity for some form of assembly intermediate between the meeting of the whole folk and the meeting of a village community" naturally led to the institution of moots for the *regiones* later called hundreds,

township as its elder men stated them, and four men were chosen to follow headman or ealdorman to hundred-court or war. It is with a reverence such as is stirred by the sight of the head-waters of some mighty river that one looks back to these village-moots of Friesland or Sleswick. It was here that England learned to be a 'mother of parliaments.'" Thus, obviously, the lyrical Green portrayed the *Markgenossenschaft*, under the name of township, as the germ of the glorious English constitution.

[36] The second volume of *The Oxford History of England* (Oxford, 1943). What follows is an elaboration of my brief remarks in *The Journal of Economic History*, IV (1944), 216 ff.

[37] Stenton, p. 310.   [38] *Ibid.*, pp. 274–75.   [39] *Ibid.*, pp. 278, 283.

[40] *Ibid.*, pp. 283–85. Mr. Stenton's "definite reason" is the fact that villages were commonly assessed in round numbers of hides long before there was a hundred court to make the assessment. But the hundred court of the tenth century is known to have inherited most of its functions from the local *folcgemot* of the earlier dooms, and it was not a "township-moot"; see Liebermann, *Gesetze der Angelsachsen* (Halle, 1903–16), II, 449 ff. ("Gericht"), 516 ff. ("hundred"). In further support of his conclusion Mr. Stenton cites Elizabeth B. Demarest's article in *The English Historical Review*, XXXIII (1918), 62 ff.; though not one of mine, in which I tried to show that Domesday provides no sure example of hidation applied to the king's *feorm—ibid.*, XXXIX (1924), 161 ff.

[41] Stenton, p. 287. The single reference provided here is to a few dubious words in a traditional life of St. Cuthbert.

where "peasants learned in the law" rendered judgments according to popular custom.[42] Albeit with some little hesitance, Mr. Stenton thus proclaims himself more orthodox even than Maitland.[43] After all, Mr. Stenton decides, Vinogradoff's thesis remains sound—and that, of course, was essentially the thesis of Georg von Maurer and his romantic precursors.

However bold it may seem to question the considered judgments of great historians, one is always justified in asking them to cite their evidence. In a previous article I have tried to give an honest summary of what the sources tell us about the classes of people in early England and have arrived at conclusions quite different from those of Mr. Stenton's recent book. And nothing presented there has led me to change my opinions. I still believe that the Anglo-Saxon sources—the dooms as well as the poems and other literary works—portray an aristocratic rather than a democratic society. I fail to find in them the slightest evidence for a self-governing township or for the warrior-peasant who is alleged to have been its typical citizen. The *ceorl*, to be sure, was legally free; but precisely what did his freedom amount to? Did he till his own land, or that of someone else?[44] Even when he could be styled a proprietor, was he not generally commended to a lord and therefore bound, together with his children, to what the Normans called a manor?[45] Was a village inhabited by such *ceorlas* a "free" village? If so, what document proves its existence—as against the hundreds which prove that, from the seventh century on, whole villages were regularly bought, sold, and otherwise alienated?

As students of early Germanic institutions have long acknowledged, the Anglo-Saxon sources cannot be matched by any contemporary series on the Continent. Why, then, should English

[42] *Ibid.*, pp. 294–95.

[43] See above, n. 34. To account for the growth of manorial economy and the concomitant degradation of the *ceorl*, Mr. Stenton naturally follows both Vinogradoff and Maitland.

[44] In this connection note particularly the verdict of Liebermann, quoted in *Am. Hist. Rev.*, XLVIII, 254.

[45] It seems to me that the evidence of Domesday, as well as that of the earlier sources, tends to make such a conclusion necessary; see my "Commendation and Related Problems in Domesday," *Eng. Hist. Rev.*, LIX (1944), 289 ff.

historians persistently accept the governing ideas which nationalists of nineteenth-century Germany chose to derive from late mediaeval documents? The constant repetition by modern scholars of an argument originally devised to justify faith in the *Markgenossenschaft* must lead one to suspect that too many of them have neglected to read the work of Fustel de Coulanges, or to examine for themselves the records of the Frankish period. To the latter subject we shall presently return. Meanwhile, here is another pertinent question: Why should our recognized authorities on pre-Norman England require us to believe that the Danish conquests of the ninth century necessarily resulted in the democratization of eastern Britain? [46] It may, indeed, be imagined that the typical Viking was a warrior-peasant who, in his isolated northland, had preserved the customs of a primitive Germany. But is there any historical evidence for that supposition?

We need only consult the index of the *Corpus Poeticum Boreale* [47] to discover that the oldest Scandinavian literature provides us with a single reference to plowing. This reference is to the famous *Rigspula*, which tells how the god Rig spent three nights in each of three homes, always sleeping between host and hostess; and how, in due time, the three wives brought forth three children. The first was Thrall (*þrael*, Anglo-Saxon *þeow*). A swarthy fellow with ugly features, thick hands and broad back, Thrall spent his life in putting up fences, spreading manure, cutting peat, and herding animals. The second was ruddy-faced Karl (Anglo-Saxon *ceorl*), who properly learned to break an ox, guide a plow, make useful tools, and build a house or barn. The third was Jarl (Anglo-Saxon *eorl*). He had blond hair, rosy cheeks, and eyes as keen as a serpent's. He took to shaping the shield, stringing and bending the bow, shafting arrows, wielding and hurling the spear, riding horses, training hounds, brandishing the sword, and swimming the sea. Finally, having been recognized by Rig as his true son, Jarl became a

[46] Cf. *ibid.*, LIX, 308, n. 6.

[47] Edited by Gudbrand Vigfusson and F. York Powell (Oxford, 1883). For the *Rigspula*, with an English translation and commentary, see I, 234 ff., 514 ff.; and for scanty references to other poems, II, 702 ("Agriculture"). A considerable part of the following summary is translated from the original poem.

landed gentleman,[48] a warrior who gloried in battle and red-dened the field with the blood of slain foes. He conquered and ruled over eighteen country estates (*buom*). He distributed largess—steeds, golden rings, and other treasure. I am convinced that this grand poem, whether written in the ninth century or somewhat later, faithfully portrays Viking society.[49] That it was as aristocratic as Anglo-Saxon society I therefore see no reason for doubting.

The present study, however, has primarily to do with Con-tinental Europe; we still have the task of reviewing the evidence presented by Tacitus and the writings of the Frankish age. This task, it seems to me, can be simplified by recognizing that a num-ber of subjects, though related, are quite subordinate to the one under discussion. In the first place, we may profitably ignore the classification of particular institutions as Roman, Celtic, Germanic, or something else; for such classification must follow, rather than precede, a good understanding of what the institu-tion was. We are not especially interested in the technical dis-tinctions of the law, except insofar as they may reflect important differences of social status. Ancient tribal arrangements, in spite of their undoubted influence upon later custom, need not detain us. And we may disregard even the question whether settlement within a certain region was commonly in nucleated villages or in scattered homesteads. As neither form was incompatible with manorial organization in the Middle Ages, so neither can be peculiarly associated with any more primitive system, manorial or nonmanorial. In other words, our central problem is the alleged warrior-peasant of Möser's frontispiece.

That illustrious character of historical literature can hardly be found in the writings of Tacitus except by one who already

[48] Literally a holder of *udal*-fields, or inherited land; see F. Seebohm, *Tribal Custom in Anglo-Saxon Law* (London, 1902), pp. 271 ff.

[49] In this respect the opinion of earlier writers (notably Vigfusson) has been supported by such modern writers as Axel Olrik, *Viking Civilization* (New York, 1930), pp. 112 ff. Cf. Karl Lehmann, "Die Rigsþula," in *Festschrift . . . Julius von Amsberg* (Rostock, 1904), which develops the thesis that the poem was a product of the feudal age. But what evidence does Lehmann present that would not like-wise hold good for *Beowulf* or the dooms of Aethelberht? It is rather surprising that so excellent a book as *Social Scandinavia in the Viking Age*, by Mary W. Williams (New York, 1920), takes no account of the problem here considered.

believes he must be there. The candid reader, I think, will inevitably see in the *Germania* the picture of an aristocracy— a people dominated by a class of warriors who, far from being also peasants, regarded agricultural labor as degrading. In this respect I heartily agree with the conclusion of Wittich noted above [50] and with that more recently stated by Marc Bloch.[51] If, indeed, the status of the primitive German was determined by military prowess, and if the German ideal was a chieftain surrounded by professional fighters, how can we suppose that German society was originally an agrarian democracy? Tacitus, for a historian whose main interest was by no means economic, gives us very satisfactory information: the *principes,* together of course with their *comites,* were supported by customary offerings of livestock and produce from their dependents. Whether these dependents were theoretically free or unfree—*servi* who resembled the *coloni* of the Roman Empire—is beside the point. They were assuredly peasants.

To one familiar with the early mediaeval sources of England those of the Continent should not appear entirely strange. Among the latter, as among the former, we can distinguish three principal groups: historical narratives, charters, and laws. What has each of the three to tell us about the common man on the Continent? And how, if at all, does their testimony disagree with that of the Anglo-Saxon records and other literature, supplemented by the oldest of the Norse sagas? In such an inquiry the burden of proof would seem to be with the scholars who try to demonstrate the existence of the *Markgenossenschaft,* or of its typical member, the warrior-peasant. For they can find no stronger support in the science of the modern anthropologist than in the sources referred to above. Thus the interested student gains considerable respite of labor; he may be sure that every available scrap of evidence in any of the Continental

[50] P. 426; cf. *Am. Hist. Rev.,* XLVI, 799–800, and XLVIII, 250, n. 22. Dopsch (I, ch. ii), after pooh-poohing the whole theory of the *Markgenossenschaft* and emphasizing the dominant position of the nobility in ancient Germany, could still hold, for some mysterious reason, that the typical German warrior tilled his own land. Cf. his remarks in W. Reeb's edition of the *Germania* (Leipzig, 1930), pp. 157–58.

[51] *Camb. Econ. Hist.,* I, 261 ff.; cf. R. Koebner's remarks, pp. 14 ff.

sources, to which no significant addition is likely to appear, has long since been discovered and repeatedly discussed.

So far as historical narratives of the Frankish kingdom and its neighbors are concerned, no one has ever been able to find in them any encouragement for the belief that the average German warrior was also a peasant, or that he somehow helped to constitute a free village community. A glance through the pages of Gregory of Tours and the subsequent writers will surely convince the reader that nothing could be farther from their view of contemporary society than a form of democracy.[52] Nor has the enormous mass of charters afforded much comfort to the believers in the *Markgenossenschaft*. On the contrary, as Wittich pointed out,[53] a single land grant that does not imply the existence of peasant cultivators, regularly bought and sold along with the estate, can hardly be adduced. There remains, accordingly, the evidence of the laws—the legal enactments of the barbarian kings, which correspond to the Anglo-Saxon dooms.

Even if I had the competence, the present essay would lack the space for a thorough analysis of the Continental *leges barbarorum*. Fortunately, with the help of Brunner,[54] it is not hard to run through them all, to gain an impression of their general character, and to examine more closely such particular articles as have been commonly cited by the upholders of the traditional doctrine. This, at least, I have done and, in the light of the foregoing discussion, have arrived at a few conclusions. They may be stated rather simply. And since the reader may not have both Brunner and Liebermann at his elbow, I insert a brief memorandum as to the relative age of the sources with which we are here concerned. The Kentish dooms, like those of the West Saxon Ine, date from the seventh century. Alfred's great doombook was written towards the end of the ninth century— to be supplemented, in almost unbroken series, by his successors during the tenth and the early eleventh centuries. Of the Continental *leges* those promulgated by kings of the Ostrogoths,

---

[52] See Dopsch, II, 128 ff.   [53] See above, n. 23.
[54] *Deutsche Rechtsgeschichte*, I, 376 ff., to which the reader is referred for bibliographical data concerning the *leges* cited below.

Visigoths, Burgundians, Salian Franks, and Lombards are contemporary with, if not older than, the earliest dooms of the Anglo-Saxons. On the other hand, we owe chiefly to the Carolingians of the eighth and ninth centuries our extant summaries of customary law among the Ripuarian Franks, Alamans, Bavarians, Saxons, Frisians, and Thuringians. Our preliminary question is whether these legal compilations of the Continent ever depict other than an aristocratic society. A rather curious answer is generally given by historians of the Germanist school, led by the distinguished Brunner.[55] The codes of the Ostrogothic, Visigothic, and Burgundian kings, we are told, naturally reflect the late Roman caste system, into which the warriors of those three nations had been drawn through settlement in the imperial provinces. Strangely enough, however, the Lombards, who entered the Italian scene a hundred years later, likewise maintained vigorous class distinctions—and the Lombard law, according to Brunner, shows remarkable affinity with the Anglo-Saxon.[56] Indeed, the *leges* of the Continental Saxons, Frisians, Thuringians, Alamans, and Bavarians all present a more or less complex differentiation of grades among *liberi* or *ingenuiles*. So Brunner has to conclude that the Frankish kingdom was peculiar in fully recognizing the social dominance of the *Gemeinfreien*. Although a *Geburtsadel* had presumably existed among the Franks, as among other Germanic peoples, it was suppressed in Gaul by the all-powerful house of Clovis, while the degenerate social structure of Rome was being swept away by the tide of Frankish conquest.[57] Such distinctions of rank as are suggested by Merovingian chroniclers resulted from the growth of inequality in landholding, which

[55] *Ibid.*, I, 339 ff. Cf. the article of Kötzschke (above, n. 21), whose conclusions were largely accepted by Brunner. In spite of all that has been written on the wergeld system throughout the barbarian kingdoms of Britain and the Continent, its social significance remains very obscure. The problem surely deserves more thorough treatment than it has yet received, but I fear our extant sources are so fragmentary that a final solution may never be possible.

[56] *Ibid.*, I, 536.

[57] "In diese kastenartig abgeschlossene und versteinerte Gesellschaft mit ausgeklügelten Titularen und pedantischen Kleiderordnungen hat die germanische Invasion Luft und Bewegung gebracht. Die fränkische Rechtsordnung ignorierte das römische Ständewesen" (*ibid.*, I, 340).

also contributed to the rise of a new Carolingian nobility. But the latter was essentially a *Dienstadel,* an aristocracy of service based on royal favor and never closed to recruitment from below.

Brunner's exposition of Frankish society, I agree with Dopsch,[58] is entirely too imaginative. If, in fact, the democratic principles of liberty and equality were unknown to the Germany of Tacitus, to the Anglo-Saxon kingdoms, to early Scandinavia, and to most of the other Germanic states, why must we strain a point to find a purer system among the Merovingian Franks? All else we know about them would hardly lead us to select them as paragons! Actually, Brunner's argument rests on little more than the absence in the *Lex Salica* [59] of any comprehensive scale of wergelds—an absence that should more probably be attributed to the vagary of a compiler than to a striving for Germanic democracy. As I have tried to show in a previous article,[60] the growth of feudal institutions in the Carolingian Empire seems to have presupposed the existence there of a warrior aristocracy—such as is portrayed, if I am not mistaken, both by Tacitus and by the whole of Anglo-Saxon literature.

We are thus brought to the more specific question whether the Continental *leges* tend to prove that the typical German warrior was also a peasant. In his noteworthy attack on the established theory Wittich, as we have seen, developed the argument that by *liber* or *ingenuus* the official compilations really designated a sort of *Grundherr,* a small proprietor whose land was worked for him by *Knechten.*[61] To declare Wittich's thesis exploded, the orthodox then had only to quote a number of texts that referred to plowing and other agricultural labor on the part of freemen. Such texts fall into two principal groups: those prohibiting to free and unfree all servile work (*opera*

---

[58] II, 96 ff. But in the following discussion, as before, Dopsch insists that German warriors regularly engaged in agricultural labor. Why in this respect he should support Brunner, Kötzschke, *et al.* I do not understand; for the evidence he presents is no better than theirs.

[59] The *Lex Ribuaria,* he points out (*Deutsche Rechtsgeschichte,* I, 444), was modeled on the *Lex Salica.*

[60] *Am. Hist. Rev.,* XLVI, 788 ff.   [61] See above, p. 268.

servilia) on Sunday [62] and those establishing penalties for men, presumably free, who plowed or otherwise injured the crops sown by another.[63] But to one who has studied the Anglo-Saxon dooms this comes as an anticlimax. The seventh-century kings of Kent and Wessex, in obedience to the church, likewise ordained that any man, free or unfree, who, with or without his lord's command, worked on Sunday should be severely punished.[64] And that the Kentish or West Saxon *ceorl* was a free peasant, protected by a two-hundred-shilling wergeld, is indisputable.[65] Must we therefore suppose that he was a true warrior and the member of a *Markgenossenschaft?*

For reasons stated above, the English evidence would seem to prove the contrary, and the inferior sources of the Continent do not lead to a different conclusion. We may surely admit that throughout western Europe some, perhaps most, peasants were legally free without regarding them as warrior-citizens of a national state. Before making any such deduction from the scanty records at our disposal, we should remember at least these facts. Under established law the Roman *colonus,* no less than the ordinary German peasant, was protected by a freeman's wergeld.[66] Besides, any such peasant could be bound to a lord by the hereditary tie of commendation, which apparently involved seignorial control of whatever land he might possess. Until the subject of commendation on the Continent has been more

[62] *Leges Alamannorum*, xxxviii; *Lex Baiwariorum*, vii, 4, which explains such *opera* to be the yoking of oxen, sowing, haying, etc. It should be noted that Brunner, Kötzschke, and other historians of the orthodox school pass over in silence the fact that agricultural labor is here described as servile.

[63] The oldest of such provisions is that of the *Lex Salica*, xxvii, 23: "If anyone plows the field of another without the consent of his lord (*extra consilium domini sui*), he shall be adjudged guilty [and liable to a fine of 15s.]." I cannot see why Kötzschke or anybody else should think that the *dominus* here mentioned was the owner of the land in question. Cf. the Anglo-Saxon dooms cited in the following note. The *Lex Ribuaria*, the *Lex Alamannorum*, and the *Lex Frisionum* merely follow the *Lex Salica*. Brunner (*Zeitschrift der Savigny-Stiftung für Rechtsgeschichte*, Germanistische Abteilung, XIX, 106) offers as additional evidence in this connection what the *Rigsþula* (above, p. 275) says about the *karl*.

[64] Wihtraed, 10–11; Ine, 3; Liebermann, *Gesetze*, I, 13, 91.

[65] For numerous references to the dooms see *ibid.*, II, 299 ("Bauer," 7).

[66] Brunner, *Deutsche Rechtsgeschichte*, I, 352.

thoroughly investigated, we cannot be sure of its precise implications. But even a cursory examination of the pertinent records tends to convince us that what Latin writers called *commendatio* was no mere survival from decadent Rome. Both the Anglo-Saxon dooms and the Continental *leges* reveal it as a significant element of Germanic custom—one that vitally affected the life of the masses in early mediaeval Europe. Too many writers continue to describe commendation as essentially the equivalent of vassalage; by doing so, in my opinion, they badly confuse the issue. The great majority of *commendati* were obviously peasants, and on that very account could not be vassals.[67]

There remains, finally, the question whether the forty-fifth title of the *Lex Salica* truly refers, as most historians have agreed, to the *Markgenossenschaft*.[68] Without stopping to comment on the lengthy discussion evoked by this famous enactment, let us see what it attempts to say. "If anyone wishes to move into a villa upon the land of another (*super alterum in villa migrare*), and one or several of those living there wish to receive him but there is one who objects, he who wishes to move there shall not have license to do so." [69] If, contrary to this prohibition, such a man refuses to leave, he must do so within thirty days or incur a judicial penalty of 30s. Should, however, no opposition arise within twelve months, he may stay there *sicut alii vicini*. That the license mentioned above might involve royal action is clearly stated by the fourteenth title, which provides that any man who wishes to move (*migrare*), and has the king's authorization (*praeceptum*), is not to be interfered with under heavy penalty (200s.). Is the *migrans* of these laws to be understood as a free peasant who can be prevented from joining a village community by the veto of a single *Markgenosse*?

[67] Many recent discussions of this complex problem, as well as some of the pertinent sources, are cited in my previous articles: *Am. Hist Rev.*, XLVI, 788 ff., and XLVIII, 245 ff.; *Eng. Hist. Rev.*, LIX, 289 ff.

[68] For the traditional view see Brunner, *Deutsche Rechtsgeschichte*, I, 281; for opposing views Dopsch, I, 226, 354, 371, and R. Koebner, *Camb. Econ. Hist.*, I, 34.

[69] This is my own translation, made to express what seems to me the obvious meaning of the text; but it is essentially the same as that of Fustel de Coulanges, *Nouvelles recherches sur quelques problèmes d'histoire*, ed. Jullian (Paris, 1891), pp. 343 ff.

Rather, I take it, the *migrans* was a person of importance—a Frankish gentleman who, according to the prevalent fashion, was transferring his domicile from the northeast to the southwest and who wanted to settle upon certain Roman property. Without a royal precept, he must not do so if one or two of the neighbors took exception to his presence. Otherwise, we may presume, the peace of the countryside would be unduly disturbed. There is nothing in our text to suggest that we have to do with other than a man of superior rank, who might be bringing with him any number of his own retainers and who might well be interested in a portion of a Roman villa, including of course the appurtenant buildings, tools, livestock, slaves, and *coloni.* Can we for a moment suppose that a king like Clovis would issue letters of protection for a simple plowman, however free, and assess a fine of 200*s.* upon anybody who molested him? To discover proof of the *Markgenossenschaft* in such meager articles of the *Lex Salica,* one must indeed have profound faith in primitive German democracy. And the rest of the Continental *leges* have been searched in vain for equally good evidence!

Our brief review of the sources thus leads us to conclude that in early mediaeval Europe the common man was at most a simple peasant. Though recognized as free, in that his body was not owned, he would normally be the humble follower of a lord—a tribal chieftain, a successful conqueror, a prelate of the church, or some other gentleman. To this lord the peasant, and his children after him, would very likely be bound by a personal tie that involved the performance of customary service. The latter would be agricultural rather than military—and so, according to the standard of the day, servile rather than honorable. The lord, as a member of the warlike aristocracy, would scorn all manual labor; like his ancestors, whether barbarian or Roman, he would gain his regular sustenance from economic dependents. The peasant would be expected to spend his life working the soil, either that of the lord or a plot to which he himself had some kind of hereditary title. In time of need his lord, or perhaps the king, might indeed call upon him for military duty of a sort. As a warrior, however, he would be considered quite inferior to the gentleman who made fighting a profession. In other words, we should not imagine the Germanic state of the early Middle Ages to have been essentially a national union formed by a citizen soldiery of free peasants.

Why do most historians still cling to the myth of the *Markgenossenschaft?* Why will they not recognize that, by gaining some measure of economic liberty, of social equality, and of political power, the common man has not returned to the sentimental primitive but has achieved the new and revolutionary? I shall be happy if this article has helped to advance that better understanding of history. Yet, in spite of the evidence, I fear that many will keep their devotion to the great romantic tradition. To them I merely suggest that they acknowledge their faith and pin up as an icon Möser's picture of the original *Markgenosse.*

Writings of Carl Stephenson

1919

"The Aids of the English Boroughs," *The English Historical Review,* XXXIV (1919), 457–75.

1922

"Les 'aides' des villes françaises aux XIIᵉ et XIIIᵉ siècles," *Le Moyen Age,* XXIV (1922), 274–328.

1924

"The *Firma Noctis* and the Customs of the Hundred," *The English Historical Review,* XXXIX (1924), 161–74.

"La taille dans les villes d'Allemagne," *Le Moyen Age,* XXVI (1924), 1–43.

1926

"The Origin and Nature of the *Taille*," *La Revue Belge de Philologie et d'Histoire,* V (1926), 801–70.

"The Origin of the English Towns," *The American Historical Review,* XXXII (1926), 10–21.

"The Seignorial Tallage in England," *Mélanges d'histoire offerts à Henri Pirenne* (Brussels, 1926), II, 465–74.

1929

"Taxation and Representation in the Middle Ages," *Anniversary Essays in Mediaeval History,* by Students of Charles Homer Haskins, ed. C. H. Taylor and John L. La Monte (Boston and New York, 1929), pp. 291–312.

1930
"The Anglo-Saxon Borough," *The English Historical Review*, XLV (1930), 177–207.

1931
"The Work of Henri Pirenne and Georg von Below with Respect to the Origin of the Mediaeval Town," *Methods in Social Science*, ed. Stuart A. Rice (Chicago, 1931), pp. 368–83.

1932
"The French Commune and the English Borough," *The American Historical Review*, XXXVII (1932), 451–67.
"Investigation of the Origins of Towns," *History*, New Series, XVII (1932), 8–14.
Article "Commune," *The National Encyclopedia* (New York, 1932), III, 192–94.
Reviews of N. D. Harding (ed.), *Bristol Charters, 1155–1373*; E. W. W. Veale (ed.), *The Great Red Book of Bristol*, I. *The American Historical Review*, XXXVII (1932), 738–40.

1933
Borough and Town: A Study of Urban Origins in England. Cambridge, Mass., 1933. Pp. xvi, 236.
Review of M. McKisack, *The Parliamentary Representation of the English Boroughs during the Middle Ages. The American Historical Review*, XXXVIII (1933), 585–86.

1934
Review of A. H. Thomas (ed.), *Calendar of Select Pleas and Memoranda of the City of London, Preserved among the Archives of the Corporation of the City of London at the Guildhall, A.D. 1381–1412. The American Historical Review*, XXXIX (1934), 363–64.

1935
Mediaeval History: Europe from the Fourth to the Sixteenth Century. New York, 1935. Pp. xviii, 797.

1936
Reviews of E. Robo, *Mediaeval Farnham: Everyday Life in an Episcopal Manor;* B. A. Lees (ed.), *Records of the Templars in*

England in the Twelfth Century. Speculum, XI (1936), 414–16.
Review of M. D. Lobel, *The Borough of Bury St. Edmund's: A Study in the Government and Development of a Monastic Town. The American Historical Review,* XLI (1936), 735–36.

1937
Sources of English Constitutional History: A Selection of Documents from A.D. 600 to the Present. Edited and translated by Carl Stephenson and Frederick George Marcham. New York, 1937. Pp. xxxiv, 906.
Review of J. Tait, *The Medieval English Borough: Studies on its Origins and Constitutional History. The American Historical Review,* XLIII (1937), 96–99.

1938
"The Beginnings of Representative Government in England," *The Constitution Reconsidered,* ed. Conyers Read (New York, 1938), pp. 25–37.
Reviews of *The Cambridge Medieval History,* Vol. VIII; *Etudes d'histoire dédiées à la mémoire de Henri Pirenne. The American Historical Review,* XLIII (1938), 351–55, 833–35.

1939
Review of J. E. A. Jolliffe, *The Constitutional History of Medieval England. Speculum,* XIV (1939), 248–51.

1940
Review of E. W. W. Veale (ed.), *The Great Red Book of Bristol* (Text, Part II). *The American Historical Review,* XLV (1940), 451.

1941
A Brief Survey of Mediaeval Europe. New York, 1941. Pp. xviii, 426.
"The Origin and Significance of Feudalism," *The American Historical Review,* XLVI (1941), 788–812.
Review of G. C. Homans, *English Villagers of the Thirteenth Century. The Journal of Economic History,* I (1941), 222–24.

1942
Mediaeval Feudalism. Ithaca, 1942. Pp. ix, 116.
Review of *The Cambridge Economic History of Europe from the Decline of the Roman Empire,* Vol. I. *The Journal of Economic History,* II (1942), 203–06.

1943
Mediaeval History: Europe from the Second to the Sixteenth Century. Revised edition. New York, 1943. Pp. xx, 700.
"Feudalism and Its Antecedents in England," *The American Historical Review,* XLVIII (1943), 245–65.

1944
Mediaeval History. Published for the United States Armed Forces Institute by Harper and Brothers. Madison, 1944. Pp. xiii, 686.
"Commendation and Related Problems in Domesday," *The English Historical Review,* LIX (1944), 289–311.
Review of F. M. Stenton, *Anglo-Saxon England. The Journal of Economic History,* IV (1944), 216–17.
Review of M. Weinbaum (ed.), *British Borough Charters, 1307–1660. The American Historical Review,* XLIX (1944), 703–04.

1945
Review of D. C. Douglas (ed.), *The Domesday Monachorum of Christ Church, Canterbury. The American Historical Review,* LI (1945), 104–05.

1946
"The Problem of the Common Man in Early Mediaeval Europe," *The American Historical Review,* LI (1946), 419–38.

1947
"Notes on the Composition and Interpretation of Domesday Book," *Speculum,* XXII (1947), 1–15.
Reviews of H. A. Cronne (ed.), *Bristol Charters, 1378–1499;* M. Sczaniecki, *Essai sur les fiefs-rentes. The American Historical Review,* LII (1947), 309–10, 771.
Review of A. Déléage, *La vie rurale en Bourgogne jusqu'au début du onzième siècle. Speculum,* XXII (1947), 635–38.

1948
"In Praise of Medieval Tinkers," *The Journal of Economic History,* VIII (1948), 26–43.
Reviews of J. F. Lemarignier, *Recherches sur l'hommage en marche et les frontières féodales;* S. L. Thrupp, *The Merchant Class of Medieval London (1300–1500). Speculum,* XXIII (1948), 713, 727–28.
Review of G. Espinas, *Les origines du capitalisme,* III: *Deux fonda-*

tions de villes dans l'Artois et la Flandre française (Xᵉ–XVᵉ siècles).
The Journal of Economic History, VIII (1948), 111–12.

1949

Reviews of R. Boutrouche, *Une société provinciale en lutte contre le régime féodal: l'alleu en Bordelais et en Bazadais du XIᵉ au XVIIIᵉ siècle;* W. M. Mackenzie, *The Scottish Burghs: An Expanded Version of the Rhind Lectures in Archaeology for 1945. The American Historical Review,* LIV (1949), 421–22, 912.

1950

Review of G. Boesch, *Sempach im Mittelalter: Rechts- und Wirtschaftsgeschichtliche Untersuchung zur Stadtgründung und Stadtverfassung. Speculum,* XXV (1950), 379.

1951

Mediaeval History: Europe from the Second to the Sixteenth Century. Third edition. New York, 1951. Pp. xxi, 551.
Review of P. W. Topping, *Feudal Institutions as Revealed in the Assizes of Romania, the Law Code of Frankish Greece. Speculum,* XXVI (1951), 224–26.
Review of C. Petit-Dutaillis, *Les communes françaises: Caractères et évolution des origines au XVIIIᵉ siècle. The Journal of Economic History,* XI (1951), 192–94.

1952

Review of E. Miller, *The Abbey and Bishopric of Ely: The Social History of an Ecclesiastical Estate from the Tenth Century to the Early Fourteenth Century. The American Historical Review,* LVII (1952), 949–50.